M000312703

DEBATING PUBLIC ADMINISTRATION

Management Challenges, Choices, and Opportunities

*Advancing excellence
in public service . . .*

American Society for Public Administration
Book Series on Public Administration & Public Policy

David H. Rosenbloom, Ph.D.
Editor-in-Chief

Mission: Throughout its history, ASPA has sought to be true to its founding principles of promoting scholarship and professionalism within the public service. The ASPA Book Series on Public Administration and Public Policy publishes books that increase national and international interest for public administration and which discuss practical or cutting edge topics in engaging ways of interest to practitioners, policy-makers, and those concerned with bringing scholarship to the practice of public administration.

RECENT PUBLICATIONS

**Effective Non-Profit Management:
Contexts, Concepts, and Competencies**
by Shamima Ahmed

Environmental Decision-Making in Context: A Toolbox
by Chad J. McGuire

**Government Performance and Results: An Evaluation of
GPRA's First Decade**
by Jerry Ellig, Maurice McTigue, and Henry Wray

**Practical Human Resources for Public Managers:
A Case Study Approach**
by Nicolas A. Valcik and Teodoro J. Benavides

The Practice of Government Public Relations
edited by Mordecai Lee, Grant Neeley, and Kendra Stewart

Promoting Sustainable Local and Community Economic Development
by Roland V. Anglin

Government Contracting: Promises and Perils
by William Sims Curry

CRC Press
Taylor & Francis Group

American Society for Public Administration
Series in Public Administration and Public Policy

DEBATING PUBLIC ADMINISTRATION

Management Challenges, Choices, and Opportunities

EDITED BY
ROBERT F. DURANT
JENNIFER R.S. DURANT

CRC Press
Taylor & Francis Group
Boca Raton   London   New York

CRC Press is an imprint of the
Taylor & Francis Group, an **informa** business

CRC Press
Taylor & Francis Group
6000 Broken Sound Parkway NW, Suite 300
Boca Raton, FL 33487-2742

© 2013 by Taylor & Francis Group, LLC
CRC Press is an imprint of Taylor & Francis Group, an Informa business

No claim to original U.S. Government works

Printed in the United States of America on acid-free paper
Version Date: 20120719

International Standard Book Number: 978-1-4665-0236-9 (Hardback)

This book contains information obtained from authentic and highly regarded sources. Reasonable efforts have been made to publish reliable data and information, but the author and publisher cannot assume responsibility for the validity of all materials or the consequences of their use. The authors and publishers have attempted to trace the copyright holders of all material reproduced in this publication and apologize to copyright holders if permission to publish in this form has not been obtained. If any copyright material has not been acknowledged please write and let us know so we may rectify in any future reprint.

Except as permitted under U.S. Copyright Law, no part of this book may be reprinted, reproduced, transmitted, or utilized in any form by any electronic, mechanical, or other means, now known or hereafter invented, including photocopying, microfilming, and recording, or in any information storage or retrieval system, without written permission from the publishers.

For permission to photocopy or use material electronically from this work, please access www.copyright. com (http://www.copyright.com/) or contact the Copyright Clearance Center, Inc. (CCC), 222 Rosewood Drive, Danvers, MA 01923, 978-750-8400. CCC is a not-for-profit organization that provides licenses and registration for a variety of users. For organizations that have been granted a photocopy license by the CCC, a separate system of payment has been arranged.

Trademark Notice: Product or corporate names may be trademarks or registered trademarks, and are used only for identification and explanation without intent to infringe.

Library of Congress Cataloging-in-Publication Data

Debating public administration : management challenges, choices, and opportunities / editors, Robert F. Durant, Jennifer R.S. Durant.
   p. cm. -- (ASPA series in public administration and public policy)
Includes bibliographical references and index.
ISBN 978-1-4665-0236-9
1. Public administration. I. Durant, Robert F., 1949- II. Durant, Jennifer R.S.

JF1351.D435 2012
351--dc23
                                                     2012028260

Visit the Taylor & Francis Web site at
http://www.taylorandfrancis.com

and the CRC Press Web site at
http://www.crcpress.com

In memory of Frederick C. Mosher

Contents

SECTION II   RECAPITALIZING ORGANIZATIONAL CAPACITY

Foreword

When Fritz Mosher ended his three-year term as editor of *Public Administration Review* (*PAR*) in 1956, he penned a perceptive wrap-up editorial that outlined several ideas for advancing public administration research. One suggestion he had was to add a regular *PAR* feature devoted to translating for practitioners the latest administrative science research developments. These would be timely in response to their needs, practical in application, and easily comprehensible. In many respects, that idea has always been the central mission of *PAR*. In *PAR*'s inaugural issue in 1940, the American Society for Public Administration's (ASPA) first president, William Mosher, set forth its goal, namely, to be "practical in content and scholarly in tone." However, with the acceleration of university-based administrative research by the mid-1950s, Fritz Mosher foresaw a pressing imperative to dedicate periodic journal pages to cover new theoretical innovations relevant for those on the "firing line."

The idea languished for a half century. In 2006, however, after our new *PAR* editorial team was appointed and assumed formal publication responsibilities, seven new journal sections were created. Each had its own associate editor and peer-review board to ensure quality. The intent was to widen significantly the coverage in *PAR* plus provide greater depth of analysis for topics that were well beyond what the journal received from the normal flow of manuscripts submitted through its general peer-review pipeline. Clearly, the sheer size, sophistication, speed, and breadth of administrative science research had grown exponentially by the twenty-first century. *PAR* needed to cover these rapidly changing developments to enhance both individual administrator's and the entire profession's capabilities to perform effectively, especially given its prime role as the journal of record for the field.

But how? The editors at the outset saw the urgent necessity for a new *PAR* section, ultimately called *Theory to Practice* (T2P), but they honestly had no idea how to make it happen. Happily, they recruited the right person six years ago. Bob Durant quickly turned a vague, fuzzy notion into an amazing, much admired, prominent *PAR* feature. From our perspective as editors, T2P ultimately surpassed our wildest expectations. Note in the table of contents the wide range of seminal contemporary public administration issues addressed and the immense number of authors and commentators recruited—senior/junior, academic/practitioner, from diverse backgrounds, regions, and institutions. These articles consistently focused on digging into what we know and do not know about salient administrative problems, and where we should go from here for developing the next steps to advance research and practice. So what you read in this book sums up intensive discussions and debates over several years among the field's best and brightest who wrestle with many of today's most vexing administrative conundrums.

Innovation is a common buzzword nowadays throughout public administration, but many remain perplexed by what it actually entails. Here are concrete examples of what it is all about, why it is so crucial, how it develops, and where it can be applied for the betterment of government and society. On a deeper level, *Debating Public Administration* permits a rare glimpse into the intriguing mental processes of successful innovation at work within contemporary administrative sciences. A new book, *The Innovator's DNA,* by Clay Christensen, Jeff Dyer, and Hal Gregersen, lays out the necessary mental habits that foster innovation and what we can learn from them. Granted, their book is written from a business perspective and based on industrial research, but the Harvard Business School authors list five ingrained habits of thinking that they characterize as follows: associating, questioning, observing, networking, and experimenting.

Little imagination is necessary to understand how these five mental habits are likewise reflected in public administration innovation as evidenced within this edited book. *Associating* to promote change and new ideas can be witnessed throughout. These contributors to T2P may not be physically connected, but the Internet allows an impressive array of experts from everywhere to "bump heads together" instantaneously. Such fruitful, often intense exchanges forge fresh thinking. Indeed, it may well be at the interstices of these prolonged arguments that innovation comes about or, rather, turns into reality. Second, *questioning* abounds in these pages. The book's very title implies that everything is up for discussion and argument as well as open to query. The essays themselves frequently begin with a question in their titles and end with more questions deemed vital to advance the next stages of research. *Observing* is also apparent, as each of these studies relies upon empirical evidence, quantitative and qualitative, to support their arguments and assertions. Conjecture without concrete, convincing evidence is unacceptable, if not deplored and disregarded. Equally apparent in the contributions to this book is *networking*. None of these contributors are lone wolves who work in solitary to spawn their innovations. All are great networkers as reflected by each chapter's diverse cluster of collaborative authors and commentators. They argue, debate, and even seek out nonconformist, odd, and offbeat ideas that are outside the box to advance research. Finally, fresh thinking demands *experimenting,* and all these authors and commentators are inveterate experimenters. They relish tinkering with theoretical models, designing and testing experiments, revamping ideas, and adapting practices to suit novel situations and changing contexts. All are unafraid of change or of embracing the new via attempts to discover something different; something better.

In the following chapters, thanks to the immense talent and hard work of the editors, authors, and commentators, readers can catch a rare, insightful glimpse of innovative minds at work within modern public administration—even whom, why, what, where, and how creative innovation is accomplished throughout the field. And maybe, just maybe, they will draw the conclusion that right now American public administration lives in an incredible golden age.

Richard Stillman, Editor-in-Chief
Jos C. N. Raadschelders, Managing Editor
Public Administration Review, 2006–2011

Preface: Theory to Practice

Advancing the "science, processes, and art of public administration" has long been a central animating purpose of the American Society for Public Administration (ASPA). Such a mission today involves practitioners and scholars providing answers to what is arguably the central animating question facing societies worldwide: how, when, and with what implications for the values treasured in a democratic republic can we best harness for public purposes the dynamism of markets, the passion and commitment of nonprofit and nongovernmental organizations, and the public interest–oriented expertise of the career public service at all levels of government. But dialogue between practitioners and academics has increasingly become the exception rather than the rule in contemporary public administration circles.

With this set of challenges in mind, the then-new *Public Administration Review* (*PAR*) editor Richard Stillman and managing editor Jos Raadschelders generously asked me to develop a feature for the journal that would be tailored to the information needs of practitioners while simultaneously affording scholars state-of-the-art summaries of the status of current research. As such, my interrelated aims as editor of *Theory to Practice* (T2P) were fourfold:

- Afford opportunities for academics, practitioners, and pracademics to inform each other's work in the hope of advancing both practice and theory building in public administration
- Facilitate cross-disciplinary, cross-sectoral (public, private, and nonprofit), and cross-professional exchanges that break down contemporary tendencies toward fragmentation and "stovepiping" of knowledge applicable to both practice and theory
- Provide for busy practitioners, scholars, and students a one-stop site for locating classics, near-classics, and future classics on topics of interest to academics and practitioners

■ Advance what former *PAR* editor Chet Newland referred to as a *floating seminar* by taking advantage of existing and future advances and developments in information-sharing technology

In pursuing these aims from 2006 to 2011, T2P featured exchanges among scholars and practitioners assessing what prominent theories and research in their areas of expertise have to say about the challenges, choices, and opportunities facing public administration today. Critical among these were calls from elected officials, popular writers, and some scholars for public administrators to

■ Reconceptualize the purpose of agencies in light of new societal challenges
■ Redefine administrative rationality to focus on outcomes rather than inputs and outputs
■ Recapitalize human resource assets
■ Reengage financial resources for new priorities
■ Revitalize constitutional values that might otherwise get lost in reform efforts

These 5 Rs served as the overarching thematic framework for articles appearing in T2P. We offered a series of blind peer-reviewed articles appearing in the hard copy of *PAR* written in language accessible to all *PAR* readers but especially to busy practitioners. These articles discussed what the best in scholarship had to say about various topics covered in the series. Each article took stock of and pondered the future of selected topics by exploring the answer to three primary questions:

■ What do we know from theory and the research literature that can help inform practice in a given topical area?
■ What don't we know and why?
■ Where do we go from here and how, in terms of research and practice?

Accepted articles appeared in two formats: a hard-copy version in *PAR* and an extended e-version of the article plus a set of e-commentaries on *PAR*'s website under *Theory to Practice*. E-commentaries were done by academics and practitioners with expertise on the topic. These e-commentators were not the persons who did the blind peer review of the article published in *PAR*. E-commentators did not know the identity of the authors and reacted to each article in terms of

■ Their perception of the contents, argument, and evidence presented
■ Any additional insights they had that might be useful for practitioners and researchers
■ Alternatively, their own perceptions regarding future research and practice on this or related topics

All articles published in T2P (hard copy) thus met all criteria for blind peer review and publication in *PAR*.

Several colleagues suggested to me that it would be useful to have a single hard-copy volume composed of the complete articles and exchanges that were published in the series. Although the articles and e-commentaries were strung out over six years in *PAR*, this edited book would afford a single source for locating condensed versions of each piece. In addition, since the e-commentaries would be removed from the ASPA website, it was all the more important to have a print record that would provide one-stop shopping for the feature as a whole to facilitate use in classrooms by academics and by practitioners. I was also persuaded to move ahead on this project for the opportunity to afford a holistic view of how the articles fit into the original aims of the series and to give readers a sense of the intellectual coherence it sought to advance. I then convinced my wife, Jennifer, to join me in this venture as coeditor, as she had served as managing editor for T2P throughout my tenure.

What follows in this volume is the product of that effort and truly has been a labor of love. And tough love had to be exercised in the process. Starting originally with 14 articles and commentaries totaling well over 1100 manuscript pages, we had to exercise ruthless editorial prerogative. Article and commentary selections, and accompanying edits, were designed to hit major points made by authors and commentators, to eliminate overlap and duplication, to ensure a wide range of perspectives, and to present a coherent overview of the five Rs that were the focus of T2P. What we cut was a reflection of these criteria and in no way should be seen as a critique of articles or commentaries not included. Although we debated asking authors to update the original articles, we opted not to for space reasons and to maintain the integrity of the original contribution. Occasionally, in section introductions, we include mention of more recent developments. In most, we leave the task of updating to readers and instructors.

Our hope is that *Debating Public Administration* will help to give MPA and MPP students a sense for some of the major challenges, choices, and opportunities they will continue to face in the years ahead. We also hope that they will gain an appreciation for the linkage between public administration and some of the major policy issues that will continue to challenge the United States. This linkage definitely gets lost in popular parlance and in pundit commentary, but it also is not made explicit often enough in public administration research. Nothing about this linkage will change in the future, and that should excite the best and the brightest of our students today and be alluring in attracting others to the field.

Our hope also is that students in traditional MPA and MPP programs—as well as students in executive programs—will see the vitality afoot among public administration scholars and practitioners and the role they can play in joining the dialogue as future scholars or practitioners. Given the challenges facing societies today, the central role that public managers play in addressing them, and the differing viewpoints expressed in these pages, the dirty little secret revealed in these pages is that we are still groping our way toward agreement on how best to proceed. Significantly, however, we hope that students do not see this as a weakness of the field they have chosen or are considering joining. Rather, we hope they see it as an opportunity for them during their public service careers to help shape the answers to these unresolved issues.

We will also be gratified if this volume makes a small contribution to disabusing those practitioners and academics who argue that they have little to say to each other. They most certainly do. As Wamsley and Wolf (1996, 30) point out, not only is public administration a "social science (albeit not merely a social science of the positivist paradigm) with a character of its own, but it is inescapably an applied field as well.... [As such, it] ... 'has to accommodate a double hermeneutic—two frames of meaning.'" Thus, practitioners need to understand that what they think, do, and say has theoretical and research grounding. It is too easy to become stovepiped in office cubicles thinking everything they deal with is unique and that researchers have not already helped shape their thinking. They have. But researchers err by thinking that staring into computer screens and having methodological arguments are activities that societies will continue to fund generously in the era of contracting resources that lies ahead if the link to practice is not clearly and convincingly made. This requires interaction not only with primary and secondary analyses of databases but also through persistent, fruitful, and respectful interaction with practitioners who are "in the arena," as Teddy Roosevelt might have put it. Researchers need to see the world through their eyes—the challenges they face, the adaptations they make in light of these challenges, and where they feel research is needed—to stay relevant in an age of turbulence.

I have many individuals to thank for this volume. First, and foremost, the series could not have taken place without the invitation, support, and advocacy of two important individuals to my professional life: Richard Stillman and Jos Raadschelders. In this case, they were willing to take a risk on a crazy idea that readers of *PAR* would go from the hard copy of the journal to the *PAR* webpage for additional text and commentaries. The hunch clearly paid off. Articles and commentaries were downloaded over 100,000 times worldwide. I am deeply grateful for the opportunity, confidence, guidance, and trust that Richard and Jos gave me and for their kind words in the foreword to this volume. That the current editorial team at *PAR*, James Perry and Michael McGuire, decided to continue this feature and place it in the extraordinarily capable hands of Don Moynihan are tributes to Richard and Jos.

My gratitude is also extended to several persons who helped to either get or keep T2P up and running over the six years. Hal Rainey and Sergio Fernandez took a huge risk when I begged them to take a manuscript that was in revise-and-resubmit status under the previous *PAR* editorial team to launch the series and be subject to public critique of their work. When they agreed, and the late Larry Terry approved the shift of the manuscript as prior editor-in-chief of *PAR*, T2P was off and running. I am also indebted to Jim Perry, Fred Thompson, David Rosenbloom, and Robert Tobias. They not only took on the T2P challenge but also served as sources of encouragement and advice in those early days and beyond.

Throughout the six years of my tenure, Matt Rankin also was a constant source of help on website postings of articles and commentaries and as an advocate within ASPA for T2P. For all this, I offer my deep thanks. Thanks as well to ASPA executive director Antoinette Samuel and Blackwell Publishers for permission to reprint edited versions and commentaries from T2P in this book. Kudos are also in order to two persons who served as coeditors for several articles in the series: William Resh, now assistant professor at Indiana University, and Robert Kramer of the Key Executive Program at American University. I also want to thank David Rosenbloom, the editor of this book series; acquisitions editor Lara Zoble; project coordinator Stephanie Morkert; and project editor Tara Nieuwesteeg for their guidance throughout the process. Finally, many thanks to all the contributors for their articles and commentaries. Without their willingness to have their work critiqued in public, their patience and confidence in us when a heavy editorial hand was necessary to meet page-length requirements, and their commitment to quality, nothing else would have been possible.

Robert F. Durant
Washington, DC

Contributors

R. Paul Battaglio, Jr., is an associate professor and assistant program head for advising and enrollment in the Public Affairs Program at the University of Texas–Dallas.

Domonic A. Bearfield is an associate professor in the Bush School of Government and Public Service at Texas A&M University.

Lisa Blomgren Bingham is the Keller-Runden Professor of Public Service in the School of Public and Environmental Affairs at Indiana University–Bloomington. She is also a visiting professor of law in the Boyd School of Law at the University of Nevada–Las Vegas and a senior research fellow in the Maxwell School at Syracuse University.

Trevor L. Brown is an associate professor in the John Glenn School of Public Affairs at The Ohio State University–Columbus. He also serves as the associate director for academic affairs and research.

Thomas Bryer is an assistant professor in the Department of Public Administration at the University of Central Florida.

Sharon L. Caudle is the Younger-Carter Distinguished Policy Maker in Residence and lecturer in the Bush School of Government and Public Service at Texas A&M University.

Stephen E. Condrey is president of Condrey and Associates, Inc., a human resources consulting firm, and president-elect of the American Society for Public Administration.

Patrick E. Connor is professor emeritus of organizational analysis in the Atkinson Graduate School of Management at Willamette University.

Brian J. Cook is a professor and program chair in the Center for Public Administration and Policy at Virginia Polytechnic Institute and State University.

Terry L. Cooper is the Maria B. Crutcher Professor in Citizenship and Democratic Values in the Sol Price School of Public Policy at the University of Southern California.

Anthony M. Cresswell is a professor and research director in the Center for Technology in Government at the University at Albany, State University of New York.

Sharon S. Dawes is a senior fellow in the Center for Technology in Government at the University at Albany, State University of New York.

Ruth H. DeHoog is a professor and master of public administration director in the Department of Political Science at the University of North Carolina–Greensboro.

Robert "Robin" H. Dorff is the General Douglas MacArthur Professor of Research in the Strategic Studies Institute at the U.S. Army War College.

Trent A. Engbers is an assistant professor in the School of Public and Environmental Affairs at Indiana University.

Richard C. Feiock is the Augustus B. Turnbull Professor in the Askew School of Public Administration and Policy at Florida State University. He is also director of the Program in Local Governance in the DeVoe L. Moore Center for the Study of Critical Issues in Economic Policy and Government.

Sergio Fernandez is an associate professor in the School of Public and Environmental Affairs at Indiana University.

Frank D. Ferris is the national executive vice president of the National Treasury Employees Union.

Bruce L. Gates is a professor of quantitative methods and public management in the Atkinson Graduate School of Management at Willamette University.

Elisabeth A. Graffy is professor of practice in the Consortium for Science, Policy and Outcomes, College of Liberal Arts and Sciences, Arizona State University and a senior sustainability scientist in the Global Institute of Sustainability.

Tanya Heikkila is an associate professor in the School of Public Affairs at the University of Colorado–Denver.

David J. Houston is a professor in the Department of Political Science at the University of Tennessee–Knoxville.

So Yun Jun is a personnel consultant in Seoul, Korea.

John M. Kamensky is a senior fellow with the IBM Center for the Business of Government and associate partner with IBM's Global Business Services.

Lael R. Keiser is an associate professor in the Department of Political Science at the University of Missouri–Columbia.

William Lyons is chief policy officer and deputy to the mayor for the City of Knoxville, Tennessee.

Sharon H. Mastracci is an associate professor and master of public administration director in the Department of Public Administration at the University of Illinois–Chicago.

Roy T. Meyers is a professor in the Department of Political Science at the University of Maryland–Baltimore County. From 1981 to 1990, he was an analyst at the Congressional Budget Office.

J. Christopher Mihm is the managing director for strategic issues at the U.S. Government Accountability Office.

M. Jae Moon is a professor and chair of the Department of Public Administration at Yonsei University, Seoul, Korea.

John C. Morris is an associate professor in the Department of Urban Studies and Public Administration at Old Dominion University.

Juliet Musso is an associate professor and master of public policy director in the Sol Price School of Public Policy at the University of Southern California.

Tina Nabatchi is an assistant professor and a faculty research associate with the Program for the Advancement of Research on Conflict and Collaboration in the Maxwell School at Syracuse University.

Sanjay K. Pandey is a professor in the School of Public Affairs and Administration at Rutgers University–Newark.

Theresa A. Pardo is the director of the Center for Technology in Government at the University at Albany, State University of New York. She is also a research associate professor at the Rockefeller College of Public Administration and Policy and an affiliated faculty member of the College of Computing and Information at the University at Albany.

Hyung Jun Park is an assistant professor in the Department of Public Administration and Graduate School of Governance at Sungkyunkwan University, Seoul, Korea.

James L. Perry is the Chancellor's Professor in the School of Public and Environmental Affairs at Indiana University–Bloomington. He also holds adjunct appointments in philanthropy and political science.

Suzanne J. Piotrowski is an associate professor in the School of Public Affairs and Administration at Rutgers University–Newark.

Matthew Potoski is a professor in the Bren School of Environmental Science & Management at the University of California–Santa Barbara.

Hal G. Rainey is an Alumni Foundation Distinguished Professor and PhD director in the Department of Public Administration and Policy, School of Public and International Affairs at the University of Georgia.

Laura A. Reese is a professor and director of the Global Urban Studies Program in the Department of Political Science at Michigan State University.

Thomas F. Reilly is the executive director of Caesars Foundation, a private foundation whose "objective is to strengthen organizations and programs in the communities where our employees and their families live and work."

Norma M. Riccucci is a professor and PhD director in the School of Public Affairs and Administration at Rutgers University–Newark.

Howard Risher of Risher Enterprises, Ltd., is a private consultant and researcher specializing in human resource management issues.

Nancy C. Roberts is a professor in the Department of Defense Analysis at the Naval Postgraduate School.

David H. Rosenbloom is a distinguished professor in the Department of Public Administration and Policy at American University.

Edella Schlager is an associate professor in the School of Government and Public Policy at the University of Arizona.

Sally Coleman Selden is a professor in the School of Business and Economics at Lynchburg College.

John Clayton Thomas is a professor in the Andrew Young School of Policy Studies at Georgia State University.

Frank J. Thompson is a professor in the School of Public Affairs and Administration at Rutgers University–Newark.

Fred Thompson is the Grace and Elmer Goudy Professor of Public Management and Policy Analysis in the Atkinson Graduate School of Management at Willamette University. He is also director of the Center for Governance and Public Policy Research at Willamette University.

Mary Tschirhart is the director of the Institute for Nonprofit Research, Education, and Engagement and a professor in the College of Humanities and Social Sciences at North Carolina State University–Raleigh.

David M. Van Slyke is an associate professor in the Maxwell School at Syracuse University.

Douglas J. Watson is a professor and director of the public affairs program in the School of Economic, Political, and Policy Sciences at the University of Texas–Dallas.

Christopher Weare is deputy director of the Civic Engagement Initiative and research associate professor in the Sol Price School of Public Policy at the University of Southern California.

Andrew B. Whitford is a professor in the Department of Public Administration and Policy, School of Public and International Affairs at the University of Georgia.

Katherine G. Willoughby is a professor in the International Center for Public Policy, Andrew Young School of Policy Studies at Georgia State University.

RETHINKING ADMINISTRATIVE RATIONALITY IN A DEMOCRATIC REPUBLIC

Building on earlier scholarly work contrasting narrow conceptualizations of economy and efficiency with the broader vision of *social economy* and *social efficiency*, Dwight Waldo argued famously in *The Administrative State* that the real question confronting scholars and practitioners was, efficiency for what? Explained Waldo (1948, 203), the "descriptive or objective notion of efficiency is valid and useful, but only within a framework of consciously held values." Waldo further noted the difficulty of assessing efficiency when disagreements over values occurred. As a person's "frame of reference" widens and "disagreement about ends" deepens, calculation of "science" and "objectivity" becomes more difficult and statements about the relative efficiency of different arrangements become "less accurate, more controversial" (205).

This challenge has grown even more pronounced for public managers in recent decades. Ascendant in salience in the post–Cold War era is a host of what scholars call *wicked* policy problems (see, for example, Rittel and Webber 1973). These are policy issues (e.g., drug abuse, reducing teenage pregnancy, terrorism, urban runoff, global warming) where no accepted definition of the problem exists. Moreover, one problem is interrelated with others, cross-sectoral (public/private/nonprofit) collaboration is essential for success, and the solutions proffered are precarious, controversial, and difficult to implement. Wicked problems are also multiattribute in nature; solutions to them require the balancing of a variety of values rather than the predominance of any one value.

These policy challenges and value choices, in turn, have raised serious questions about the ability of conventional bureaucratic models to address them. Wicked problems beg cross-functional and cross-jurisdictional solutions, procedural flexibility and discretion wielded by administrators closest to the situation, outcomes-based measures of success, and stakeholders involved in defining both problems and solutions. Yet the conventional bureaucratic structure is not noted for embracing these traits. As such, agencies must be empowered to work with elected officials to reconceptualize their purpose, to reconnect with citizens, and to redefine administrative orthodoxy.

But how can public administrators and elected officials best align organizational, interorganizational, and cross-sectoral strategies, structures, and incentives to realize economy, efficiency, and effectiveness without sacrificing other values we cherish in a democratic republic? Sergio Fernandez of Indiana University and Hal Rainey of the University of Georgia cull eight lessons for practice from the bountiful, rich, yet often perplexing literature on understanding, promoting, and sustaining large-scale organizational change. Moreover, although prior research generally treated these determinants as having additive effects, the authors treat each factor as interacting with the others.

Responding to their analysis, Patrick Connor and Fred Thompson of Willamette University embrace much of what Fernandez and Rainey offer as advice for large-scale organizational change, adding their own research insights and role theory to help elaborate and extend the analysis. However, they are critical that the authors' propositions and subpropositions exhibit a preference for top-down, managed organizational change. Christopher Mihm of the Government Accountability Office (GAO) also embraces the authors' lessons for practitioners, noting their scholarly consistency with GAO's best-practice analysis of effective change. He elaborates on the specific processes and nuances that the authors emphasize but also highlights the importance to success of employee involvement, human capital strategies, and external communication strategies. Mary Tschirhart of North Carolina State University–Raleigh also finds much merit in the prescriptions Fernandez and Rainey offer to practitioners but shares Thompson and Connor's worry about top-down perspectives. She advises that change—and resistance to change by employees—can be appropriate and needs further research. She recommends a greater focus on interorganizational dimensions of change in our contemporary networked state.

One of the most persistent initiatives to rethink administrative rationality launched by elected officials at all levels of government over the past three decades has involved efforts to establish pay-for-performance reward systems for government employees. But have pay-for-performance systems lived up to the promise that proponents have held out for them? Have the basic theories underlying them proven valid? What lessons can be drawn from prior experiences with pay-for-performance systems? In Chapter 2, James Perry of Indiana University, Trent Engbers of DePaul University, and So Yun Jun, a personnel consultant in Seoul, Korea, coffer lessons from their meta-analysis of research assessing pay-for-performance systems in the United States from 1977 to 2008. Overall, they find little evidence that this approach works effectively in public agencies, note the barriers to successful applications in the public sector, and ponder why it continues to be embraced by elected officials.

Commentators David Houston of the University of Tennessee and Sanjay Pandey of Rutgers University–Newark find much to support in the original *PAR* article and elaborate in greater detail than did Perry and his colleagues the findings of research on public service motivation for agency performance. Houston argues that performance-related pay fails to appreciate adequately the importance of intrinsic motivation. He notes that individuals engage in work tasks out of an inherent interest in the activities (enjoyment-based) and find the work to be meaningful due to a commitment to self-defined goals or social norms. Pandey does the same but challenges what he sees as an implicit assumption that past failures with pay-for-performance are doomed to repeat themselves in future efforts. His call is for a greater appreciation for organizational context and for greater heed to literature showing the conditions under which success is more likely to occur. In contrast, Howard Risher—a private consultant who focuses on pay and performance in government, higher education, and health care—takes strong issue with the interpretation of prior research by Perry and his colleagues and offers arguments for the necessity and utility of pay-for-performance in all types of organizations.

As pressures and advocacy by administrative reformers to engage in cross-agency and cross-sectoral partnerships became more widespread in the face of wicked policy problems, budget cuts, and the need to leverage interorganizational capacity in the last three decades, barriers to information sharing immediately became a daunting aspect of public administration. In Chapter 3, Sharon Dawes, Anthony Cresswell, and Theresa Pardo of the University at Albany, State University of New York, offer a baker's dozen of lessons they have culled from prior information technology (IT) research and their own action research agenda on the building of public sector knowledge networks (PSKNs) in New York. Grounded in a multidisciplinary, experientially based, and street-level view of the obstacles to and tactics for building successful PSKNs, the authors warn practitioners to conceive of collaborative information-sharing efforts as governance rather than IT challenges.

In response, Lisa Bingham of Indiana University emphasizes the legal barriers alluded to in the original *PAR* article and offers a more detailed analysis of their sources and implications for information sharing in a networked state. She argues that a new legal infrastructure has to be designed if information sharing is to improve; it should address how agencies can (1) exercise delegated authority in networks, (2) reconcile networks with transparency in government, (3) foster citizen participation in networks, (4) get networks to use more innovative deliberative processes with citizens, and (5) ensure that the network is adequately accountable to the public. Sharon Caudle of Texas A&M University, and formerly an analyst at

GAO, buttresses the authors' findings but criticizes them for not incorporating a range of applicable research from the collaborative governance literature. In relating that literature to PSKNs, she also critiques the original article for not paying sufficient attention to the variety of PSKNs that exist and that require lessons more specific to their contexts and dynamics. Relatedly, she argues that different lessons would likely emerge at different stages of the life of PSKN development and implementation, and she emphasizes that a focus on the purpose of the PSKN might also produce different results.

With faith in government waning, cultural and ethnic diversity spiraling, and fiscal stress straining the ability of policy makers to address the policy challenges accompanying these developments, the salience of (re)connecting citizens with government was also afoot in the United States. Perhaps nowhere were these challenges more prevalent than in urban America. So-called global cities teeming with ethnic diversity and controlling a disproportionate amount of global business in the world economy confronted profound citizen participation challenges, choices, and opportunities. In their chapter, Juliet Musso, Christopher Weare, and Terry Cooper of the University of Southern California and Thomas Bryer of the University of Central Florida cull lessons from these efforts to rethink administrative rationality from their ten-year action theory-based assessment and participation in Los Angeles's neighborhood council experience. Comparing and contrasting their findings in this global city with those from related studies on participatory mechanisms and deliberative processes more generally, they offer six lessons for those seeking to build stronger democracy in urban areas. They also argue that further advances require a greater research focus on the longitudinal implementation of these efforts rather than just on their design and contend that university researchers have a role to play in these efforts as long as they appreciate the paradoxical nature of their participation.

Responding to these arguments, Brian Cook of Virginia Tech, Tina Nabatchi of Syracuse University, and John Thomas of Georgia State University offer largely laudatory commentaries of the work and arguments proffered by Musso and her colleagues. Yet each also offers important refinements to their lessons. Cook, grounding his position in Woodrow Wilson's vision of civic vibrancy in urban areas as laboratories of citizenship, argues that the power of the arguments made by the authors are nevertheless limited in their immediate benefit by the lack of an adequate theory of democracy for the American republic. Nabatchi feels that the power of the claims made could be enhanced if arguments for and against greater citizen participation in agency decision making are resolved. She argues that doing so requires thinking more systematically about design choices as well as about how these design choices contribute to (or detract from) desired outcomes. Two design choices are critical and require attention by researchers and practitioners: systems design and process design.

Thomas agrees and elaborates and extends several of Musso and her colleagues' points. In particular, he stresses the importance of institutionalizing participatory reforms because of the fluidity of reform champions, and he argues for two-way capacity building. In the latter, he emphasizes the need not only for citizens to learn substantive knowledge about policies from public managers but also for managers to learn from citizens. Relatedly, public managers must learn how best to incorporate citizens in timely and meaningful ways in agency policy deliberations, understanding the benefits of doing so under various conditions. Public managers, he avers, must be given training stressing how best to reconcile technical standards and public preferences.

One of the most significant challenges facing practitioners and scholars today in reconsidering administrative rationality in public agencies is how to protect the constitutional values one cherishes in a democratic republic. In his William E. Mosher and Frederick C. Mosher Award-winning article in *PAR*, David Rosenbloom of American University spiritedly argues that it is long past time to "reinvent" the administrative reform movement itself. Reformers, he argues, have slighted democratic-constitutional values in the prescriptions they have offered, with serious consequences for citizens, public employees, and respect for government. Rosenbloom argues that these values have been conspicuously absent in prior reform efforts and proposes that reformers' prescriptions be formally assessed both prospectively (through impact statements) and retrospectively (through scorecards) to gauge their consequences for democratic-constitutional values. His argument is grounded in public administrative history, steeped in American political traditions, and buttressed by illustrations of why and how reinventing administrative reform cannot be ignored.

Responding to Rosenbloom, commentator John Kamensky of the IBM Center for the Business of Government and a leader in reinventing government initiatives in the United States during the 1990s is deeply skeptical. Kamensky questions Rosenbloom's underlying assumptions and supporting arguments, claiming that practitioners are unlikely to find them compelling, that his proposals are impractical to implement, and that they could actually halt needed agency actions. He also urges greater precision in defining democratic constitutional values, doubts that value tradeoffs can be made without more definitional precision, and argues that elected officials are already making those decisions implicitly—to which Rosenbloom responded that post hoc evaluation by elected officials can come only after harm is done. He adds, "I fear he [Kamensky] is projecting his own bewilderment with democratic-constitutionalism onto the field as a whole. I assumed—and continue to assume—that most *PAR* readers are familiar enough with the substantial literature on public administration and U.S. democratic-constitutionalism to know what constitutional rights and integrity, transparency, and the rule of law are and are not."

Chapter 1

Managing Successful Organizational Change in the Public Sector[*]

Sergio Fernandez and Hal G. Rainey

Contents

Can government organizations change? Reform initiatives have swept through governments in the United States and overseas, again and again bringing news about efforts to reinvent, transform, or reform government agencies (Barzelay 2001; Kettl 2000; Pollitt and Bouckaert 2000; Stillman 1999). Curiously, however, this recurrent theme of change in government agencies has not induced a high volume of

---

[*] Adapted from Fernandez, S., and H. G. Rainey. 2006. Managing successful organizational change in the public sector. *Public Administration Review* 66(2): 168–176.

articles in public administration journals that explicitly address the topic. There are prominent exceptions to this observation (e.g., Bryson and Anderson 2000; Chackerian and Mavima 2000; Mani 1995; Wise 2002) and journal articles on topics related to organizational change (e.g., Berman and Wang 2000; Brudney and Wright 2002; Hood and Peters 2004). Articles reporting research and theory with titles containing "organizational change" and with that theme as a focal topic, however, appear with much less regularity in public administration journals than in research journals focusing on general management and organization theory.

In that literature on organization theory, Van de Ven and Poole (1995) report a count of one million articles relating to organizational change. This vast body of work abounds with complexities, including multiple and conflicting theories and research findings and a good bit of inconclusiveness. This complexity presents a challenge to public administrators and public administration researchers alike. To aid them in their efforts, we identify points of consensus among researchers on what are commonly called organizational transformations: initiatives involving large-scale, planned, strategic, and administrative change (Abramson and Lawrence 2001; Kotter 1995). These points serve as testable propositions for researchers to examine in future research and as major considerations for leaders of change initiatives in public organizations.

Theoretical Perspectives on Successfully Implementing Organizational Change in Public Organizations

The variety of theoretical perspectives on organizational change presents a confusing picture, but they provide important insights about the causes of change and the role of the manager in the change process. Some of the theories downplay the significance of human agency as a source of change (e.g., DiMaggio and Powell 1983; Hannan and Freeman 1984; Scott 2003). Conversely, other theories view managers' purposeful action as driving change (e.g., Lawrence and Lorsch 1967; Pfeffer and Salancik 1978), although environmental, cognitive, and resource constraints place limits on such action (Van de Ven and Poole 1995). Despite the conflicts among theorists, however, a significant body of private sector research indicates that managers frequently do make change happen in their organizations (Armenakis, Harris, and Feild 2001; Burke 2002, 271; Judson 1991; Kotter 1995, 1996; Yukl 2002). Public sector studies also have offered evidence of the critical role that public managers play in bringing about organizational change (e.g., Abramson and Lawrence 2001; Bingham and Wise 1996; Borins 2000; Doig and Hargrove 1990; Hennessey 1998; Kemp, Funk, and Eadie 1993).

Noting that managers can effect change tells us little, however, about whether an intended change actually occurs and about the best strategies for effecting change. Fortunately, a stream of research exists that contains various models and frameworks—many of them loosely based on Lewin's (1947) steps or phases of change. These studies describe the process of implementing change within organizations and point to factors contributing to success (e.g., Armenakis et al. 2001; Bingham and Wise 1996; Burke 2002; Greiner 1967; Kotter 1995, 1996; Rainey and Rainey 1986; Thompson and Fulla 2001).

Despite some differences in these models and frameworks, one finds remarkable similarities among them, as well as empirical studies supporting them (Armenakis and Bedeian 1999). As Table 1.1 illustrates, one can discern from this body of research a consensus that change leaders and change participants should pay special attention to eight factors suitable for further testing and refining. Since it draws on points of consensus among researchers and experienced observers, the set of factors discussed here resembles, but differs in significant ways from, certain other frameworks (e.g., Kotter 1996, 21).

Some experts portray the change process as a linear progression through successive stages represented by the factors discussed herein (e.g., Armenakis et al. 2001; Greiner 1967; Kotter 1995). The process, however, rarely unfolds in such a simple linear fashion (Amis, Slack, and Hinings 2004; Van de Ven 1993). The following eight factors and propositions can influence the outcome of change initiatives at different points of the process. Moreover, researchers generally have treated these determinants of effective implementation of organizational change as having additive effects. The present analysis, in contrast, treats each determinant as potentially contributing to the successful implementation of change, or making implementation smoother, by interacting with the other factors. Despite what might seem like their commonsense nature, examples and prior research indicate that change leaders ignore, overlook, or underestimate them quite often (Kotter 1995, 1996).

Factor 1: Ensure the need. Managerial leaders must verify and persuasively communicate the need for change.

Research indicates that the implementation of planned change generally requires leaders to verify the need for change and to persuade other members of the organization and important external stakeholders that it is necessary (Armenakis et al. 2001; Burke 2002; Judson 1991; Kotter 1995; Laurent 2003; Nadler and Nadler 1998). The process of convincing individuals of the need for change often begins with crafting a compelling vision for it. A vision presents a picture or image of the future that is easy to communicate and that organizational members find appealing (Kotter 1995); it provides overall direction for the change process and serves as the foundation for developing specific strategies for arriving at a future end state.

Table 1.1 Determinants of Successful Implementation of Organizational Change in the Public Sector

Proposition	Subpropositions
Ensure the need. Managerial leaders must verify and persuasively communicate the need for change.	• Convince organizational members of the need and desirability for change. • Craft a compelling vision of change. • Employ written and oral communication and forms of active participation to communicate and disseminate the need for change.
Provide a plan. Managerial leaders must develop a course of action or strategy for implementing change.	• Devise a strategy for reaching the desired end state, with milestones and a plan for achieving each one of them. • The strategy should be clear and specific, avoiding ambiguity and inconsistencies in the plan. • The strategy should rest on sound causal theory for achieving the desired end state.
Build internal support and overcome resistance. Managerial leaders must build internal support for and reduce resistance to change through widespread participation in the change process and other means.	• Encourage participation and open discussion to reduce resistance to change. • Avoid criticism, threats, and coercion aimed at reducing resistance to change. • Commit sufficient time, effort, and resources to manage participation effectively.

Ensure top-management support and commitment. An individual or group within the organization should champion the cause for change.	• An "idea champion" or guiding coalition should advocate for and lead the transformation process. • Individuals championing the change should have the skill and acumen to marshal resources and support for change, to maintain momentum, and to overcome obstacles to change. • Political appointees and top-level civil servants should support the change.
Build external support. Managerial leaders must develop and ensure support from political overseers and key external stakeholders.	• Build support for and commitment to change among political overseers. • Build support for and commitment to change among interest groups with a stake in the organization.
Provide resources. Successful change usually requires adequate resources to support the change process.	• Provide adequate amounts of financial, human, and technological resources to implement change. • Avoid overtaxing organizational members. • Capitalize on synergies in resources when implementing multiple changes simultaneously.

Continued

Table 1.1 (*Continued*)   Determinants of Successful Implementation of Organizational Change in the Public Sector

Proposition	Subpropositions
Institutionalize change. Managers and employees must effectively institutionalize changes.	• Employ a variety of measures to displace old patterns of behavior and institutionalize new ones. • Monitor the implementation of change. • Institutionalize change before shifts in political leadership cause commitment to and support for change to diminish.
Pursue comprehensive change. Managerial leaders must develop an integrative, comprehensive approach to change that achieves subsystem congruence.	• Adopt and implement a comprehensive, consistent set of changes to the various subsystems of the organization. • Analyze and understand the interconnections between organizational subsystems before pursuing subsystem congruence.

Some research on private organizations indicates that it is easier to convince individuals of the need for change when leaders can craft a vision that offers the hope of relief from stress or discomfort (Kets de Vries and Balazs 1999). Nadler and Nadler (1998) even suggest creating dissatisfaction with the current state of affairs in order to get members of the organization to embrace change. Also, to convince individuals of the need for and desirability of change and begin the process of "unfreezing" the organization, Armenakis, Harris, and Feild (2001) suggest the need to employ effective written and oral communication and various forms of active employee participation.

In addition, the public management literature contains evidence of the importance of determining, framing, and communicating the need for change through a continuing process of exchange with as many stakeholders and participants as possible (Abramson and Lawrence 2001; Rossotti 2005; Young 2001). For instance, Kemp, Funk, and Eadie (1993) and Bingham and Wise (1996) conclude that successful implementation of new programs depends on top management's ability to disseminate information about the change and convince employees of the urgency to change. Denhardt and Denhardt (1999) describe how effective local government managers verify the need for change through "listening and learning" and then communicate those needs in ways that build support for change. Relatedly, researchers also note that leaders in the public sector take advantage of mandates, political windows of opportunity, and external influences to validate and convey the need for change (Abramson and Lawrence 2001; Harokopus 2001; Lambright 2001; Rossotti 2005).

Factor 2: Provide a plan. Managerial leaders must develop a course of action or strategy for implementing change.

Convincing the members of an organization of the need for change is obviously not enough to bring about actual change. The new idea or vision must be transformed into a course of action or strategy, with goals and a plan for achieving it (Abramson and Lawrence 2001; Carnall 1995; Judson 1991; Kotter 1995; Lambright 2001; Nadler and Nadler 1998; Young 2001). This strategy serves as a road map for the organization, offering direction on how to arrive at the preferred end state, identifying obstacles, and proposing measures for overcoming those obstacles. As Kotter (1995) explains, this is necessary so that the transformation does not disintegrate into a set of unrelated and confusing directives and activities.

Two aspects that appear crucial for organizational change in the public sector include the clarity, or degree of specificity, of the strategy and the extent to which the strategy rests on sound causal theory (Bishop and Jones 1993; Grizzle and Pettijohn 2002; Mazmanian and Sabatier 1989; Meier and McFarlane 1995). As Bingham and Wise (1996) and Meyers and Dillon (1999) discover, policy ambiguity can sow confusion, which allows public managers to reinterpret the policy and implement it in a fashion that brings about few of the changes that policy makers intended (see also Montjoy and O'Toole 1979). Finally, a mandate for change based on sound causal theory helps to eliminate inconsistent or conflicting directives that can undermine efforts to implement change.

Factor 3: Build internal support and overcome resistance. Managerial leaders must build internal support for and reduce resistance to change through widespread participation in the change process, among other means.

Students of major organizational changes typically report that successful leaders understand change to involve a political process of developing and nurturing support from major stakeholders and organizational members. Individuals in organizations resist change for a variety of reasons (Kets de Vries and Balazs 1999), including that some change ideas are simply ill conceived or unjustified, or pose harmful consequences for members of the organization. Even assuming a well-justified and well-planned change initiative, however, leaders must build internal support and overcome resistance.

Several researchers have observed that a crisis, shock, or strong external challenge to the organization can help reduce resistance to change. Van de Ven (1993) explains that because individuals are highly adaptable to gradually emerging conditions, a "shock" or stimulus of significant magnitude is typically required for them to accept change as inevitable. In a similar vein, Kotter (1995, 60) warns managers against the risk of "playing it too safe" and notes that "when the urgency rate is not pumped up enough, the transformation process cannot succeed." He even observes that in a few of the most successful cases of organizational change, the leadership manufactured crises (see also Laurent 2003; Thompson and Fulla 2001).

For many decades, other social scientists have emphasized the value of effective and ethical participation, as well as other means, in supporting group and organizational change and in lowering the resistance to change (Coch and French 1948; Lewin 1947). More recently, experts have further explored ways of reducing the resistance to change. Judson (1991) identifies a variety of tactics managers can employ to minimize the resistance to change, including threats, compulsion, criticism, persuasion, inducements and rewards, compromises and bargaining, guarantees against personal loss (e.g., offering job security or retraining to employees), psychological support, employee participation, ceremonies and other efforts to build loyalty, recognition of the appropriateness and legitimacy of past practices, and gradual and flexible implementation of change. With the exception of threats, compulsion, and criticism, which can be counterproductive and further increase resistance, he argues that these approaches can be effective at reducing the resistance to change (see also Kets de Vries and Balazs 1999). A "dual approach" that creates pride in the organization's past success, while also arguing for a new way of doing things, seems also to be effective at reducing the resistance to change.

The scope of participation is also important. Widespread participation in the change process is perhaps the most frequently cited approach for overcoming resistance to change (e.g., Abramson and Lawrence 2001; Young 2001). Many scholars focusing on private organizations have asserted that planned change requires extensive participation by members at multiple levels of the organization during the various stages of implementation (Bunker and Alban 1997; Greiner 1967; Johnson and Leavitt 2001; Nadler and Nadler 1998; Pasmore 1994). The literature indicates that involving organizational members helps to reduce barriers to change by creating psychological ownership, promoting the dissemination of critical information, and encouraging employee feedback for fine-tuning the change during implementation.

Participation presents a particularly important contingency in the public sector. As Warwick (1975) asserts, career civil servants, allegedly motivated by caution and security, can use to their advantage the frequent turnover among top political appointees; they can simply resist new initiatives until a new administration comes to power. However, their participation in the various stages of change can help to reduce this kind of resistance. Rossotti (2005), for instance, recounts a continuous process of meetings with all types of stakeholders—including frontline employees, union leaders, taxpayers and taxpayer groups, managers, Treasury Department executives, and members of Congress (see also Denhardt and Denhardt 1999; Poister and Streib 1999). Goldsmith (1999, 68ff), too, describes how employee "empowerment" played a key role in his change efforts as mayor of Indianapolis.

Interestingly, Kelman's (2005) analysis of the federal procurement reform process suggests that one should avoid *overestimating* change resistance. A significant number of employees welcomed reforms, and their support needed only to be "unleashed." Buttressing Kelman's point, Thompson and Sanders's (1997) analysis of change within the Veterans Benefits Administration suggests that success may require various bottom-up participatory elements, such as delegating decision making to middle management and granting frontline workers greater discretion to implement changes. They note, however, that top-management must still encourage and reward innovation and express continuing support for the change. Successful implementation of organizational change, therefore, often resembles a hybrid form that combines elements of lower-level participation and top management direction. Even widespread participation, however, does not offer a magic bullet for overcoming resistance to change (Shareef 1994). Bruhn, Zajac, and Al-Kazemi (2001) advise that participation be widespread and span all phases of the change process, but they stress that leaders must take participation seriously, commit time and effort to it, and manage it properly. The failure to do so can lead to wasted time, morale, and resources (also see Bryson and Anderson 2000).

Factor 4: Ensure top-management support and commitment. An individual or group within the organization should champion the cause for change.

Top-management support and commitment to change play an especially crucial role in success (Burke 2002; Carnall 1995; Greiner 1967; Johnson and Leavitt 2001; Kotter 1995; Nadler and Nadler 1998; Yukl 2002). Some studies of organizational change have stressed the importance of having a single change agent or "idea champion" lead the transformation. An idea champion is a highly respected individual who maintains momentum and commitment to change, often taking personal risks in the process (Kanter 1983). Other authors have stressed the need to have a guiding coalition to support the change. A guiding coalition is a group of individuals who lend legitimacy to the effort and marshal the resources and emotional support required to induce organizational members to change (Carnall 1995; Kets de Vries and Balazs 1999; Yukl 2002). Kotter (1995, 62) asserts that one or two managers often launch organizational renewal efforts, but "whenever some minimum mass is not achieved early in the effort, nothing much worthwhile happens."

Whether in the form of a single change agent or a guiding coalition, however, top-management support and commitment play an essential role in successful change in the public sector (Abramson and Lawrence 2001; Berman and Wang 2000; Bingham and Wise 1996; Denhardt and Denhardt 1999; Harokopus 2001; Hennessey 1998; Kemp et al. 1993; Lambright 2001; Laurent 2003; Rainey and Rainey 1986; Thompson and Fulla 2001; Young 2001). Barzelay's (2001) analysis of new public management reforms in various nations, for instance, supports this claim. It reports that Aucoin (1990) attributes failure of these reforms in Canada to lack of support from the cabinet ministers.

Finally, in the public sector, top-management support for change often requires the support of top-level career civil servants in addition to politically appointed executives. Moreover, the need for leadership continuity and stability raises particular challenges in the public sector, given the frequent and rapid turnover of many executives in government agencies, as compared to business executives. This may explain why many significant changes in government need to be, and have been, led by career civil servants (Holzer and Callahan 1998).

Factor 5: Build external support. Managerial leaders must develop and ensure support from political overseers and key external stakeholders.

Organizational change in the public sector also depends on the degree of support from political overseers and other key external stakeholders. The impact of these actors on the outcome of change efforts stems in part from their ability to impose statutory changes and control the flow of vital resources to public organizations. Political overseers also can influence the outcome of planned change by creating and conveying a vision that explains the need for change, as well as by selecting political appointees who are sympathetic to the change and have the knowledge and skills required for managing the transformation.

As Golembiewski (1985) suggests, attaining support from governmental authorities and political actors involves serious challenges. Public agencies often have multiple political masters pursuing different objectives, and politically appointed executives often have very weak relationships with career civil servants. Despite these challenges, public managers implementing change in their organizations must display skill in obtaining support from powerful external actors (Berman and Wang 2000; de Lancer Julnes and Holzer 2001; Wallin 1997). Berry, Chackerian, and Wechsler (1999), for instance, note that the governor's high level of commitment and support for particular reforms in Florida had a substantial influence on the degree of implementation (see also Chackerian and Mavima 2000). Changes that could be implemented quickly and cost-effectively generated more support from elected officials than those with higher implementation costs and requiring much more effort and time to implement.

Support from other key external stakeholders also figures prominently in successful change efforts (Abramson and Lawrence 2001; Denhardt and Denhardt 1999; Harokopus 2001; Mazmanian and Sabatier 1989; Rossotti 2005; Wallin 1997). Thompson and Fulla (2001) conclude that the interest group environment acted as an important determinant of agency adoption of National Performance Review (NPR) reforms, with strong interest group opposition to an agency's NPR reforms constraining change. One caveat noted by Weissert and Goggin (2002), however, is that proceeding with implementation without garnering the support of interest groups can speed up the implementation process but at the cost of dissatisfaction and criticism among these groups.

Factor 6: Provide resources. Successful change usually requires adequate resources to support the change process.

A fairly consistent finding in the literature is that change is not cheap or without tradeoffs. Planned organizational change involves a redeployment or redirection of scarce organizational resources toward a host of new activities, including developing a plan or strategy for implementing the change, communicating the need for change, training employees, developing new processes and practices, restructuring and reorganizing the organization, and testing and experimenting with innovations (see Burke 2002; Mink et al. 1993; Nadler and Nadler 1998). Failure to provide adequate resources in support of a planned change leads to feeble implementation efforts, higher levels of interpersonal stress, and even neglect of core organizational activities and functions.

Boyne's (2003) review of research, for example, finds that *resources* was one of the important factors for improving public services (and, hence, bringing about change). Rossotti (2005, 40) invested heavily in resources for major changes at the IRS and expressed regret that he had not sought stronger assurances of budgetary support for the reforms at the outset from Treasury Department officials. He is supported in his view by students of recent administrative reforms in the public sector who have found that resource scarcity can hinder organizational changes (Berry et al. 1999; Bingham and Wise 1996; Chackerian and Mavima 2000; Kemp et al. 1993).

As Chackerian and Mavima (2000) discover in their analysis of government reform in Florida, the issue of resource munificence becomes even more complex when multiple organizational changes are implemented as part of a comprehensive reform agenda. The authors find that multiple changes interact with one another, causing synergies and tradeoffs. For example, the pursuit of multiple changes that demand *modest* amounts of similar resources can lead to synergies, which increase the likelihood that all changes will be implemented successfully. The pursuit of multiple changes that require *large* amounts of similar resources, on the other hand, tends to result in tradeoffs. Tradeoffs, in turn, create winners and losers, with low-cost changes taking precedence over, or even displacing, more costly changes.

Factor 7: Institutionalize and embed change.

To make change enduring, members of the organization must incorporate the new policies or innovations into their daily routines. Virtually all organizational changes involve changes in the behavior of organizational members. Employees must learn and routinize these behaviors in the short term, and leaders must institutionalize them over the long haul, so that new patterns of behavior displace old ones (Edmondson, Bohmer, and Pisano 2001; Greiner 1967; Kotter 1995; Lewin 1947).

Doing so, however, is not easy. Armenakis, Harris, and Feild (2001) developed a model on how to reinforce and institutionalize change. They argue that leaders can modify formal structures, procedures, and human resource management practices; employ rites and ceremonies; diffuse the innovation through trial runs and pilot projects; collect data to track the progress of and commitment to change; and engage employees in active participation tactics that foster "learning by doing." Judson (1991), too, strongly emphasizes the need to collect data and monitor the implementation process to keep managers aware of the extent to which organizational members have adopted the change. Evaluation and monitoring efforts should continue even after the change is fully adopted to ensure that organizational members do not lapse into old patterns of behavior.

The evidence, however, is mixed as to the optimal pace for institutionalizing change. Some experts underscore the need to adopt a change gradually or incrementally on a small scale to build momentum and demonstrate the benefits of change (Armenakis et al. 2001; Cohen and Eimicke 1994; Greiner 1967; Kotter 1995; Rainey and Rainey 1986). Others have argued that a rapid pace of change can overcome inertia and resistance (Tushman and Romanelli 1985). Small-scale or gradual implementation, however, may pose more of a challenge in the public sector than in business, since frequent shifts in political leadership and short tenures for political appointees can cause commitments to change to wane.

Factor 8: Pursue comprehensive change. Managerial leaders must develop an integrative, comprehensive approach to change that achieves subsystem congruence.

Many researchers stress that for fundamental change in behavior to occur, leaders must make systemic changes to the various subsystems of their organization. These must be aligned with the desired end state. Changing only one or two subsystems will not generate sufficient force to bring about organizational transformation (Meyers and Dillon 1999; Mohrman and Lawler 1983; Nadler and Nadler 1998; Tichy 1983). Still others have warned, however, that implementing multiple changes without understanding the structure and nature of the interconnections among subsystems can result in additional costs and a longer implementation period than anticipated (Hannan, Polos, and Carroll 2003).

Amis, Slack, and Hinings (2004) go even further, arguing that the actual sequence of change matters; they find that beginning the transformation process by changing "high-impact" decision-making elements of the organization helps to build momentum for the broader array of changes that follow. Likewise, Robertson, Roberts, and Porras (1993, 629) conclude from their study of business firms that practitioners should begin any change effort with systematic changes in the work setting and ensure "that the various work setting changes are congruent with each other, sending consistent signals to organization members about the new behaviors desired."

Support for these arguments is also present in public sector research. Shareef (1994), for instance, finds that an effort to implement a participative culture in the United States Postal Service fell short due to management's failure to modify organizational subsystems to make them congruent with the desired cultural change. Golembiewski (1985) emphasizes the fruitlessness of attempting to change attitudes and behaviors toward more teamwork and participation if the organizational structure remains strictly hierarchical and fails to support a team orientation (see also Meyers and Dillon 1999). The wisdom of this strategy notwithstanding, Robertson and Seneviratne's (1995) study suggests that subsystem congruence may be more difficult to achieve in the public than in the private sector, because change agents in the public sector exercise less discretion than their private sector counterparts.

Conclusion

The factors and propositions offered in this chapter should serve not as a roadmap but as a compass for researchers and practitioners seeking to find their way amid the sustained, persistent, and challenging pressures for change that they confront daily. These factors and propositions, in turn, suggest a robust, varied, and quite challenging agenda for future research. Such an effort is timely, important for both practice and theory building, and long overdue.

Commentary

Patrick E. Connor and Fred Thompson

In summarizing the vast literature on organizational change, Fernandez and Rainey's otherwise informative analysis provokes several questions. The second proposition in Table 1.1 says (simply), "provide a plan … a course of action … a strategy … with milestones" and offers some subpropositions for doing so. But what does it mean to provide a plan? At a minimum it means answering the following questions (Connor, Lake, and Stackman 2003). What are the *objects* of change; that is, what needs to be changed—tasks or activities that individuals perform, routines and procedures, or mechanisms and processes, such as how decisions get made, how information flows, and how control is exercised? What *methods* will be employed in carrying out a particular large-scale change? There are several that are available, ranging from technological to structural. What *strategies* are most appropriate under the circumstances—providing the participants with a new script, developing their capacity to perform their assigned roles, or coercing them into doing so?

These questions, in turn, suggest a number of research lines of inquiry. How do the members of organizations reliably identify the "objects" on which change-energy should be spent? What governance mechanisms should the members of organizations use to choose change methods? If different circumstances call for different strategies, what distinguishes one "circumstance" from another? And how does that translate into a choice of strategy?

Fernandez and Rainey also speak specifically to "managerial leaders," "top management," "change agents," "idea champions" (although the latter two seem to be treated as if they are roughly the same), and more generally, to a number of other roles that must be performed to accomplish social change. These might more usefully be conceptualized (see Connor et al. 2003, 140–143 for an elaboration) as follows. *Catalysts* acknowledge, sometimes encourage, dissatisfaction with the status quo. They might be thought of as *agents provocateurs*, leading others to feel sufficiently frustrated or perturbed to call for change. *Solution givers* suggest what can be done to solve problems or take advantage of opportunities. *Process helpers* assist change managers and organization members in understanding how the process of change should work—both in general, as with the models referred to above, and in the specific case at hand. *Resource linkers* bring together various financial, people, and knowledge resources. These are all leadership roles. These roles, in turn, suggest the following avenues for research: (1) what knowledge, skills, and attributes of individuals are associated with success in performing each role; (2) what contextual—that is, organizational and environmental—conditions are associated with success in performing each role; (3) which roles are critical to each phase of a successful change process; and (4) how do the roles differ in relative importance, by phase?

The authors also allude to one of the most useful devices for thinking about the conduct of organizational change. They refer to "forces in the desired direction [and] opposing forces." The reference, as they note, is to Lewin's (1947, 1951) conceptualization of a change process as taking place within a sort of force field. There is a key piece that is missing from this formulation, however. As an executive friend of ours is fond of saying, in talking about moving from the current state to the end state, "Meanwhile, we have a business to run." The phase to which "meanwhile" refers is known in the literature as the *transition* phase.

Bridges (2003) argues that this phase consists of the following sequence: first, members of the organization let go of the past; second, they endure a kind of limbo between the old and the new, in which they experience a certain level of disorientation—a confused feeling of "what in the world is going on here?"; and, finally, they reorient themselves so that things make sense again. Successful management of the transition phase requires three timing questions to be answered: where should the first change action occur, when must the change be essentially complete, and what are the optimal sequence and timing for applying whatever strategies and tactics have been decided upon? In turn, these suggest some intriguing research questions pertaining to the key variables integral to transition management: (1) in successful change efforts, how do organizations help their members to "let go"; (2) what—empirically, not anecdotally—works and what does not; (3) in successful change efforts, what decision rules govern the staging—the sequence and timing—of strategies and tactics; and (4) are there activities at each stage that the participants must get absolutely right?

Finally, we are concerned about the authors' implicit attitude toward the recipients of change—the organization members upon whom a particular change is visited. Consider the language in several propositions and subpropositions: "convince organizational members," "craft a compelling vision," "employ … communication … [to] disseminate the need for change," "build internal support and *overcome resistance*," and "encourage participation and open discussion *to reduce resistance to change*" (emphasis added in both cases). There is a clear contradiction between these words—*employ … active participation* and *encourage … open discussion* and these words—*overcome, convince, disseminate* and *manage participation*. The language of the propositions and subpropositions is altogether consistent with a top-down, managed perspective on effecting organizational change. Management knows that it is the employee's job to follow.

But there is an alternative perspective which argues that organizational change occurs most successfully when organization members are truly engaged, when they actually care about the outcome, and when they "have the necessary ownership, commitment, and will to implement" change strategies (Axelrod 2000, 2). From this perspective, engagement, caring, ownership, and commitment are not the result of being overcome, convinced, disseminated to, or, we daresay, managed. Rather, they come about by virtue of organization members' views, in fact, being taken into account and considered; by *many*—read, most—members being involved in the design and implementation of a change process; by members' ideas and information being systematically shared widely; and by the formation of "communities" of members who share interests, knowledge, and abilities.

Commentary

J. Christopher Mihm

Our work at the Government Accountability Office (GAO) on transformation and the resulting advice we have been giving to federal agencies and the Congress are broadly consistent with the eight determinants of successful implementation of organizational change in the public sector identified by Fernandez and Rainey. As such, I will elaborate a bit more on the specific processes and nuances that the authors highlight. The opinions expressed in this commentary are mine and not those of the GAO.

First, as the authors note, leadership must set the direction, pace, and tone for the transformation and must provide a clear, mission-related, consistent rationale for the organizational change. Second, the mission and strategic goals of a transformed organization must become the focus of the transformation, must define the culture, and must serve as a vehicle for employees to unite and rally around. Mission clarity is especially essential to defining the purpose of the transformation to employees, customers, and stakeholders. The mission and strategic goals must be clear to employees, customers, and stakeholders and must be seen as the driving force of the changes that are being made. Indeed, these are essential to helping agency leadership and its customers and stakeholders make intelligent tradeoffs among short-term and long-term wants, needs, and affordability.

Third, and relatedly, organization leaders must have a clear set of principles and priorities that serve as a framework for change. Principles define the attributes that are intrinsically important to what the organization does and how it will do it. This, in turn, leads to a fourth critical factor: because the transformation will take years to complete, action-oriented implementation goals and timelines with milestone dates must be established to track the organization's progress toward its intermediate and long-term transformation goals. By demonstrating progress toward these transformation goals, the organization also builds momentum and demonstrates that real progress is being made.

Fifth, the primary goal of the strong and stable implementation team that Fernandez and Rainey identify as critical to the day-to-day management of the transformation is to ensure that various change initiatives are sequenced and implemented in a coherent and integrated way. The team must have direct access and be accountable to top leadership. In turn, top leadership must vest the team with the necessary authority and resources to set priorities, make timely decisions, and move quickly to implement top leadership's decisions regarding the transformation.

Sixth, leaders must ensure that the organization's performance management system creates a "line of sight" that shows how team, unit, and individual performance can contribute to overall organizational results. The performance management system also can help manage and direct the transformation process. To be successful, transformation efforts also must be led and managed by individuals who know how to integrate and create synergy among the multiple organizations involved in any large-scale transformation effort. Successful efforts measure individual performance and contributions on competencies such as change management, cultural sensitivity, teamwork and collaboration, and information sharing. Leaders, managers, and employees who demonstrate these competencies must then be rewarded.

Seventh, an effective and ongoing internal and external communication strategy is essential to making transformation happen. Moreover, a successful communication effort requires twice the time and effort that was at first planned—no matter how ambitious the original plan was. Communication is most effective when done early, clearly, and often and is downward, upward, and lateral. A transforming organization must develop a comprehensive communication strategy that reaches out to employees, customers, and stakeholders and seeks genuinely to engage them in the transformation process.

Employee involvement strengthens the transformation process by including frontline perspectives and experiences. By participating in transformation task teams, employees have additional opportunities to share their experiences and shape policies and procedures as they are being developed. Communications with employees must include topics such as the new organization's strategic goals, customer service, and in particular, employee concerns. It is important to help employees understand how the changes from the transformation process will affect them and to address the immediate and natural question: "What's in it for me?" Employees and other stakeholders will be concerned about whether their jobs will be affected, what their rights and protections will be, or how their responsibilities and existing access and influence might change yet still benefit them. Still, there are cautions. Day-to-day operations, service quality, and mission accomplishment must continue to take first priority. Organizations and their employees must guard against being so involved in implementing their transformation initiatives that they lose sight of the fundamental reason for the transformation—improved results.

Eighth, human capital strategies are at the center of any serious change management initiative. An organization's people define its culture, drive its performance, and embody its knowledge base and thus are the keys to a successful transformation. Therefore, it is not surprising to find that a failure to address adequately—and often even to consider—a wide variety of people and cultural issues is at the heart of unsuccessful transformations. The key to success is to recognize the "people" element of a transformation and implement strategies to help individuals maximize their full potential in the new organization while simultaneously minimizing the duration and significance of reduced productivity and effectiveness that inevitably occur as a result of the changes.

Finally, an argument can be made that the essential ingredients of improved public performance in the twenty-first century are not so much strengthened internal workings of agencies. Rather, they are improvements in how agencies collaborate and interact with other organizations through networks to achieve results. To ignore this dimension is to miss much of what is important in public management today.

Commentary

Mary Tschirhart

Fernandez and Rainey outline eight factors that they say condition the success of change efforts. Their first proposed determinant for successful implementation of organizational change in the public sector is to ensure the need, which involves the subproposition of convincing organizational members of the need and desirability for change. This implies that any desired change by managerial leaders will, if successfully implemented, result in organizational success. But is an intended organizational change that is accomplished also a successful change?

Perhaps, given an assumption that some change is inevitable, we simply accept that internally driven change is better than more random, organic, or externally controlled change. But is that necessarily the case? I would contend that scholars and practitioners writing about organizational change neglect an important part of the picture if they fail to address how to differentiate and conceptualize successful change, successful implementation of an intended change, and a successful organization produced by the intended change.

Fortunately, there are literatures that can help guide us in this direction. The stakeholder (e.g., Freeman 2005), values (e.g., Amis, Slack, and Hinings 2002), and ethics (e.g., Durand and Colari 2006) literatures offer some tools for justifying prioritization of some objectives and strategies over others. A psychological contract orientation (Rousseau 1995) may help us relate change efforts to employees' sense of their own and their employers' obligations related to the change. Organizational justice approaches help us to understand issues of fairness related to change (e.g., Hosmer and Kiewitz 2005; Wooten and White 1999). Theories and analyses of how different stakeholders judge the success of a change and its implementation may lead to a better understanding of the potential winners and losers from a change effort and encourage more thoughtful and ethical decision making about desirable changes and change strategies. By surfacing patterns showing what tends to be *lost* as well as gained with specific types of changes and change techniques, we may gain an insight into common tradeoffs that can then aid strategic decision making. This may reorient us to see Fernandez and Rainey's propositions less as "determinants" of successful change than as options that are more or less likely to have specific outcomes whose value can be judged by a range of criteria.

If we accept that successful implementation of an intended organizational change is not the same as successful organizational change, then we also need to look more carefully and critically at the literature on resistance to change. We need to know more about how to uncover and understand the norms, attitudes, and beliefs that may be behind resistance. Change-agent prescriptions tend to focus on how to reduce resistance to change. An acceptance that some resistance may be appropriate and beneficial to organizational success (Piderit 2000) comes with the implication that scholars and managers should consider strategies and incentives for appreciating and fostering resistance (e.g., Mabin, Forgeson, and Green 2001) as well as overcoming it. In addition, it calls attention to the positive aspects of employee deviance from formal organizational practices as a potential asset for change initiation and acceptance and encourages organizational leaders to be facilitators of change efforts rather than originators (Pascale and Sternin 2005).

Anyone interested in change in the public sector should also consider the applicability of Fernandez and Rainey's advice to groups of organizations. This is especially true in the contemporary networked state. By focusing on the organization as the unit of analysis, we fail to see the boundary blurring that may affect when and how members of different organizations interact in the development of change goals, design of change processes, implementation of change efforts, and evaluation of change outcomes.

It is not that Fernandez and Rainey ignore the external environment of organizations. Some of the theoretical streams (e.g., institutionalism) they briefly note focus on changes in populations of organizations rather than change in individual organizations. But in their adoption of a rational, strategic lens and focus on the proactive management of change, the authors acknowledge and then set aside these theoretical perspectives in their discussion of prescriptions for successful change. However, a network perspective encourages us to go beyond seeing other organizations simply as sources of support and tangible resources. It encourages research on network-level effects of changes and the network characteristics and interorganizational dynamics that may affect implementation outcomes. For recent network perspectives on change, readers may wish to see Balogun, Gleadle, Hailey, and Willmott (2005), Bramson and Buss (2002), and Vogel (2005). Research designed to help refine change-management techniques for single organizations is limited in telling us what is needed to create and improve networks of interacting organizations with compatible or conflicting objectives.

To be sure, there has been little effort to synthesize the numerous theories on organizational change. I am, however, less interested in learning which theories offer the most explanatory power than in how to integrate knowledge gained from multiple theoretical perspectives to inform practice and develop better models and tools for research and practice. Not surprisingly, much of the prescriptive literature, as demonstrated by Fernandez and Rainey's distillation of it, focuses on practical implications from theories asserting the importance of human agency in change efforts. However, by expending more effort to understand what they cannot control, individuals may become better at influencing what they can manage and reducing the psychological strain that can come with organizational change (Bordia et al. 2004).

Chapter 2

Back to the Future? Performance-Related Pay, Empirical Research, and the Perils of Persistence*

James L. Perry, Trent A. Engbers, and So Yun Jun

Contents

---

* Adapted from Perry, J. L., T. A. Engbers, and S. Y. Jun. 2009. Back to the future? Performance-related pay, empirical research, and the perils of persistence. *Public Administration Review* 69(1): 39–51.

One of the by-products of new public management (NPM) is the resurgence of interest in performance-related pay. This is consistent with NPM's view of "organizations as a chain of low-trust principal/agent relationships (rather than fiduciary or trustee-beneficiary ones), a network of contracts linking incentives to performance" (Dunleavy and Hood 1994, 9). And the most prominent examples of the application of these principles to federal agencies occurred during the George W. Bush administration when Congress approved performance-related pay reforms in the Department of Homeland Security (DHS) and the United States Department of Defense (DOD).

The reform of human capital policies was a bone of contention in the 2002 legislation creating DHS. President Bush, however, succeeded in winning the legislative contest to "design a modern human resources management system that is mission-centered, fair, effective, and flexible" (DHS 2005). DOD also introduced a pay-for-performance system in the context of the National Security Personnel System (NSPS) approved by Congress in 2004 (Office of the Secretary of Defense 2007). DOD issued final regulations for NSPS in November 2005 and implemented regulations for performance management on April 30, 2006. The performance management regulations, which run thirty-four pages with appendices, cover details ranging from setting performance expectations, to monitoring performance, to pay pool policies and procedures.

Curiously, the resurgence of performance-related pay in the U.S. federal government comes more than a decade after Congress abandoned the Performance Management and Recognition System (PMRS), which was the pay-for-performance policy from 1984 to 1991. The demise of PMRS resulted from a variety of flaws, including poor discrimination among performance levels, inadequate funding, and little demonstrable evidence that the system improved performance (Perry, Petrakis, and Miller 1989). Although PMRS was abandoned, it was considered a significant improvement over its predecessor, the Merit Pay System, which was ushered in with great fanfare by the Civil Service Reform Act (CSRA) of 1978.

The recent about-face on performance-related pay raises questions about whether anything has changed in the intervening period. What evidence do we have that performance-related pay is now likely to work when it did not before? Do we have new research addressing this question that suggests optimism that this latest effort will succeed? What conclusions can we draw from that literature about what it would take to create an effective pay-for-performance system in the public sector? Do public sector institutions affect prospects for success?

To answer these questions, this chapter begins by reviewing syntheses of evaluations of pay-for-performance systems research conducted in the late 1980s and early 1990s. With this as an evaluative baseline, we offer a comprehensive analysis of fifty-seven studies assessing performance-related pay in government conducted from 1977 to 2008. From this analysis, we identify seven important lessons for improving the performance of public servants in the bureaucracy.

Assessing the Effectiveness of Pay-for-Performance Systems: A Review of Prior Research, 1977–1993

Support for performance-related pay theoretically is grounded in expectancy theory (Pearce and Perry 1983) and reinforcement theory (Perry, Mesch, and Paarlberg 2006). Expectancy theory is predicated on the belief that individuals will exert effort if they expect it will result in an outcome they value (Van Eerde and Thierry 1996). In the case of performance-related pay, employees will work harder if they value monetary rewards and believe that those awards will result from their increased efforts. Reinforcement theory posits a direct relationship between a desired target behavior (e.g., performance) and its consequences (e.g., pay). It suggests that pay can be used to create consequences for desired behaviors, such as high performance, that will, in turn, reinforce the behaviors (Perry et al. 2006).

The straightforwardness of this causal theory, however, is belied by the number of important variables and the complexity of relationships identified in prior research. Figure 2.1 provides a schematic of these variables and relationships. A variety of antecedent employee and organizational characteristics and environmental

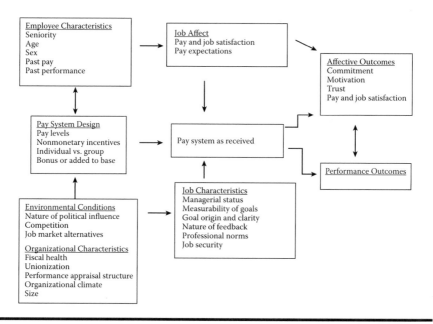

Figure 2.1 Key variables in performance-related pay research.

conditions, together with pay-system design, affect critical intermediate variables. Among these are job characteristics, job affect, and the perceived pay system. These variables influence affective and performance outcomes.

Because most prior reviews of research were published in the late 1980s and early 1990s (Ingraham 1993a; Kellough and Lu 1993; Milkovich and Wigdor 1991; Perry 1986, 1988, 1992), which coincides with reforms triggered by the CSRA, summarizing them tells us what scholars had concluded about performance-related pay prior to its recent resurgence. The first review of the effects of merit pay reforms emanating from the CSRA was Perry's (1986) assessment of contingent pay for public managers. The scope of his review was limited to research on individual contingent pay systems that added performance increments to base pay. Using research conducted prior to 1985, he could not identify any study that found positive effects. Although the evidence was limited, he concluded that merit pay in the public sector was plagued by invalid contracts, information asymmetries where the supervisor lacked accurate information about subordinate performance, and diminished capacity to coordinate interdependence.

A National Research Council (NRC) panel, convened under contract to the U.S. Office of Personnel Management, subsequently reviewed both public and private sector research on pay for performance (Milkovich and Wigdor 1991). Composed of members from academia, business, and government, the NRC panel offered a sobering assessment of the possibilities for successful performance-related pay based on federal experience and research prior to 1990. Directly acknowledging the gap between the promise and reality of pay for performance in the federal government, the panel wrote

> ... In the federal government, the absence of organizational trust and shared values and objectives may be an obstacle to effective pay for performance. Expectations have been high for previous reforms; in most cases, the reality has not approached the expectations. At the same time, increased efforts at political control and rhetoric that has devalued the public service have created high levels of dissatisfaction and demoralization among members of the career service. In such a setting, common goals and objectives, consensus, and trust may be difficult to achieve. (Milkovich and Wigdor 1991, 32)

To be sure, the panel did conclude that "empirical research indicates that individual incentive plans can motivate employees and improve individual performance" (Milkovich and Wigdor 1991, 153). They qualified this conclusion, however, by observing that individual incentive schemes are most likely to succeed for simple, structured jobs and in contexts where trust is high and fair performance goals can be set.

Two additional reviews of pay-for-performance research were published in 1993. Ingraham (1993a) assesses pay for performance using secondary sources on federal programs, a 1991 survey of states that had adopted pay for performance, and interviews conducted in Europe and the United States in 1991 and 1992. She concludes that, "to the extent that success can be demonstrated to exist, it occurs in the context of organizational characteristics not likely to be found in most public sector organizations under existing civil service laws and procedures. Further, budget reductions and economic constraints in many organizations render adequate and stable financial resources unlikely" (354). Ingraham's conclusion about the likely success of performance-related pay is pessimistic, but her inference is qualified by circumstances (e.g., laws, procedures, and funding) and not grounded in fundamental flaws in the approach.

In that same year, Kellough and Lu (1993) afford the last major synthetic review dedicated entirely to this topic by examining fourteen empirical studies of merit pay. The studies covered federal, state, and local managers; public school administrators; and nonsupervisory local government employees. Much like their predecessors, Kellough and Lu conclude: "Generally, merit pay systems have had little positive impact on employee and organization performance" (48). They refer to one application, a demonstration program in the Navy that produced positive effects, but note that the impact of performance-related pay was confounded by other simultaneous changes (e.g., broadbanding, simplified classifications) and higher pay overall. Among the specific reasons Kellough and Lu give for merit pay not being more successful are difficulties with performance evaluation, such as rater leniency and lack of resources to fund the systems at appropriate levels. They also raise similar questions as their predecessors about the environment precluding managerial discretion to link pay to performance and the validity of the motivational assumptions underlying the systems.

The most recent review of pay-for-performance-related research appears as a subset of a study on motivation in the public sector (Perry et al. 2006). As part of a larger review of research on motivation in the public sector, the authors analyzed seventeen review articles, including three meta-analyses and nine research syntheses on financial incentives. Although this analysis does not focus on individual studies and reaches beyond public sector research, it develops several generalizations about financial incentives that are relevant to the present study. The analysis concludes that individual financial incentives are ineffective in traditional public sector settings and joins prior reviews of pay-for-performance systems in concluding that the effectiveness of financial incentives is dependent on organizational conditions.

Pay for Performance Revisited: Getting Our Research Bearings

Do these findings still hold up in research conducted since 1993? In our effort to answer this question, we defined performance-related pay as compensation, contingent on performance, that is awarded to individuals or groups either as permanent increments to the base salary or as a bonus (Milkovich and Wigdor 1991). The aims of our effort were to (1) critically analyze the relevant literature on the topic, (2) attempt to resolve conflicts in the literature, and (3) identify central issues for future research (Cooper and Hedges 1994). The methodology used for this synthesis was drawn from Cooper and Hedges, who apply a five-stage process: (1) formulating the problem, (2) searching the literature, (3) coding the literature, (4) analyzing and interpreting the literature, and (5) presenting to the public. The studies examined were published over a thirty-one-year period, from 1977 to 2008.

To ensure we did not bias our review by excluding new or unpublished studies, we used three primary search processes. The initial search began with the four literature reviews on performance-related pay previously discussed (Ingraham 1993a; Kellough and Lu 1993; Milkovich and Wigdor 1991; Perry 1986). The studies listed in these reviews were included, and the references were examined for other relevant studies. Citations were followed backward from recent articles by using the process of footnote chasing (White 1994), which produces branches of studies progressing backward from current research. Second, we conducted natural language searches in three online search engines and databases—Google Scholar, Academic Search Elite, and JSTOR—using the following terms: *performance-related pay, performance-based pay, merit pay, incentive pay,* and *pay for performance.* Each of these terms was searched independently and in combination with the word *group* (e.g., group performance-related pay). Third, our search process sought sources such as conference papers, unpublished research, and current papers under production by colleagues. Municipal government reports were excluded from the analysis, because they proved too difficult to locate and were often of low quality.

Ultimately, sixty-eight studies were identified for the 1977–2008 time period, and they were assessed for appropriateness of their inclusion in the synthesis. The collection of studies was screened according to four inclusion criteria. Studies had to (1) directly address performance-related pay; (2) be empirical, including case studies, surveys, cross-sectional longitudinal studies, and panel studies; (3) report on immediate, intermediate, or long-term results; and (4) be set in the public sector, which includes nonprofit service providers and organizations delivering services traditionally delivered or funded by government. The use of these criteria reduced the initial list of sixty-eight studies to fifty-seven for final analysis. The eleven studies excluded from the analysis included three studies of for-profit organizations that were not delivering public services, one pre-implementation study, and seven studies that did not deal with performance-related pay. Twenty-five of the fifty-seven studies were published after 1993. A summary of all these studies is provided in Table 2.1 (see Appendix A).

We then coded the following variables in each of the studies: report identification (e.g., author); setting (public, private, nonprofit); subjects; and methodology (see Stock 1994). A series of variables affording insights on performance-related pay also were coded: functional area (general government, medical, human services, professional, regulatory, educational, transit, public safety/military, public services, technical, and financial); type of compensation (bonus or additions to base pay); level of incentive (individual or group); level of government (municipal, state, and national); nature of outcomes studied (affective, performance, implementation, and climate); and managerial status (manager, nonmanager, or nonmanagement professional).

Although we developed a set of codes a priori, we modified them as the analysis progressed. Each study was coded independently by one of the researchers. Studies that proved difficult to code were discussed among the researchers to identify the appropriate code. If no information could be identified for a variable, it was coded as missing. The limited sample size and diversity of variables prevented formal statistical analysis.

We also screened for quality of study by using two measures. One was an ordinal indicator of research methodology, ranging from case studies to quasi-experimental studies to longitudinal and experimental studies. A second was journal impact scores, computed using counts of citations in Google Scholar and the Social Sciences Citation Index and standardized for years since publication. Studies identified vary widely in quality, with impact ratings ranging from 0 to 13.50 and an average impact of 2.33. Variations in quality as judged by methodological sophistication were also wide, ranging from six randomized experiments on the high end to nine case studies on the low end. Twenty-seven of the studies use post-test-only designs.

Of the articles included in our analysis, fourteen studies comprise for-profit public service providers and four studies assess nonprofit public service providers. Three studies from the 1970s and twenty-four studies from the 1980s met our inclusion criteria. Seventeen studies in the database are from the 1990s, and thirteen were published since 2000. A variety of public services is represented in the sample. Twenty-six studies, just under 50 percent of the total, focus on general government. Eleven medical service studies are the next most frequently represented, followed by ten studies of public safety/military and six studies each of human services and education.

The Past as Prologue: The Pay-for-Performance Problematic Revisited

Our analysis confirms past inferences about the limited efficacy of contingent pay in the public sector. Summative results do not appear to differ for the periods prior to 1993 and from 1993 to the present, and isolating post-1993 studies leads to conclusions identical to the pre-1993 studies. Thus, at the aggregate level, our analysis finds that performance-related pay in the public sector consistently fails to deliver on its promise. Aside from this bottom line, disaggregating our analysis offers a more contingency-based response and several additional lessons for practitioners to ponder and researchers to explore further.

Lesson 1: Performance-related pay often has failed to trigger expected intermediate changes in employee perceptions necessary to change motivation.

In addition to assessing whether performance-related pay affects individual and organizational performance, scholars also have been attentive to its effects on several intermediate outcomes portrayed in Figure 2.1, in particular employee perceptions (Egger-Peitler, Hammerschmid, and Meyer 2007; GAO 1984; Heneman and Young 1991; Nigro 1981). Researchers have looked at perceptions integral to the success of pay programs from a motivational perspective and at attitudes toward program implementation. In regard to employee perceptions of variables such as expectancy, instrumentality, and valence (drawn from expectancy theory), researchers have found mixed results. In studies where goals were clear, compensation adequate, and a significant amount of support for merit pay plans existed, performance-related pay resulted in positive outcomes (Greiner et al. 1977). In many cases, however, the underlying foundation of expectancy theory failed to materialize. Some researchers found that respondents perceived little relationship between performance and compensation (Daley 1987), that few believed higher pay would materialize (Pearce, Stevenson, and Perry 1985), and that financial incentives were too small to be valued (Heinrich 2007). Other researchers found that a lack of financial motivation existed (Dowling and Richardson 1997) and that distaste among employees for the divisive side effects among employees occasioned by merit pay was an issue (Marsden 2004).

Although the results of contingent pay systems for intermediate outcomes such as these were generally negative for the articles analyzed in our study as a whole, the results for high-quality studies (i.e., randomized experiments and time-series analyses) were mixed. When focusing on just fourteen high-quality studies, four were found to exhibit negative effects (Bullock 1983; Heinrich 2007; Pearce and Perry 1983; Pearce et al. 1985), five were inconclusive (Allan and Rosenberg 1986; Heckman, Heinrich, and Smith 1997; Hutchison et al. 1996; Perry et al. 1989; Schay 1988), and five were favorable (Davidson et al. 1992; Hickson, Altemeier, and Perrin 1987; Kouides et al. 1998; Krasnik et al. 1990; Orvis, Hosek, and Mattock 1993). The five favorable studies were conducted in healthcare settings and assessed piece-rate compensation programs. Consequently, it is difficult to determine if the high-quality studies showed greater general support for performance-related pay or merely situational support based on the service context or the design of the pay systems that were the focus of the research. No other studies included used piece-rate compensation methods. Despite the results of the studies involving piece-rate plans, analysis of the fifty-seven studies found no differences in performance outcomes between plans using bonuses or those that added to the base pay.

Lesson 2: A variety of contextual factors appears to moderate the effectiveness of performance-related pay systems, especially the type of public service industry involved.

Several contextual factors appear to be associated with the success of performance-related pay. These include high levels of trust, adequate rewards, effective performance appraisals, geographic proximity (Brudney and Condrey 1993; Condrey and Brudney 1992), and degree of professionalism (Andersen 2007). Although the results are open to interpretation, a particularly significant contextual factor appears to be the type of public service industry involved. As noted, studies within the medical context were largely positive (also see Andersen 2007; Davidson et al. 1992; Dowling and Richardson 1997; Heneman, Greenberger, and Strasser 1988; Hickson 1987; Hutchison et al. 1996; Kouides et al. 1998; Krasnik et al. 1990; Shaw et al. 2003). In contrast, research in the regulatory and financial sectors found that performance-related pay generally was perceived as divisive (Bertelli 2006; Gaertner and Gaertner 1985; Gaertner, Gaertner, and Akinnusi 1984; Marsden 2004; Marsden and Richardson 1994; Nachmias and Moderacki 1982; O'Toole and Churchill 1982). Results for education and public safety lay somewhere between those for the medical and the regulatory and financial sectors. Studies on performance-related pay within the education sector found that, except in the most unique situations, the impact on employee attitudes and intrinsic motivation was negative (Andersen and Pallesen 2008; Heneman and Young 1991; Murnane and Cohen 1986). Early studies of police officers using clear goals based on specific crime reduction found a positive impact on crime reduction (Greiner et al. 1977), but subsequent research was less conclusive (Allan and Rosenberg 1986; Schay 1988; Siegel 1987).

Lesson 3: Performance-related pay may have more effect at lower organizational levels where job responsibilities are less ambiguous, contradicting assumptions that contingent pay plans will be more effective at higher levels of organizations.

A factor that appears to affect the efficacy of public performance-related pay is whether it is applied to managers or nonmanagers. Although a significant majority of the studies in our research involved managers, research on nonmanagers accounts for a disproportionate share of positive performance results. This is consistent with the earlier NRC study (Milkovich and Wigdor 1991) cited already, which found, among other things, that performance-related pay systems are best suited for positions where job responsibilities are fairly concrete and measurable. Similarly, Lee and Whitford (2008) find that the use of performance-related pay programs has a disproportionate impact in crowding out intrinsic motivation for nonmanagers.

We need to be cautious, however, not to overstate differences in the effectiveness of performance pay between managers and nonmanagers. Studies on both populations generally showed no effects, but 20 percent of nonmanagerial studies appeared to produce positive performance-related outcomes compared with 14 percent for managerially focused studies. This contradicts existing sentiment that performance-related pay plans will be more effective at higher organizational levels (Risher and Fay 2007).

Importantly, results involving attitudinal changes after introducing performance-related pay are less conclusive. Nachmias and Moderacki (1982) find lower-ranking employees to be more supportive of performance-related pay after contingent pay systems were introduced. However, Gabris (1986) and Kellough and Nigro (2002) find that supervisors and political appointees are most supportive. This may be attributed to involvement in the policy development process. Those most involved in the process of policy development were most supportive of performance-related pay plans (Gabris and Mitchell 1986).

Nevertheless, employees generally perceive the implementation of performance-related pay as unfair (Gabris and Mitchell 1988; Kellough and Selden 1997). The reasons behind the perceptions are varied and sometimes difficult to identify. They include low levels of organizational trust (Condrey and Brudney 1992), lack of transparency of the systems for employees (Egger-Peitler et al. 2007), lack of trust in performance-rating systems (Kellough and Selden 1997), and lack of leadership credibility (Gabris and Ihrke 2000).

Finally, regardless of organizational level, enhancements in performance measurement and management that are independent of pay incentives may account for performance increases by improving goal setting. The beneficial aspect of performance-related pay that emerges from prior research appears not to be the product of the pay scheme but rather the development of performance standards. The use of performance standards has repeatedly been shown to be the most beneficial aspect of performance-pay plans (Fletcher and Williams 1996; Gaertner and Gaertner 1985). In one instance, the introduction of pay into the performance measurement process resulted in a negative impact on performance (Hatry, Greiner, and Gollub 1981).

Avoiding Buyer Remorse: Theoretical Traps and Institutional Constraints

Our review of prior research provides in some ways a pessimistic view for the future of performance-related pay in the public sector. Although research has identified occasional performance-pay successes, the programs typically have fallen short of intermediate and long-term expectations. We argue, however, that our findings are less cause for despair than for caution and more strategic thinking. The reasons for a persistent failure of performance-related pay are more likely its incompatibility with public institutional rules, proponents' inability or unwillingness to adapt it to these values, and its incompatibility with the more powerful motivations that lead many people to pursue public service in the first place. Consequently, our analysis offers three additional lessons for those looking for more than symbolism and political points with voters than for performance results.

Lesson 4: Implementation breakdowns account for some failures of performance-related pay but not all. Institutional differences between the public and private sectors may be the source of these problems and may be the more fundamental constraints on success. Consider them in shaping any performance-based motivational approach to public organizations.

Multiple studies have found employees supporting the idea of pay for performance in the abstract but finding its implementation in their organization plagued by problems (Egger-Peitler et al. 2007; Kessler and Purcell 1992; Marsden and Richardson 1994). In addition, one of the most consistent findings on public sector performance-related pay initiatives in our research is that the absence of good performance management practices is a critical flaw. Not surprisingly, then, the difficulties of implementing performance-related pay in the public sector often generate optimistic "if only" attributions, such as "if only more money were available for payouts" or "if only managers gave more time to appraising employees."

We believe, however, that "poor implementation" explanations for the failure of performance-related pay mask more fundamental deficiencies rooted in basic institutional differences between market and nonmarket settings. These differences include transparency, budget, and stewardship constraints embedded in public institutions that impede the success of performance-related pay. These institutional differences are seldom acknowledged by advocates of performance-related pay.

One distinctive characteristic of public institutions is transparency, which safeguards public trust in a democracy. Transparency also brings with it, however, greater scrutiny of performance-related pay decisions by employees and external constituencies. Within the Senior Executive Service, for instance, the subjective nature of performance-related pay is magnified when inconsistencies are easily identifiable by employees or the media (Bonosaro 2008). Performance-related pay depends, to some extent, on maintaining perceptions that the system is valid, fair, and nonpolitical. These perceptions are harder to maintain when a performance-based pay system operates in transparent settings.

The transparency constraint that public institutions face contrasts with secrecy (Colella et al. 2007) in many private organizations where contingency pay is introduced. Research on pay secrecy is inconclusive (see, e.g., Bartol and Martin 1989; Burroughs 1982; Pfeffer and Langton 1993; Schuster and Colletti 1973), but it does suggest that private organizations rely on secrecy for success (Colella et al. 2007). A study by Pfeffer and Langton (1993) of college and university faculty, for instance, finds that greater wage dispersion (i.e., differences in wages) results in decreased productivity, decreased collaboration, and reduced satisfaction. Yet it has fewer adverse effects in private colleges and universities where pay is less likely to be known. Some states have tried to limit public records laws to expand compensation flexibility and reduce transparency constraints. The courts, however, have tended to support public disclosure lawsuits filed by citizens and media organizations (Poston and Marley 2008).

Budget constraints are a second feature of public institutions that challenge the viability of public performance-related pay. Given the unique nature of public tax revenue streams, institutional rules have been established that constrain public performance-related pay. Market-based revenue streams do not have the same limits as budgets; private salary budgets can increase with expanding revenue. Moreover, when the operative rule is "payroll cost-containment," as in government, it is unlikely that performance-related pay will be designed in a way or at the levels of annual pay increments that expectancy or reinforcement theory require. Edward Lawler (1990, 17) indicates that annual increments ought to be between 10 and 15 percent to be motivationally meaningful, but this level is seldom achieved in public sector salary budgets.

The third implementation constraint faced by public institutions involves external expectations about responsible stewardship of resources. Like the nondistribution constraint that defines nonprofit institutions, public institutions operate in nonmarket conditions subject to rules and expectations regarding how financial resources may be used. Because of these stewardship expectations, even when public employees earn large compensations within the rules, they may face public backlash and outrage. This is precisely what happened when the first round of senior executive bonuses was paid under the CSRA of 1978.

Concerns among politicians that public employees might be overcompensated are responsible for rules that seek to operationalize the stewardship constraint. In Minnesota, for instance, salaries of state agency heads, who must be the highest paid employees in their departments, are capped at 95 percent of the governor's salary (Poston and Marley 2008). It is ironic that the same politicians who promote performance-related pay also may vote against appropriations to fund it if they perceive fiscal restraint serves larger political ends. Miller and Whitford (2007) call this the "principal's moral hazard constraint," where bonuses large enough to produce an efficient incentive effect are prohibitively expensive for the principal. These kinds of institutional rules limit the prospects for effective performance-related pay.

Lesson 5: Don't despair. Public service motivation theory and self-determination theory may be more applicable levers for improving performance in public agencies than approaches applying expectancy theory and reinforcement theory.

Other empirical research suggests that self-determination theory (Deci and Ryan 2004) and public service motivation theory (Perry and Hondeghem 2008a) may be more suitable for public institutional settings. As we imply above, performance pay has roots in the widespread belief that pay-for-performance compensation systems are fair and an appropriate foundation for managerial control. Other motivation theories contend, to the contrary, that the external controls performance pay imposes on employees have the potential to diminish overall motivation, especially when intrinsic motivations direct and sustain employee behaviors. Negative employee reactions to performance pay could reflect their disapproval of external control rather than a self-serving or irrational resistance to change (Brehm and Gates 1997). Motivation-crowding research in economics also reinforces the growing credibility of this explanation for persistent findings of failure (Frey 1997b; Frey and Jegen 2001; Frey and Osterloh 2005).

Lesson 6: Don't adopt conventional pay-for-performance systems simply because everyone else is doing it. Consider the contextual contingencies and adapt accordingly.

The results of our research synthesis confront us with a puzzle: performance-related pay continues to be adopted but persistently fails to deliver on its promise. What accounts for the persistence not only of the failure of performance-related pay but for repeatedly pursuing a failed course of action? An institutional explanation for the persistence of public jurisdictions to adopt performance-related pay begins with an argument originating in sociology. Sociologists argue that organizations that confront uncertainty about performance criteria—and public organizations typically are offered up as exemplars for such uncertainties—seek alternative ways to justify or legitimate themselves to external stakeholders.

In lieu of definitive evidence of high performance, public organizations will either acquiesce to external demands about what is "good management" or seek proxies to signal to stakeholders that they conform to how effective organizations behave (DiMaggio and Powell 1983). The result of such processes is that organizations tend to become more alike, or isomorphic. Thus, public organizations adopt performance-related pay because they are coerced (i.e., "coercive" isomorphism), because they seek to mimic private practices that have achieved high degrees of legitimacy across society (i.e., "mimetic" isomorphism; Meyer and Rowan 1977), or because they try to conform to professional standards or social norms (i.e., "normative" isomorphism). The 1978 adoption of merit pay in the federal government was clearly the result of mimetic isomorphism. When founding U.S. Office of Personnel Management director Scotty Campbell was asked why he had not provided for experimentation prior to government-wide implementation, his reply was simple: "I saw no need. It was my perception that it worked fine in the private sector" (Ingraham 1993a, 349).

Press accounts leave little doubt that the latest round of performance-related pay adoptions is the result of coercive isomorphism. Politicians who press for performance-related pay see it as a mechanism to call bureaucrats to account, to punish them for noncompliance with politicians' preferences, and to make them conform to public and political expectations (Kellough and Lu 1993; March and Olsen 1983; Perry 1988). President George W. Bush's and Congress's support for the DHS's ill-fated MaxHR is an excellent illustration of both institutional isomorphism and the detachment of these processes from effectiveness.

Conclusion

Our journey back in time has yielded important lessons for the future of public performance-related pay. An especially important lesson is that institutional differences between the public and the private sectors—such as transparency, budget limitations, and stewardship expectations—need to be considered in shaping pay-based motivational strategies. Greater scrutiny of performance-related pay accompanying public sector transparency, insufficient financial resources to satisfy motivational theory, and public expectations about the stewardship of resources all limit the potential of public performance-related pay.

Commentary

David J. Houston

In responding to this chapter, it is important to point out that variable pay is not the only external incentive that managers have at their disposal when balancing internal and external motivators. Other tools for encouraging extrinsic motivation are base pay, fringe benefits, commands (rules and regulations), promotion, job security, status, and recognition (social and professional). That said, performance-related pay fails to appreciate the importance of intrinsic motivation. At times, individuals engage in work tasks out of an inherent interest in the activities (enjoyment-based) and because they find the work to be meaningful due to a commitment to self-defined goals or social norms (obligation-based; Deci, Koestner, and Ryan 1999; Frey 1997a; Osterloh, Frey, and Frost 2001).

One aspect of internal motivation that Perry has been instrumental in developing but does not develop in this chapter is that of public service motivation (PSM). Perry and Hondeghem (2008b, vii) define PSM as "an individual's orientation to delivering services to people with a purpose to do good for others and society." It focuses attention on intrinsic motives such as commitment to the norms of service to the public, making a difference in society, and social equity. I would argue that PSM not only is a critical component of motivation but also offers ways to overcome the downsides of pay-for-performance systems.

One major and useful summary critique of such systems is offered by Frey and Osterloh (2005). They argue that variable pay for performance (1) gives a signal to managers that doing one's duty without extra pay is not appropriate; (2) approximates within the firm the conditions of a competitive market in which prosocial behavior is inadequate; (3) changes relational contracts into transactional contracts, which include fewer socioemotional elements; (4) undermines the neutrality of superiors, therewith reducing perceived procedural fairness; and (5) enlarges the self-serving bias of managers and directors (106).

As DiIulio (1994, 281) writes, though a principal-agent approach may explain why bureaucrats "shirk, subvert, and steal on the job," it cannot explain why they "strive ... support ... and sacrifice on the job." And compared with private sector workers, public employees place less of an emphasis on higher pay as a job motivator (Jurkiewicz, Massey, and Brown 1998; Rainey 1982; Wittmer 1991) than on service to society and the importance of meaningful work (Crewson 1997; Houston 2000; Rainey 1982; Steijn 2008; Wittmer 1991). PSM is also positively correlated with organizational citizenship behavior (Kim 2006; Pandey, Wright, and Moynihan 2008) and whistle-blowing (Brewer and Selden 1998). Public sector workers are more likely to be civically engaged, to donate money and time to charitable organizations, and even to give blood (Brewer 2003; Houston 2006, 2008; Rotolo and Wilson 2006; Wilson and Musick 1997).

It is often hypothesized that individuals with high PSM needs will self-select to public sector jobs (Perry 2000; Perry and Wise 1990). However, most evidence in support of this hypothesis is indirect in that it focuses on those already employed (Lewis and Frank 2002; Steijn 2008; Vandenabeele, Hondeghem, and Steen 2004). Still, Leisink and Steijn (2008) argue that qualifications for public service occupations should be expanded beyond a focus on education, previous experience, and job-specific knowledge and skills to include the level of intrinsic motivation encompassed by PSM (Vandenabeele et al. 2004).

The relevance of the work environment for fostering PSM is also important to understand. Moynihan and Pandey (2007) find that bureaucratic red tape is negatively correlated with employee PSM, while the presence of employee-friendly reforms is positively correlated. Camilleri (2007) reports that an employee's PSM is positively correlated with clear organizational goals, performing significant tasks that are varied and challenging, dealing with others, strong manager–employee relations, and friendship opportunities at the workplace. Leadership also has been found to be correlated with PSM (Park and Rainey 2008).

The opportunity to make meaningful contributions to a community, and to see the effect that one's work has toward that end, should also be an especially important management technique for satisfying the intrinsic motivational needs of public employees. Although not examining PSM directly, an experiment conducted by Grant (2008) indicates that making employees aware of the contribution their work ultimately has on organizational outcomes can enhance employee attitudes and behavior. Pandey and Stazyk (2008, 109) review research on the antecedents of PSM and suggest that "nonmonetary, intrinsic rewards may be as important, if not more so, than pecuniary motivators." An organization could foster the desire to perform public service by encouraging or presenting organized activities beyond job-related tasks to engage employees in prosocial acts for the community. PSM thus has the potential to expand appreciably public managers' motivational toolkits.

Commentary

Sanjay K. Pandey

The careful and succinct overview of earlier research synthesized in this chapter serves a valuable purpose, reminding us that the motivational terrain in the public sector is powerfully shaped by its unique institutional constraints. If there is one critique I have, it is that, implicit in the authors' invocation of "Back to the Future," implementation of performance-related pay going forward is likely to suffer from the missteps and failures experienced earlier as well. One way to avoid that future is to recognize, as they do, that simplistic cause–effect relationships devoid of institutional context should neither inform our efforts nor be the standard against which their effectiveness is evaluated.

Misguided theory is one major simplistic assumption that can be avoided in the design and evaluation of pay-for-performance systems in the public sector. The authors correctly point out that broad acceptance of principal–agent models and a global resurgence of new public management have renewed interest in performance-related pay. But principal–agent theory makes somewhat simplistic assumptions about the nature of goals that can foil successful implementation of pay-for-performance systems.

At the heart of principal–agent models is the idea that principals know their goals, can specify them clearly, and can transmit this awareness and knowledge to agents. But what if principals face *unclear* goals and thus find it difficult to specify clear goals for agents to pursue? The idea that public managers face goals that can be characterized as multiple, conflicting, and ambiguous is an old one and can be traced to a number of scholars (see Pandey and Rainey 2006, 87; Rainey, Backoff, and Levine 1976). Thus, any theory of performance of public organizations and individuals—and, by implication, efforts to improve performance—needs to account fully for organizational goal ambiguity.

All this leads to three questions that need to be answered in this regard. First, what are the sources of organizational goal ambiguity for employees of public organizations? Second, how is organizational goal ambiguity experienced at the individual level and at the task level? Third, and relatedly, what can be done to mitigate any negative effects? To some, goal ambiguity is a given; public organizations are not subject to price-based market signals and must respond to a variety of external forces in the political environment. But Rainey and Bozeman (2000) ably summarize a host of empirical studies showing that public and private managers face similar levels of organizational goal ambiguity. Regardless, goal ambiguity poses significant contextual problems for pay-for-performance systems. Wright and I, for example, show that unclear goals have a direct effect on job-level goals: "vague, multiple, and conflicting goals distract attention and do not provide clear guidelines on searching for alternative solutions. The net result of organizational goal ambiguity is to increase information deficiency about job processes and salient outcomes" (Pandey and Wright 2006, 517).

We also highlight how unclear organizational goals can indirectly lead to increased job-level ambiguity as organizations try to compensate for unclear goals by creating structural mechanisms to bring about behavioral consistency. However, these structural mechanisms often institute standardized and routine responses that are not oriented toward goal clarification or achievement. More directly, when organizational goals are hard to define and measure, they create challenges to developing well-defined and measurable goals at the individual level. Prescriptions for pay for performance must take this variation in goal clarity into account.

To be sure, performance objectives can still be developed for individuals and groups when goals are ambiguous. But if success of pay-for-performance systems is defined as better aligning individual and group behavior with an organization's mission, vague goals will make the ultimate purpose impossible. Proponents of these systems must appreciate this problem and modify their proposals accordingly.

Commentary

Howard Risher

I am far more optimistic about the use of pay-for-performance systems in the public sector than are Perry, Engbers, and Jun. Of course, there have been problems, but the alternatives are worse. Moreover, prior research has failed to consider the deleterious effects of the alternatives: step increases or across-the-board increases. Either employers can treat every employee the same or they can differentiate, and if they choose to differentiate, they need a credible rationale. Neither is anyone defending current step-increase policies. There is a reason the federal community and perhaps others use derogatory phrases such as "living and breathing" in referring to the step system. Nor is the pressure to improve government performance going to lessen.

I would also argue that if agency performance is to improve, public employers—like their private sector counterparts—will need to explore strategies to realize gains through improved employee performance. Indeed, it is very difficult to identify any element of the private sector of the United States economy where performance-related pay is not the dominant policy. This is not surprising, as research in the private sector has consistently shown that employers who adopt a new work management paradigm can expect productivity increases of at least 30 to 40 percent, and the business press has documented dramatic gains over the past decade (Macy and Izumi 1993). As the authors correctly note, several employers maintain successful policies.

I am sensitive to the argument that government is "different." Every employee in a company understands the importance of continued profitability. Another fundamental difference is the emphasis on confidentiality for personnel actions in public organizations as opposed to private organizations. A third difference that varies from state to state is the presence of labor unions, as pay for performance is a threat to unions. A closely related difference is that public employees always seem to have someone in an elected position who will support efforts to kill or change proposed policies or procedures. There is also the argument that public employees are not driven by pay. However, by the time they reach mid-career, have a mortgage, and are looking ahead to the cost of college for their children, my interaction with federal employees is that they are not disinterested in how much they are paid. Also implicit in the Perry, Engbers, and Jun article is the notion that public employees are the only ones who are inspired strictly by the opportunity to serve a "higher calling." To the contrary, I am convinced that most employees want to do a "good job" and be valued.

Relatedly, the authors' argument that performance-related pay reduces intrinsic motivation seems to have emerged from laboratory studies that have little resemblance to actual work situations. First, salary increases in the real world are granted once a year, and the actual difference between an average increase and what might be granted to a star performer is nominal. For example, an average increase currently might be 3.5 percent, and a "star" performer might see a 6.0 percent increase.

That means a star with a $50,000 base salary would earn a difference in weekly pay of $23.55—that is, before taxes. Pay increases, of course, compound over time, so the advantage increases—high performance pays off—making it difficult to understand how that undermines intrinsic motivation throughout the year. Second, I would also argue that jobs in organizations with performance goals and measurable results in the private sector trigger greater satisfaction and motivation.

Legitimate differences notwithstanding, public organizations *can* take the steps necessary to overcome resistance to the policy change. My experience tells me that the following are important for improving the success of pay-for-performance systems:

Have a policy change champion: Managers and employees need to understand that the change in policy is important to the organization. When there is a champion, he or she makes it clear that the change is a management initiative and not a human resource initiative. David Walker, when he was the head of the General Accountability Office, exemplified the importance of having a champion.

Focus on performance planning: When organizations develop strategic plans, install measurement systems, and adopt a cascading goal-setting process, it sends a message that everyone understands: performance is important. This contributes to a culture where performance is a shared priority. When an organization has realistic goals, employees generally want to contribute to the achievement of those goals.

Involve managers and employees: Traditionally, the planning for a new salary program or policy was done "behind closed doors." Yet managers need to "own" the system or process; they are in the best position to know what will be accepted. On a related issue, research some years ago by an Air Force group showed that job incumbents know what is needed for good performance. When managers and employees are involved in the planning, they will take "ownership" and help to "sell" the new system to their peers.

Know the difference between performance management and performance appraisal: There is a decided difference between these two concepts. The traditional appraisal often was limited to a few checkmarks on a form and a brief meeting between a supervisor and one of his or her direct reports. Performance management starts with a planning session to define goals or performance standards early in the year, includes feedback and coaching throughout the year, and finishes with the completion of the form at the end of the year. If the manager has been effective, there are no surprises in the year-end review.

Provide manager training: Effective performance management requires soft, behavioral skills to handle the planning, feedback, and year-end discussions. Too many employers limit manager training to an explanation of the policy and instructions for completing the appraisal form. Training is an important investment.

Have job-specific performance criteria: Experience shows that the best basis for evaluating employee performance is an agreed-upon set of goals or objectives.

Realistically, goal setting does not "fit" every job or every organization, but the track record confirms the value of investing in job-specific performance indicators. The same logic applies to the use of competencies so employees can identify what is expected. The criteria through the 1980s were generally generic—for example, dependability, job knowledge, and teamwork. The use of generic criteria as the standard of performance also suggests that performance management involves a comparison of employees, when the relevant assessment is how well an employee performs his or her specific job duties. The notion that it is a comparison is counterproductive.

Create "calibration" committees: This is a relatively new idea in industry, although it was used a decade or so ago in the demonstration projects to "test" performance pay in United States Department of Defense research labs. The role of the committee is essentially the same as a promotion-and-tenure committee in higher education. It reviews at least the high and low performance ratings. In some situations, managers are asked to present the evidence and defend their ratings. The committee provides quality control and consistency.

Emphasize communications: Pay for performance sends messages that inform employees of management priorities; the most obvious is that senior management wants to encourage good performance. Corporations tend to place more emphasis on employee communications than the typical public jurisdiction. They are more sensitive to the importance of marketing and "selling" important organizational changes. In high-performance organizations, communications are used extensively to highlight results and achievements and to recognize the contributions of employees. Employers of choice typically make this a priority.

Use performance management software: A growing number of software products are available for performance management. The systems are designed to facilitate recordkeeping, collect feedback from others, and record decisions.

Last, my experience also suggests that it is best to eliminate all vestiges of the former evaluation program that give employees a reason to think about what would have been. This introduces another important consideration—that the introduction of the new program is best understood as organizational change. The change in policy involves a change in the psychological contract between each supervisor and his or her staff. Those relationships will be redefined permanently. A mixed record of successes and failures should not be surprising. The "technical" planning issues are straightforward compared with the process considerations. It may be the most difficult organization change a public employer can undertake.

Appendix A

Table 2.1 Summary of Studies Reviewed in Meta-Analysis

Study	Sample	Study Focus	Institution Type	Pay Type	Governmental Level	Research Design	Job Status	Relevant Results
Allan and Rosenberg (1986)	2,000 New York City police managers	Effects of managerial traits on performance appraisals and merit pay	Public safety/ military	Added to base	Municipal	Time series	Managers	Performance appraisals and pay were correlated, but this correlation decreased over the course of the study.
Andersen and Pallesen (2008)	27 Danish research centers	Effects of merit pay on publications of Danish researchers	Educational	Bonus	Nongovernmental	One group pretests/ posttests	Nonmanagement professionals	Perception of the financial incentive is important for motivational-crowding theory. The amount of the incentive is also important.
Andersen (2007)	Danish dentists and doctors	Effects of performance-related pay on Danish dentist and doctor performance	Medical	Not specified	National	One group posttest	Nonmanagement professionals	When strong professional norms existed, then incentives were not important. The inverse was also true.
Bebchuk and Fried (2004)	Fannie Mae employees	Effects of performance-related pay on executive compensation	Financial	Bonus	National	Case study	Managers	Performance-related pay resulted in perverse incentives and decreased transparency.

Continued

Table 2.1 (*Continued*) Summary of Studies Reviewed in Meta-Analysis

Study	Sample	Study Focus	Institution Type	Pay Type	Governmental Level	Research Design	Job Status	Relevant Results
Bertelli (2006)			Financial	Added to base	National	Nonequivalent groups with posttest only	Managers	IRS reward structures crowd in motivation for those with low levels of intrinsic motivation but crowd out intrinsic motivation for those with high intrinsic motivation.
Brown (2001)			General government	Not specified	National	Randomized experiment	Not specified	Perceptions of procedural justice had the strongest relationship with support for merit pay, followed by market comparability, job security, and supervisory appraisal ratings.

Brudney and Condrey (1993)		General government, public safety/ military, regulatory	Added to base	National	One group posttest	Managers	The effectiveness of performance-related pay as a motivational tool was moderated by attitude toward merit pay, organizational trust, organizational commitment, salience of monetary rewards, perceived fairness of the plan, and closeness of link between pay and performance.
Bullock (1983)		Technical	Added to base	Regional	Time series	Managers and nonmanagers	Merit award status did not significantly predict changes in pay satisfaction but did significantly predict increases in job satisfaction.

Continued

Table 2.1 (*Continued*) Summary of Studies Reviewed in Meta-Analysis

Study	Sample	Study Focus	Institution Type	Pay Type	Governmental Level	Research Design	Job Status	Relevant Results
Condrey and Brudney (1992)	4 federal agencies in southeast U.S.	Impact of agency characteristic on the effectiveness of performance-related pay	General government, technical	Added to base	National	One group posttest	Managers	Performance-related pay was more effective at agencies with high levels of trust, adequate rewards, effective performance appraisals, and close geographic proximity. In general, negative attitudes existed toward performance-related pay.
Daley (1987)	315 mid-level managers and senior executives	Effects of federal merit pay systems on motivation	General government	Bonus	National	Non-equivalent groups with posttest only	Managers	Intrinsic satisfaction and equity are the same regardless of pay scheme; perceived performance–reward relationship significantly greater for recipients of merit pay.

Davidson et al. (1992)	80 primary care physicians	Effects of performance-related pay on health-care services provided	Medical	Piece rate	Nongovernmental	Randomized experiment	Nonmanagement professionals	Patients received better treatment as measured by a number of measures with performance-related pay than with flat-rate payment.
Deadrick and Scott (1987)	222 mass transit directors	Effects of performance-related pay on public sector productivity	Transit	Added to base	National	One group posttest	Managers	Financial incentive programs are being used within the transit industry and these programs are for the most part evaluated positively.
Deckop, Mangel, and Cirka (1999)	8 utility companies in the United States	Effects of performance-related pay on organizational citizenship behavior	Public services	Not specified	Nongovernmental	One group posttest	Nonmanagers	Performance-related pay had a negative impact on extra role behaviors for employees low in value alignment but not for employees high in value alignment.
Dowling and Richardson (1997)	114 managers at the National Health Service	Effects of performance-related pay and levels of challenge and motivation	Medical	Added to base	National	One group posttest	Managers	Performance-related pay was challenging for employees but not motivating. In general, money was not a primary source of motivation.

Continued

Table 2.1 (Continued) Summary of Studies Reviewed in Meta-Analysis

Study	Sample	Study Focus	Institution Type	Pay Type	Governmental Level	Research Design	Job Status	Relevant Results
Egger-Peitler, Hammerschmid, and Meyer (2007)	1,417 Austrian municipal employees in 14 departments	Effects of attitudes toward work motivation on incentives	General government	Not specified	Municipal	One group posttest	Managers and nonmanagers	Employees had a high degree of dissatisfaction with performance-related pay execution, handling, and transparency, yet 81 percent said it should be retained.
Fletcher and Williams (1996)	Eight organizations with 800 private and 300 public employees	Relative impact of performance-related pay in public and private organizations	General government	Not specified	Municipal	One group posttest	Managers and nonmanagers	Performance-related pay led to clear goals, a short-term work orientation, and peer conflict. Effort appears to have no relationship to performance-related pay.
Gabris and Mitchell (1986)	City employees in Biloxi, MS	Effect of participation in policy adoption on perception of performance-related pay	General government	Bonus	Municipal	One group posttest	Managers and nonmanagers	Merit council participants were more satisfied with performance-related pay and perceived supervisors more fairly than non-participants.

Gabris and Mitchell (1988)	160 city employees in Biloxi, MS	Effects of performance scores on opinions of performance-related pay	General government	Bonus	Municipal	One group posttest	Managers and nonmanagers	Employees with low performance scores perceive performance-related pay as unfair and have negative views of management.
Gabris (1986)	280 city employees in Biloxi, MS	Effects of employees' attitudes toward supervision based on the introduction of performance-related pay	General government	Bonus	Municipal	One group posttest	Managers and nonmanagers	Supervisors have more favorable perceptions of performance-related pay than nonsupervisors and consider it more accurate. A minority of supervisors and nonsupervisors find it effective.
Gabris and Ihrke (2000)	125 professional employees of Midwestern county government	Changes in professional attitudes' impact on merit pay implementation	General government	N/A	Municipal	One group pretest/ posttest	Managers and nonmanagers	Leadership credibility and leader motivation to change significantly increase employee acceptance of performance appraisal and merit pay.

Continued

Table 2.1 (*Continued*) Summary of Studies Reviewed in Meta-Analysis

Study	Sample	Study Focus	Institution Type	Pay Type	Governmental Level	Research Design	Job Status	Relevant Results
Gaertner and Gaertner (1985)	5 units in two federal agencies	The relationship between performance standards and performance-related pay	Regulatory	Added to base	National	One group pretest/posttest	Managers	Most employees were invested in their performance standards and that contributed to more positive perceptions of performance-related pay. A full 75 percent said it is not an improvement over previous non-performance-related pay systems.
Gaertner, Gaertner, and Akinnusi (1984)	213 management employees	The implementation of personnel reforms in the federal government	Regulatory	Added to base	National	One group posttest	Managers	Managers in more responsive organizations were significantly less positive than managers in the mechanistic organizations.
GAO (1984)	3 federal agencies	Evaluation of federal performance-related pay plans	General government, profession, public safety/military	Added to base	National	One group posttest	Managers	Problems with consistency, distribution, and agency formulas. A total of 5 to 10 years needed for implementation.

Greiner et al. (1977)	Orange County police	Effects of performance-related pay on performance	Public safety/military		Municipal	Case study	Nonmanagers	Adoption of performance-related pay decreased crime and improved job satisfaction and union relations.
Greiner et al. (1977)	Waste collectors in Flint, Michigan	Effects of performance-related pay on performance	Public service	Bonus	Municipal	Case study	Nonmanagers	Adoption of performance-related pay increased productivity and lowered cost but had an unclear impact on customer service and mildly negative impacts on safety.
Greiner et al. (1977)	Philadelphia water repair workers	Effects of performance-related pay on performance	Public safety/military	Bonus	Municipal	Case study	Nonmanagers	Adoption of performance-related pay increased performance, job satisfaction, and quality of union relations.

Continued

Table 2.1 (*Continued*) Summary of Studies Reviewed in Meta-Analysis

Study	Sample	Study Focus	Institution Type	Pay Type	Governmental Level	Research Design	Job Status	Relevant Results
Hatry, Greiner, and Gollub (1981)	Municipal departments in four cities	Effects of performance-related pay on performance and satisfaction	Public service, general government, human services	Bonus and added to base	Municipal	Case study	Managers	Performance measures were used prior to performance-related pay without negative consequence, but the addition of pay yielded problems regarding sufficient compensation, objective measures, and perceived fairness. No impact on performance.
Heckman, Heinrich, and Smith (1997)	16 job training centers	Effects of organizational merit incentives on outputs	Human services	Bonus	National	Time series	Nonmanagers	Introduction of performance-related pay resulted in more short-term orientation, "gaming," and cream skimming for job coaches.
Heery (1998)	Local officials around London	Effects of performance-related pay on performance and motivation	General government	Not specified	Municipal	One group posttest	Nonmanagers	Little effect on performance or motivation.

Citation	Sample	Purpose	Sector	Pay type	Level	Design	Employee type	Findings
Heinrich (2007)	State Department of Human Resources	Effects of state-level reforms on social worker performance	Human services	Bonus	State	Time series	Managers and nonmanagers	Financial incentives must be sufficient to impact performance. Employee bonuses were too low to impact performance.
Heneman, Greenberger, and Strasser (1988)	104 nursing, technical, professional, and managerial employees of Midwest hospital	Relationship of performance-related pay perceptions and pay satisfaction	Medical, technical, professional	Not specified	Regional	One group posttest	Managers	Positive relationship between pay-for-performance perceptions and pay satisfaction.
Heneman and Young (1991)	100 Midwest administrators	Implementation of a merit pay plan	Educational	Bonus	Municipal	One group pretest/posttest	Managers	Implementation of performance-related pay resulted in unfavorable perceptions of merit pay by managers.
Hickson, Altemeier, and Perrin (1987)	18 medical residents	Effects of performance-related pay on services provided	Medical	Piece rate	Nongovernmental	Randomized experiment	Nonmanagement professional	Introduction of performance-related pay resulted in improved performance as measured by more contacts, less emergency treatment, and more visits with physicians.

Continued

Table 2.1 (Continued) Summary of Studies Reviewed in Meta-Analysis

Study	Sample	Study Focus	Institution Type	Pay Type	Governmental Level	Research Design	Job Status	Relevant Results
Hutchison et al. (1996)	116 physicians	Effects of performance-related pay on medical service provided	Medical	Piece rate	Nongovernmental	Randomized experiment	Nonmanagement professional	Performance-related pay had no impact on hospitalization.
Ingraham (1993b)	20 state personnel directors	Performance-related pay use by the states	General government	Not applicable	State	One group posttest	Managers	Many states have decreased use of performance-related pay. State HR directors approve of performance-related pay. Adoption is most commonly initiated by the governor.
Kellough and Nigro (2002)	350 personnel managers in 30 states	Performance-related pay use by the states	General government	Not specified	State	One group posttest	Managers	Performance-related pay had a mild effect on motivation and performance, decreased confidence, and was perceived as administered ineffectively. It did help clarify goals and communication. Political appointees are most supportive.

Study	Sample	Focus	Sector	Added to base	Level	Design	Subjects	Findings
Kellough and Selden (1997)	2,500 nonsupervisors and 450 supervisors in Georgia state government	Effects of performance-related pay on job satisfaction, trust, and confidence in human resources	General government		State	One group pretest/posttest	Managers and nonmanagers	Employees and managers lack trust in performance ratings and perceive politics as being involved. Many believe ratings are changed and that they do not reflect performance. A total of 70 percent disagreed that performance-related pay was motivating.
Kessler and Purcell (1992)	7 public and 2 private organizations	Challenges to implementing performance-related pay	Not specified	Not specified	Not specified	Case study	Not specified	A total of 54 percent considered performance-related pay fairer but listed many challenges in implementation, including specifying objectives, evaluating performance, managing paperwork and constraints, and confidence in the relationship between management and pay.

Continued

Table 2.1 (Continued) Summary of Studies Reviewed in Meta-Analysis

Study	Sample	Study Focus	Institution Type	Pay Type	Governmental Level	Research Design	Job Status	Relevant Results
Kouides et al. (1998)	54 solo or group medical practitioners	Effects of performance-related pay on medical services provided	Medical	Piece rate	Nongovernmental	Randomized experiment	Nonmanagers	Better immunization rates were achieved with performance-related pay than with traditional compensation methods.
Krasnik et al. (1990)	265 primary care physicians	Effects of performance-related pay on medical service provided	Medical	Piece rate	Nongovernmental	Randomized experiment	Nonmanagers	Patients received better treatment with performance-related pay than with traditional compensation methods.
Langbein (2006)	Over 7,000 courses at American University	Effects of performance-related pay on faculty behavior	Education	Added to base	Nongovernmental	One group posttest	Nonmanagers	Tying faculty pay to student evaluations resulted in grade inflation.
Lovrich (1987)	400 Washington state employees	Effects of performance-related pay on motivation	General government	Not specified	State	One group pretest/ posttest	Not specified	Workplace participation was the only significant motivator of performance. Performance-related pay had no influence on motivation.

Marsden and Richardson (1994)	2,423 employees in the Inland Revenue Service	Effects of performance-related pay on motivation	Financial, human services, education, medical	Added to base	National	One group posttest	Managers and nonmanagers	Most employees supported the idea of performance-related pay but considered implementation ineffective.
Marsden (2004)	Employees and managers at 6 British public agencies (income, health, job placement, and education)	Effects of performance-related pay on job renegotiation	Financial	Added to base	National	One group posttest	Nonmanagers	Job setting and performance appraisals helped renegotiate jobs and influenced motivation. Yet many considered performance-related pay divisive.
Mesch and Rooney (in press)	2,439 fundraising professionals	Effects of performance-related pay on performance differences	Nonprofits	Bonus	Nongovernmental	One group posttest	Nonmanagers	Correlation between compensation method and performance.
Murnane and Cohen (1986)	6 school districts with large merit-related bonuses for more than 5 years	Performance-related pay effectiveness for teachers	Educational	Added to base	Municipal	Case study	Nonmanagers	Schools where merit pay was successful were different from most schools and used merit pay in nontraditional ways.

Continued

Table 2.1 (Continued) Summary of Studies Reviewed in Meta-Analysis

Study	Sample	Study Focus	Institution Type	Pay Type	Governmental Level	Research Design	Job Status	Relevant Results
Nachmias and Moderacki (1982)	463 managers and nonmanagers in the IRS in Wisconsin	Effects of performance-related pay on satisfaction	Financial	Added to base	National	One group posttest	Managers and nonmanagers	Perceptions of performance-related pay were generally negative, but women and lowest grade levels were most supportive.
Nigro (1981)	14,500 participants in the Office of Personnel Management and 2,068 in the Navy	Public employee opinions about merit pay	General government, technical, public safety/military	Added to base	National	One group posttest	Nonmanagers	Managers expressed dissatisfaction with pre-CSRA appraisal system but were uncertain about the new system. They did not believe it improved performance.
Orvis, Hosek, and Mattock (1993)	Department of Defense test site	Effects of gain sharing on productivity	Military/public plus safety	Bonus	National	Time series	Managers and nonmanagers	Gain sharing resulted in improved work-life quality, sustained production quality, and increased productivity.

O'Toole and Churchill (1982)	EPA managers	Implementation issues with the adoption of performance-related pay	Regulatory	Added to base	National	Case study	Managers	Performance-related pay inhibited risk taking and increased red tape, conflict, and competition. Managers cited implementation problems (timing, who is involved, clarity of goals).
Pearce and Perry (1983)	5 divisions of the SSA	Effects of performance-related pay on performance	General government	Added to base	National	Nonequivalent groups with posttest only	Managers	Performance-related pay had no impact on performance and was perceived as poorly implemented. Managers were concerned about long-term consequences of financial rewards.
Pearce, Stevenson, and Perry (1985)	5 federal units in the Social Security Administration	Federal attitudes toward performance-related pay plans	General government	Added to base	National	Time series	Managers	Performance-related pay had no effect on organizational performance.

Continued

Table 2.1 (*Continued*) Summary of Studies Reviewed in Meta-Analysis

Study	Sample	Study Focus	Institution Type	Pay Type	Governmental Level	Research Design	Job Status	Relevant Results
Perry, Petrakis, and Miller (1989)	Randomly selected managers from the General Services Administration	Performance Management and Recognition System	General government	Added to base	National	Time series	Managers	Rankings were inconsistent across departments. Most employees ranked high so there was no discrimination. Performance-related pay was significant for the first round but not the second.
Schay (1988)	2,072 employees in scientific, technical, administrative, and clerical positions in the Navy	A comparison of two models of performance-related pay systems	Public safety/ military	Added to base	National	Time series	Managers and nonmanagers	Performance-related pay perceptions increased for the experimental groups and did not change for the control groups. Pay satisfaction did not change for the experimental groups and decreased for the control groups.

Study	Sample	Focus	Setting	Pay	Scope	Design	Population	Findings
Shaw et al. (2003)	157 employees of Midwestern university hospital	Effects of performance-related pay on employee attitudes	Medical	Added to base	Nongovernmental	One group pretest/posttest	Not specified	Merit increases were significantly related to pay level satisfaction, pay raise affect, and pay raise behavioral intentions.
Siegel (1987)	Employees at the Naval Weapons Center	Effects of performance-related pay on administrative performance	Public safety/military	Added to base	National	Nonequivalent groups with posttest only	Managers and nonmanagers	Most performance-related pay has implementation problems, but if properly implemented, then it is effective.
Wisdom and Patzig (1987)	26 public sector managers, 1,130 private sector managers	Merit systems and employee expectations about pay and performance	General government, medical	Not specified	National	Simple descriptives	Managers	Perceptions of employee performance were higher for private than public sector managers.

Chapter 3

From "Need to Know" to "Need to Share": Tangled Problems, Information Boundaries, and the Building of Public Sector Knowledge Networks[*]

Sharon S. Dawes, Anthony M. Cresswell,
and Theresa A. Pardo

Contents

[*] Adapted from Dawes, S. S., A. M. Cresswell, and T. A. Pardo. 2009. From "need to know" to "need to share": Tangled problems, information boundaries, and the building of public sector knowledge networks. *Public Administration Review* 69(3): 392–402.

For public managers, the importance and challenges of networking and knowledge sharing for attacking wicked problems are well-known and well-founded (Weber and Khademian 2008). We argue, however, that a broader category of more common, day-to-day "tangled" problems lies in a vast middle ground between routine and wicked problems that are equally as challenging. Think of the tangle of actors involved in operating a public school or a military base, or the tangle of programs that a social worker must navigate to help the families he or she serves. Success in coping with these kinds of challenges depends on finding ways to overcome the "need-to-know" default option in most organizations and moving to a "need-to-share" network culture.

One way to do so involves creating public sector knowledge networks (PSKNs). Unlike other types of networks, PSKNs have information and knowledge sharing across traditional organizational boundaries as a primary purpose while addressing public needs that no single organization or jurisdiction can handle alone. PSKNs are social–technical systems in which human, organizational, and institutional considerations exist in a mutually influential relationship with processes, practices, software, and other technologies. They have emerged in tandem with the adoption of advanced networking technologies and the development of e-government.

Examples of PSKNs include efforts to share geospatial information and expertise, such as the National Spatial Data Infrastructure; networks to support sharing public health data, such as the BioSense system backed by the Centers for Disease Control and Prevention and the Department of Health and Human Services; and networks to share environmental data, such as the Environmental Protection Agency's AirNow program. Other efforts aid communities of practice with information systems, communication tools, and data resources that improve professional practice. These PSKNs also gather, analyze, and share information about program performance among participating agencies or establish monitoring and communication functions for such fields as public health, financial management, and national security.

But building and nurturing PSKNs is no easy matter. Drawing on prior research on collaboration and networking, along with our own fifteen years of action research and theory building involving public management projects in New York State, our argument is threefold. First, although problems in starting and sustaining PSKNs are formidable, they are not beyond the capabilities of astute, strategic, and tactically adept network builders. Second, it is misguided to conceive of information-intensive public management problems as mainly information technology (IT) problems and thus useless to consider IT as a silver bullet. Instead,

IT considerations must be appreciated as nested within a variety of organizational, sociological, ideological, and political contexts that all need considerable attention. Third, governments need to invest in developing as fundamental public management skills a broad and deep understanding of the realpolitik of PSKNs.

PSKNs in Analytical Perspective

PSKNs potentially offer substantial benefits. They constitute communication channels that give participants access to others' information and knowledge with the expectation that better quality, more timely, and more complete information will be available to those who need it at the time that it is most useful. From an organizational learning perspective, they provide a connection to others' knowledge and experiences (Galaskiewicz 1985; Hall 1999; Powell 1998), which can help public organizations improve their ability to react to uncertainty and complexity in their environments. In addition, interorganizational knowledge sharing is a major source of organizational innovation (Powell, Koput, and Smith-Doerr 1996).

Shared knowledge and information integration can also help agencies better define and solve joint problems; coordinate programs, policies, and services; and prompt improvements in both IT infrastructure and information content (Dawes 1995). Sharing also facilitates integrated functions (Landsbergen and Wolken 2001) that, in turn, provide citizens with convenient access to diverse information and services. Furthermore, positive sharing experiences can help government professionals build and reinforce professional networks and communities of practice, which can be valuable resources of information about programs, best practices, politics, and environmental conditions (Kraatz 1998; Powell 1998; Zucker et al. 1996).

Importantly, however, PSKNs are not all alike. One way to understand their variety is to see them as varying substantially across two salient theoretical dimensions: focus and extensiveness. As Table 3.1 illustrates, two kinds of focus are prevalent: (1) a narrower focus that uses knowledge networking to help meet a specific need or solve a specific problem, and (2) a broader focus that aims to create systemic capacity to share knowledge and information whenever it is needed within a domain of action.

The narrower focus has the advantage of clarity: regardless of their organizational home or professional background, the actors involved are pursuing a particular goal that presumably has a desired end point. However, this type of focus lacks staying power. The knowledge and information-sharing network formed to solve a specific problem generally is considered a temporary necessity rather than a permanent resource. By contrast, the broader focus offers more permanence and versatility. However, it is more difficult to design and implement, requires more fundamental capability, and faces different challenges to sustain its operations, including finding an appropriate and acceptable permanent organizational home for the network.

Table 3.1 Types of Public Sector Knowledge Networks

	Focus of Knowledge Networking	
Extent of organizational network	*To address a specific need or solve a particular problem*	*To create systemic capacity to share knowledge and information within a domain*
Across organizations in multiple jurisdictions, sectors, or levels of government	Annual reassessment Homeless services	GIS cooperative
Across organizations in the same jurisdiction	Statewide accounting system	Justice information sharing
Across units within the same organization	Municipal affairs	No illustrative case available

In terms of network extensiveness, three levels theoretically exist: (1) an intraorganizational network, where sharing takes place across different units of the same organization; (2) an interorganizational network that lies within a single government jurisdiction; and (3) an interorganizational network that crosses jurisdictions, sectors, or levels of government. Typically, more extensive and varied organizational networks have greater depth and breadth of knowledge to share, but the greater number and variety of stakeholders and contexts present more risks, costs, and barriers to overcome.

Thus, as we move from bottom to top and from left to right in Table 3.1, the costs and risks increase but so, too, do the potential benefits and overall public value. Specific problem-oriented initiatives have the potential to meet a particular need and perhaps to generate learning that can be applied in similar settings at other times. By contrast, systemic initiatives have the potential to create ready capability not only to address current problems but also to tackle new problems as they emerge. These systemic knowledge and information-sharing capabilities also can support ongoing innovation and value creation within their policy or problem domains.

Lessons from the Field: Challenges, Choices, and Opportunities

Prior research and our fifteen years of action research in New York State suggest important lessons for those contemplating or trying to sustain PSKNs. We illustrate these lessons by referencing our experiences with six (falling into five of the quadrants of our theoretical construct) PSKNs that we worked with extensively in our research program. These PSKNs all involved information-intensive problems, including managing and evaluating homeless shelters and services, changing the basis for real property assessments, creating a geographic information coordination program, revitalizing the state central accounting system, enabling justice information sharing, and shifting from a regulatory to a service orientation in overseeing municipal finances.

The homeless services project is an example of an effort to share knowledge and work practices across many organizations and levels, all focused on a specific need (see Table 3.1, top left cell). This project involved building a multiorganizational, information-sharing system to consolidate information about homeless families and single adults, shelters, and related service programs across several dozen public and nonprofit organizations. In the real property assessment project, which was the same type, state and local participants held very different views about the definition of tax equity, the practices and processes of assessment, and the costs and benefits of relying on sales information instead of direct observation of real property characteristics to set assessments. The Geographic Information System (GIS) case (Table 3.1, top right) aimed at building systemic capacity for a state–local data coordination program, including a shared governance structure involving representatives of all stakeholder groups; a web-based clearinghouse of metadata, data sets, and related information; and tools and policies that would promote the sharing of spatial data sets.

The accounting case is an example of problem-oriented sharing within the same jurisdiction (Table 3.1, middle left cell). An aging central accounting system—a legacy mainframe application involving hundreds of public and private entities—was the backbone of New York's financial management. It needed replacement to allow the state to keep up with changing financial management standards with the help of modern information technologies. In turn, the initial goal of the justice information-sharing initiative (Table 3.1, middle right cell) was a systemic one involving a set of state-level justice agencies (including police, corrections, parole, and a central coordinating agency) in joint development of e-Justice New York, an interagency IT framework and portal to give users of criminal justice data and systems "one-stop" access to mission-critical information. Finally, the municipal affairs project (Table 3.1, bottom left cell) sought to improve a particular kind of performance within one agency. This effort aimed at generating consistent and shareable information about local finances, local political and economic conditions, and state interventions in local government practices and was part of a transition from a regulatory to a service-oriented program in the Office of the State Comptroller. No cases are available for the bottom right cell of our theoretical construct.

The Tough News First

Although PSKNs offer significant potential benefits for dealing with both wicked and tangled problems, our research suggests they also face challenges that make them difficult to develop and sustain.

Lesson 1: It is dangerous to assume meanings are clear, context is understood, and quality is acceptable to all participants in PSKNs.

Effective knowledge sharing depends heavily on shared understandings, and these must be actively developed. Assuming that language is "clear" or that meanings are "obvious" usually leads to confusion, wasted effort, or costly errors. The social processes necessary to develop shared understandings and standard definitions of key terms and concepts require at least minimal levels of trust and support if open dialogue and compromise are to result.

The ease of knowledge sharing through a PSKN will depend on the nature of the knowledge itself. Moreover, different kinds of knowledge are likely to coexist in any given setting, and the same sharing strategies will not work for all kinds. Some elements of knowledge are explicit, formal, and embodied in written policies, procedures, standards, and databases—and are thus readily conveyed to others through structured data and information systems. Other elements of knowledge are likely to be more tacit, embedded in social contexts and practices, and conveyed through "learning by doing" rather than explicit means (Cohen and Bacdayan 1994; Wenger 1998). So, too, may knowledge be embedded in organizational forms (historical, material, and cultural) (Gherardi and Nicolini 2000). Knowledge management studies also show that what is information to some is knowledge to others. Information forms the basis for knowledge development on the one hand, and knowledge often is required to assimilate and interpret information on the other (Davenport, DeLong, and Beers 1998). Moreover, important aspects of knowledge sharing go beyond simple information or data exchange to focus on knowledge as *knowing*, implying the ability to use knowledge to accomplish some task or reach some level of performance (Brown and Duguid 2001).

Data quality is a further challenge. Quality most often is characterized as simple accuracy, but research shows that high-quality data should be not only intrinsically good but also contextually appropriate for the task, clearly represented, and accessible to users (Wang and Strong 1996). The same information may be "fit for use" (Wang and Strong) for one application but completely inappropriate for other applications that have different temporal, security, granularity, or other requirements. In addition, unrealistic assumptions about the quality and usability of information are common problems, including the widespread belief that information is objective, neutral, and readily available (Radin 2006).

In New York's annual reassessment project, for example, the basic argument for making annual statistical adjustments based on real property sales data presumed that there were enough sales in each town every year to make up a reasonable body of evidence for adjusting all property values in the town. Where this assumption did not hold, assessors refused to even consider the new process. When the state argued that sales data from "similar" towns might be used instead, assessors rejected the idea as politically untenable.

Lesson 2: As a potentially sharable resource, knowledge varies in several essential respects—codifiability, embeddedness, and dynamics—and each variation demands substantially different treatment within a PSKN.

Variations in the nature of information and knowledge resources can be summarized in terms of three dimensions. One is *codifiability*: the ease of expressing knowledge in language, numbers, formal procedures, and explicit techniques. A second is *practice embeddedness*: the degree to which knowledge is situated in or generated by ongoing practice and learning by doing (Cohen and Bacdayan 1994). Information and knowledge are also very much embedded in temporal, physical, and programmatic contexts that must be conveyed along with the information if someone working in a different context is to understand it. The third dimension is *dynamics*: the degree to which knowledge is constantly recreated and transformed by use, including the development of new knowledge. The usefulness or validity of some kinds of knowledge may be subject to rapid or unpredictable changes over time. The GIS cooperative faced all these challenges when it sought to make geospatial data sets widely available for sharing. Because the data had seldom been intended for use outside the programs that collected them, almost no metadata existed to aid new users to understand their contexts, how they changed over time, their known weaknesses, or how key elements were defined and used in practice. Before the cooperative could become operational, significant investments were made in developing and implementing a common metadata standard to describe data resources.

Lesson 3: PSKNs are a form of cross-boundary exchange. The boundaries of organizations, jurisdictions, and sectors present the most obvious challenges, but subtler boundaries related to ideology, professional norms, and institutional divisions can be equally problematic.

Although networks of information systems may be relatively new to the public sector, the historical and institutional relationships among agencies are often many generations old. Moreover, sharp lines of authority divide branches of government as well as local, state, and federal levels. These may compose the most deeply embedded and pervasive boundaries to be crossed by PSKNs. Widely different roles and functions at the federal, state, and local levels; enormous variation in local conditions and capabilities; inconsistent physical and technical infrastructure; and diverse and competing missions all contribute to misunderstandings that can foil collaborative work.

The annual reassessment case is again instructive. Real property assessment is mainly a municipal function in New York. Assessments are conducted by more than 1,000 cities and towns ranging in size and sophistication from New York City, to diverse suburban areas, to towns of only a few hundred people. Accordingly, their ability to finance and manage the assessment process, handle the data management and analysis responsibilities, and interact with and educate the public varies in every possible way. Combining diversity with a lack of state-level authority over these functions means that prospects for success rapidly fade.

Boundaries also typically occur in complex combinations. Policy and legal constraints on collaboration and knowledge sharing may involve program boundaries and goals (LaPorte and Metlay 1996; Milward and Rainey 1983) in addition to matters of cost allocation and authority across jurisdictions. Agencies also will have different policy agendas and competing priorities that flow from their different missions. Other boundary concerns include control of collaboration activities and rules on participation and decision making. Consider the knowledge exchanges necessary to establish new data-sharing relationships: data policies and standards, timing and methods of data collection, and access to information all can vary widely across organizations (Landsbergen and Wolken 2001). Unless knowledge about these differences is also shared, they cannot be reconciled. Once made explicit, however, they *can* be taken into account. In the homeless services case, for instance, the state agency and homeless shelter providers worked for months to agree on policies and practices to protect the confidentiality of shelter residents. The agreement rested on a hard-won common understanding about how to shield individual identity. However, for a certain type of client—a victim of domestic violence—they also had to learn that the overriding confidentiality concern was not a client's identity but her physical location.

Experience with and attitudes toward the kinds of collaboration needed for knowledge and data sharing also may vary widely across organizational boundaries. Innovative capacity (Pardo et al. 2006)—or the attitudes, resources, and skills necessary to organize and facilitate collaboration and knowledge sharing— may differ widely as well. Key elements of innovative and collaborative capacity building for PSKNs include managerial support and leadership (Eglene, Dawes, and Schneider 2007), facilitative skills (Bryson 2004b), attitudes toward power and trust (Huxham 2003), and available resources and infrastructure. Innovative capacity also reflects a willingness to change attitudes and to master new managerial and technical tools as well as a willingness to serve collective and individual agency missions and goals.

Crossing boundaries also means interaction with "alien" business processes and practices. The knowledge necessary to interpret many kinds of information is intricately linked to the business processes from which it arises and where it is used. As with information systems, the logic and details of a process may be poorly documented, causing fragmented understanding of the complete process. Thus, effective data sharing and integration often require cross-boundary examination of diverse business processes and practices. In the justice case in New York, an important requirement was assuring secure access to justice information systems through a single portal. A new joint management arrangement was needed to supersede multiple agency–based processes, one that authoritatively issued and maintained user authentication and access permissions for thousands of workers in multiple organizations. This shift to a unified system required difficult negotiations, including crafting a formal interagency contract to deal with costs, processes, and authority relationships.

Organizational and professional cultures pose other kinds of boundaries. Knowledge often is embedded in these cultures and thus is not easily extracted or transferred (DeLong and Fahey 2000). The way a police officer interprets criminal history data, for instance, will not be consistent with or easily transferred to someone without that particular training and experience. For information systems, the "knowledge wrapper" that holds the logic of data structures, definitions, collection methods, and related processes is unique to the organizational setting in which it was created. This knowledge may be poorly documented and distributed in ways that make it difficult to aggregate and share. Without sharing this knowledge, however, the transfer of data across organizations is unlikely to produce meaningful results.

In the New York municipal affairs case, for example, regional staff used the general term *technical assistance* to mean a wide variety of activities under quite diverse circumstances. Only by actively engaging in comparisons and debates were they able to come to a common definition and set of services that could be deployed (and understood) consistently in every region. A similar process took place in the homeless services and annual reassessment cases, where critical concepts such as recidivism and tax equity had to be explained, debated, and harmonized before the networks could really begin to work.

Physical distance poses a final boundary challenge. Despite great expectations for network technologies to allow remote collaboration, face-to-face contact is often important, even indispensable, for PSKNs to collaborate and share knowledge. This is especially true in the early stages of network exploration and formation. Personal engagement, however, often is inhibited by the costs of travel or lack of access to synchronous telecommunications—such as video conferencing—and incorrect assumptions about the nature and meaning of the knowledge and information to be shared. As is probably true in most states, there is a common expectation in New York that local and regional officials will come to the state capital to be involved in discussions of statewide programs. As a consequence, however, only those with enough discretionary money and full-time staff, or those in proximity to the capital, actually participate. In five of our six cases, it was necessary to go out physically on the road to engage these critical stakeholders in an evenhanded way.

Lesson 4: Trust, like knowledge, comes in different forms that work best under different conditions. Lack of sufficient trust and lack of the right kind of trust can be powerful inhibitors to PSKNs.

Trust influences how culture, values, and personal and organizational relations affect the processes and outcomes of knowledge sharing (Cresswell et al. 2006). When trust is low, transaction costs rise as a result of efforts to implement management and oversight controls to prevent exploitation (Jones, Hesterly, and Borgatti 1997). Three kinds of trust are salient in knowledge networks. Calculus-based trust (Williamson 1993) rests on information-based rational decisions about the organization or person to be trusted. Identity-based trust (Coleman 1990) stems from familiarity and repeated interactions among the participants and emerges from joint membership in a profession, a team, a work group, or a social group. Institution-based trust (Gulati 1995; Ring and Van de Ven 1992) rests on social structures and norms, such as laws and contracts, that define acceptable behavior.

Different kinds of interactions in PSKNs demand different sorts of trust (Lewicki, McAllister, and Bies 1998). The sharing of codifiable information (such as in the GIS cooperative) may need only calculus-based trust or some combination of institutional and calculated trust. However, sharing practice-embedded knowledge (such as among the assessors or shelter providers) requires at least some identity-based trust, a development that takes considerable time and interaction.

The quality of preexisting personal and professional relationships makes a big difference in determining how long it takes to build sufficient trust for new undertakings. In the homeless services case, the relationships between the state agency and the nonprofit shelters had not always been smooth but were consistently respectful. The shelter providers approached the project with healthy skepticism, but they also had many past experiences of fair dealing that gave them some confidence to try new ways of working. By contrast, the annual reassessment project started from a basis of long mutual distrust across state and local levels. Many tentative steps were taken, withdrawn, and taken again as a long mutual adjustment process played out. Financial incentives, training programs, and grant-funded demonstrations all helped to encourage small but positive engagements that eventually moved the program forward.

Lesson 5: Risk is inevitable in PSKNs and is perceived and handled differently by different players.

Substantial risks inherent in knowledge sharing and collaboration can greatly interfere with effective PSKNs. Parties may not share the same understandings of risk and thus disagree over what may or may not be shared (Pardo et al. 2006). Common areas of disagreement include privacy, confidentiality, and security concerns; ambiguity about statutory authority to collect, share, or release information; and different degrees of openness to public access. Moreover, agencies that compete for budget, control of scarce resources or infrastructure, or dominance in a policy domain may be reluctant to reveal any knowledge assets that reduce or threaten their discretion and autonomy (Rourke 1978) or their ability to compete for power and influence (Provan and Sebastian 1996). Revealing information to outsiders also may pose a threat of embarrassment or sanction, or invite invidious comparisons of one agency or jurisdiction against another (Dawes 1995). In addition, knowledge may constitute highly valued organizational or personal assets that actors are loath to relinquish. Even if no financial or tangible value is at risk, some may resent another person or agency getting a "free ride" on their hard-won knowledge.

If the benefits of sharing are not clear, or if the exchange appears to be too one-sided, barriers go up. Strategies to address these perceptions of risk are therefore critical to the success of knowledge-based collaboration. In the New York municipal affairs case, the regional staff were initially reluctant to share knowledge about how they advised local governments, fearing they would be criticized for giving bad advice. To build trust, agency leaders reassured them that the information gathered would not be used for personal evaluation and that good practices would be highlighted and replicated.

But There Is Also Good News

All is not lost for those seeking to develop, nurture, and sustain PSKNs.

Lesson 6: The processes of PSKN engagement build professional networks, organizational connections, and reusable capabilities regardless of the level of substantive network success.

Substantive PSKN success seems to depend on leadership and management practices, good quality data and appropriate infrastructure, and a culture that provides incentives and rewards for knowledge and information sharing. In contrast, successful processes and relationships—what we call *networking success*—rest on a combination of reputation, trust, competence, and supportive culture. In the cases we studied, networking success was achieved more often and to a greater degree than substantive project success. Indeed, substantive success aside, it seems that trusted networks among individuals and organizations are an explicit positive outcome as well as a precondition for eventual long-term substantive success. In addition, organizational and individual networking success can outlive a particular project and go on to strengthen and deepen working relationships that can pay off in later projects (Zhang and Dawes 2006). The homeless services project, for example, achieved a high level of networking success yet was not implemented because of a lack of political and financial support. Nevertheless, the project leaders from both the government and nonprofit shelter groups continued to work together successfully on new program initiatives.

Regardless, networking success is much less visible than project success to external constituencies and political leaders. It is a challenge to gain the time and support to work past early difficulties that are an inevitable part of the PSKN maturation process. However, persistence and focus on the ultimate goal can pay off. The GIS project, arguably the most substantively successful of the knowledge networks in our research, actually failed several times over nearly ten years to garner political support and legal legitimacy before it eventually succeeded in achieving both its networking and substantive goals. Over this time, the professional GIS community persisted in demonstrating the practical value of its ideas until the political and managerial climate of state government was ripe for acceptance.

Lesson 7: Acquiring legal authority for a PSKN is a necessity, but there is no one-size-fits-all approach to structuring formal authority. Regardless of structure, mobilizing political support really helps.

Some legal basis for a knowledge network is necessary for legitimacy, but no particular structure of formal authority seems best. We have studied successful networks created specifically in law or by executive order or formed under the general authority of an existing statute. None of the PSKNs we have studied would have survived without this legitimating authority. In the annual reassessment project, for example, statutory authority was essential just to get started. Local government assessors are independently appointed or elected officials and very few would consider a radically different way of working without a legal foundation to justify their actions with their constituencies.

However, although formal legal authority appears to be necessary to launch a knowledge network, it may not be sufficient to sustain it through implementation. In the projects we worked with, legal authority bolstered by political support provided a more conducive environment for project development. These political linkages, usually associated with the explicit support of an elected official such as the governor or mayor, were especially useful in bringing reluctant parties to the table, clarifying leadership responsibilities, and negotiating powerful bureaucratic processes such as budget formulation. In the justice network, for example, difficult negotiations over authority relationships and resource allocations depended on the direct and ongoing involvement of the governor's criminal justice coordinator. In the municipal affairs project, internal agency conflicts could be confronted by the project leaders, because they were carrying out their elected chief executive's call to change the agency's culture from one based on audits and compliance to one emphasizing prevention and assistance.

Lesson 8: Policy barriers are the greatest obstacles to substantive success in building PSKNs, but they often can be navigated by early intervention, focused action, and consistent attention.

Policy and legal barriers, especially the lack of formal support mechanisms, appear to present the greatest obstacles to achieving the expressed program or policy goals of PSKNs. These barriers are not so much restrictions on sharing as they are failures to support collaboration with appropriate resource allocations and policy mechanisms. In our research, general lack of legislative support, misallocated funding, and simple lack of funding were perceived as more severe barriers than laws that specifically restricted knowledge and information sharing. This is troubling because so much of the promise associated with public sector innovation depends on the ability of agencies to share information about clients and services and to share knowledge about their professions and practices. Without an enabling policy framework, the risk-averse culture of government is likely to dominate decisions and actions and produce missed opportunities and half-measures that achieve little.

Astute PSKN leaders find ways to deal with these challenges. In the statewide accounting system case, the project leader built a policy cabinet of "strategic partners" (representing both houses of the legislature, the state budget office, and the statewide IT agency) into the governance structure of the project. This ensured their ongoing attention, created a venue for policy discussions, and prevented surprises from derailing the effort. The GIS cooperative shows how formal policies can work to allow and encourage information sharing. Through the creation of a formal standardized data-sharing agreement, the cooperative members established the rules, responsibilities, and benefits of sharing geospatial data across state and local government. The agreements assured access to data holdings, established primary data custodians for all data sets, and specified practices to enhance data use and quality for all members. By contrast, New York's annual assessment project was stymied by a lack of specific statutory and regulatory authorization to use market information to assess property values.

Lesson 9: Organizational barriers are serious but amenable to innovation and creative management.

Organizational barriers negatively affect both substantive and networking success, but in our research, participants were resourceful in dealing effectively with some of them. Their efforts included building enduring relationships among key individuals with a shared vision, a practice notable in the GIS cooperative program. Professional commitments to innovative programs also carried the annual reassessment project through a long period of negotiation and learning until it finally was adopted by a significant number of local governments. Likewise, long experience in working with certain organizations and skills in negotiating familiar bureaucratic constraints were instrumental in planning to replace the statewide accounting system. Here, veteran state officials designed the project in phases to coincide with budget and legislative cycles, ensuring that they would have the evidence necessary for decisions that would move the project forward and keep it visible to those with approval and budget authority.

Lesson 10: Multiple leadership behaviors are associated with success, including mission focus, emphasis on people and communication, willingness to experiment, and nurturing a culture of joint responsibility for success.

The leaders of knowledge networks need a repertoire of behaviors and skills that support collaboration and trust. In another multicase evaluation study (Eglene et al. 2007), we found that these personal qualities of leadership were much more important than the network leader's expertise in the program or policy domain. Leaders who inspired trust, commitment, adaptation, and mutuality set a positive tone for behavior throughout the network. The most successful projects were led by people who emphasized the mission value of the effort and who focused first on the people involved rather than on the rules of engagement, the information content, or the material resources. They engaged in open communication with all players and used example and persuasion to convince participants of the collective and self-interested benefits of the effort. Successful leaders also were candid and realistic about the costs and risks to all concerned. In the state-wide accounting system and homeless services projects, for example, we found that leaders refrained from using the formal authority of their positions to compel participation by others. Instead, they sought practical solutions through wide consultation and experimentation. Moreover, they encouraged informal leaders to take responsibility for parts of the effort, especially when certain kinds of expertise or resources were needed.

Lesson 11: Early experience sets the tone and direction of cross-boundary relationships—unrealistic, incorrect, or mis-aligned expectations, processes, incentives, and assumptions are hard to change once set.

Unrealistic expectations and unexamined assumptions plague PSKN projects. Thus, the early planning process needs to facilitate candid discussions that explicitly identify and engage stakeholders; fully describe benefits, barriers, and risks; and state underlying assumptions about the problem, the participants, and how they will make decisions and work together. Nor can we overstate the importance of aligning goals and incentives through careful stakeholder analysis. An early understanding of the history, policy constraints, organizational capabilities, and technological limitations allows participants to plan projects wisely and manage interorganizational dynamics and implementation processes more effectively. In the justice project, participants initially thought they needed a common portal to link their information systems together. Through weeks of difficult and mostly unproductive early discussions, however, they learned that their most pressing need was not for a technological tool but for a governance process to evaluate alternatives, consider divergent views, and make decisions about their joint responsibility for the justice enterprise. In addition, our research indicates that higher levels of government tend to oversimplify and underestimate the needs of lower levels. State officials often wanted to rely on their own assumptions about what "locals" think, need, and do, but when local officials spoke for themselves, the picture of risks, benefits, and capabilities was much more accurate, diverse, and authentic. In fact, local government stakeholders were considerably less optimistic about achieving goals and more concerned about a variety of organizational, technological, and financial barriers than their state-level counterparts.

Lesson 12: Learning and adaptation are essential to PSKN development and survival.

PSKNs are inherently learning organizations that need to adapt to changing economic conditions, political priorities, social trends, and their own experiences. The interactions among individuals, organizations, and communities are the channels through which knowledge is exchanged, examined, and integrated. In the central accounting system project, for example, the lead agency staff thought they were well versed in the uses made of accounting information. Thirteen stakeholder workshops later, they recognized how little they had appreciated the myriad cross-boundary business processes that linked their agency to all the other government and private sector organizations that receive, handle, or disperse state funds. The agency subsequently refocused on detailing and accommodating these critical linking processes.

Our research indicates that experience makes PSKN participants more realistic: in our project evaluations, none of the benefits were as great as initially expected and none of the barriers were as formidable. Moreover, the top benefits that participants believed had actually been achieved were somewhat different from their initial predictions. The number one predicted benefit was better quality information, but the top benefit achieved was wider professional networks. In addition, participants initially overstated the severity of all barriers, but they did accurately predict the top three: lack of funding, overly ambitious goals, and different organizational priorities.

Conclusion

We have argued that public managers confront tangled problems every day across all policy domains and levels of government, and they need to be ready to deal with them through networked forms of engagement and action. Knowledge networking—the ability to create PSKNs suitable for addressing these problems—requires a certain set of skills and attitudes as well as interpersonal and other kinds of trust. PSKN development processes that emphasize early open dialogue and examination of assumptions and expectations do better than those that rush forward with a fixed IT solution in mind. Those that adapt and learn from experience are more likely to succeed in achieving their substantive project and networking goals.

Finally, to be sustainable as organizational forms, knowledge networks need some legal foundation, access to resources, supportive policies, and innovative forms of leadership. Thus, the challenge to public managers is not so much a matter of successfully carrying out a particular networking project. Rather, it is one of building institutional, managerial, and professional capabilities to engage cross-boundary, knowledge-intensive problems whenever they appear.

Clearly, sharing and integrating knowledge and information in multiorganizational settings involve complex, sociotechnical interactions embodied in work processes, organizational forms, and institutional contexts. These are challenges of governance as well as issues for administration. They have implications for efficiency, performance, and public value that are ripe for multidisciplinary investigation as well as for usefully linking research and practice. To work well, they require that information-sharing and knowledge-sharing capabilities be woven deliberately into the fabric of organizational and partnering work. The wicked and tangled problems of the future will require no less.

Commentary

Lisa Blomgren Bingham

Governance is about sharing information, building knowledge, and using these together to make policy. Employing their fifteen years of action research, Dawes, Cresswell, and Pardo argue that astute, strategic, and adept managers can build effective PSKNs, that these are not simply IT but rather structures for governance, and that political leaders and public managers must master fundamental skills to function in PSKNs. I agree. Questions remain, nevertheless. What kind of legal foundation might we need? How and with what skills do we conduct the necessary dialogue? And where is public voice in this vision of PSKNs?

The authors observe that policy and legal barriers are the "greatest obstacles to achieving the expressed program or policy goals," in part because government is risk averse. Federal agencies have substantial discretion to choose among different governance processes under the Administrative Procedure Act (APA, 5 U.S.C. §§551 *et seq.*). Roughly the same structure and distinctions exist in state administrative procedure acts across the fifty states. Agencies also derive their authority in part from the APA, Freedom of Information Act (5 U.S.C. §552), Federal Advisory Committee Act (5 U.S.C. Appendix II), Negotiated Rulemaking Act (5 U.S.C. §§561, *et seq.*), and Administrative Dispute Resolution Act (5 U.S.C. §§571, *et seq.*). They become barriers to interagency collaboration, however, because none are drafted to authorize agencies to collaborate in networks with other actors. Their unit of analysis, the obligations they impose, and the processes they authorize all take individual agency action as their starting point. Nor do they contemplate the dramatic evolution of technology related to communication and online citizen participation and deliberation, such as wikis, blogs, or the Internet.

I have argued elsewhere (Bingham 2008) that a new legal infrastructure must address several questions. These include how agencies can (1) exercise delegated authority in networks, (2) reconcile networks with transparency in government,

(3) foster citizen participation in networks, (4) get networks to use more innovative deliberative processes with citizens, and (5) ensure that the network is adequately accountable to the public. The advantage of a statute is that in one simple act Congress can eliminate many of the legal obstacles that currently exist.

Dawes, Cresswell, and Pardo also suggest that collaborative capacity depends on a willingness to "change attitudes" and "serve collective as well as individual agency missions and goals." How exactly should managers do this? The authors argue that trust building and negotiation are critical, but they do not go deeply into operationalizing these tactics. They do identify different understandings of risk as a source of disagreement. Importantly, the negotiation literature offers some answers by arguing that actors can use differing perceptions of risk as an avenue for dovetailing interests (Fisher, Ury, and Patton 1991).

Informed by that literature, O'Leary and I (2007) argue that managers should resolve network conflict using principled or interest-based negotiation as essential skills. In interest-based negotiation, participants satisfy as many interests or needs as possible through a problem-solving process aimed at reaching an integrative solution, as Follett (2003) advocates. This distinguishes it from competitive or hard bargaining, in which participants distribute rewards in a win–lose process. Participants learn to identify interests by focusing on basic human needs for security, economic well-being, belonging, recognition, and autonomy (Fisher et al. 1991). Interest-based negotiation involves defining the issues, framing them as a joint task to meet all parties' needs, educating each other about their respective agency's interests, looking for ways to create value or expand the pie, and brainstorming or generating multiple options for a settlement.

Importantly, this literature suggests that networks should engage in the conscious design of governance rules at the earliest stage of their work. This includes identifying network members whose agreement is necessary, ascertaining the scope and jurisdiction of the network, addressing issues of the network's legitimacy, setting the ground rules, negotiating the processes governing exchanging views, discussing administration and allocation of responsibilities, negotiating the decision rules for closure on an issue, identifying a system for resolving an impasse, and figuring out a decision process for ending the network.

Finally, public organizations in networks owe a unique responsibility to citizens, because they often address issues of public concern. Many networks, however, do not afford sufficient transparency or accountability. Dawes and her associates do not address this issue. Yet, in several of their cases, one might logically ask whether including public voice might strengthen the PSKN. For example, they describe an annual reassessment project involving a network of state and municipal actors that ran up against unanticipated problems with real-property sales data. What might have happened if the network had consulted with the public about this problem? Instead, the authors refer to the public in a top-down fashion: assessors "interact with and educate the public." Indeed, they do not discuss the obvious remedy: transparency to the public. Likewise, in the criminal justice case, they look only to political linkages, such as the explicit support of an elected official, governor, or mayor; the governor's criminal justice coordinator; or project leaders responsive to a chief executive. They look "up" to others in the hierarchy, not "across" to citizens as partners.

Fung, Graham, and Weil (2007, 17) introduce the breakthrough concept of *collaborative transparency*, which they define as the use of IT to enable communities of users to both shape information content and act as self-disclosers. Consider the SARS epidemic. Through private emails, cell phone calls, and Internet chat room messages, Chinese citizens reported an illness whose existence the Chinese government denied (151). Private trackers picked up this traffic and warned of an outbreak. The United Nations World Health Organization could act only on an official government alert but used the information to pressure China. In collaborative transparency, the power of IT allows users of information to become disclosers.

Thus, within the context of PSKNs, this chapter by Dawes and her colleagues suggests issues that apply universally to collaborative public management and network governance. Three issues for the future stand out. First, we need a better legal framework for collaboration in governance. Second, we need to train managers in interest-based negotiation and conflict management skills. Finally, we need to incorporate the public's voice into the work of networks.

Commentary

Sharon L. Caudle

I do not have major disagreements with what the authors present in this chapter. However, they have missed an opportunity to weave in the findings of others that have a direct bearing on their observations of PSKNs. For example, they might have drawn on the extensive work in the *Public Administration Review* special issue on collaborative management (2006, vol. 66) as well as work by Agranoff (2005), Goldsmith and Eggers (2004), Kelman (2007), Klitgaard and Treverton (2003), Provan and Milward (2001), Sanderson, Gordon, and Ben-Ari (2008), and the General Accounting Office (GAO 2001, 2003a).

The authors might also have separated out those critical factors or practices important to developing, implementing, and sustaining any new cross-organizational relationship from those specific to a successful PSKN. Virtually any successful boundary-spanning relationship calls for strong leadership and management practices, competencies, and cultural acceptance of collaborating and integrating efforts with others. But the most important factors for PSKNs may center on the quality of information and knowledge flow, such as the timeliness and quality of the data, the infrastructure to handle the flow to the right actors practically, the policy and legal requirements regarding information sharing and intellectual property, and the actual personal relationships across PSKN participants.

In this regard, the authors might also have considered identifying the critical success factors for the different *phases* of the life of a PSKN, from deciding to form a PSKN to sustaining effective sharing and collaboration. In research on regional partnerships (Caudle 2006), I describe initiation factors, such as evaluating in what environment the partnership must perform, what the right mix of capable partners should be, who the potential partners are, and what value each partner brings. Once a partnership becomes operational, then partner contributions and renegotiation of the partnership compact occurs. Partners can become rivals in securing funding, have changed missions, or have major changes in the mix of products and services. Partners also can be terminated if there no longer is synergy for added value, whether due to one partner's lack of contribution or other partners deciding they are strong enough to jettison a partner. Relatedly, Snyder and de Souza Briggs (2003) describe the evolution of communities of practice and the different activities, methods, and tensions that occur at each stage of evolution. At each stage, different management tasks and challenges emerge.

Dawes and her coauthors also contend that PSKNs are best classified in terms of their "focus" and "extensiveness." The authors might have considered fashioning their analysis of focus and extensiveness into more explicit "bad" or "good" findings to help guide those creating and implementing a PSKN. What costs would outweigh the benefits for each type? Should each PSKN type be approached differently in terms of strategies, policies, and practices? Are there different barrier issues or factors? In this regard, they might have incorporated Agranoff's (2008) and Chen's (2008) discussion of network process and collaboration outcomes. These factors include partner knowledge, resource exchange, goal achievement, and power relationships.

Finally, a more robust categorization scheme than focus and extensiveness should be pursued. Various networks have different purposes, targets, and perspectives, and I would argue that these might be more useful bases for categorization. For example, direct service delivery networks are those designed to determine client needs, the availability of services and products, the crafting of those services and products to meet client needs, and a delivery and accountability mechanism. Communities of practice are informal social learning systems where practitioners voluntarily participate and connect in problem-solving—sharing ideas, setting standards, building tools, and developing relationships with peers and other stakeholders (Snyder and de Souza Briggs 2003, 7). Kerno (2008) points out that learning for a community of practice relies on a high interactive process that bridges those who are new to a community of practice (amateurs) and those who are experienced (masters). A community of practice's main value is the synergistic creation and dissemination of knowledge, whereas direct service delivery is more grounded in consistent information flow and integration for a client's benefit.

As such, the barriers, challenges, and lessons of PSKNs should be somewhat different if community of practice and direct client service delivery are the units of analysis. For example, the authors say that the risk-averse culture of government runs counter to the ability of organizations to share information about clients, services, and knowledge of their professions and practices. Actually, there are good reasons to protect information about clients and services in partnerships servicing the same clients. Thus, a client service delivery PSKN requires considerable structure, skills, resources, management attention, and accountability. A community of practice requires some of these same elements but is much more contingent on those participating in the community, and information control may be very fluid. Kerno (2008) and Probst and Borzillo (2008) also discuss "lessons" for an effective community of practice, including a flatter, horizontally linked organizational structure; commitment of a core group to engagement in the community; importing external expertise into the community; and weighing differences in the societal context in which the community is situated. These differences are likely more effective in understanding PSKNs, with focus and extensiveness nested within each category.

Chapter 4

Toward "Strong Democracy" in Global Cities? Social Capital Building, Theory-Driven Reform, and the Los Angeles Neighborhood Council Experience[*]

Juliet Musso, Christopher Weare, Thomas Bryer, and Terry L. Cooper

Contents

---

[*] Adapted from Musso, J., C. Weare, T. Bryer, and T. L. Cooper. 2011. Toward "strong democracy" in global cities? Social capital building, theory-driven reform, and the Los Angeles Neighborhood Council experience. *Public Administration Review* 71(1): 102–111.

Perceptions of the appropriate role of citizens and other stakeholders in governance have evolved through several historical transitions, from the limited direct involvement established by the nation's founders to the more recent emergence of community-based institutions for participation (Sirianni and Friedland 2001). Most recently, an interest in "strong democracy" and building "social" and "civic" capital has seized the popular imagination in the United States, especially in urban areas. Strong democracy refers to overcoming the "conduct of politics for private advantage" and building self-government involving citizens rather than representative government conducted solely in the name of the people (Barber 1984, 4).

Strong democracy has spawned citizen participatory initiatives across the United States, initiatives that have generated excellent studies assessing their success. We argue, however, that the broad institutional prerequisites for successful participatory institutions that have been the focus of much of the existing literature are insufficient for developing a vibrant participatory system—especially in "global" cities with highly diverse and mobile populations. A global (or "world" or "alpha") city is one recognized as a strategic geographic node creating, facilitating, and sustaining the global economic system (e.g., New York or Los Angeles). We contend that the focus of study should shift to the processes of implementation and their relationship to outcomes—that is, a shift to factors that go beyond the design of a strong democracy initiative and that can advance, foil, or attenuate prospects for success. We also argue that universities and foundations have constructive roles to play in advancing this cause, as long as they understand the paradoxical nature of their involvement as neutral facilitators of that process.

Our argument is founded on a longitudinal study involving years of action research and evaluation of the neighborhood council system in Los Angeles (LA). We focus our analysis on two independent but related projects: participatory budgeting and facilitated collaboration (The Collaboration Learning Project) between neighborhood council and city agency officials. We compare this experience to studies on participatory mechanisms and deliberative processes more generally. We offer six key lessons that can help identify the conditions under which effective neighborhood councils are more or less likely to be implemented successfully. All can serve as propositions for researchers to test, elaborate, and refine in future research. An overarching theme of the essay could be described as "design is not enough!"

Bringing Citizens Back In? Best Practices, Deliberative Design, and the LA Neighborhood Council System

Researchers are divided over the effects of citizen engagement in governance. Some cite an array of benefits associated with "stronger" democratic practice (Barber 1984): participatory institutions develop citizenship by helping individuals strengthen civic skills, increasing their knowledge about civic issues, and promoting more informed and better reasoned political judgment (Barber 1984; Berry, Portney, and Thomson 1993; Carpini, Cook, and Jacobs 2004; Chaskin et al. 2001; Fung 2004). Others find that the benefits of public deliberation are highly context-dependent, shaped by—among other things—the structure of discourse, who participates, and relationships to decision makers (Carpini et al. 2004). A more fundamental critique is that many individuals are disinclined or unable to voice demands constructively, with the result that involvement promotes alienation and conflict rather than trust (Mansbridge 1980).

These diverse perspectives were echoed in the political debate surrounding the formation of neighborhood councils in LA. Supporters argued that it would transform the civic fabric of the city, while detractors marked it as a vehicle for NIMBYism or a tokenistic sop to neighborhood gadflies. Nonetheless, in 1999, LA voters approved a new charter that created a citywide system of neighborhood councils. The political impetus for the councils was a threat of secession sparked by complaints that some neighborhoods did not get a "fair share" of services, that administrative agencies were unresponsive, and that downtown development interests imposed unwanted land-use decisions (Hogan-Esche 2002). Still, the neighborhood council provisions of the new charter were included in the face of opposition from business and development interests, Mayor Richard Riordan, and a majority of the city council. On the other hand, the councils were given only an advisory role, despite strong pressure from neighborhood advocates and some charter commission members who sought legal authority over land-use decisions.

The charter directed that neighborhood councils were to be open to anyone who lived, worked, or owned property in the neighborhood. It also contained several provisions intended to create arenas for engagement, including an early warning system to alert neighborhoods of impending decisions and to provide them with a reasonable opportunity to respond. The charter also directed LA to engage neighborhood councils in the budget process, to establish regular meetings between neighborhood councils and departmental general managers, and to support a Congress of Neighborhoods—all best practices culled from the literature on neighborhood boards. In addition, neighborhood councils were allowed to emerge through a community planning process intended to produce councils that recognized a historical sense of community (rather than being mapped along city council district lines). Councils were given independence to design their bylaws and to determine how members would be elected. To provide necessary administrative support, the charter created the Department of Neighborhood Empowerment (DONE), which was charged with overseeing the system.

The formulation of ordinances to implement the charter mandate and to develop a plan for this global city required an additional two years. Again following the example of other cities with similar systems, LA provided technical assistance targeted at self-organization and certification of neighborhood councils and began certifying them in late 2001. As of 2008, there were 88 councils representing neighborhoods, averaging about 38,000 residents. As of 2010, 340 board elections were held, with neighborhood council seats often contested. On average, these elections had about 300 voters, with more prominent elections attracting more than 2,000 voters. The city has given consistent, if modest, financial support for the system, providing a budget of about $3.3 million and each neighborhood council a grant of $50,000 per year.

Getting Real: Six Lessons from the LA Experience for Anticipating and Coping with Implementation Deficits

What has been the evolving fate of this effort? The following integrates research findings from a multiyear action research project studying neighborhood council implementation in LA in which we have been engaged with studies of neighborhood participation in other cities. The research underlying the broader project was multimethodological, with specific approaches varying across research initiatives. The neighborhood council evaluation combined documentary research, field observation, focus group research, and two network surveys of neighborhood council board members. Semi-structured interviews also were conducted with an array of city officials and neighborhood stakeholders, and these were complemented by two evaluative surveys of DONE project coordinators. Unless otherwise indicated, the evaluation findings cited were drawn from a final evaluation report on the initiative (Musso, Weare, et al. 2007).

Lesson 1: Participatory systems are politically vulnerable because of the fluidity of participation of elected and administrative actors involved, and even "model" charter designs for citizen participation in global cities require considerable attention to micro details that are frequently misunderstood or subject to implementation conflict.

The literature on participatory reforms identifies a number of critical features of institutional design, and LA adopted many of these features. That literature, however, often frames the benefits of participation noted above in administrative terms and absent elevated conflict (Berry et al. 1993; Fung 2004; Thomas 1986). In particular, the citizen participation literature has tended to downplay political obstacles highlighted routinely in the literature on implementation (e.g., Brodkin 1990; Hill and Hupe 2009; Mazmanian and Sabatier 1989). As noted, however, the LA charter reform process produced strong opposition from business and political elites that contributed to vague language on the form or operation of participatory arenas. Moreover, the city has since resisted specific organizational reforms designed to engage neighborhood councils with city agencies. As students of policy design (Ingram and Schneider 1990; Matland 1995) would have predicted when mandates are vague, the implementation of participatory arenas has faltered over time, while halting progress has been contingent on shifting leadership by the mayor's office, DONE, and external actors such as the University of Southern California, Coro Southern California, and local foundations. Under these circumstances, the expectations of the implementation literature were validated: the predisposition of leaders involved played a critical role (Hill and Hupe 2009).

In particular, mayoral support for neighborhood councils wavered during critical periods of implementation. Early disinterest from Mayor Riordan's administration contributed to the lack of strong arenas for involvement in budget development and service delivery. James Hahn, who followed Riordan as mayor from 2001 to 2005, provided some support for neighborhood councils, pursuing his campaign pledge to develop a neighborhood-friendly agenda in the midst of an active secession campaign. Hahn appointed a new DONE general manager—Greg Nelson—a city hall insider who had helped write the charter language. Under Nelson's leadership, and consonant with the implementation literature's emphasis on creating a climate of compliance expectations and regimes (Stoker 1989), his staff institutionalized a more interactive budgetary process and supported university engagement in action research to empower neighborhood councils. Hahn, however, was a single-term mayor, and many of his institutional initiatives were abandoned or deemphasized following his departure and Nelson's ensuing retirement.

Elected in a hard-fought campaign against Hahn in 2005, Mayor Antonio Villaraigosa's administration viewed neighborhood councils as a distraction at best and took several early actions to circumscribe council engagement. Moreover, under Villaraigosa, DONE has not had steady administrative leadership, having experienced four different general managers during his administration. Although it has become less negative toward neighborhood councils over time, the Villaraigosa administration assumed a standoffish role toward them.

These fluctuating political fortunes have directly affected participatory budgeting and service engagement. Despite charter language requiring neighborhood council advisement in budgetary processes, progress developed haltingly from a largely symbolic "Budget Day" but with no interaction on the budget. And although it has become better institutionalized over time, the process remains far less deliberative and empowering than oft-cited best practices of participatory budgeting in the literature (Baiocchi 2001; Musso, Sithole, et al. 2007). For example, it does now include best practices such as advance education of citizens regarding city budget processes and fiscal issues, a survey collecting information about stakeholder preferences, and facilitated regional deliberation providing an opportunity for representatives to develop informed viewpoints. However, the information provided to participants is broad, the survey of stakeholder budget preferences has varied highly in quality, and the information from deliberations has seldom been used by decision makers (Musso, Sithole, et al. 2007).

Meanwhile, LA has never systematically developed systems for monitoring service delivery or engaging neighborhood councils with general managers. Thus, when the city did not implement the charter provision requiring neighborhood council engagement with departments, the Collaborative Learning Project (CLP) got involved (Kathi and Cooper 2005). The CLP at times faced misunderstanding of its role; an example was criticism by neighborhood councils when researchers acted as observers and note-takers rather than active participants. Nonetheless, the CLP achieved some success in producing a memorandum-of-understanding process that later was emulated by neighborhood councils dealing with the city's Planning Department and the Department of Water and Power.

However, Mayor Villaraigosa prohibited memorandum-of-understanding processes early in his first term, and there has not been any ensuing systematic effort to comply with this provision of the charter. Continuing disinterest in neighborhood councils exists at the departmental level in LA, and a survey of midlevel departmental administrators found that they perceived neighborhood councils to be even less important for setting goals and getting information than other informal civic associations such as homeowner groups. The LA experience suggests that more detailed mandates requiring specific types of deliberation processes are required to ensure that deliberative processes involving citizens occur.

> **Lesson 2:** The representativeness of participatory bodies influences their substantive focus and perceived legitimacy, but realizing diversity on those boards can be a challenge.

A thorny issue for developing participatory institutions is their vulnerability to the socioeconomic biases that characterize political participation in the United States and, in particular, high-effort activities such as those required of voluntary boards (Verba, Schlozman, and Brady 1995). These biases call into question the extent to which participatory institutions fairly and effectively speak for their communities. The LA experience confirms the entrenched nature of these biases while at the same time pointing to new challenges to the legitimacy of participatory bodies in global cities.

The LA charter required that neighborhood councils reflect the diversity of their neighborhoods and precluded dominance by any one type of stakeholder. Nonetheless, the members of LA neighborhood council boards have been disproportionately white, highly educated, and wealthy homeowners. Given the high housing costs and mobility found in LA, the homeowner bias is acute. More than 80 percent of neighborhood council board members are homeowners, whereas LA's homeownership rate of 38.6 percent is the lowest of any major U.S. city. In comparison, the cities studied by Berry, Portney, and Thomson (1993), Fung (2004), and Thomas (1986) had homeownership rates ranging from 63 percent to 76 percent. Likewise, although more than 39 percent of LA residents are foreign born, less than 2 percent of respondents to neighborhood council member surveys were noncitizens, and not a single member had been living in the United States for less than five years.

Other studies confirm that volunteer bodies can attain representative legitimacy in substantive terms (e.g., the degree to which the council acts in the community's interests) or participative terms (e.g., the degree to which the council provides opportunities for stakeholders to be active within the organizations) (Berry et al. 1993; Fung 2004; Guo and Musso 2007; Mansbridge 1980). Other studies have found that more homogeneous forums may operate more effectively (Chaskin 2003; Williamson and Fung 2005). In LA, however, descriptive biases skew the substantive representativeness and the perceived legitimacy of neighborhood councils. Because homeowners dominate board membership, planning and transportation issues dominate, even though the general public is more concerned with crime, schools, and jobs. Moreover, the lack of representative diversity has weakened agency perceptions of the political legitimacy of the neighborhood councils, as city officials and administrators frequently call critical attention to the underrepresentation of Latino constituents on them. As ethnic diversity and economic inequality rise in the United States, the legitimacy issues that have encumbered the LA system are likely to challenge participatory systems in other global cities.

Verba, Schlozman, and Brady (1995) argue that citizen participation requires motivation (a reason for citizens to participate), invitation (specific opportunities and outreach to encourage participation), and resources (financial and cognitive capacity and attitudes of political efficacy). In LA, considerable attention has been paid to resource constraints, and many neighborhood councils provide translation and child care at meetings. More challenging are motivation and invitation. When councils are dominated by higher-income individuals, such forums may fail to motivate diverse participation in that they focus on issues of less interest to historically disadvantaged groups (e.g., land use rather than education or jobs). This is consistent with the historical institutionalism literature (Mettler 1998), which finds that policy and institutional design can negatively shape feelings of citizen efficacy and, hence, their motivation to participate. Thus, the relative success of Chicago's participatory governance efforts identified by Fung (2004) may be attributable to the city's focus on schools and public safety, issues that are much more salient for minority residents than the land-use problems emphasized in LA.

Localities can improve motivation by providing targeted grants or other incentives to engage community groups around issues that cross the income divide. At the same time, higher-income citizen representatives need to be motivated to be inclusionary. A tactic that has been employed successfully in participatory budgeting is to allocate resources to neighborhoods contingent on the mobilization of community residents (Baiocchi 2001). Another option is to incentivize agendas of broad interest through targeted categorical grants. For example, the Minneapolis Neighborhood Revitalization Program has provided grants funded by tax increment monies to eighty-one 501c(3) residential organizations (Fagotto and Fung 1995). The program requires resident organizations to pursue an inclusive community planning effort that produces "Neighborhood Action Plans" that are a basis for the funding.

A capacity constraint is that community volunteers often lack skills in organizing across cultural differences. In LA, there has been a tendency to rely on outreach fliers translated for diverse language groups. This is necessary but not sufficient. The community capacity literature suggests that outreach efforts must move beyond impersonal and passive media campaigns. They must strategically deploy nonprofits and their associated community networks to mobilize disadvantaged populations using personal connections and invitations (Chaskin et al. 2001). An issue that is subtler and more difficult to address is that community meetings may not feel familiar or socially welcoming to people who are not members of the dominant cultural group (Fischer 2006). Prior research suggests that a more hospitable atmosphere may be created by systematically engaging leaders from nonprofit organizations or churches that represent historically disadvantaged groups.

Lesson 3: Deliberation in global cities requires two-way capacity building to address mismatches between citizen and administrator knowledge and attitudes. These efforts at capacity building should not be so complex as to confuse or intimidate citizens, will need to be repeated, and should not unduly raise expectations of citizen influence.

Innovations in deliberative practice are theorized to enhance government responsiveness, trust in government, and policy making (Forester 1999). The experience of the CLP shows that a well-designed deliberative forum can achieve trust, partnerships, and new discourses (Cooper, Bryer, and Meek 2008). The LA experience also suggests, however, that design alone is not sufficient to ensure success;

capacity building for both government agencies and citizen groups is a necessary precondition for successful deliberative practice (also see Fishkin 2009).

Both the CLP and budgeting processes faced challenges that required two-way capacity building aimed at citizens and administrators. In the case of the budgeting process, city officials and neighborhood stakeholders identified gaps in stakeholders' knowledge of the budget process that were barriers to substantive neighborhood council deliberation. In the beginning, LA's information forums were at such a level of discursive complexity that they confused rather than enlightened. At the same time, participants had conflicting and sometimes unrealistic perspectives of their role. Some neighborhood councils sought full audit authority or demanded city actions that were not part of the budget process, such as land-use concessions. Six iterations of the budget process were required for the city staff to develop an understanding of what information was helpful and for a core of neighborhood council participants to develop a base of knowledge and reasonable expectations. In turn, city finance staff needed to develop and implement a role definition for themselves that emphasized engaging stakeholders in the process.

The CLP was designed in large part to address the need for two-way capacity building through direct and open interaction between administrators and neighborhood activists. Difficulties, nevertheless, remain evident. The best example is from the first collaborative process with the Department of Public Works. The department developed an individualized service plan for every neighborhood council in the city. However, the plans were so complex that they overwhelmed the capacity of neighborhood councils to respond to them. Success means that agencies must understand their audience better and provide information accordingly.

Unfortunately, following the completion of the CLP experiments in 2007, LA has done little to develop the capacity for deliberation among either neighborhood council staff or city administrators. A leadership academy initiative faltered politically, and surveys found that agency administrators did not view the councils as important stakeholders. As a result, neighborhood councils appear to be developing more adversarial than deliberative relationships with the city. For example, neighborhood councils have used horizontal networks to mobilize opposition to several citywide initiatives.

Thus, the LA experience confirms findings from other studies showing that administrators frequently resist citizen engagement, because they do not perceive citizens to be in conformance with norms of agency decision making (Kweit and Kweit 1980). Addressing such perceptions is critical to ensuring that citizens are not marginalized or disadvantaged in deliberations (Fung and Wright 2001). Here, enlightened self-interest can be cultivated and leveraged. As Renn and his coauthors (1993) discuss, whereas administrators bring expertise that may be critical for the design of alternatives, citizens bring street-level knowledge vital for administrators to understand the value tradeoffs among different options.

Lesson 4: Strong elected and administrative leadership can overcome organizational barriers, develop sustained deliberation, build trust, and improve administrative responsiveness in global cities. Tactics for doing so include aligning incentives and standard operating procedures with cooperation and deliberation, improving role coherence and redefinition, modeling appropriate behavior, and calculating first-, second-, and third-order effects.

Prior research suggests that administrative and cultural changes are key to integrating neighborhood councils as productive partners in administrative processes, as is a similar cultural shift among elected officials. In Cincinnati, the development of programmatic incentives for neighborhood engagement in governance changed the attitudes of local elected officials and reduced their tendency to "succumb to pressure rather than risk open conflict" (Thomas 1986, 157). What is less clear is how this cultural change in administrative values came about. Berry, Portney, and Thomson (1993) likewise identify the importance of political support in general terms but do not describe the role that leadership played in changing the culture of the city council or administrative agencies. What we do know from prior research, however, is that altering perverse incentives for cooperation, modeling desired behavior by leaders, and manipulating organizational levers for change are critical (Fernandez and Rainey 2006).

The LA experience provides examples of how these strategies can be employed with some effectiveness. LA city government places a strong value on technical expertise, which not unexpectedly has contributed to a dismissive attitude toward neighborhood councils. Cultural change was accomplished by a leader in the Department of Public Works, director William Robertson of the Street Services Bureau. Robertson sought to remove his staff's fear of working with the public, and he modeled desired behavior by visiting neighborhood council meetings and engaging members in open discussion (Cooper and Bryer 2007). His leadership promoted the success of the first memorandum-of-understanding experiment, as administrators within the department came to perceive their role as a partner with neighborhood councils that supported joint problem identification (Bryer 2009). An important contrast, however, was presented by top managers in LA's Department of Transportation. They perceived their own roles as prescriptive, wherein neighborhood councils might describe a perceived problem but would depend on expert administrators to diagnose the root issue and prescribe the solution.

Similarly under Hahn and Villaraigosa, members of the mayor's budget team and the city administrative officer staff were technical analysts who were inclined to resist neighborhood involvement in budgeting processes. But budget staff resistance was overcome by commitment on the part of the deputy mayor for neighborhood and community service, Larry Frank. As a city staff member involved with the budgeting process put it, the budget staff "received the memo" and, over time, became accustomed to presenting at Budget Day (a role previously handled by staff from DONE).

In the LA cases, a more participative budgetary process slowly evolved partly because of a realignment of incentive systems—a realignment that allowed the staff to experience role coherence. The traditional role of budget staff in most public agencies emphasizes the translation of expertise and advice to decision makers, which could become coherent with their new role of delivering information to neighborhood council representatives. Thus, a fit between administrative culture and the participatory budgeting process gradually emerged. In contrast, the CLP took on a more challenging venture—to help agency staff to reexamine their role assumptions and modify operating procedures to engage the citizenry—which provoked heavy resistance (Cooper et al. 2008).

Lesson 5: Universities and foundations have a critical role to play in supporting deliberative reforms in global cities, including overcoming informational impediments and bringing institutional innovations to the process. Paradoxically, however, the neutrality that makes their contributions useful can compromise the impact of their prescriptions.

Previous research has noted that foundations have played an important role in successful experiments with citizen participation (Berry et al. 1993; Lagemann 1999; Thomas 1986). For example, the Mott Foundation supported the development of Cincinnati's neighborhood governance reforms, while the Ford Foundation assisted neighborhoods in some cities studied by Berry and his colleagues. Although much of this research acknowledges the supporting role played by foundations, little explanation is given to the types of roles third parties usefully play.

Our experience with foundation/university partnerships suggests that third parties can be particularly useful in helping participatory systems overcome information impediments by serving as politically neutral sources of knowledge and policy ideas at important junctures. Our research teams, supported by foundations, played an important role as conveners and distributors of information at a number of points. Soon after enactment of the charter reform, we brought neighborhood stakeholders and city officials together in a series of facilitated workshops where they began deliberating over such design issues as boundary designation, organizational structure, and stakeholder designation. At these workshops, many actors met for the first time and developed relationships that became a basis for continued engagement.

University researchers also successfully introduced a number of institutional ideas that were eventually incorporated (e.g., the memorandum-of-understanding process). Likewise, researchers proposed a regional model for deliberating budget preferences and developed a survey instrument that allowed respondents to weigh in on specific budget options being considered by city hall. These innovations continue today. However, outsiders can do little to introduce institutional innovations in the face of political and administrative opposition (e.g., the Villaraigosa administration not permitting departments to participate in later CLP processes).

The research mission of universities also can clash with the action orientation of neighborhood groups (Lagemann 1999). In the CLP process, for example, a number of citizens were skeptical of the motives of university researchers and perceived them to be treating neighborhood councils as an academic exercise. In budget workshops, some activists reacted angrily when researchers pointed out the difficulty of making anything more than marginal changes to a complex budget with limited discretionary spending. Paradoxically, although involvement of neutral and trusted outsiders may assist participatory efforts by providing information and neutral facilitation, their function as neutral brokers also may constrain their ability to assist in overcoming political barriers to neighborhood empowerment.

Lesson 6: Participatory institutions can develop and unleash social capital beyond the original goals of innovation, but then they are likely to produce less deliberation than hoped for.

Although theory suggests that the benefits of participatory institutions accrue to the broader community, much research focuses more narrowly on effects among direct participants (Fung 2004; Mansbridge 1980). Berry, Portney, and Thomson (1993) provide an exception, finding that cities with strong participation systems have higher-quality civic participation, improved government responsiveness, and increased citizen levels of political efficacy. The LA experience provides additionally textured findings on the promise of participatory reform.

The ability of the neighborhood council system to emerge attests to the power of such reforms to unleash social capital. Contrary to the conventional wisdom that LA lacks a civic culture or neighborhood identification (Sonenshein 2004), the opportunity to organize neighborhood councils was met by citizens with enthusiasm. Organizing efforts developed rapidly throughout the city, even in the absence of city resource support. Existing social capital was clearly a facilitator, according to an analysis of the factors that influenced time to formation (Jun 2007). Despite early concerns that self-organization might be difficult for lower-income or migrant communities, the neighborhood council system is citywide, and the few areas without neighborhood councils are very wealthy communities that resisted the procedural requirements placed on certifying neighborhood councils. Indeed, the political networks that have formed around the neighborhood councils connecting them to their communities, city agencies, and other neighborhood councils have been shaped by council members' prior experiences in visiting and volunteering in their neighborhoods and by their past associational memberships (Weare, Musso, and Jun 2008). Moreover, social capital, in fact, had stronger effects than income or education, the attributes commonly predictive of civic involvement.

The political networks that have arisen, however, primarily are "bridging networks" connecting disparate neighborhoods across the city. The number of contacts between neighborhood councils increased fourfold between our 2003 and 2006 surveys of neighborhood council members. In contrast, the frequency of contacts between neighborhood councils and stakeholders in their own community decreased by 25 percent between the surveys, suggesting that neighborhood councils are less successful at generating "bonding" social capital that can build community capacity (Weare et al. 2008).

Importantly, the evolution of these networks over time highlights how the effects of institutional innovations extend beyond the specific deliberative goals, designs, and forums that are created initially. Although many have struggled, networked neighborhood council activists have become important change agents in pushing for collaborative work with the departments, lobbying for a more inclusive budgetary process, and organizing citywide campaigns to support or oppose city initiatives. Moreover, the LA experience shows that a networked core of individuals who are interested in seizing participatory opportunities exists even in global cities.

At the same time, however, the LA case also highlights the difficulties of connecting the activities of core participants to a broader community of interests or to connect agencies with their constituencies at the grassroots. In the absence of a broad and extended feedback loop, the interaction of core participants may have limited benefits for councils and their communities or lead to community fissures. For example, when the resources necessary for collaborative learning forums necessitated a focus on a limited number of neighborhood councils, the process was challenged by activists who were excluded. This lack of connection became manifest in fissures between local communities, their neighborhood councils, and city agencies.

The long-term effects of the emphasis on bridging social capital remain to be seen. Surveys of the general LA population have shown a decline in support for the council system. At the beginning of the reform, 68 percent of survey respondents believed that neighborhood councils would improve the quality of LA city government, and 71 percent believed that they would improve citizen participation. After five years, the percentage of residents holding these favorable views dropped to 41 percent and 51 percent, respectively (Guerra et al. 2007).

Conclusion

The LA experience suggests that best practice lessons from an array of cities can inform the institutional design of a participatory system in a highly diverse global city. Despite thin and inconsistent political support, a citywide system emerged through volunteer excitement about the opportunities for self-determination offered by the flexible charter design. The most important theme of our research, however, is that the politically contested nature of participatory reforms geared toward "strong democracy" poses an array of implementation hurdles that can diminish the benefits of institutional reform, constrain participatory opportunities, and shape the political and social networks that ensue from reforms.

Previous studies have identified challenges to participation across a range of city types but have not fully explored the implications of specific design features on the implementation of participatory initiatives. These include designs that can enhance the presence or absence of continuing political support, administrative leadership, outreach to encourage diversity of engagement, facilitative support from neutral outsiders, and the latent nature of social capital. The nature of these design features in the LA experience has led to an implementation structure that is horizontal in nature ("bridging") rather than bringing together neighborhood stakeholders ("bonding"), that is politically reactive rather than deeply deliberative, and that lacks needed capacity building within deliberative arenas in this most global of U.S. cities. Our research also shows that although universities can serve as neutral experts helping to reduce participatory transaction costs (e.g., information about processes), the legitimacy that neutrality brings is vulnerable to attack by citizens doubting third-party commitment.

In addition to the specific suggestions we have offered in this article, future research needs to go beyond a focus on the study of successful systems at one point in time and produce fine-grained, comparative work that examines the effect of design features on implementation over time. A key question is how the proper confluence of political and administrative supports can be crafted—perhaps with the aid of universities and foundations—to support implementation and maintenance of more successful systems for citizen engagement. A more thorough examination of the relationship between civic participation initiatives, barriers to implementation, and the building of a strong democracy in increasingly diverse global cities merits more attention than it has garnered to date.

Commentary

Brian J. Cook

I find the lessons that the authors of this chapter have drawn from their systematic observations and experience persuasive and intriguing. Their work is quite valuable and stimulating in its own right. It is nevertheless limited in its immediate benefit by the lack of an adequate theory of democracy or, to be more precise, an adequate theory of democracy for the American republic.

As most readers are aware, Woodrow Wilson has had a very confusing relationship with the self-aware study and practice of public administration. Wilson
has been honored as a founder of the field and for being prescient in recognizing
the need to treat administration as a distinctive dimension of democratic governance. In nearly the same breath, however, he has been denigrated or dismissed for
bequeathing to us the unreal and thus reviled politics–administration dichotomy
and for promoting a hierarchical form of governing inconsistent with the spirit and
reality of American constitutional design. Rarely noticed, however, is that Wilson
tried to think about administration and citizen participation in broad, integrated,
and systemic terms, offering a critical role for cities in democratic governance.

Wilson portrayed modern cities as combining both politics and commerce in
complex and often socially stressful ways and as following both natural and artificial
developmental forces. He argued that although they were neither the semi-indepen-
dent polities of medieval times nor the relatively self-contained units for experiencing
self-government represented by early American townships, modern cities were nevertheless still primarily responsible for direct citizen experience with, and instruction
and engagement in, self-government. Seeing cities as important sources of political
and economic differentiation within the essential unity of the nation, Wilson concluded that considerable administrative decentralization and local autonomy were
warranted within American federalism. Decentralization that put everything "local
and peculiar" in the hands of cities and city councils would better sustain civic
"health and vigor" throughout the body politic (Link 1969, vol. 6, 504).

In turn, Wilson argued that it was the duty of citizens to participate directly
in the administration of their cities. He envisioned this happening through an
extensive system of citizen-filled committees and insisted that such engagement in
local administration was true self-government. Voting was not enough, amounting
to a mere act of selection and something of an abrogation of power at that. Direct
engagement aimed "to get and hold the attention of the community for the tasks"
of self-government (Link 1968, vol. 5, 712).

Later, when the community centers' movement emerged and burned brightly
for a brief time coincident with Wilson's service as governor and president, he
took note of its potential to reinforce the lessons of self-government learned at the
municipal level. Community centers, he contended, would open up the channels
of communication among the several parts of the local body politic, where the
core sections—residential, commercial, and industrial—were separated and out of
touch with one another. Bringing citizens together in community centers from
many different stations and walks of life, opening up a dialogue, and creating channels of communication among them would make citizens "conscious that they have
things in common" and that they actually share a "single point of view, namely, the
point of view of the general interest" (Link 1977, vol. 23, 482). Community centers
would thus empower localities to cope with the problems of modern society created

by the forces of specialization and disconnection, which tended to dampen severely the vitality of community life.

What is most important to recognize about Wilson's attention to direct citizen engagement in the administration of the local public realm is that it was part of the top-to-bottom systemic reform of American government, and especially of American public administration, advocated by Wilson (see Cook 2007). He sought a major redesign of municipal government, including its role in a national governing system and its internal structure. This, as part of an overall enterprise to construct the systemic, institutional, and organizational structures necessary for the effective governance of a liberal democracy facing the pressures of the modern age. These included, one may fairly say, the growing global forces impinging on American localities.

Wilson's concern for this systemic political and administrative integration reflected his organicism. He saw the polity as an organism that required harmony in its working parts if it was to survive and thrive amid the daunting forces of social entropy. Overall, his reconstructive effort aimed to further regime adjustment by bolstering the forces of unity, better balancing them against the modern pressures for social division and political disaggregation based on self-interest. The result, Wilson surmised, would be better accommodation of diverse interests and strengthened liberty by facilitating the individual's "accommodation to the whole," as well as the "adjustment of the whole" to the individual's "life and interests" (Link 1977, vol. 23, 485).

As part of this systemic integration and careful fitting of parts to the whole, Wilson gave some thought to the confounding problem of the differences between citizen and administrative expert. He did not reflexively champion the primacy of technical expertise in government. He expressed on occasion, in both scholarly and more overtly political forums, considerable skepticism about rule by technical experts. Much of his thinking about administration and democracy, in fact, can be understood as his attempt to reconcile the citizen and the expert in an age dominated by administration. His solution was to diminish direct citizen contact with expert administration at the national level while facilitating much greater direct citizen engagement with administrative expertise at the local level. He concluded that whatever form a reconstructed American regime reconciling democracy and administration would take, it would require legitimation on a scale that only a new kind of national leadership could achieve.

I find it especially fascinating, not to mention ironic, that Musso and her colleagues have discovered the necessity of top-down political and administration leadership in facilitating bottom-up citizen engagement. The possibility that the strengthening of citizen engagement is dependent on formal leadership seems antithetical to principles of citizen self-rule. Yet this relationship is the great bugbear of democratic theory and practice. From the founding of the republic down to the present day, theories of American self-government have been flawed by inadequate conceptions of both citizenship and statesmanship.

James Madison sold his theory of the extended republic in *Federalist No. 10* as distinctive in part because it did not require "enlightened statesmen ... at the helm." And he based his design of "auxiliary precautions" (*Federalist No. 51*) on a well-articulated liberal model of human behavior but not on anything except the thinnest reed of a concept of citizenship (Elkin 2006, 65–68). It was not too long after Madison's theory was put into practice that he and Thomas Jefferson realized the serious need for a patch in the form of the political party, a patch that Martin Van Buren improved upon mightily, providing a vehicle for citizen engagement and political leadership that stood a developing nation in good stead for about a century.

With the rise of the administrative state, the patch has long since outlived its usefulness. Instead of taking heed of Wilson's insight and engaging in a concerted effort to devise a systemic reconstruction that would address the flaws in Madison's design with respect to citizenship and leadership, however, politicians, political commentators, and many scholars across the ideological spectrum have wasted a great deal of time and energy trying to subdue the bureaucracy and restrain administrative expertise. A far more productive theoretical and practical enterprise would have entailed fully defining the proper roles of citizens and administrative experts and devising the most productive arrangement of relations between them.

Strong democracy may, in fact, offer us the integrating theory for the American regime that we need. I have my doubts, however, because—especially in the new edition—Barber (2003) promotes strong democracy as transcending regime boundaries, though what is politically rational for one time and place may not be so for another. In any case, Musso and her colleagues invoke strong democracy only in passing rather than anchor their efforts to a fully fleshed out articulation of its tenets. They choose instead to tie their research to middle-range theories of local citizen engagement. Until the theory and practice of citizen engagement at the ground level is tied to an adequately formulated theory of self-government for the American regime as a whole, we will suffer with unhappy citizens, cynical politicians exploiting citizen anger and frustration, and scholars who misdirect their intellectual powers.

Commentary

Tina Nabatchi

For the lessons that Musso and her colleagues offer to have the most value for theory and practice, they need to be unpacked and assessed for their design implications. From a normative perspective, citizen participation is an almost universally accepted foundation of democracy. Moreover, scholars throughout the history of public administration have emphasized the integration of administrative practices and democratic values (e.g., Appleby 1945; Follett 2003; Gaus 1923–1924; Lindblom 1990; Lippmann 1957, 1961; Long 1962; Mosher 1982; Sayre 1951; Waldo 1948, 1980; Wildavsky 1979). Likewise, given democratic ethos, public administration has an important role to play in addressing the public's declining confidence in government (for a discussion, see Nabatchi 2010). Additionally, over the past few decades, demands for direct citizen participation have grown tremendously at all levels of government and in nations around the world. Direct citizen participation can be defined as the "process[es] by which members of a society (those not holding office or administrative positions in government) share power with public officials in making substantive decisions related to the community" (Roberts 2008a, 5). Thus, the field needs to move beyond normative arguments to include examinations of the instrumental benefits of citizen participation. By neglecting to think systematically about design choices, as well as how these design choices contribute to (or detract from) desired outcomes, both research and practice are impaired.

Advocates have long asserted the potential benefits of public participation (see, generally, Carpenter and Kennedy 2001; Roberts 2008a). For example, the authors point to literature suggesting that participation can "strengthen civic skills, increase knowledge about civic issues, and promote more informed and reasoned political judgment." In addition, other scholars assert that direct citizen participation can be developmental, educative, therapeutic, integrative, legitimating, protective of freedom, instrumental, and realistic (see Roberts 2008b, 10–11). Still others assert that direct citizen participation can facilitate public learning (Ventriss 2008); build community (Nalbandian 2008); improve responsiveness (Rosener 2008); serve and empower citizens (Denhardt and Denhardt 2007, 2008); build trust in government, citizen efficacy, and a shared conception of the common good (Levine 2008); and reduce citizen discouragement and apathy (King, Feltey, and Susel 2008).

On the other hand, not all are supportive of direct citizen participation. Aside from the critiques noted by the authors, some scholars claim that direct participation is based on a false notion, inefficient, politically naïve, unrealistic, disruptive, and dangerous (see Roberts 2008b, 12–13). It can have high transaction costs for both citizens and government officials (e.g., Irvin and Stansbury 2004; Rydin and Pennington 2000) and limit the ability of officials to broker policy compromises (Ostrom 1990; Sunstein 2003). It may also reduce the ability of government officials to satisfy citizen demands and thereby injure citizen perceptions of efficacy and power (Hibbing and Theiss-Morse 2002). Finally, it may increase the potential for cooptation by more powerful groups or individuals (Arnstein 1969; Young 2003).

It is likely, however, that the diverse outcomes of citizen participation (good or bad) are, in part, a function of design. Not all participation processes are equally endowed in their abilities to produce positive outcomes. Indeed, as the authors rightly note, the evidence suggests that participation is "highly context-dependent, shaped—among other things—by the structure of discourse, who participates, and relationships to decision makers" (see also, Delli Carpini, Cook, and Jacobs 2004). Dewey (1988, 365) recognized long ago that the challenge of public participation lies in the "improvement of the methods and conditions of debate, discussion, and persuasion."

Thus, ultimately, the question is how to design public participation in a way that maximizes the likelihood of achieving positive outcomes (and minimizes the likelihood of achieving negative outcomes). Some important theoretical work on this issue has been done (e.g., Fung 2003, 2006). There are two design levels: system design and process design. System design refers to choices made about the overall system for participatory endeavors, whereas process design refers to choices made about the specific elements within an individual participatory event. This distinction between system design and process design is common in the dispute systems design literature (e.g., Bingham et al. 2009; Elangovan 1995, 1998), and these works are very worth reviewing by interested readers.

The lessons offered by Musso and her colleagues suggest several considerations for the design of both participatory systems and processes. In particular, the study raises salient issues at the system design level, including fostering the embeddedness of, and generating buy-in for, the participatory system, in part through the education of political and administrative officials; making choices about participant representativeness, diversity, and recruitment in the overall system; creating incentives, invitation, and resources for participation; building capacity in terms of role definition, communication, and information sharing; and making decisions about third-party partnering. Salient issues raised by the article for process design include decisions about participant selection and recruitment; choices about incentives, motivation, and invitation or outreach; and decisions about the proper role of parties in the participatory process, as well as how to communicate that role to participants and how to distribute necessary information that is clear and balanced. Future research should give more methodologically sophisticated consideration to these and other salient design choices and options regarding participatory systems and processes.

Commentary

John Clayton Thomas

As I have argued elsewhere (e.g., Thomas 1995, 2010), scholarship on engaging the public in public administration lacks for counsel on how managers should behave to maximize their effectiveness, the effectiveness of government, and the engagement of the public. Our field needs more contributions along the lines of the "design principles" Nobel laureate Ostrom (1990, 90) proposed for the related area of managing common-pool resources, and Musso and her colleagues advance this research agenda appreciably.

In terms of specific lessons offered, I begin with the political vulnerability of neighborhood governance, where the authors make their most significant contribution. Students of participatory reforms might take two pieces of counsel from the LA experience. First, the probability of a reform initiative succeeding will be much greater if reformers can find someone in high elected office to champion their cause. By their nature, participatory initiatives may favor bottom-up, grassroots strategies. However, despite many virtues, that approach may have limited potential for success if proposed reforms do not capture the imagination of someone in authority. Yet finding a political champion carries its own risk in that political champions may not stay in place. All this suggests that proponents of participation must give high priority to seeing reforms institutionalized as much and as fast as possible while under the protection of a political champion. There may also be value in not placing too much weight on the support of any one individual, instead continuing to pursue new political converts even when a political champion is on board.

The authors also nicely capture one of the vexing dilemmas of participatory initiatives: ensuring representativeness. Therein lies a difficult irony of participatory reforms. Envisioned as a means to correct some deficiencies of representative democracy, these reforms typically fail to represent the diversity of the public, as well as do traditional forms of political participation, such as voting. The difficulties in achieving representativeness in these nontraditional forms of participation are multiple. First, people are much less aware of these opportunities for participation than they are of opportunities for voting (see Laurian 2004). Elections generate attention and interest, which stimulate turnout and enhance representativeness, in a manner inconceivable with opportunities for involvement in neighborhood governance. Second, with the competing demands people feel on their time, it can be difficult to arouse broad citizen interest in a participatory initiative. Add to that the fact that participatory involvements usually require more effort than voting. Voting may require only a few minutes' time to get to a neighborhood polling place and complete a ballot. In contrast, involvement in neighborhood governance likely requires attending one or more meetings, each of an hour or more in duration. Third, as participatory initiatives grow toward deliberative democracy, the demands of involvement only grow. This, in turn, further undermines the potential for representativeness. The broader the target population to "represent," the greater the diversity of demographics, socioeconomics, and values to be represented in deliberations.

To their credit, the authors also suggest what might be done to combat these biases, offering some intriguing suggestions regarding focusing on salient issues (e.g., schools and public safety), showing how targeted grants to neighborhood groups have proved successful at mobilizing their residents and broadening participation, and demonstrating how nonprofit agencies can be used to target underrepresented groups. Granted, ensuring representativeness is difficult. But whatever their biases, efforts such as LA's still provide another channel for communication from the public to government that should be considered *with* rather than *instead of* input from other channels.

The authors' focus on two-way capacity building to enhance citizen participation also addresses a gap in the literature. Public administrators often resist citizen engagement, an unsurprising tendency given that the technical training of many administrators often inclines them to look for technical solutions, not solutions that should necessarily please citizens. How can that resistance be overcome? I have argued that administrators, as part of their capacity building, must be trained to look for solutions that both satisfy technical standards and reflect public preferences (e.g., Thomas 1995). It is both demonstrably false and democratically destructive to describe technical standards and public preferences as typically opposed. And even when they appear to be opposed, experts may change their technical judgments on an issue after hearing the public's perspectives, and public preferences may change in the face of more information from experts (see Freudenberg 2004).

For this to happen, however, administrators must receive appropriate training. For institutions such as city governments, the principle of two-way capacity building implies the need for on-the-job training programs. More attention should be paid to building the capacity of citizens, too. Administrators sometimes complain about the low levels of knowledge that citizens exhibit in public involvement efforts, yet they do little to build that knowledge. The city of LA appears mostly to have failed at operationalizing two-way communication and capacity building.

Going beyond administrators and citizens, the authors offer an additional important observation in asserting that "universities and foundations have a critical role to play in supporting deliberative reforms" at the local level. Foundations have underwritten or assisted participatory reforms in many cities, including LA and Cincinnati (Thomas 1986), as when a foundation funds a university program to facilitate neighborhood–city interactions. And one major lesson from these joint initiatives is to seek out these third-party institutions, as the chances for success will increase if their support can be gained. Still, as the authors note, universities and foundations as third parties mostly cannot "make things happen." They can only help to facilitate action that has been initiated by the primary parties: citizens and government. They can be allies, too, but advocates should look elsewhere to find their political champions.

In a public sector environment where efficiency may be the predominant value for the foreseeable future, participatory reforms face an uncertain future. Increasing the role of citizens in government and governance promises many benefits, but greater efficiency (i.e., reducing costs) is not first on the list. However, public projects continue to falter or fail as a consequence of the inadequate or flawed involvement of the public (e.g., Irvin and Stansbury 2004; Welsh 2004). The need to coproduce public services appears to have grown as the work of government has evolved away from products and toward services (Alford 2009).

Chapter 5

Reinventing Administrative Prescriptions: The Case for Democratic-Constitutional Impact Statements and Scorecards*†

David H. Rosenbloom

Contents

---

* Adapted from Rosenbloom, D. H. 2007. Reinventing administrative prescriptions: The case for democratic-constitutional impact statements and scorecards. *Public Administration Review* 67(1): 28–39.
† Recipient of the 2008 William and Frederick Mosher Award for Best Article by an Academician in *Public Administration Review*.

Policy impact statements and scorecards are common tools for prodding public administrative organizations to pay attention to specific concerns and values. In federal administration, environmental impact statements, which were first broadly mandated by the National Environmental Policy Act of 1969 (Public Law 91-109), are complemented by impact statements and assessments regarding the potential effects of agency rules and policies on family values, federalism, environmental justice, and other matters (see Executive Orders 12606 [1987], 12612 [1987], and 12898 [1994]). The contemporary widespread use of scorecards began following the publication of Kaplan and Norton's (1992) now-classic article, "The Balanced Scorecard: Measures That Drive Performance." We have scorecards for the war on terrorism, freedom, civil liberties, school breakfasts, legislative performance, and corporate social responsibility, among others (American Civil Liberties Union of Northern California 2002; Fluke and Kump 2004; Food Research and Action Center 2005; Human Rights Campaign n.d.; Levitt 2002; Marcus 2006). During the George W. Bush administration, the U.S. Office of Management and Budget (OMB) used a scorecard to assess agencies' progress toward the goals of the President's Management Agenda (PMA; OMB 2001).

Conspicuously missing from the plethora of impact statements and scorecards available today are those focusing on the protection and promotion of democratic-constitutional values, including individual rights, constitutional integrity, transparency, and the rule of law. This chapter proposes (1) that democratic-constitutional impact statements be required as part of all substantial prescriptions for administrative reform and (2) that evaluations of program and policy implementation routinely include democratic-constitutional scorecards. The term *democratic-constitutional* refers to those aspects of American government and politics that have democratized the original constitutional design, as amended. Examples include freedom of information, open meetings, the Administrative Procedure Act of 1946 (Public Law 79-404), and the expansion of individual rights through constitutional law. It is understood that the United States is a republic, not a democracy.

The chapter begins by placing the contemporary failure to consider democratic-constitutional values in context as a recurring historical failure of U.S. public administration. Reviewed are reasons practitioners and public administration scholars have, at best, marginalized and, at worst, been contemptuous of democratic-constitutional values as well as reasons why such disregard matters. Next, the logic of impact statements and scorecards is discussed, including how these might be developed, administered, and used to inform administrative reforms in the future. Illustrated subsequently are the differences that impact statements and scorecards might make in protecting values that are typically slighted—if not ignored—by administrative reformers in their prescriptions for improving public management. Several likely arguments against impact statements and scorecards are then confronted.

Misplacing the Keys to Better Government?

Off and on since Woodrow Wilson (1997, 15) famously proclaimed, "It is getting harder to run a constitution than to frame one," public administrative reformers have paid cursory attention to democratic-constitutional concerns in their prescriptions. Most commonly, reformers view variants of cost-effectiveness as the "key to better government" (Savas 1987). They frequently assume that greater cost-effectiveness will automatically improve democratic constitutionalism. For example, in 1937, the President's Committee on Administrative Management (PCAM; also known as the Brownlow Committee) argued that an aggrandized presidency, diminished Congress, and, consequently, a less vigorous separation of powers were necessary "to make good our democratic claims" while warning that "if America fails" for want of administrative efficiency, the "hopes and dreams of democracy all over the world go down" (PCAM 1937, 2). Today's reformers in the Departments of Defense and Homeland Security have followed suit, claiming that the cost-effective defense of democracy requires curtailing employees' rights (McGlinchey 2005; Rutzick 2005a, 2005b, 2005c; Shoop 2005).

Likewise, proponents of other keys to better government have a tendency to slight democratic-constitutional considerations. Reinventers who advocate a heavy emphasis on results offer no plan for protecting values that are not mission based, such as freedom of information and democratic procedures. The National Performance Review, for example, ultimately devalued elections because they have little to do with the ability of administrative agencies to satisfy customers (Gore 1995, 93). Better government reforms in the new public administration tradition could easily promote social equity at the expense of the rule of law (Rosenbloom 2005).

A benign view of reform prescriptions that potentially weaken democratic-constitutional government assumes that advocates take the stability and durability of the U.S. constitutional system for granted. After all, the "miracle at Philadelphia" in 1787 was said to have produced a "machine that would go of itself" (Bowen 1966; Kammen 1986). No need to worry about constitutional government in this view—ambition will counteract ambition, and checks and balances will prevail (Madison 1788/2001, 268–269). Of course, there is still reason for concern. When Benjamin Franklin, a member of the 1787 Constitutional Convention, was asked, "Well, Doctor, what have we got—a Republic or a Monarchy?" he replied, "A Republic, if you can keep it" (Platt 1989, 1593). Ambition may not immediately check ambition, and institutional imbalances may take time to recalibrate. President George W. Bush's ability to assert expansive, largely unchecked executive power from September 11, 2001, until the U.S. Supreme Court handed down its decision in *Hamdi v. Rumsfeld* (542 U.S. 507 [2004]) is a recent example.

A less sanguine view is that administrative prescriptions for better government are based on disaffection with U.S. constitutional design and democratic values. Waldo (1984, 104) noted that orthodox public administration was "hostile to the tripartite separation of powers." Gulick, a pillar of the administrative orthodoxy, only begrudgingly accepted grassroots democracy: "We are in the end compelled to mitigate the pure concept of efficiency in the light of the value scale of politics and the social order. There are, for example, highly inefficient arrangements like citizen boards and small local governments which *may* be necessary in a democracy as educational devices" (quoted in Waldo 1984, 192; emphasis added).

Whether hostile to the constitutional system or confident in its durability, prescriptions for better government and their administrative impacts are incomplete without an assessment of their potential effects on democratic constitutionalism. As Lynn (2001, 155) correctly observes, "Often missing in the literature and discourse is recognition that reformers of institutions and civic philosophies must show how the capacity to effect public purposes and accountability to the polity will be enhanced in a manner that comports with our Constitution and our republican institutions. Basic political and legal issues of responsible management in a postmodern era are inadequately defined and addressed." Arguably, democratic-constitutional impact statements and scorecards would force attention at least to individual rights, constitutional integrity, transparency, and the rule of law.

The Logic of Administrative Prescription Impact Statements

Impact statements are prospective assessments of the probable impact of administrative initiatives on particular concerns. For example, the National Environmental Policy Act requires federal agencies to develop impact statements whenever a proposed action will have a substantial effect on the environment. These statements address possible adverse impacts, alternatives, long-term consequences, and irreversible and irretrievable commitments. In the absence of impact statements and attendant public discussion, an agency charged with developing nuclear power might not view conservation as an alternative to energy generation (*Vermont Yankee Nuclear Power Corp. v. Natural Resources Defense Council, Inc.*, 435 U.S. 519 [1978]). Impact statements can address virtually any political, social, economic, or other matter touched by public administration. The Assessment of Federal Regulations and Policies on Families Act of 1998 (Public Law 105-177) currently requires "family policy-making assessments" to evaluate the impact of agency actions on marital commitments, the authority and rights of parents, and the overall performance of family functions.

Although impact statements have been criticized for creating layers of additional requirements before agencies can issue rules or take other actions, their utility is obvious. If used to assess the democratic-constitutional impact of administrative reforms, they may highlight values that are typically neglected by reformers. For example, if there is any mention of the impact of outsourcing on democratic-constitutional government in Savas's (1987) 308-page book on privatization, it is not prominent. Yet anyone with a basic understanding of constitutional government and administrative law would know that privatization almost automatically incurs three consequences.

First, rights are lost because, with the exception of the Thirteenth Amendment's ban on slavery and involuntary servitude, private sector workers have no constitutional rights with regard to their employers. By contrast, public employees have a wide (if currently narrowing) array of constitutional rights within the context of their government employment. These include freedom of speech and association, personal privacy, procedural and substantive due process, and equal protection (DiNome, Yaklin, and Rosenbloom 1999). In some areas, such as civil rights, there are similar protections in private employment, and there are other areas in which private employees have greater rights, including the broad right to strike.

However, public employees generally have greater protection against reprisals for whistle-blowing, workplace searches and drug testing, invasions of personal privacy, and adverse treatment based on sexual orientation (DiNome et al. 1999). Ordinary citizens also have constitutional and administrative law rights when dealing with government that are not pertinent to their interactions with private organizations. If, as the Declaration of Independence states, governments are instituted to secure rights such as these, then it follows that better government requires an assessment of whether rights will be diminished, enhanced, or unaffected by administrative prescriptions.

Second, privatization typically reduces transparency. At the federal level, legal requirements for freedom of information and open meetings do not apply to private organizations that perform outsourced government work.* Under the Freedom of Information Act (FOIA) of 1966 (Public Law 89-487), one can obtain information from government agencies but not from the contractors whose work is paid for with the same taxpayer dollars (Rosenbloom and Piotrowski 2005). Likewise, under the Government in the Sunshine Act of 1976 (Public Law 94-409), commissioners of federal regulatory agencies may have to hold open meetings when they draft rules.

---

* The Openness Promotes Effectiveness in our National Government Act of 2007 (OPEN Government Act) expands the Freedom of Information Act's reach to include as a "record" information "maintained for an agency by an entity under Government contract, for the purposes of record management" (PL 110-175, December 31, 2007, Section 9). This provision establishes that the records produced by outsourced records management are agency records potentially subject to release under FOIA. For additional consideration of the OPEN Government Act, see the section of this chapter on reflections, *infra*.

However, when the task of writing a draft proposed rule is outsourced, contractors are subject to no such statutory requirement.

Third, privatization diminishes oversight. Federal executives and administrators are routinely summoned to testify before and submit documents to congressional committees. The process of obtaining information becomes arduous when Congress has to subpoena private sector executives and employees in order to obtain basic answers regarding the implementation of federal programs and the use of government funds. Being a tool of adversary legal procedure, subpoenas highlight the involuntary quality of individuals' appearances and their unwillingness to cooperate on their own. Testimony and the provision of documents are likely to be less forthcoming—and personal legal counsel more intrusive—than when federal employees, who are generally deferential to members of Congress, testify before legislative committees. Subpoenas also are subject to challenge in court, related delay, and restriction in scope. The enforcement of subpoenas is by contempt of Congress, which is generally viewed as a drastic last resort involving prosecution by the Department of Justice.

Some might argue that these concerns are overstated because core government functions are not being privatized. However, the differences in legal obligations faced by government agencies and their contractors should not be trivialized on this basis. Contractors today analyze proposed legislation; draft reports to Congress; write testimony that agencies deliver to congressional committees; prepare budget documents, proposed rules, and preambles to final rules; respond to public comments submitted as part of the rulemaking process; and conduct public hearings. Even inspector general functions are sometimes outsourced (Light 1999b, 14; U.S. Congress 1989, 63, cited in Guttman 2000, 873).

Table 5.1 presents an example of what a democratic-constitutional impact statement for key National Performance Review prescriptions might look like. Impact statements would consider the specifics of the prescribed administrative reforms, assess their potential implications for key democratic and constitutional values, and suggest means of mitigating or eliminating any threats to democratic-constitutional values that might be present. Ideally, the impact statements would be submitted to the relevant congressional committees, the OMB, the Government Accountability Office, and the Congressional Research Service, as well as published in the Federal Register for comment by members of the general public, stakeholders, and experts in public administration and related fields. These impact statements, in turn, might even note greater or lesser threats when applied within the context of specific programs. Regardless, the rebuttable presumption is that the implications noted are threats, and the burden of persuasion rests on reformers, who must demonstrate why the concerns are overstated or how they intend to mitigate them in practice. These can then become grist for broader debate among elected officials, attentive publics, and citizens about administrative reforms.

Table 5.1   Example of a Democratic-Constitutional Impact Statement for the Clinton–Gore National Performance Review

Specific Components and Implications for Democratic-Constitutionalism
Steering, not Rowing (Outsourcing)
• Individual Rights: Reduction of constitutional and administrative law rights for individuals • Transparency: Freedom of Information Act and Government in the Sunshine Act inapplicable; congressional oversight more difficult
Results Orientation
• Rule of Law: Loss of attention to non-mission-based values may compromise rule of law • Transparency: Accountability for procedure may be weakened
Biennial Budgeting and Budget Rollovers
• Constitutional Integrity: Weakens congressional power of the purse • Rule of Law: "No year money" reduces legal controls on agency spending
Internal Deregulation and Employee Empowerment
• Rule of Law: Enhances agency and employee discretion • Constitutional Integrity: Weakens prospects for effective judicial review
Potential Mitigations
• Tailor overall prescriptions to specific programs • Include protection of democratic-constitutional values in contracts, such as whistle-blower protections, equal employment opportunity, and transparency requirements

The Logic of Administrative Prescription Scorecards

In contrast to impact statements, scorecards are retrospective. They provide evaluative feedback on how organizations are performing on various dimensions. The balanced scorecard, which is said to be used by 50 percent of Fortune 1000 companies, looks at performance along four dimensions: financial, customer service, internal business process, and learning and growth (Kaplan and Norton 1992; Niven 2003, x). It prevents organizations from neglecting a critical dimension of their overall business strategy or organizational strategic plan. Unfortunately, reinventers' fixation on results parallels the tunnel vision of Kaplan and Norton's hypothetical pilot who has just one cockpit gauge—for airspeed—and none for altitude or fuel consumption (1–2). Getting agencies and contractors up to speed in delivering administrative services and constraints is but one aspect of better government.

Using the OMB's scorecard approach to the Bush administration's PMA, red, yellow, and green lights could be assigned to agency performance on dimensions of importance to democratic-constitutional government (OMB 2006a). The PMA "focuses on five areas of management weakness across the government where improvements and the most progress can be made" (OMB 2006b): strategic human capital, competitive sourcing, financial performance, e-government, and budget and performance integration. Following the OMB format, democratic-constitutional scorecards would be a relatively easy step toward improved awareness of the impact of reforms on democratic-constitutional processes and values (see Table 5.2).

Certainly, the Government Accountability Office, the OMB, and the Congressional Research Service would be appropriate scorers, as might be the National Academy of Public Administration. To the extent feasible, inspectors general could periodically include democratic-constitutional scorecards in their semiannual reports. An agency receiving a red light on a democratic-constitutional dimension from one or all of the scorers would be alerted to the need for improvement. An agency receiving a green light might decide that future resources would be better devoted to different functions, either those on the democratic-constitutional scorecard or others more closely connected to achieving mission-based results. Regardless of choice—and using the same logic of impact statements noted previously—elected officials, attentive publics, and citizens would benefit from the enhanced dialogue requirements imposed on agencies. Similar to the PMA and other scorecards, scoring could involve a mix of quantitative and qualitative measures developed in the context of each agency's activities. For example, some agencies receive thousands of FOIA requests and others receive very few. Some have few direct dealings with the public in which individual constitutional rights are pertinent. Others, such as the Bureau of Prisons, are so highly constrained by constitutional law that they might consider periodic "constitutional audits" (Feeley and Hanson 1990, 26). The important point is that the scorecard would keep agencies focused on democratic-constitutional concerns.

From Theory to Practice: Scorecards and Impact Statements in Action

The following examples are offered as illustrations—and illustrations only—of how impact statements and scorecards could work in practice. These are intended for purposes of argument only. The merits of democratic-constitutional impact statements and scorecards should not prevail or fail on the basis of the particulars of the illustrations, which are well-researched and reasonable (if not definitive) interpretations.

Table 5.2 Example of a Democratic-Constitutional Scorecard Modeled on OMB's PMA Scorecard

PMA Initiative	Individual Rights	Constitutional Integrity	Transparency	Rule of Law
Strategic Human Capital	Yellow Light: Reduction of due process	Yellow Light: Enhances executive authority	Yellow Light: Individualized financial arrangements	Yellow Light: Enhanced agency discretion
Competitive Sourcing	Red Light: Loss of constitutional and administrative law rights	Yellow Light: Legislative oversight more difficult	Red Light: Freedom of information, sunshine laws inapplicable	Yellow Light: Requires effective contract monitoring
Financial Performance	GreenLight: No impact	Green Light: Enhanced financial accountability	Green Light: Enhanced financial reporting	Green Light: Enhanced control of spending
E-Gov	Green Light: Can inform public of legal rights	Yellow Light: Executive-centered control under OMB	Green Light: Enhances transparency	Green Light: Publicizes legal requirements
Budget and Performance Integration	Green Light: No impact	Yellow Light: Can weaken legislative role in budget decisions	Green Light: Greater information about agency performance	Yellow Light: Potential inattention to non-mission-based legal requirements

Note: In the PMA Scorecard, red indicates at least one serious flaw, yellow indicates success on some but not all criteria, and green indicates success on all criteria. Here, red means danger, yellow means caution, and green means positive or no impact.

Protecting Individual Rights

The free exercise of religion is a fundamental human right protected by the U.S. Constitution's First Amendment. The Constitution mandates that "no religious Test shall ever be required as a Qualification to any Office or public Trust under the United States" (Article VI, Section 3). This clause applies at all levels of the federal government (*Torcaso v. Watkins*, 367 U.S. 488 [1961]). However, it did not protect an employee working for the Kentucky Baptist Homes for Children, a contractor providing at-risk youth services for the state of Kentucky. Although conceding she was an excellent worker, the contractor's president explained that the employee had been fired because to "employ a person who is openly homosexual ... does not represent the Judeo-Christian values which are intrinsic to our mission" of providing "Christian support to every child, staff member and foster parent" (Press 2003, 187–188).

If this woman had been employed directly by a state agency, her situation would have been radically different as a matter of law. The agency could not have a mission of providing Christian support to anyone without violating the First Amendment's establishment clause. It could not have made adherence to Judeo-Christian values a job requirement without violating religious freedom. At a minimum, the Fourteenth Amendment's equal protection clause would require the governmental employer to have a rational, job-related basis for firing an employee for his or her homosexuality. Substantive due process under that amendment might require a more stringent standard of review if the dismissal were deemed an interference with the fundamental personal liberty to "engage in [homosexual] conduct without intervention of the government" (*Lawrence v. Texas*, 539 U.S. 558, 578 [2003]).

A comprehensive democratic-constitutional impact statement would raise these concerns for individual rights as part of the process of prescribing the faith-based delivery of public services. Assuming faithfulness to the Declaration of Independence, the Constitution, and national ideals, potential contractors would be notified that all personnel actions involving outsourced government work must comport with the clearly established constitutional standards that apply to public employment. Kentucky Baptist Homes could forego government contracts and continue its refusal to employ openly homosexual persons. However, it would not be free to repress them gratuitously while performing government work.

Preserving Constitutional Integrity

Reform prescriptions often seek to alter constitutional checks and balances by enhancing executive power while reducing legislative roles in public administration. Confusing the president as "chief executive officer" with "sole executive officer" (Rohr 1986, 139), the Brownlow Committee asserted that the "responsibility for the administration of the expenditures under [a legislative] appropriation is and should be solely upon the executive" (PCAM 1937, 22). It viewed checks on the executive's "final authority to determine the uses of appropriations, conditions of employment, the letting of contracts, and the control over administrative decisions, as well as the prescribing of accounting procedures" (49–50), as interferences with the president's constitutional responsibility to "take Care that the Laws be faithfully executed" (Article II, Section 3). This view is so alien to the constitutional design for "joint custody" over federal administration that, in 1937, members of Congress rejected it as dictatorial (Karl 1963, 24; Rourke 1993). By 1946, Congress had responded to the growth of the executive branch (in size and in power) by designing a substantial and coherent role for itself in federal administration. In much the same vein, the Supreme Court rejected President Bush's blank-check approach to implementing the 2001 congressional Authorization for Use of Military Force (*Hamdi v. Rumsfeld*, 542 U.S. 507 [2004]; *Hamdan v. Rumsfeld*, 548 U.S. 557 [2006]).

Undeterred by history, reinventers in the 1990s echoed the Brownlow Committee in calling for fewer congressional earmarks, line items and other spending directives, reporting requirements, and agency staffing floors (Gore 1993, 13, 17, 34). They also sought greater presidential rescission power and agency budgetary flexibility, including the authority to roll over 50 percent of unspent, unobligated year-end budget balances (Gore 1993, 20). Not prone to view its supervision of federal administration as micromanagement, Congress failed to go along with the reinventers' design for a weaker institutional role in the separation of powers.

President Bush's PMA is another example of administrative prescription with potentially significant implications for constitutional integrity (OMB 2001). Bush successfully used the tools of executive dominance—appointments, executive orders and agreements, proclamations, and signing statements—to such a degree that it is fair to ask "whether the extensive use of administrative actions for governance has jeopardized the balance of power between the executive and legislative branches" (Warshaw 2006, 23). Less tentatively, an American Bar Association report indicated that "if left unchecked," Bush's practice of issuing signing statements "does grave harm to the separation of powers doctrine and the system of checks and balances that have sustained our democracy for more than two centuries" (CNN 2006).

Intentionally or not, the PMA also served the interests of expansive executive power. Implementation in each of its five areas provided political appointees with greater flexibility to manage career employees and afforded additional strength to the OMB's already powerful role in federal administration. Briefly, strategic human capital looks toward initiatives at the Departments of Homeland Security and Defense that serve as a model for future personnel reforms that would enhance managerial flexibility while reducing federal employees' collective bargaining rights and protections against unfair or illegal adverse actions (McGlinchey 2005; Rutzick 2005a, 2005b, 2005c). Likewise, OMB Circular A-76, "Performance of Commercial Activities," is the instruction manual for organizing competitive sourcing exercises and decisions (OMB 2003). At the same time, improving financial performance requires the OMB to play a more vigorous role in designing agencies' financial systems. The OMB also has a major role in overseeing agencies' e-government activities and executive branch efforts to institute performance budgeting.

Whether efforts to improve administrative cost-effectiveness—such as those associated with the Brownlow Committee, the Clinton–Gore reinvention, and the PMA—truly threaten constitutional integrity could be addressed through democratic-constitutional impact statements and scorecards when reforms are first proposed and again after they are implemented. Writes Warshaw (2006, 23), a leading expert and author of seven books on the presidency:

> When the Justice Department argues that the president does not need to adhere to legislative actions that unconstitutionally infringe on his authority, what is the recourse in our political structure? The recourse must emanate from Congress itself, but seems unlikely since both Houses are controlled by Republicans whose leadership remains dominated by conservatives. The issue is problematic through the courts. Matters between the executive and legislative branches often fall under the rubric of a "political question" which the Supreme Court refuses to adjudicate. Thus, unless the public can put substantial pressure on Congress, which is unlikely, the continued use of administrative actions will continue to dominate the policy process. The most likely recourse will be when divided government returns.

Many reasonably consider sacrificing constitutional integrity and then restoring it through divided government a very high price to pay for whatever gains in administrative cost-effectiveness or policy goals might accrue as a result of straying from the Madisonian system. Some tradeoffs are obviously tempting and may be necessary. It is important to remember that the definitive guide for making them lies in constitutional law requirements for different degrees of judicial scrutiny rather than the preferences of reformers, officials, or the public. Recall the Supreme Court's words in its ruling on *INS v. Chadha* (462 U.S. 919 [1983]), in which the Court checked what it perceived to be a legislative power grab:

> The choices we discern as having been made in the Constitutional Convention impose burdens on governmental processes that often seem clumsy, inefficient, even unworkable, but those hard choices were consciously made by men who had lived under a form of government that permitted arbitrary governmental acts to go unchecked. There is no support in the Constitution or decisions of this Court for the proposition that the cumbersomeness and delays often encountered in complying with explicit constitutional standards may be avoided, either by the Congress or by the President.... With all the obvious flaws of delay, untidiness, and potential for abuse, we have not yet found a better way

to preserve freedom than by making the exercise of power subject to the carefully crafted restraints spelled out in the Constitution.

Enhancing Transparency

Two illustrations of recent administrative prescriptions for greater cost-effectiveness that have diminished transparency readily come to mind. First, as noted earlier, although the work may be identical, regulations requiring freedom of information and open meetings typically apply when work is done by government agencies but not when it is outsourced. This lesson was brought home to the media after the space shuttle *Columbia* disintegrated in 2003. The National Aeronautics and Space Administration (NASA) generally responded well to FOIA requests for emails and other sources of pertinent information. However, NASA's chief contractor, United Space Alliance, had no legal responsibility to be as forthcoming and was less so. Much of the information held by United Space Alliance—said to do roughly 90 percent of the launch work (Bonné 2003)—became widely available only after the Columbia Accident Investigation Board was convened and released its report.

Importantly, several states provide models of how freedom of information can be applied to contractors, as does the U.S. Department of Energy Acquisition Regulation (Rosenbloom and Piotrowski 2005, 116–117). Nevertheless, as a rule, when government work is outsourced, the public loses the right to know how it is being performed. If James Madison is correct, cumulatively, this is no small matter because "a people who mean to be their own Governors, must arm themselves with the power which knowledge gives" (1999, 790; see also U.S. Senate 1974, 37–38).

Second, as a practical matter, results-oriented public administration has difficulty accommodating and funding non-mission-based activities. For example, improving performance in meeting FOIA requests received very limited attention in federal agencies' Government Performance and Results Act (Public Law 103-62 [1993]) performance plans for fiscal year 2001 (Piotrowski and Rosenbloom 2002, 650–653). Nevertheless, the fact that four of 24 major agencies included specific goals or targets for FOIA requests in their plans demonstrates that appropriate measures exist. For one of those agencies, the National Archives and Records Administration, freedom of information is mission based. The other three were the Departments of State and Energy and the Office of Personnel Management. Eleven cabinet departments and six agencies made no mention of freedom of information in their performance plans. This group included the Department of Justice, which spent about $69 million on FOIA and related transparency activities; the Department of Defense ($36.5 million); and the Department of Veterans Affairs ($25 million). The remaining agencies mentioned FOIA in their performance plans but without specific goals or targets (ibid., 651–653).

The lack of attention to non-mission-based activities in results-oriented public administration is not surprising. It is axiomatic, as an FOIA expert at the Defense Department explained, that "we all struggle with insufficient funds, insufficient staff, and too many requests to handle in a timely fashion. The people who run the daily mission programs in the agencies find it hard to devote the time to FOIA" (Foerstel 1999, 94). The predictable shortchanging of non-mission-based demo-cratic-constitutional values, procedures, and programs is not evitable. It might have been prevented by subjecting the Government Performance and Results bill to a democratic-constitutional impact analysis and modifying it accordingly. Including democratic-constitutional scorecards in agencies' annual performance reports would almost certainly help protect these values, procedures, and programs by making them more salient in evaluating administrative performance.

Ensuring the Rule of Law

Contemporary administrative prescriptions for greater cost-effectiveness, better customer service, and other objectives emphasize the desirability of increasing managerial flexibility, employee empowerment, deregulation, and client and contractor self-regulation (Gore 1995, 11–33; Sparrow 1994). The National Performance Review was particularly hostile to rules: "The perverse effect of 'rule by rules' is that instead of reducing arbitrariness it appears to increase it; instead of fostering cooperation it destroys it; instead of solving problems it worsens them" (Gore, 19). Deemphasizing rules and enforcing fewer of them translates into greater reliance on discretionary administration and compliance. Yet, from a legal perspective, discretion is generally viewed as antithetical to the rule of law, potentially fostering tyranny and even evil (Warren 2004, 345–347; *Delaware v. Prouse*, 440 U.S. 648 [1979]). Two examples, one routine and the other extraordinary, should make the point.

The National Performance Review showcased the Cooperative Compliance Program of the Occupational Safety and Health Administration (OSHA) as a model of commonsense, collaborative regulation. Under the program, OSHA offered employers a choice: voluntarily complying with the standards developed by OSHA in consultation with employers and employees or incurring a 70 to 90 percent greater chance of being inspected, perhaps wall to wall (Gore 1995, 25–27, 32–33; Graves n.d.; LaBombard 1998). Viewed and sued by industry for being a "shakedown," "more like coercion than cooperation," and "ambush rulemaking" in violation of the Administrative Procedure Act of 1946, a federal court declared it illegal and the program was terminated (Harris 1999; LaBombard 1998; *Chamber of Commerce v. Occupational Safety and Health Administration*, 174 F.3d 206 [D.C. Cir 1999]). Ironically, OSHA's "Maine 200" initiative, on which the Cooperative Compliance Program was based, received the Innovation in American Government Award from the Ford Foundation and was celebrated with a coveted Hammer Award from the National Performance Review. A democratic-constitutional impact statement addressing the core issue of whether the prototype or the national program circumvented the Administrative Procedure Act's rulemaking requirements could have obviated OSHA's misguided peremptory steps, litigation, and the embarrassment of showcasing a program that so obviously flouted the rule of law.

A second example—outsourcing a part of the Iraq War—resulted in a much more disturbing breach of the rule of law. In spring 2006, President Bush said, "The biggest mistake that's happened so far, at least from our country's involvement, is Abu Ghraib" (Elliott 2006; Thomas 2006). Were those who issue administrative prescriptions held to the same liability standards as medical doctors who prescribe drugs, the mistake might have been avoided. A doctor who prescribes a dangerous or addictive drug without taking predictable patient behavior into account engages in some level of malpractice.* The same is true of administrative reformers who prescribe outsourcing, administrative entrepreneurship, and partnering with contractors in an environment in which violation of the rule of law is all but inevitable.

These are the pertinent administrative facts regarding Abu Ghraib: The U.S. Army needed interrogators to obtain information from some of the prisoners held at Abu Ghraib. It turned to the Department of Interior's National Business Center to find a private contractor who could supply interrogators. Using a professional engineering services schedule to procure interrogators, the National Business Center issued a contract to CACI International, despite prior federal government experience that had led the General Services Administration to conclude that it is "inappropriate to use [a] technology contract for interrogation work" (Harris 2004b). On the ground at Abu Ghraib, a CACI employee "supervised" military personnel, which is illegal but far from the greatest abuse that occurred (Crawley and Adelsberger 2004). Further breakdown of the rule of law was abetted by the Army's failure to send to Iraq the military officer responsible for overseeing the contract interrogators' performance. Investigators concluded that "it is very difficult, if not impossible, to effectively administer a contract when the [contracting officer's representative] is not on-site" (Harris 2004a; see also Crawley and Adelsberger 2004).

The Army broadly followed administrative prescription in outsourcing interrogation through the entrepreneurial National Business Center. However, this attenuated approach to getting its work done and its failure to supervise CACI personnel all but ensured inadequate accountability for the abusive interrogations. Could a democratic-constitutional impact statement for contracting out work in prisons have stopped the depravity at Abu Ghraib? Perhaps. Domestic experience with contracting out prison health services has established that exceptional measures are necessary to protect the rule of law in penal environments (von Zielbauer 2005).

Conclusion: "You Get What You Measure"

The rationale for impact statements and scorecards is clear. In today's performance-oriented world, what is not assessed or measured is apt to be ignored (Radin 2006). Democratic-constitutional values are weakened by default when not addressed in

---

* Note the conviction of Dr. Conrad Murray for his alleged role in the death of Michael Jackson.

administrative prescriptions. Although tradeoffs may be necessary, democratic-constitutional impact statements and scorecards could help institutionalize Radin's call for the political system, not administrative reformers, to make them. Requiring impact statements and scorecards also could help to recover the "impressively deep insight into public administration in a representative democracy" that public administrative professionals "once owned" (Lynn 2001, 155).

Historically, administrative reforms were often presented as a means of perfecting or democratizing constitutional government. Thomas Jefferson, Andrew Jackson, the civil reformers of the late nineteenth century, and the Progressives of the early twentieth century viewed their reforms in this way (Goodnow 1900; Rosenbloom 1971, 39–41, 47–50, 70–80; Skowronek 1982). In retrospect, some of these reforms were misguided despite ultimately being thoughtfully presented in terms of democratic constitutionalism.

Regardless of what drives today's administrative reformers—cost-effectiveness, business-like models, faith in executive power, social equity, accountability for results, or other concerns—they infrequently focus on whether their prescriptions will promote or diminish individual rights, constitutional integrity, transparency, and the rule of law. In some cases, such concerns are an afterthought at best. Without further explanation—much less analysis of the foreseeable impact of its strategies on democratic constitutionalism—the National Performance Review declared that it sought to "transform bureaucracies precisely because they have failed to nurture" the values of "democratic governance—values such as equal opportunity, justice, diversity, and democracy" (Gore 1993, 8).

Given the tenor of contemporary administrative reforms, the need for democratic-constitutional impact statements and scorecards is probably greater now than ever. Are there obstacles to requiring them? Three objections are predictable. First, some may argue that democratic-constitutional impact statements and scorecards are a solution in search of a problem. The examples presented in this chapter should caution otherwise. Despite some prescient warnings (Moe and Gilmour 1995), the field of public administration lags the courts and legal scholars in addressing the problems illustrated (Rosenbloom and Piotrowski 2005).

Second, adding costs and impediments to administrative action is always a concern. However, in terms of democratic-constitutional impact statements and scorecards, the underlying question is not one of additional cost per se. It is one of priorities, and a key question is whether the money spent could be better used in some other fashion—or, put differently, whether public funds spent for other purposes might be better used to ensure that administrative prescriptions do not detract from U.S. democratic constitutionalism. As for encumbrances, Supreme Court Justice Felix Frankfurter may have said it best: "Remember, there are very precious values of civilization which ultimately, to a large extent, are procedural in their nature" (U.S. Congress 1940, 13664). Although the National Performance Review claimed that "process sometimes cost[s] more than what [is] protected" (Gore 1995, 33), procedure also significantly reduces litigation. Moreover, impact statements and scorecards also can help attenuate a more intangible but nonetheless costly dimension of failing persistently to consider the democratic-constitutional impacts of reforms: an increase in citizen cynicism, the diminution of public trust in government, and bureaucracy bashing. These are, after all, outcomes that administrative reformers typically claim their prescriptions are designed to combat.

Third, developing best practices for implementation may take time and involve a moderate learning curve, especially at a time when a great deal of results-oriented activity is devoted to the war on terror. Initial difficulties can be expected, but democratic-constitutional impact statements should be no more difficult than environmental impact statements or impact assessments regarding families and other matters. "Enacting democracy" through them might even help strengthen public administration's "moral and intellectual authority" in the polity (Lynn 2001, 155). There is already substantial guidance for adapting, developing, and implementing scorecards in the public sector (Kerr 2002; Niven 2003).

The particular challenge posed by democratic-constitutional scorecards is to develop appropriate measures for different programs and agencies. The risk is two-fold: measures must be appropriate because "you get what you measure" (Niven 2003, 185); not measuring may be tantamount to neglect. This challenge should not prove insuperable to practitioners who are well versed in the use of scorecards and performance measurement. In this area, as in others, public administration depends on them to be at the forefront of implementation.

Will Franklin's republic be preserved or lost based on the use of democratic-constitutional impact statements and scorecards? Neither is likely to be the case. However, they can contribute to its strength by guarding against the weakening of individual rights, constitutional integrity, transparency, and the rule of law by default. Reinventing administrative prescriptions in light of the importance of these values in our constitutional republic is important, long past due, and within the grasp of administrators and scholars in the years to come.

Commentary

John M. Kamensky

Rosenbloom's general proposal for governments to assess their reform initiatives both proactively and retroactively will probably come across as a reasonable idea to persons interested in good government. I would argue, however, that his underlying assumptions and supporting arguments may not be effective in selling his general proposition to practitioners. I also think that his specific proposals may not be practical to implement.

Rosenbloom's proposition seems to be that administrative reformers consistently slight democratic and constitutional values and that safeguards—in the form of impact statements and scorecards—are needed. But in the world of practice, a constantly shifting emphasis exists among value sets, largely because these values depend on where stakeholders stand. In addition, management values are seen as being politically determined and evolving over time. He also assumes that these values are well-defined absolutes, but practitioners tend to see them as relative or context-dependent. At the same time, one set of values may be in ascendance at any point in time depending on the political trends and values in either the White House or the Congress. There is also a lack of philosophical consistency in existing management laws (e.g., the Governmental Performance and Results Act [GPRA] and the Paperwork Reduction Act). And these values and principles seem to evolve, ebb, and flow over time. Given this, can there be a consensus around what would be the underlying values in any assessment process, either via an impact statement or a scorecard?

Rosenbloom also proposes the preparation of an impact statement or scorecard on administrative reforms that would focus on the impact of these reforms on the protection and promotion of "democratic-constitutional values." These values are defined as including "individual rights, constitutional integrity, transparency, and the rule of law." These are further deemed to be "central features of U.S. democratic-constitutional government...." As a result, however, anyone wanting to support such a proposal could read anything into it. For example, he defines *democratic-constitutional* as "those aspects of U.S. government and politics that have democratized the original constitutional design, as amended." However, it would have to be defined in far more precise terms to be used in the implementation of either an impact statement or a scorecard. Others (see Dahl 2001; Moe 2004) have offered evaluation criteria for democratic constitutional values that differ with each other and with Rosenbloom's.

Having a clear, bounded definition, which is commonly seen as legitimate, is a crucial first step to creating an impact statement or scorecard that can be impartially implemented. However, creating a definition for administrative implementation efficiency may be counter to political values—defining and bounding "democratic constitutional values" may inadvertently begin to limit those values commonly seen as inherent. In other words, some ambiguity may be healthy for democracy, but it is not healthy for an administrative program requiring precision to prevent misuse by partisans.

To be sure, in describing the value "constitutional integrity," Rosenbloom specifically cites examples of balance-of-power issues. These examples are a clearer explanation of what he is seeking to address, but the broader term, *constitutional integrity*, would need to be further defined to be useful to practitioners. A definitive set of agreed-upon elements, such as a list of constitutional checks and balances, would be needed so an impartial analyst of a management reform proposal would know what "counts" in relation to a program or policy review.

Rosenbloom also expresses concern over how GPRA contributes to a lack of transparency. Again, it depends on relative values—there are always tradeoffs among the levels of enforcement of different laws that are rooted in different philosophical values. GPRA has led to increased transparency in what agencies do and the results they produce. Yet it may have indirectly contributed to decreased funding for nonmission functions—such as the Freedom of Information Act. But could this tradeoff have been predicted in advance via an impact statement?

On another point, his proposal needs to have its scope better defined. In his discussion of the misuse of the Department of the Interior's contracting authority to hire private interrogators for the military, for example, Rosenbloom poses a question: "Could a democratic-constitutional impact statement for contracting out work" have prevented this misuse? This instance of abuse was a contracting decision, not a conscious policy action. Administratively, is Rosenbloom recommending that all individual contracts be subjected to his proposed impact statement requirement? In fiscal year 2004, the federal government awarded nearly 1.7 million contracts valued at nearly $311 billion. This might create a major bottleneck in the government's ability to deliver services. Again, the question is a tradeoff in priorities. And, again, this is a value judgment by political leaders. A related "scope" question is whether the intent of the impact statement is to conduct an assessment on the process of reform or on its results.

Finally, our field is prone to propose rules and administrative processes as a solution to problems—it is in politicians' and managers' genetic code. However, I would argue that an educated citizenry and a caring political and career leadership are probably more effective means of providing oversight of activities, such as reforms, that could affect national values. "Caring leadership" is critical to sustaining important values. So who would champion Rosenbloom's proposal? Proposals to create permanent administrative institutions legislatively—such as a permanent National Performance Review or a separate Office of Federal Management—have been rejected historically because no political champion existed for them.

The Office of Management and Budget's Program Assessment Rating Tool (PART) was an administrative initiative President George W. Bush used to assess the performance of programs. It was effective because he cared, and his staff used it to make decisions. If Rosenbloom's proposals were required in legislation, a future president might not be committed to their use, and the proposals would become another useless compliance requirement that agencies would have to go through the motions of completing—at some cost to program performance. Moreover, from a practitioner's perspective, outside efforts to preassess a reform initiative (impact statements) would be perceived as slowing things down, while a postreform assessment (scorecard) would be perceived as unwanted interference.

But even assuming a political champion for the idea of conducting assessments emerged, who could develop and apply criteria that would be seen as credible by the public, the politicians, and the agencies and programs assessed? This is not an insignificant question. The constitutional role for oversight of the executive branch resides with the Congress. Would Congress be interested in such assessments? So far, it has expressed anywhere from mild to no interest in other forms of assessments, such as GPRA or PART scores. Rosenbloom offers several options, including the

Government Accountability Office, the Office of Management and Budget, the Congressional Research Service, the National Academy of Public Administration, and inspectors general in affected departments and agencies. But each of these (and other) institutions could be perceived as biased and would tilt the balance of power toward either one branch of government or the other (which undermines one of his earlier stated values).

RECAPITALIZING ORGANIZATIONAL CAPACITY

In his classic, *Big Democracy*, Paul Appleby (1945, 33) insisted that the United States needed "philosophers of administration" who have an "ingrained disposition to put the public interest first and, thus, to recognize the great, essential, and pervasive difference that distinguishes public administration from the management of private enterprise." Yet the last three decades have seen a resurgence of faith in markets and private sector techniques. These were attempts to avert what proponents termed *government failures* in the wake of Great Society programs of the 1960s.

Spawning these demands was the interaction of several large-scale demographic, social, and political forces. The aging of the U.S. population occasioned spiraling fiscal demands combined with downward pressures on tax revenues due to economic globalization, thus arousing calls for the downsizing of federal agencies, budget cuts, the devolution of federal responsibilities to the states, and the contracting out of service provision at all levels of government. This occurred as elected leaders responded to countervailing pressures to take on new obligations while cutting taxes without trimming entitlement programs and without increasing the visible size of government (Light 1998).

The most notable manifestations of these trends came packaged in the new public management (NPM) and new governance movements. Embraced typically by minimal state proponents, NPM is an administrative theory that accords no special role for either the public service (in Washington or elsewhere) or the public interest, aside from what market forces and competition allow or dictate. In contrast, the movement is attractive to positive (i.e., activist) state proponents. It affords an administrative theory that better links the "essential unity of politics and administration and recognizes the importance of the state in balancing market forces" (Wettenhall 2003, 80). Both sets of administrative theories, however, embrace to varying degrees the following concepts as central animating principles of administrative reform: downsizing, contracting, competition, decentralization, defunding, deregulation, partnerships, and economism (i.e., economic, human resource, and technical efficiency).

As such, finding the financial wherewithal to deal with old, new, and emerging public policy problems stands front and center as an immediate challenge for public managers. And endemic to this challenge is anticipating and stewarding the revenue flows that administrators need to address societal problems amid economic volatility. Fred Thompson and Bruce Gates of Willamette University tackle this issue directly. They argue that new financial theories and tools used in the private sector can inform this fiscal challenge and should be in the toolkits of budget professionals at all levels of government.

Responding to their arguments, Roy Meyers of the University of Maryland–Baltimore County, and previously an analyst at the Congressional Budget Office, and Katherine Willoughby of Georgia State University both doubt the practicality of Thompson's and Gates's prescriptions, stressing that it is political risk, not fiscal risk, that most animates elected officials' concerns. For Meyers, the decision rules and techniques advocated by the authors require daunting foresight that is beyond the ken of elected officials, and he doubts that—as the authors claim—politicians would adopt rules they fail to understand. Willoughby is equally skeptical: "adoption by governments of toolkit components is one step, agreement as to application in the budget process is a second step, and then consistent championing and use of the component over time is a third step. All of this is complicated by the politics of state budgeting, the fluidity of the process, and the timeliness of the budgeting cycle."

No aspect of recapitalizing agency capacity and linking it to agency downsizing draws more opprobrium from public administration scholars than the contracting of agency activities to the private and nonprofit sectors. Trevor Brown of Ohio State University, Matthew Potoski of the University of California–Santa Barbara, and David Van Slyke of the Maxwell School of Syracuse University tackle this issue by integrating theoretical insights from three research traditions—strategic management and planning, public law and administration, and economics. They offer a multiple-values framework for practicing and studying public sector contracting and then draw lessons from that framework for different stages.

Reacting to their article, Ruth DeHoog of the University of North Carolina–Greensboro, Suzanne Piotrowski of Rutgers University–Newark, Thomas Reilly of Clark County, Nevada, and Andrew Whitford of the University of Georgia are impressed about the breadth of value coverage but have important refinements to offer. DeHoog and Whitford are the most critical out of hand, with the former claiming that the authors underplay political realities in contracting that public managers and elected officials ignore at their peril. DeHoog worries that readers will leave the authors' work thinking contracting is merely a management process instead of a "messy, confusing, and conflictual process fraught with opportunism, both political and financial." For Whitford, the enterprise of linking theory to practice, while affording general lessons, is impossible in principle. In his judgment, the value of the original article is in shifting the research focus toward understanding how managers should strategically implement political directives to contract out as they balance multiple values.

In contrast, Piotrowski focuses on the costs to transparency of government contracting—a key aspect of the process that has drawn little concern from administrative reformers and that reaps little attention from Brown, Potoski, and Van Slyke. Pointing out that most of the limited research on the relationship between transparency and contracting has focused on other nations, she notes how transparency-seeking U.S. legislation such as the Freedom of Information Act faces obstacles to implementation when applied to private rather than public organizations. For then–county manager Reilly, the lessons gleaned from prior research and theory by Brown and his coauthors are on target but need refinement in terms of realpolitik. In particular, he calls readers' attention to various games that contractors play, the importance of aligning service delivery goals across contracts, the ways that contractors increase costs, and the need to consider the venues in which dispute resolution occurs.

Next to contracting out, the most controversial aspect of market-inspired administrative reforms for recapitalizing agency capacity has been a state-based movement to end tenure in employment. So-called radical civil service reforms (RCSRs) launched in many states prompted a host of claims by proponents and a raft of concerns by critics. Proponents promised more effective, responsive, and adaptable government performance, whereas opponents were wary of threats to merit protections. Personnel specialists Stephen Condrey of Condrey and Associates, Inc., and Paul Battaglio of the University of Texas–Dallas draw lessons, offer propositions, and assess the durability of civil service reform efforts from prior studies and their own research on at-will employment in Georgia. Their survey of state agency human resource managers reveals, among other things, that the claims of NPM proponents were overstated in Georgia but that a generational and gender component related to support for RCSR also existed. Younger human resource personnel, those with less public employment experience, and women were more supportive of RCSR than were their older, male, and more experienced colleagues. Since the publication of this article, the authors contend that the Georgia reforms have continued apace and were the harbinger of a sustained assault on employees' rights in the United States. The most egregious examples at the state level came in Ohio and Wisconsin with efforts to abolish collective bargaining rights. At the federal level, similar efforts occurred to freeze pay and alter federal employee benefits, particularly retirement benefits.

Commentators Frank Ferris of the National Treasury Employees Union, Norma Riccucci of Rutgers University–Newark, and Frank Thompson of Rutgers University–Newark find much of interest in Condrey and Battaglio's research and arguments. Ferris takes solace in their finding that more experienced workers were less supportive of RCSRs and hopes that younger state workers will grow similarly opposed as they spend more years in government and appreciate the downsides of this approach to recapitalizing agency assets. He also criticizes the focus on human resource managers, arguing that more negative results would have been likely if first- and second-line program managers had been surveyed (as had been the case in the federal government). He also argues that administrative reformers are too detached from practice (e.g., academics and the National Academy of Public Administration) and should have less influence. Riccucci focuses on the role of labor unions and the courts in countering RCSR initiatives in the federal government, recounting in the process the ill-fated efforts of the George W. Bush administration to rein- vent personnel management at the United States Department of Defense and the Department of Homeland Security. With no clear trends regarding the impact of unions and the courts in the states, she urges a robust research agenda on these topics. Thompson wants the implications of certain findings either reconsidered or explored more fully: Were attitudes toward RCSR really generational, or might they be maturational—with decidedly different implications? Might the finding that RCSR increased responsiveness to political appointees indicate an undesirable centralization of power in agencies, as opponents of RCSR feared? Before infer- ences regarding RCSR are accepted, might one not want to examine the interaction of all aspects of the agenda rather than merely at-will employment?

But if contracting and RCSR sparked the most heat among public administra- tion scholars, the most contentious among citizens involved efforts to recapitalize public agencies by increasing their representativeness through affirmative action (AA). In her chapter, Sally Coleman Selden of Lynchburg College leaps into the controversy by asking whether AA policies are really needed anymore to increase both passive and active representation of the public service. The major lesson she draws from her review of citizen surveys, prior research on passive and active repre- sentation, and evolving court doctrine is that it is necessary but has to be revamped in light of these factors.

Responding to Selden's arguments, Domonic Bearfield of Texas A&M University, Lael Keiser of the University of Missouri–Columbia, and Sharon Mastracci of the University of Illinois–Chicago are largely sympathetic with Selden's findings and interpretations of ongoing trends. However, Bearfield takes a different tack by arguing that treating historically disadvantaged groups as homo- geneous—a key element of AA—is increasingly misguided. Not only are many of these groups becoming mixed race in origin, but also discriminatory barriers believed to impact all people within a given group (e.g., barriers to college admis- sion, employment, or home ownership) are felt differentially by various subgroups (Wilson 1987, 1996). He notes, too, that the greatest long-term threat to AA comes less from public opinion and court cases than from a supply-side problem generated by the prison incarceration rates of young black males. Similarly, Mastracci complements Selden's analysis by citing prior research suggesting that a more profitable way to approach AA in light of public opinion and court suits is to focus on class rather than race or gender, while Keiser takes issue with Selden's characterization of the literature as offering only mixed results for the linkage between passive and active representation.

Chapter 6

Betting on the Future with a Cloudy Crystal Ball? How Financial Theory Can Improve Revenue Forecasting and Budgets in the States[*]

Fred Thompson and Bruce L. Gates

Contents

[*] Adapted from Thompson, F., and B. L. Gates. 2007. Betting on the future with a cloudy crystal ball? How financial theory can improve revenue forecasting and budgets in the states. *Public Administration Review* 67(5): 825–836.

Accurately predicting revenue growth is nearly impossible. Predicting the peaks and valleys of the business cycle is even more hopeless. This matters because tax revenues are largely driven by economic growth. Volatile, unpredictable revenue growth causes all sorts of unpleasant governmental responses, most commonly manic-depressive patterns of spending and taxing. Moreover, the further governments look into the future, the murkier the outcome.

We contend that although predicting the future is truly a "mug's game," part of the problem is that, historically, the mugs playing the game have been asking the wrong question. The question should not be, "How much will revenue grow?" Rather, the more appropriate question is, "Given that we can't predict the future, how can we get a good result no matter what the economy throws at us?" We contend that the latter question is a more analytically feasible one to answer because of recent developments in financial theory.

Interestingly, the American Finance Association started the same year as the American Society for Public Administration. Its official organ, the *Journal of Finance*, began in 1947, seven years after *Public Administration Review*. In this relatively short time, finance has undergone a revolution that has transformed its conceptual frame, its methods, and even its subject matter. This revolution has profoundly influenced nearly every branch of economics, especially macroeconomics (Boskin 2000; Eisner 1986; Kotlikoff 1986; Kotlikoff and Burns 2004). In the long run, we contend that it should have an equal effect on public financial management, public budgeting, and government accounting.

In making this argument, we show how two basic ideas that have dominated modern financial theory—variance and drift—can enhance crystal-ball gazing for budget practitioners and theorists alike. More precisely, although financial outcomes are uncertain, they are predictable in an actuarial sense. That is, we can quantify expectations in terms of growth rates and risk. The technical term for actuarial risk is *variance*. *Variance* means distance from an average or mean, and in this instance, the mean we are talking about is the expected rate of growth of a financial variable. At the same time, movements in financial variables over time are more or less random. In other words, the future is typically assumed to be a random walk, albeit, perhaps, one with a long-term trend. More technically, we refer to this as *drift*.

In this chapter, we focus on how four tools of financial analysis—growth analysis, portfolio analysis, hedging, and consumption smoothing—can help elected officials, budgeters, and scholars anticipate the answers to four basic questions about forecasting uncertain financial futures. First, how much can revenues be expected to grow? Second, how much revenue volatility is likely to occur? Third, how much can volatility be reduced without jeopardizing growth expectations?

And finally, how long is it safe to wait before acting? In the process of introducing this toolkit—which we argue ought to be part of the standard repertoire of all public sector financial managers—we also cull from prior research and practice six lessons for managers engaged in financial forecasting.

Growth Analysis: Through a Glass Darkly

Rapid and sustained revenue growth tends to encourage unsustainable spending increases or tax cuts. When a recession strikes, governments facing a "hard budget constraint" and not able to practice discretionary monetary and fiscal policy engage in a variety of expedients—many of them quite wasteful—to cope with the emergency.[1] These expedients include cutting maintenance or deferring the replacement of assets, raiding trust funds (which is costly because governments are implicitly borrowing at the taxable rate, which is higher than the tax-exempt rate on state debt), and shifting fiscal obligations to local governments.

As long as recession is fresh in the minds of public officials, their control of the purse strings will remain tight. Gradually, however, funds accumulate and the need to spend becomes overriding. This is costly, both directly as a result of the expedients taken to balance budgets (Cornia, Nelson, and Wilko 2004; Hou 2006) and indirectly from a macroeconomic perspective. This occurs because spending increases and tax cuts add force to booms, and spending cuts and tax increases deepen cyclical troughs (Levinson 1998; Poterba 1995). So what can budgeters do to get a good result no matter what the economy throws at them?

Lesson 1: The simple average of past revenue growth rates is the best estimator of expected growth rates when decomposed into systematic and nonsystematic components using mean-variance analysis. We argue that although they cannot accurately predict revenue growth from one year to the next or the timing of the business cycle, budget makers can make actuarial appraisals by quantifying revenue expectations in terms of average growth rates and the variance (or volatility) of actual revenue growth from that average.

Whenever the distribution of revenue growth rates around the average growth rate is stable over time, and as long as periodic growth rates are independent of one another, the simple average of past growth rates is the best estimator of expected growth rates. However, budgeters should appreciate that the arithmetic mean must be distinguished from the geometric mean, which measures the compound rate of growth over several periods. This is the case because the geometric mean will always be less than the arithmetic mean unless the rate of growth is constant. Indeed, the gap between the two will widen as variance in the growth rate increases.

With this caveat in mind, how might practitioners and scholars take advantage of mean-variance analysis? As done already by sophisticated revenue forecasters (Bowerman, O'Connell, and Koehler 2005; Makridakis, Wheelwright, and Hyndman 1998), they should start by breaking historical data into three components: (1) the trend or rate of long-term growth or decline; (2) cyclical or regular, periodic oscillation in growth rates; and (3) a random component. The trend is simply the mean growth rate and the other two components, the variance.

Standard approaches to revenue forecasting do not offer a discernible cyclical component related to growth in the economy as a whole, because the relationship is not known until after the fact. In contrast, mean-variance approaches allow budgeters to decompose revenue volatility into an *unsystematic* component and a *systematic* component. The former is random and can be managed partly through diversification of revenue sources; the latter reflects changes in the underlying economy and can be managed, at a cost, through hedging and buffering strategies. Moreover, once these components are identified, the advances in financial theory that follow in this chapter suggest additional tools for anticipating and coping with revenue volatility.

Using Portfolio Theory to Manage Unsystematic Volatility

Effective diversification of revenue sources (i.e., expanding the types of revenue sources on which governments depend) is widely seen as a way of reducing revenue volatility without also reducing revenue growth. In turn, the effectiveness of diversification depends less on the number of tax types used than on the way they perform relative to one another—or covariance. Covariance analysis is one of the main ideas that tax specialists have adopted in recent years from modern financial theory. Prior research in this tradition (Gentry and Ladd 1994) leads to a significant conclusion for practitioners and researchers.

Lesson 2: Governments cannot significantly reduce volatility in revenue growth by merely substituting one tax type for another. Volatility in revenue growth can be significantly reduced by a well-designed portfolio of tax type. Once an efficient frontier has been identified, changes in the portfolio of tax types to increase tax equity, however, can also increase volatility in revenue growth. But even the best-designed tax portfolio cannot eliminate all revenue volatility.

Covariance analysis and its extension, portfolio theory, are conceptually and mathematically similar to such traditional elements of public finance as analyses of vertical and horizontal equity and revenue elasticity. The former is usually done with cross-sectional data on personal income and tax payments, the latter with time-series or panel data on personal income and tax yield. However, portfolio theory differs from these traditional approaches by looking at how types of taxation that incorporate different design elements covary with each other and with the underlying economy. In this way, one can understand how a portfolio of tax types can help manage volatility in revenue growth. This is, again, subtly different from the traditional view of tax specialists, which holds that inherent tradeoffs exist between revenue growth and stability (Groves and Kahn 1952). According to this view, income-elastic tax bases (i.e., those with greater progressivity) tend to grow faster than the economy, but fluctuations in income over the business cycle cause them to be unstable. In contrast, inelastic tax bases grow more slowly or not at all, but they are highly stable.

This traditional view certainly has a basis in fact. Governments that rely heavily on highly progressive, comprehensive income taxes have both high growth rates and high revenue volatility. Nevertheless, empirical research demonstrates that the tradeoff between revenue growth and stability is not as acute as once thought and varies across different tax types. Income taxes, for example, are not necessarily more volatile or faster growing than broad-based consumption taxes. Likewise, corporate income taxes grow more slowly than personal income taxes and are more volatile; even some specific excises, such as motor fuel taxes, are fast growing, and some are quite volatile (Bruce, Fox, and Tuttle 2006; Dye and Merriman 2004; Otsuka and Braun 1999; Sobel and Holcombe 1996).

Still, Bruce, Fox, and Tuttle (2006; see also Fox 2003) show that the composition of the tax base, rate structures, and elements of administration can have bigger effects on volatility and growth than tax type. For example, state policy makers can often significantly lower the revenue volatility from broad-based taxes without adversely affecting revenue growth by eliminating exemptions or equalizing marginal rates—that is, by reducing the progressivity of the overall tax structure. But governments can also reduce volatility by diversifying their tax portfolios without reducing the progressivity of their tax base. This is because the volatility of a tax portfolio depends on how its components covary, not on the average of its individual tax types (Gentry and Ladd 1994). This is a special application of ideas formulated in corporate finance having to do with risk and return (see Lintner 1965; Markowitz 1952; Sharpe 1964).

Though a variety of consequences flow from this observation, some of the more remarkable implications of portfolio theory are as follows:

■ The average volatility of tax revenues will usually be reduced by adding tax sources, except where yields from the two taxes are perfectly correlated.
■ Hypothetically, a two-tax portfolio could be developed to eliminate revenue volatility completely but only if their yields are inversely correlated (i.e.,

coefficient of correlation = −1.0) and the two taxes are weighted equally (i.e., produce equal yields over time). Unfortunately, there are no such tax types. The closest we can come to one is the lottery, which has a coefficient of correlation between −0.08 and −0.20. Thirty-one states had both a state income tax and a fully operational lottery for fiscal years 2000–05. We looked at the annual percentage change in both personal income tax revenues and net lottery income, which is pretty close to the net revenue from this source. For all thirty-one states, we calculated a correlation coefficient of −0.16 on percentage change for a sample of 155 observations. So, although lottery transfers are quite small (averaging somewhere around 3 percent of state own-source revenues), they do help offset the volatility of personal income taxes.

■ In general, tax sources have coefficients of correlation that average about 0.65, so adding taxes to the portfolio tends to reduce but not eliminate volatility.

■ Only if one looks at efficient tax portfolios is there a necessary tradeoff between stability and growth. Moreover, it is possible to construct an efficient growth frontier showing this tradeoff. All one needs is information on the covariance of the growth rates of each of the different tax types and designs that obtain in the different states.

Instead of calculating the covariance of each pair of possible tax designs and using that information to construct an efficient frontier, an analyst can more simply calculate the relationship of each tax type to gross domestic product or state product, whichever is the single most important influence on revenue growth. If the growth of a tax type is more volatile than the economy, that tax type will make the portfolio more variable than it would have been otherwise. If the tax type is less volatile, it will make the portfolio less risky. The volatility of the portfolio is the weighted average of these relationships (Gentry and Ladd 1994). Lacking negatively covariant tax types, the best that tax-portfolio designers can do is to eliminate the unsystematic or random portion of the variation in revenue growth. The systematic portion would remain. Moreover, portfolio analysis tells us that we need a lot of tax types to eliminate all unsystematic variance in revenue growth, but we may not have enough tax types with which to work.

Managing Systematic Risks with Hedges and Buffers

How can practitioners best manage the second component of risk—systematic risk—in making projections? One way to reduce the volatility in revenue growth caused by an unpredictable underlying economy is to offset these types of changes with a revenue flow of equal size and opposite volatility. This is called hedging. As noted, if we could find two tax types that produced revenue flows of the same size and that were perfectly but inversely correlated with each other, we could eliminate all volatility in revenue growth. Though there are no such tax types, it is possible to design hedges against the systematic component of revenue volatility.

Lesson 3: Hedging with futures and options contracts is potentially the cheapest, most direct way to deal with systematic volatility in revenue growth, but these approaches are not without their own problems.

Hedging with futures and options contracts is the most direct way to deal with systematic volatility in revenue growth, at least in theory (Swidler, Buttimer, and Shaw 1999). Indeed, many of the expedients that governments currently use to offset systematic volatility in revenue growth are conceptually analogous to the use of futures and options contracts. For example, governments issue variable-rate bonds precisely because of the inverse correlation between the prime interest rate and revenue flows, which means that they work like futures contracts. They could go even further in this direction by directly indexing debt service on their bonds to revenue growth. And, of course, many government debt issues feature an embedded *call option*, which gives the issuer the right to *buy* them back at a fixed price at a future date.

Governments also can offset systematic revenue risk and stabilize revenue growth by *selling* futures contracts on an index based on probably the single most important macroeconomic factor influencing revenue growth, gross state product. The underlying asset values would covary with the systematic portion of the government's revenue flows. This is a fancy way of saying that the profit or loss from the sale of these futures contracts would vary inversely with the systematic component of the variance in government revenue growth. This could be accomplished, in theory, by selling futures contracts on state revenue, but problems of moral hazard and, perhaps, adverse selection would probably make the design and operation of such markets prohibitively costly.

Taking this approach to managing systematic risk also is not without its own inherent problems. As Hinkelmann and Swidler (2005, 129) observe, "A futures contract is … a zero sum game in which the profits of one party equal the losses of the counterparty." Using futures contracts to hedge revenue flows means sacrificing higher than expected revenue flows, not just avoiding revenue shortfalls. If governments wanted only to protect themselves against revenue shortfalls (keeping high revenue inflows for themselves), they would have to purchase *put options* on the covarying financial asset. A put gives the buyer the right, but not the obligation, to sell the underlying financial asset for a fixed price, called the *strike price*. Of course, a government would exercise its option to sell the asset only if its spot price fell below the strike price. Unfortunately, however, options are not free. Governments would have to pay hefty premiums to purchase enough put options to provide meaningful insurance against unwanted revenue shortfalls. Moreover, the greater the volatility of a government's tax portfolio relative to the volatility of the index, the larger the hedge needed.

Thanks largely to Yale professor Robert Shiller (2003), there is a movement afoot to create hedging instruments based on indices of macroeconomic aggregates. Goldman Sachs and Deutsche Bank already offer derivatives on nonfarm payroll and initial jobless claims. The Chicago Board of Trade offers futures and options contracts based on indices such as gross national product and personal income. None of these indices represents a perfect hedge (a one-for-one offset for gains or losses) against all revenue volatility, but they work pretty well. Derivatives based on personal income (either futures or put options) could reduce systematic revenue volatility by 60 to 80 percent in about twenty states, including New York, Ohio, Pennsylvania, and Massachusetts (Hinkelmann and Swidler 2004, 2005). Nevertheless, it is unlikely that governments will soon embrace the use of futures and options contracts to hedge against systematic revenue volatility, both for technical and political reasons.

Lesson 4: Participating in self-insurance pools is similar to the use of put options in managing systematic risks, and their downsides can be attenuated through the use of Markov and Monte Carlo processes.

The two most common suggestions for dealing with systematic revenue volatility are (1) putting money aside to deal with revenue shortfalls in what is commonly called a "rainy day fund" and (2) participating in a multigovernment risk pool, with specific experience ratings created to reflect revenue volatility. The former involves a program of self-insurance and the latter is comparable to buying an insurance policy, with the annual contribution analogous to an insurance premium. The problems raised by a policy of self-insurance against revenue shortfalls are twofold, however. The first is the difficulty of estimating the size of the rainy day fund needed to stabilize spending, given systematic variations in revenue flows. The second is the challenge of formulating a contribution or savings rule to achieve the desired fund size.

To resolve these issues, Wagner and Elder (2004) use a Markov-switching model to estimate real per capita personal income for each state during booms and busts as well as the probability of switching from economic expansion to contraction and back again. Based on these results (together with the assumption that state revenues vary directly with personal income), they compute the savings rate needed to buffer state governments against revenue shortfalls. To provide a 90 percent buffer against cash shortfalls, the required contribution rate would be $19 million per

$1 billion of revenue on average. At the time of their analysis, ten states would need contribution rates of less than $10 million per billion, with Kansas requiring none. Eight states would need contribution rates of more than $30 million per billion, with Wyoming topping the list at $45 million per billion.

According to Kriz (2003), the level of savings needed depends on several factors: average revenue growth, revenue volatility, average return on investments, the volatility of investment returns, and the desired rate of revenue growth. To compute this value, Kriz assumes that revenues and investment returns can be modeled by a Markov process called geometric Brownian motion. This is a type of stochastic process, also known as a random walk, in which the distribution of future values of a financial variable (conditional on current and past values) is identical to the distribution of current values. Future values are conditional on growth increments being independent of one another and on the variance of change growing linearly with the number of years projected (the "growth horizon").

Kriz (2003) uses a Monte Carlo simulation to replicate this process and thereby to estimate the level of savings needed to sustain a given rate of expenditure growth. As he notes, Monte Carlo simulation is widely used to assess financial strategies in the face of uncertainty in the private sector but is rarely used in public finance. If a jurisdiction wished to "sustain a three percent expenditure growth rate with a 75 percent confidence level, it would need savings equal to 91 percent of total revenues" (891). This is a lot more expensive, however, than investing in futures or options contracts. Moreover, rainy day funds with high balances represent an almost irresistible source of ready cash to some public officials, who are often unwilling to bear the substantial opportunity costs of maintaining them until they are needed.

Lesson 5: Investing in rainy day fund pools that operate independently of their members can be a less expensive way than self-insurance to deal with revenue volatility, reduce perverse incentives by individual states to spend down funds with higher balances, and reduce state borrowing costs.

The recognition that many governments fail to adopt contribution and withdrawal rules adequate enough to safeguard their rainy day funds led Holcombe and Sobel (1997) to suggest that states establish a pool that would operate independently of its members. Mattoon (2004, 289) argues that a "quasi-governmental agency created by the states would be the logical organization to administer the fund. The agency would need to be autonomous enough to enforce rainy day fund rules and to have sufficient expertise to adjust rainy day fund structure to reflect emerging conditions. If specific experience ratings were created to reflect state revenue and expenditure volatility, the agency would need to have the staff expertise to calculate annual experience ratings. The agency would need to function as an independent third party administrator." Holcombe and Sobel further note that clear rules governing contributions and withdrawals would improve state credit ratings and thereby reduce capital financing costs for states. Finally, they note that by pooling their funds, states could significantly reduce the amount of money each would have to contribute to achieve a given level of stability.

This last conclusion logically follows from treating the determination of cash balances in rainy day funds as an inventory problem to be managed. The standard formulation holds that the minimum inventory needed to buffer against shortages for any specified percentage of time is a function of the square root of the size of the pool. But Holcombe and Sobel (1997) also assess how the revenue yields of various types of taxes covary with macroeconomic aggregates, demonstrating in the process that the collective or pooled state variance of revenue volatility is substantially less than the sum of the variance of the individual states. Based on their calculations, state participation in a savings pool would average about $15 million for each $1 billion of revenue collected, making pooled approaches 15 to 25 percent less costly than self-insurance.

Mattoon (2004) has also designed a national state rainy day fund modeled on the unemployment compensation trust fund, a widely used countercyclical risk management tool. Unemployment compensation payments tend to go up during recessions, but premiums fall. The system is designed to accumulate reserves during booms to meet the needs of the unemployed during busts. He proposes creating an experience ratings system that would trigger differential fund contributions for each state and permit state borrowing from the national fund, with borrowers charged interest for the use of their own funds.

Using Stochastic Process Analysis to Formulate Spending Rules

Consumption or expenditure smoothing is the last approach that we will consider to managing revenue volatility. Under consumption smoothing, governments use borrowing as well as savings to smooth out consumption over time. Formally put, this means that a *present-value balance* must be calculated. This term means that the present value of a state's projected revenues plus its net financial assets (assets minus liabilities) is equal to or greater than the present value of its projected outlays (Baker, Besendorfer, and Kotlikoff 2002). When a state's present-value balance is violated, permanent reductions in spending or increases in taxes are unavoidable. Hence, the problem faced by budgeters is to identify the maximum rate of growth in the spending level that is consistent with the present-value balance, given the government's existing revenue structure and volatility. To see how and why this is the case, we discuss indirect approaches to smoothing and then offer our own more direct model.

Lesson 6: Governments should balance budgets in a present-value sense, using savings and debt to smooth consumption (expenditure or spending). This is the case because optimal rates of expenditure growth can be identified using stochastic techniques with considerable precision from one year to the next. However, although indirect means to calculating sustainable rates of revenue growth are adequate, more direct approaches hold great promise.

Indirect Methods

As a first approximation in using smoothing techniques, Schunk and Woodward (2005; see also Hou 2006) restrict the planning horizon under consideration to the business cycle, thus clouding its duration. Specifically, they do not describe fiscal sustainability as present-value balance but as *sufficient revenue to meet a state's fiscal obligations over the course of the business cycle.* This prompts governments to achieve balance, in theory, by offsetting revenue shortfalls in bad times with revenue windfalls in good times. That is, they offset deficits during recessions with surpluses accumulated during periods of boom.

Schunk and Woodward (2005) conclude that the answer to the problem of revenue sustainability lies in stabilizing spending growth during business cycles through target budgeting. They propose a spending rule for state governments: spending is allowed to increase no faster than the sum of population growth, inflation, and 1 percent real growth. Revenue in excess of this amount would be partly diverted to a stabilization (rainy day) fund, with the rest returned to the taxpayers. This model is tested using aggregate spending and revenue data from the 50 states for the period 1992–2002. They find that with only a modest portion of surplus revenues partially invested in a rainy day fund, their spending rule resulted in "stable growth of state budgets throughout the recession and sluggish recovery of the early 2000s" (105).

Looking at California and South Carolina individually, Schunk and Woodward (2005) find that California diverged from a sustainable path as early as 1996 or 1997, but it would have been fine if it had merely practiced a little spending restraint over the next four or five years. Likewise, South Carolina would have survived intact had it followed their spending rule, but it would have needed to put a higher portion of its surplus revenues into a rainy day fund than California. Moreover, that fund would have been almost completely depleted by 2004.

As such, this spending rule is but a variation on the rainy day fund theme: instead of focusing on the size of the contribution needed to support a given rate of revenue growth, it focuses on the allowable rate of revenue growth. However, one weakness of this rule is that it is an arbitrary, one-size-fits-all solution. It also ignores the unpredictability of the business cycle and variations in revenue codes and, therefore, differences in growth trends, revenue volatility, and investment returns on savings. Nor does the rule allow for annual adjustments of spending levels on the basis of new information. The rule also seems like a rather roundabout way of addressing the question of consumption or expenditure smoothing. Why not address it directly?

A More Direct Answer

Current savings (net financial assets, which could be either positive or negative), average revenue growth, revenue volatility, average return on investments, the volatility of investment returns, and the cost of debt service are all eminently knowable. Thus, it is possible to reformulate Kriz's (2003) model (explained earlier) so there is a single unknown—the maximum rate of growth in the spending level that is consistent with present-value balance. Put more formally, if we treat revenue and savings growth as continuous-time, continuous-state stochastic processes, a budgeter ought to be able to calculate a spending rule directly using optimal control theory.

In a recent paper, Dothan and Thompson (2006) do this by analyzing the interaction of government revenues, the investment performance of stabilization accounts, and optimal expenditure levels in cases where budget balance in a present-value sense must be respected and the jurisdiction uses savings and debt to smooth spending. Then, using optimal control theory and martingale methods, they derive time-consistent government spending rules that depend only on current state variables. Dothan and Thompson's results differ from most other, largely inconclusive attempts in the literature to use optimal control theory to derive optimal spending rules for national governments, because they take the existing revenue structure as given and ignore the effect of government taxes and spending on the rate of economic development. By contrast, most optimal growth/tax theorists seek to determine how to adjust fiscal and monetary policy to produce the mix of savings, investment, and consumption that is consistent with the highest sustainable rate of real economic growth. This is a very hard puzzle to solve. It is not surprising that the answers are not conclusive. By comparing proposed spending levels (including tax cuts and debt service) against the maximum rate of expenditure growth calculated, however, it is possible to say whether a specified spending level is sustainable.

Because Dothan and Thompson's (2006) formulation accounts for a government's net financial assets and the returns on those assets (positive or negative) as well as the government's tax structure, it can be used to assess a government's saving and borrowing policies, not just its spending proposals. Moreover, although the mathematics needed to identify a time-consistent spending rule are technically demanding, those needed to calculate expenditure growth rates are not. Nor does one have to understand how a rule is derived to use it.

Granted, American state and local governments deal with a variety of regulatory ordinances (many of them self-imposed) intended to make them live within their means. These include expenditure, debt, and tax limitations, as well as rules aimed at enforcing annual budgetary balances. These regulations not only are arbitrary and capricious in their effects but also discount the effectiveness of markets in providing incentives that encourage fiscal accountability. For example, efficient land markets penalize poorly performing local governments through the capitalization of debt, and inadequate services are translated into local property values. Likewise, well-developed, efficient bond markets can discipline fiscal behavior by imposing higher borrowing costs and limiting access to credit markets for governments that perform poorly (Inman 2003).

On the other hand, bond markets and bond raters often fail to recognize that governments are in trouble until it is too late to avoid problems (Burnside 2004, 1). Dothan and Thompson's (2006) model faces this conundrum head-on by providing a clear-cut rule identifying the maximum sustainable rate of growth in spending for any given jurisdiction and revenue structure. If that rate of spending increase is too low, the model can be used to calculate the increase in tax rates needed to sustain the desired rate of spending growth. Hence, the advantage of this formulation is that it can be used to assess a government's spending, taxing, saving, and borrowing policies in periods of booms and busts. Thus, it provides an early warning signal to public officials, bond raters, and the market that a government is on its way to a financial crisis.

Conclusion

In her magisterial review of the literature on state budgeting and finance, Rubin (2005, 47–48, 65) writes

> Much of the literature on state-level budgeting follows the states' adaptation to and responses to cycles of boom and bust in the economy, including prevention (building up reserve funds that can be used in time of recession), temporizing (using delaying tactics to tide the state over until the economy improves), and balancing (increasing revenue and/or decreasing spending).... What would be useful here is an index of prevention of and perhaps a second and related one of preparation for recessions.

What we have done in this chapter is to provide the indices of preparation and prevention called for by Professor Rubin. In doing so, we have described several concepts: risk, stochastic processes, present-value balance, optimal spending, diversification, systematic and unsystematic risk, buffering, and hedging.

We have also identified some of the analytical tools needed to use these concepts—mean-variance analysis, Monte Carlo simulation, optimal control theory, and covariance analysis. These concepts, techniques, and applications are all borrowed from modern financial theory, and they can be applied to a wide array of public sector financial management problems. As such, they ought to be part of the standard repertoire of all public sector financial managers.

Using them could help public officials produce a good outcome no matter what the economy does. Without question, betting on the future in revenue forecasting and budgeting will always be a challenging exercise as policy makers try to discern the fiscal future of their governments with cloudy crystal balls. We have tried, however, to show how recent developments in financial theory can enhance crystal-ball gazing for practitioners and theorists alike.

Commentary

Roy T. Meyers

To truly understand the authors' arguments, readers will have to immerse themselves in a finance textbook. But that is exactly the point, is it not? And in my judgment, it is a defensible one. Having said this, it is political risk, not fiscal risk, that most animates elected officials' concerns. Consequently, technical prescriptions must be calculated to fit into the realpolitik of electoral politics. If they are not, they will not be taken seriously or will be jettisoned quickly once adopted, if they yield politically risky or deleterious consequences. Trust in technique can be a risky venture for politicians and citizens. Thus, at a minimum, elected officials are unlikely to accept the authors' assumption that techniques will be embraced, even if they are not understood. To make my point, let us examine the realpolitik of two of Thompson and Gates's proposals.

On its surface, the estimate of an $8 to $10 million price for a put of $1 billion hedged revenues looks pretty attractive. The authors note, however, that this alternative is unlikely for both technical and political reasons but do not specify them. What political factors might have held them back, besides the obvious difficulty political leaders would have convincing voters that selling futures is a desirable practice? Perhaps the answer is that not all politicians find "manic-depressive patterns of spending and taxing" undesirable and, therefore, value hedges at exactly zero (or less). As the cutback management literature generally shows, state and local governments often balance budgets by wasteful expedients. Some political leaders do not understand they are doing this, but some simply do not care about those costs.

From experience, many politicians know that the best time to cut spending and avoid political retribution is when revenues go bust. In states and localities with advanced systems of performance budgeting and priority setting, the picture may be prettier. However, I suspect most governments fit the first pattern. Similarly, after cutting spending during a recession, politicians can then feel justified in expanding tax bases and raising rates to close any remaining gap. Knowing of these possibilities only encourages them to *not* set "enough" aside in budget stabilization funds, particularly because they can generate political benefits with spending increases or tax cuts during flush times and with myopic voters.

This is not to suggest that states utterly fail to smooth consumption at some level, for the literature says otherwise. In Maryland, for example, some of the dot. com-era revenue boom was not used to start new programs but was either saved or invested in capital assets (displacing planned borrowing). With this record, *manic depressive* would be a bit too strong a term. But consider also Maryland's later transfer of monies to the general fund from two major special funds: the transportation trust fund and the program open space fund. The former combines capital and operating expenditures for all modes of transportation and is financed with excise taxes, fees, and bonds. The latter finances public lands acquisition from the proceeds of a dedicated tax on the sales of real property.

These transfers were widely interpreted as budget balancing, since the budget was defined as the general fund, which is only about one-half of the state's budget. In effect, however, the state just shifted spending from transportation and land protection to, say, education, without changing the financial position of the government. To smooth total state consumption effectively, the then-required reductions in transportation and open-space spending would have to be prevented by borrowing more for these purposes. This is more likely to work when interest rates are relatively low. My point is that just focusing on the budget in Maryland and other states is not enough to understand consumption smoothing because of the political games that are played.

In this same regard, Thompson and Gates propose a spending rule and a method to calculate it. However, present-value balancing would require farsightedness—calculating in present-value terms projected revenues, projected outlays, and net financial assets. This is a brave stance for an article that begins with the phrase, "prediction is a mug's game!" However, what they argue in practice is "predict what you can about what really matters," and the method they propose has real potential. On the other side of this argument, however, is the ghost of Bob Citron, an example that is relevant not only to present-value balancing but also to the topics discussed previously. As treasurer of Orange County, California, Citron bet on interest rates using highly leveraged funds, eventually driving Orange County into bankruptcy. That he did so was certainly his fault, but it was also the fault of the many political leaders who looked away when they should have been watching closely (Baldassare 1998). Thus, naiveté is *not* always acceptable: just as we teach children to moo so they know where milk comes from, we should expect political leaders to understand the basis of fundamental government decisions about finance and budgets. Thankfully, most leaders will be unwilling to defer to a model that they do not understand when it would set the parameters for one of the most important things that they do.

Commentary

Katherine G. Willoughby

Thompson and Gates present a financial management toolkit to support state government navigation through fiscal storms. This toolkit suggests analytical methods, rules, and institutions that can help states reduce revenue volatility of tax structures. But how likely are governors and other elected state officials to follow their advice? The greatest challenge for their proposals is realistic application of their toolkit to current state budget and financial management processes. For example, revenue estimates must be packaged into a final state revenue forecast that legislators use to deliberate and pass the budget each fiscal year. Analytical tools support one form of rationality, but such analyses must be coupled with the formal and informal aspects of the budget process. This means gaining agreement on the revenue forecast itself.

Of the dozen states indicating a strong, as opposed to a weak, long-term budgeting perspective in a 2005 Government Performance Project (GPP) study, ten use a consensus method of forecasting state revenues. Consensus methods include the participation of members from the executive and legislative branches and from other external stakeholders. These groups develop revenue and (sometimes) expenditure estimates as well as the final revenue forecast. Interestingly, states combining multiple methods of analysis (including simple trend analysis) with consensus forecasting produce the most accurate revenue forecasts, if one compares general fund revenue estimates with actual revenues. Mathematical accuracy of forecasting notwithstanding, agreement among stakeholders on the forecasted amount is thus the primary constraint on the next year's spending plan.

Consensus-based or otherwise, broadening the amount, type, and quality of information used to make decisions about the revenue future can certainly be useful. Consequently, Thompson and Gates's effort to provide a better understanding of the random versus systematic components of revenue volatility may aid state budget stakeholders to focus on possible methods to reduce such volatility. However, the "essential prerequisite of economic rationality is that multiple ends have been specified and valued" (Thurmaier and Willoughby 2001, 103). Also, within a technical–political framework, there are a number of feasible options to solve whatever budget problems are identified. Thus, agreement on which option to choose is paramount to taking action. Even then, adoption by governments of toolkit components is one step, agreement as to application in the budget process is a second step, and then consistent championing and use of the component over time is a third step. All of this is complicated by the politics of state budgeting, the fluidity of the process, and the timeliness of the budgeting cycle.

A look at a state with a weak structural balance in 2005—Wisconsin—illustrates how politics has compromised fiscal discipline in the government. Wisconsin's weak structural balance is partly due to political leaders having "made an extraordinary financial commitment to local governments and to K–12 schools" and partly due to their acquiescing to other citizen demands for funding (Conant 2006, 248). As such, the state has used a compendium of revenue and expenditure strategies to manage chronic budget imbalances, demonstrated an inability or unwillingness by legislators to fund Wisconsin's rainy day fund, and typically produced negative general fund balances each year. Conant emphasizes that the "structural dimension of the FY 2001–2003 and 2003–2005 budget problems was largely the result of gubernatorial and legislative policy decisions made during the 1990s, add[ing] more than $2 billion worth of expenditure increases to the base budget and cut[ting] taxes by almost $2.6 billion" (252).

At the same time, Thompson and Gates's proposal for pooling state rainy day funds to advance budget balancing is intriguing and, over time, might find traction in some states. States in the habit of keeping rainy day funds replenished might be lured by the possibility offered of increased revenues. But states completely depleted rainy day funds during the period from 2002 to 2004. Moreover, many continue to struggle to keep these funds at legally prescribed levels, if they fund them at all.

To be sure, the strictures the authors suggest placing on depositing and accessing funds in a rainy day pool could foster greater fiscal discipline in the states and help abate revenue volatility. Yet a healthy number of states would first have to join the pool and are likely to be put off by the inflexibility that pooling would bring. Pooling rainy day funds and providing comprehensive oversight of these funds inevitably reduce individual state flexibility to manage them as they might wish.

Anyone applying financial theory to address revenue volatility in state governments must recognize the political messiness of dealing with such uncertainty. Citizen expectations are often contradictory. This is most overtly exhibited when they press state governments for tax reductions or eliminations while simultaneously demanding program and service delivery increases. Political leaders react as expected: they push tax cuts and spending increases during periods of revenue growth. These choices then exacerbate fiscal stress in periods of recession when new revenues must be found and spending must be cut. Amid these contradictions, prior research finds no one technical path to structural balance within the states. Of the eight states that score well on structural balance in the 2005 GPP survey, tax structures range from highly diverse to almost sole sourced. Nor does any one tax structure emerge in the states as the means to structural balance. Rather, it is a state's use of its management tools and rules (formal *and* informal), as well as the politics of budgeting, that either support or compromise structural balance. Bringing technical rationality as an input into the political discussion is not an insignificant contribution. Turning technical rationality into decision rules for making political choices, however, is likely to be a "mug's game."

Chapter 7

Managing Public Service Contracts: Aligning Values, Institutions, and Markets*

Trevor L. Brown, Matthew Potoski,
and David M. Van Slyke

Contents

* Adapted from Brown, T. L., M. Potoski, and D. M. Van Slyke. 2006. Managing public service contracts: Aligning values, institutions, and markets. *Public Administration Review* 66(3): 323–331.

Contracting proponents, who often have roots in public sector economics, champion contracting as a way to reduce service costs through competitive efficiencies and economies of scale. Contracting critics, who often have roots in traditional public administration fields, counter that contracting tends to sacrifice key public interest values (e.g., equality of treatment) and reduces service delivery capacity. Several things are clear, however, in the evolution of the contract state. First, contracting is and will continue to be a major task facing public managers. According to the U.S. Government Accountability Office, contracting is the most used alternative to direct service provision (GAO 1997). Second, public managers do not always have a choice about contracting and may be required by elected officials to do so under less-than-optimal market conditions. Research on contracting at the local level indicates that governments often contract even when circumstances suggest they should not, such as when insufficient numbers of competing bidders exist (Brown and Potoski 2003b). Third, public managers charged with contracting operate in politically charged environments that put a premium on balancing competing stakeholder values (Van Slyke and Hammonds 2003). Finally, one-size-fits-all judgments about contracting are generally unrealistic: contracting can improve service delivery or it can be a disaster, depending on the underlying market conditions and management efficacy (Brown and Potoski 2005; Kelman 2002a; Van Slyke 2003).

So what are managers to do? The prescriptive literature on contracting tends to offer step-by-step procedures for managers to identify service delivery decisions and apply contract management techniques. However, it fails to provide a strategic foundation for managing the complicated and often politically charged tradeoffs of contracting. Step-by-step procedures thus are ill suited for offering managers practical advice across diverse contract settings. Meanwhile, strident ideological debates have crowded out discussion of rigorous, theory-driven, multidisciplinary analyses of how contract management can improve service delivery. These analyses still can be valuable, however, particularly if viewed through an integrated analytic framework.

With this aim in mind, we offer public managers a comprehensive strategic framework for practicing contract management. It is founded on the interaction of three central factors culled from the strategic management and planning, public law and institutions, and economics literatures. Respectively, these are public values, institutions, and service markets. In our framework, (1) stakeholder preferences and democratic processes establish the values to be optimized in service delivery, (2) public law and organizational arrangements determine the contracting tools available for balancing competing values, and (3) the characteristics of service markets influence which contracting tools and vendors are suited to achieve stakeholder values.

In elaborating our approach, we illustrate what the existing research suggests about how managers can use the lenses of public values, institutions, and service markets to improve service delivery. We examine the interaction of these factors in three key stages of contract management: (1) deciding whether to deliver services directly or through contract, (2) selecting vendors to produce services, and (3) deploying monitoring tools for overseeing the implementation of contracts. Our goal is to reveal the tradeoffs inherent in managing service delivery, to illustrate which tradeoffs vary across circumstances (e.g., political and market conditions or types of service providers), and to suggest how contracting can be improved through more effective public management.

The Foundation of Government Contracting: Public Values, Institutions, and Service Markets

We posit that contracting is an economic exchange among actors in which the government's central management challenge is to align public values, institutions, and service market conditions for effectiveness across the three principal contracting phases. The first stage—the make-or-buy stage—centers on whether conditions are suitable for contracting (e.g., Donahue 1989). Managers decide whether market conditions are likely to support a competitive environment for contract service delivery (e.g., Sclar 2000) and identify the service production and management components for outsourcing (e.g., Brown and Potoski 2006). After the decision to contract, the second stage involves the need for public managers to structure and execute a competitive bidding process (e.g., Lavery 1999). This contract specification stage requires public managers to make many complex decisions, including specifying a vendor's obligations and tasks, defining the contract's renewal provisions, and specifying its incentive and performance measurement systems (e.g., Shetterly 2000). Once a vendor has been selected and the contract awarded, public managers must shift their focus to the third stage: managing the contract. This stage includes monitoring vendor performance, communicating with service recipients, and executing incentive programs (e.g., Kelman 2002a, 2002b).

As they make decisions across these three phases, public managers operate in a crucible of swirling and often competing political values, including effectiveness, efficiency, accountability, responsiveness, equality of treatment, and service quality (Frederickson 1997; Moe 1996; Rainey 2003; Rosenbloom 1983). Managers experience these values as pressures from internal and external stakeholders that they must variously balance or optimize as they deliver services. In some cases, these values are codified through the political process into institutions, public laws, and organizational arrangements that determine the range of tools and resources that public managers can employ for service delivery. The services and the character and composition of their markets influence the ability of public managers to optimize or balance competing values through service delivery. In particular, transaction costs—"the comparative costs of planning, adapting, and monitoring task completion under alternative governing structures" (Williamson 1981, 552–553)—make achieving values such as effectiveness and efficiency throughout all phases of contracting more challenging for some services than for others.

Values

Whether government provides services directly or through contract, managing service delivery is as much about identifying, balancing, and targeting shifting stakeholder values as it is about services such as operations management and vendor relations (deLeon 1995; Van Slyke, Horne, and Thomas 2005; for a review, see Boyne 1998). For any service, the list of potential stakeholders is long: interest groups and attentive segments of the general public, elected officials, the media, public employees, administrative superiors, collaborators and partners, service recipients, and vendors. Service recipients and their interest groups may be primarily concerned with equality of treatment. Elected politicians may focus on political accountability and responsiveness. Administrative superiors may be most attuned to cost efficiency. Consequently, these values sometimes conflict—for example, ensuring equality of treatment may reduce cost efficiency—so managers must either frame the tradeoffs for key decision makers or, as is often the case, use their discretion to make these tradeoffs as they implement services (deLeon 1995; Moe 1996; Seidman 1998; Van Slyke et al. 2005).

In practice, the degree to which managers can achieve values through service delivery is likely to vary across circumstances. Some conditions lie beyond a manager's control. For instance, managers typically have little influence over the laws and rules governing service delivery, such as those that allow the use of some management practices or service delivery approaches but prohibit others. Still, all things being equal, services with inherently lower transaction costs are more favorable contracting targets, freeing resources to lower costs or improve service quality. On the other hand, services with higher transaction costs pose greater contracting problems, consuming more resources and inhibiting a manager's ability to optimize competing values.

An important first step for either practicing or studying contracting is identifying and prioritizing the often politically contentious stakeholder preferences at each stage. In this way, public managers can weigh relevant public values (e.g., equity and efficiency) against one another in the context of externally imposed constraints (e.g., disagreements about the contract among city council members).

Effective management requires going beyond passively receiving value signals from stakeholders; it means identifying stakeholder preferences and framing value trade-offs among them.

A rich literature describes how public managers can gauge and manage stakeholder values (Kraft and Clary 1991; Serra 1995; Thomas 1995). Surveys can reach large numbers of people, but they are quite expensive. To reach stakeholders with more intensely held preferences (e.g., interest groups, service recipients, elected officials), public managers can rely on public meetings and hearings, requests for comment and information, advisory committees, and focus groups. Recently, managers have invited stakeholder participation in developing service delivery goals prior to beginning the contract process to help prioritize competing values and preferences.

Several strategies can frame the use of these different tools. Notable examples include stakeholder value mapping (e.g., Bryson 2004a; Elmore 1979–80) and the balanced scorecard approach (e.g., Kaplan and Norton 1996; see Rosenbloom in this volume for a discussion of constitutional scorecards). These strategies are designed to serve three purposes: assess the needs, demands, and value preferences of key stakeholders (i.e., to establish goals and objectives); identify the opportunities and constraints in employing different service delivery approaches; and evaluate alternative courses of action for achieving goals and objectives (i.e., deciding what contracting tools are likely to be most effective). Consider, for example, Kaplan and Norton's (1996) balanced scorecard approach, where managers simultaneously and continuously develop metrics, collect data, and analyze them from multiple perspectives. For contracting, public managers align managerial actions with targeted goals and objectives by explicitly linking internal business processes (i.e., contract management) with external outcomes (i.e., the achievement of targeted stakeholder values) as they construct organizational arrangements (i.e., the use of contract rather than direct service provision).

Institutions

As managers identify stakeholder values, they also need to identify the tools, resources, and constraints that define the range of actions they might take in delivering services. Here, two "institutions" are central to the contracting process: public law and organizational arrangements. These define the "rules of the game" (North 1991) that managers must follow as they deliver services. Public law sets the boundaries within which public managers must operate, thereby permitting, authorizing, or requiring the range of managers' actions. At its root, a contract is a legal instrument, an "agreement by particular parties [who] accept a set of rules to govern their relationship, whether it is for the purchase of services or for a cooperative working agreement" (Cooper 1996, 125). As the law establishes what is authorized and prohibited, it also defines a manager's zone of discretion, either through legal ambiguity or direct delegation. Discretion allows for flexibility, creativity, and innovation in contracting, whereas legal fiat can restrict discretion to such an extent that managers have trouble managing contracts effectively. Thus, managers need a sound understanding of the laws, ordinances, and administrative statutes (e.g., the Administrative Procedure Act) governing both the contracting process generally and the contracted services they are considering (Rosenbloom and Piotrowski 2005).

Simultaneously, organizational arrangements define the capacity and resources available and necessary for managing service delivery contracts. In particular, they influence a manager's ability to achieve targeted stakeholder values. If the goals are innovation and efficiency in service provision, then contracting with a private vendor may be more desirable; private employees typically operate with higher-powered, compensation-based, and profit-oriented incentives. If the goal is more government control over service provision, then internal production may be preferred; government employees' motivations typically are better aligned with the agency's mission. Yet, as we will discuss later, even this basic tradeoff is conditioned by the institutional and market contexts of the contracting decision.

Effective contract management is necessary to monitor the ways vendors and public employees are achieving service delivery values (e.g., efficiency, quality, and equity). This includes acquiring and nurturing physical infrastructure, financial resources, and human capital. For example, prior research (Brown and Potoski 2003b; Van Slyke and Hammonds 2003) suggests that building human capital for contract management involves developing several basic skills in one's workforce for planning and coordinating service delivery, negotiating with vendors, monitoring task completion and executing performance incentives, and ensuring technical skills, such as writing contracts. Unfortunately, public sector contract management has received a low priority in recruitment, training, and retention (Kelman 2002b). But government officials must understand that weak contract management capacity, contentious political environments, and few career rewards for attracting the best and brightest managers not only increase the risks of failed contracts but also often result in embarrassing government scandals (Brown and Brudney 1998; Van Slyke 2003).

Service Markets

A final set of factors in our framework involves determining whether service and market conditions favor contracting. Effective markets provide managers with important information about prices and service quality across vendors and facilitate disciplining vendors who fail to meet contract standards (Hart and Moore 1999; Niskanen 1971). Moreover, in well-functioning markets, competition for contracts can help overcome what are known in the economics literature as principal–agent problems. Such problems stem from relationships where a principal (a contracting government) contracts with an expert agent (a vendor) for the production of goods and services. The principal looks to prevent the agent from exploiting its information advantages by carefully designing contracts, offering incentives, and monitoring the agent so that it performs to contract specifications.

Strong and effective markets, however, require some fairly strict conditions. They need large numbers of buyers and sellers, participants should be well informed about products and each other's preferences, and actors must be able to enter and exit the market and exchange resources at low costs. Markets can fail because of high transaction costs, limited information, uncertainty about the future, and the prospect that people or organizations will behave opportunistically in their interactions (Coase 1937; Williamson 1981, 1991, 1996).

Of particular importance in this decision are the varying transaction costs inherent in different market and service arrangements. Because the parties cannot fully predict all possible future scenarios, contracts typically are underspecified (i.e., incomplete) and may allow vendors to take advantage of contracts at the expense of the government's goals. To minimize this, the contracting government must incur transaction costs by clearly specifying the values sought in performance measures, writing more detailed contracts, monitoring vendors' performance, and enforcing sanctions when necessary.

Consider two notable service-specific sources of transaction costs: asset specificity and ease of measurement. Asset specificity refers to the need for physical infrastructure, technology, or knowledge, skills, and abilities that can only be acquired through on-the-job experience or highly specialized investments (e.g., high-cost investments in computer technology). For winning and losing vendors, investing in an asset-specific service that cannot be readily translated to other economically valuable activities (i.e., used for other organizational purposes or marketed to others) leaves them vulnerable to a single (i.e., monopsonistic) service purchaser. This not only raises the costs for vendors to compete in the market, but it can also make it unlikely they will bid in future rounds for the contract. Conversely, asset-specific services can dangerously privilege vendors that win the first contracts, thus constraining future competition. Under such monopolistic conditions, the winning vendor can exploit the contracting government by raising prices or reducing service quality with impunity.

Ease of measurement, in turn, refers to how easily and well public managers can assess the quantity or quality of services. Easily measured services have identifiable and accurate performance metrics for either the outputs or outcomes of service quantity and quality. Still, even if performance outcomes are difficult to measure, service performance can be assessed if it is relatively straightforward to monitor vendor activities and if these activities are reasonable proxies for desired outcomes.

As with asset-specific services, difficult-to-measure services make governments vulnerable to unscrupulous vendors who may exploit their information advantage by lowering service quality and quantity. Here, the best option is to avoid the market altogether through internal service delivery. The advantage of producing difficult-to-measure services internally is that managers can monitor and reward their own employees more easily than they can vendors. Prudence aside, however, legal mandates, financial stress, and political realities sometimes require governments to contract for difficult-to-measure or asset-specific services. In these cases, managers must do the best they can to ensure management monitoring capacity to mitigate transaction-cost risks.

The Framework in Action

The Make-or-Buy Decision

Proponents of contracting argue that it is more cost-efficient and better stimulates innovation than direct service delivery. Scholars such as Tiebout (1956) argue that competition can occur across jurisdictions, perhaps improving efficiency and innovation as governments look to attract mobile residents. But this depends on the level of competition among vendors and governments. On the other hand, proponents of direct service delivery argue that it promotes political account-ability, stability, and equality of treatment (DeHoog 1984; Donahue 1989; Kettl 1993). But the relative strengths of direct versus contract service delivery on these values appear to vary across circumstances (Brown and Potoski 2006; Morgan and England 1988; Sclar 2000). For example, the returns from contracting versus direct service delivery depend in part on legal requirements. Federal and state administrative procedure acts mandating whistle-blower and other employee protections, as well as open records and meeting requirements, create both costs and constraints for government managers under direct service delivery (Cooper 1996). Legal requirements also can restrict contracting practices (e.g., some require that a percentage of contracts be awarded to female- or minority-owned firms; DeHoog 1997). Moreover, private firms and nonprofits sometimes avoid competing for public sector contracts because of time-consuming and procedur-ally complex legal requirements (MacManus 1991; Praeger 1994). By reducing competition, the advantages of contracting relative to in-house service delivery are diluted in the process. Consequently, examining the legal and political con-text of make-or-buy decisions is critical for managers and scholars studying con-tracting dynamics.

Other characteristics of the service market can play an even more fundamental role in determining the returns from contracting. Political pressures, of course, may lead governments to retain what should be contracted and to contract what should be produced in-house. Proactive managers, however, need not be helpless victims to thin markets. They can recruit new vendors (Brown and Potoski 2004), split service delivery into multiple contracts (Osborne and Plastrik 2000), allow public employees to compete against private vendors (Goldsmith 1999), and employ "joint contracting" by retaining a portion of service delivery in-house to provide informa-tion on service quality and cost while also ensuring there is an alternative provider of the service (Shleifer and Vishny 1998; Williamson 1991).

Contract Specification

Assuming that a government elects to buy (contract) rather than make (provide) the service in question, public managers must decide on and implement a bid process, select a vendor, and craft contract terms. Within the contours of legal requirements, public managers typically have discretion in contracts to specify several features, including vendor tasks (e.g., the nature and scope of work), outcome measures (e.g., performance-based contracts), vendor qualifications (e.g., licensing or accreditation issues), vendor compensation (e.g., time and materials versus cost plus fee), contract duration, contractor incentives and sanctions (e.g., rewards versus punishments), renewal provisions, payment schedules, and reporting requirements. Each of these features potentially plays an important role in determining the returns from contracting. For example, alternative compensation schemes and incentive systems motivate vendors differently (e.g., Lavery 1999).

Although our framework applies to each of these tasks, we focus here on one central contract specification decision: the type of vendor selected. Contracting governments can choose among three types of vendors: private firms, nonprofits, and other governments. Private firms, whether they are publicly or privately held, are motivated by profit; consequently, they may focus more on innovation and efficiency (Hart, Shleifer, and Vishny 1997). However, achieving these goals may come at the expense of other public values and goals, such as service quality or equality of treatment (Durant, Legge, and Moussios 1998; Moe 1996).

For example, when private contractors are forced to choose between maintaining or upgrading service quality and keeping costs low, public managers should be alert that vendors may favor reducing expenses and thus substituting their own profit for the public interest. In contrast, nonprofit organizations are thought to share similar missions with government and thus may be more reliable contract partners (Hansman 1987; Salamon 1995). Rather than behaving opportunistically, a nonprofit might tap its own private philanthropic resources (e.g., volunteers, endowments) to augment its contract commitment. Caution is still warranted, however. Nonprofits' goals may not always be aligned with public objectives and may instead channel residual revenue from contracts into subsidizing their other programs (Van Slyke 2007).

Finally, other governments also can be service vendors. As with nonprofits, they are thought to have values aligned with the contracting government because they share a similar public mission and a workforce more committed to public values. However, contracting with other government agencies is also not without risks and transaction costs. Intergovernmental contracts may actually do less than private contracts to solve the inefficiency, lack of innovation, weak incentives, and other bureaucratic ills that can plague public service delivery (Niskanen 1971). Nor is contracting with vendors that purportedly share the same goals without risk. Van Slyke (2003) finds that governments often establish long-term contractual relationships with nonprofits for social services, but then they neglect oversight and monitoring responsibilities. In addition, nonprofits reliant on public sector contracts may behave like conventional monopolists to maintain their resource streams.

Institutional arrangements also play an important role in determining the relative superiority of these vendors in achieving different stakeholder values. Other governments, for instance, often are subject to the same legal requirements as the contracting government, such as promoting service quality and equity at the expense of efficiency and innovation. Nonprofits, in turn, are regulated as tax-exempt organizations and, as such, are prohibited from distributing profits to their employees or volunteer boards. Consequently, there may be fewer incentives for them to engage in opportunistic behavior, at least compared with private firms. Yet public managers should take into account that this also may curb their ability to be innovative.

Importantly, the type of vendor may be less important for low transaction-cost services in competitive markets. This is the case because the risk that vendors will become monopoly service providers is low, performance can be easily measured, and contracts are easier to enforce. Indeed, prior research suggests that governments understand this already. They tend to contract more with for-profit vendors in such circumstances (Brown and Potoski 2003a), exploiting their competitive zeal and relatively lax legal requirements through contract specifications and enforcement mechanisms (Brown and Potoski 2004). The type of vendor becomes more relevant when contracting for high transaction-cost services in thin markets—for example, when a small government needs to deliver a service that requires large asset-specific investments beyond what it can afford or to procure a service that resists performance measurement. In these instances, public managers would be wise to solicit bids in each sector and perhaps even favor nonprofits or other governments, selecting a vendor whose values best align with their own objectives. Again, the literature suggests that governments are already understanding this; they more frequently choose nonprofit and other governments when contracting for high transaction-cost services and in thin markets (Brown and Potoski 2003a).

For governments that are willing and able to invest in sufficient contract management, certain types of long-term contractual relationships can foster mutual support and sharing (Artz and Brush 2000; Hart and Moore 1999; Levin 2003). Using incomplete or relational contracts, public managers work with vendors to build long-term relationships based on trust, reciprocity, and joint involvement in developing and implementing the contract. In fact, relational contracts increase the possibility that governments and vendors can build trust and common understandings to buttress incomplete contracts. Relational contracts may be particularly attractive for asset-specific services where monopsonistic markets provide the winning vendor and government with good reason to fear each other given their resource-interdependent needs.

When compared with conventional arm's-length contracting, successful relational contracting has higher short-term transaction costs for both parties. Over time, though, effective relational contracts may lower transaction costs through reduced bidding, monitoring, and legal costs (Hart and Moore 1999; Tadelis 2002). Nevertheless, public managers must balance the returns from building a cooperative relationship with a single vendor against the continued risk of opportunism and the perception that the vendor's long-term relationship stems from political favoritism. Prior research, unfortunately, is relatively silent on the conditions under which the choice of conventional and relational contracts is most likely to be effective.

Contract Management

Once governments select a vendor and turn to contract implementation, managers face more decisions regarding tradeoffs among public values. Although the contract cements the tools available to public managers as they engage the vendor, the implementation of these tools ultimately determines the returns from contracting. Perhaps the most central of these tasks involves monitoring and evaluating the performance of vendors working under contract (Kettl 1993; Praeger 1994). Well-monitored vendors are more likely to perform according to contract specifications, thereby improving returns from contracting (Brown and Potoski 2003b).

Effective contract monitoring requires a solid legal grounding. In some circumstances, information from monitoring practices that are not contractually authorized may not legally be used to evaluate vendors. For example, public managers must be legally authorized through the contract to audit and analyze vendors' records and performance data or to conduct scheduled or random field audits. In others, managers may be authorized or required to establish formal systems for tracking and monitoring citizens' complaints about service delivery or to gauge public sentiment through citizen surveys (Miller and Miller 1991; Swindell and Kelly 2000). In these monitoring approaches, citizens can serve as "fire alarms" (McCubbins and Schwartz 1984), calling attention to occasional vendor transgressions without requiring governments to constantly monitor vendors' activities.

These monitoring activities, of course, vary in their costs and efficacy depending on the nature of the service and existing service market conditions. In particular, the relative ease of identifying and measuring performance outcomes conditions the desirability of various monitoring techniques. In cases where governments face vendor opportunism stemming from difficult measurement, for instance, managers cannot simply purchase service outcomes and ensure desired outcomes. Moreover, arm's-length contract monitoring tools such as reports and field audits may be less effective in these circumstances.

One countermeasure for these monitoring problems is for managers to develop a deeper understanding of the service production process. This can be an onerous undertaking, beginning with uncovering the logic behind the vendors' service delivery techniques and then identifying and monitoring each step in the service production process. Alternatively, public managers may again rely on a more relational approach to contracting, where each party learns experientially how the other conducts its work within the framework of the contract. In this way, ensuring alignment between government and the vendor may require that the parties discuss the specific program goals and approaches to intervention and jointly agree to the types of measures that would best represent successful service delivery. They also may discuss the formal and informal practices for addressing future uncertainties (Baker, Gibbons, and Murphy 2002; Bernheim and Whinston 1998; Hart 2003). Once again, however, additional research on the comparative efficacy of these approaches is needed.

Conclusion

Our argument in this chapter has been that effectively managing or researching the three stages of the contracting process requires an appreciation of the intersection of three factors: public values, institutions, and service markets. Values, including public interest values, are the stakeholder preferences that public managers must balance or optimize as they deliver services. Throughout the phases of contracting, public managers should continually identify and prioritize the often politically contentious public value preferences of key stakeholders. To the degree that managers have discretion, these values or value tradeoffs should guide the use of different contract management tools as well as inform the research strategies of scholars.

Institutions, or the laws and organizational arrangements that frame service delivery, determine the range of tools and resources that public managers can employ to achieve stakeholder values. Public managers need to identify (and researchers need to consider) the legal architecture that governs contracting. Legal mandates define the boundaries within which public managers can operate to optimize and balance targeted values, while a lack of contract management and monitoring capacity increases the risk of failed contracts.

The characteristics of services and their markets influence which contracting tools are best suited to achieve stakeholder values. Public managers should determine whether service and market conditions favor contracting. Of particular importance are factors that increase the risks of contract failure—for example, thin markets and asset-specific and difficult-to-measure services. When these factors are present, public managers should internalize service delivery (if they can), pursue joint production, and expand contract management capacity.

Importantly, we argue that these factors should not inform practice in isolation. Public values, institutions, and service markets are interrelated and should be viewed by practitioners and scholars as interacting to produce contracting outcomes. Thus, before applying prescriptive step-by-step approaches or developing propositions suitable for testing in future research, public managers and scholars should map all three sets of factors to determine value targets, the steps managers can legally take to achieve these targets, and the likelihood of success given existing service market conditions.

Commentary

Ruth H. DeHoog

Brown, Potoski, and Van Slyke present a comprehensive framework for studying and practicing contracting—clarifying and explaining the values, institutions, and service markets that influence how contracting choices should be made. This is a worthwhile effort, and I find the research and approach both comprehensive and useful. Nonetheless, their presenting of a rational framework for contracting decision making underplays certain political realities in contracting that should be understood by practitioners.

Although public choice economists were among the first to promote privatization and contracting out, public administration scholars, many of whom initially resisted its practice and research, embraced it in their research agendas in the 1990s, often as part of the new public management effort. Slower to develop until recently is an understanding of contracting out as part of the shift in the broader political system in the United States and elsewhere to a less hierarchical, often more fluid governance system with multiple actors playing various roles. In particular, the private sector's roles as political actors, contractors, and interest groups affect contracting choices and performance.

This chapter might encourage students and scholars to understand contracting as merely a management process in which various choices can be made in a rational and orderly way. Perhaps this is a potential landmine in any effort to lay out a comprehensive approach that relies on strategic management and economics for its literature base and is directed toward the public administration audience. But contracting for services in many environments can be a messy, confusing, and conflictual process fraught with opportunism, both political and financial. Although the authors acknowledge the complications, and Van Slyke's prior research in particular (e.g., Van Slyke 2003; Van Slyke and Hammonds 2003) has contributed to the understanding of these political forces and complications, I would not want anyone who reads this chapter to be misled into thinking that the pressures and processes are necessarily manageable. The framework seems just too tidy.

Perhaps my view has become more jaundiced in recent years with cases of contracting scandals and opportunism becoming almost weekly media fare, from the federal government (e.g., Hurricane Katrina response, Iraq reconstruction) to state and local governments (e.g., North Carolina's affordable housing scandal). How did the values get so skewed, the institutions so limited in managing the process, and competitive service markets so irrelevant? How does opportunistic behavior so often get rewarded? These notorious cases force us to question why contracting systems can lead to such huge financial and management failures in large and professional organizations where competent and ethical public managers were employed.

In addition, the authors' framework requires some additional explanation or nuances that may lead us to understand how the political and organizational environments of contracting can complicate or even overwhelm the procedures of a rational contracting process. First, in discussing the values of contracting, the authors fail to name some core political values that often are present in discussions about contracting. These are economy (cut costs and taxes if at all possible), a pro-business philosophy (use private contractors whenever possible), and an election coalition-building value (strengthen opportunities to support powerful business interests or nonprofits).

Unaware practitioners may not detect immediately the subtle or even obvious pressures to contract out or to award contracts to particular organizations. Yet they should be able to identify and then balance these values along with those mentioned by the authors or challenge elected officials to provide a clearer justification for their decisions. Additionally, managers must be aware of the potential for powerful stakeholders and long-term contractors to bypass or subvert the contracting process. These stakeholders can do so by developing strong relationships with political officials who can overturn or change the normal contracting procedures, whether in award decisions or contract management and auditing. They also should have some legal and procedural tools at their disposal to challenge these end-runs of normal procedures.

Although competition for contracts often is stated as a primary reason for efficiency gains, we do not often hear how political associations or coalitions of contractors also can promote contracting out due to self-interest. Both nonprofit agencies and businesses are more likely to organize effectively with a financial incentive at stake than are clients or the public at large. These organizations can mobilize clients at times to support their contracts or oppose threats to continuation of the services they provide.

Second, the authors' discussion of institutions emphasizes the importance of the rules and types of contractor agencies, from public to nonprofit to for-profit businesses. Their discussion about the distinctions among these types of vendors is useful. Yet one point that needs to be stressed is that the nonprofit sector is also a mix of types of agencies, with a range of incentives and accountability measures. Some of these agencies can be as opportunistic as private contractors to ensure survival, growth, personal ambition, and even higher income. This can produce innovation, perhaps more often in service delivery methods than in cutting costs. But, as the authors note, it can also result in the triumph of private over public interest.

Third, an important point missing in the authors' discussion of institutions involves the reality of organizational culture, transaction costs, and resource constraints. At times, institutions have to use shortcuts and "satisficing" approaches in their contract decision making as well as in the monitoring and reporting phases. Contracting personnel also may have somewhat conflicting values and goals within the contracting system, choosing expediency and responsiveness to political pressures over thorough, often time-consuming procedures that take advantage of service markets. Moreover, although program managers may have a better sense of the service needs, service delivery methods, and characteristics of quality service delivery, they often do not receive the staff or have the time to devote to contract administration and monitoring (and thus cannot mount credible threats of contract termination).

Finally, the authors' point that transaction costs are particularly high in relational contracting may be misleading. Even in strong and somewhat competitive service markets, competitive bidding involves significant transaction costs for, among other things, planning contract specifications, making announcements, conducting the competitive proposal process, and holding pre-proposal meetings (DeHoog 1990). Relational contracting does have some disadvantages, as the authors suggest, but it can avoid some of the costs encountered in competitive bidding. Moreover, if a particularly reputable and experienced agency is chosen, the process has some significant benefits in weak markets and new service areas.

Commentary

Suzanne J. Piotrowski

Brown, Potoski, and Van Slyke make a valuable contribution to the public service contracting literature. I supplement the authors' argument by addressing this question: What functions does transparency play within the "values, institutions, and service markets" contracting framework that they offer? Transparency, along with competitive bidding and the prevention of conflicts of interest, has been identified as a basic requirement of contracting out to serve the interests of the public (Baar 2001). Moreover, the need for transparency is eminently clear and highlighted by examples of waste and abuse of federal contracting dollars following Hurricane Katrina. Although the authors implicitly address access to government contracting issues, a dearth of literature exists on this topic in the United States. In fact, most work on contracting transparency is based on non-U.S. or comparative examples (Baar 2001; Cho and Choi 2004; Deng et al. 2003; Magrini 2005; Roberts 2000).

Brown and his colleagues argue, "Public managers operate in a crucible of swirling and often competing political values, including effectiveness, efficiency, accountability, responsiveness, equality of treatment, and service delivery." One value not explicitly identified is governmental transparency. Transparency usually is achieved through legal mechanisms such as freedom of information laws to access documents, open public meetings, or whistle-blowing. Increasingly, websites are used as a conduit of proactively released government information. Of course, transparency also can be achieved through illegal channels such as leaked information. Fortunately, a growing research interest exists in the role of transparency in public administration in general (Cleveland 1986; Cooper 1986; Feinberg 1986, 1997, 2004; Relyea 1986, 2003; Roberts and Darbishire 2003), as well as in contracting in particular. As Baar (2001, 104) notes, "Without transparency, the general public is excluded from the contracting out process. As a result, the potential benefits of independent public review, criticism, and expertise are lost."

The authors also identify public law and organizational processes as institutions, and certain aspects of transparency *have* been codified in this way through freedom of information and open meetings laws. An overlooked point, however, is that although freedom of information acts can be used to constrain contractors, this is not always the case. At the federal level, for example, contractors generally are not covered under the Freedom of Information Act (FOIA). Only in specific circumstances are contractor documents accessible through the federal FOIA (for more on this point, see Rosenbloom in this volume). Among the states, there is variation as to which governmental partners are covered under open public records acts (Campbell 2005; Feiser 2000). As such, the public administration community needs to think and write more about what the appropriate level of access should be when private entities conduct the public's business.

The authors provide nine features that managers typically have discretion to specify within contracts. A level of transparency easily could be included in the list of possible contract specifications. At the federal level, after all, personal privacy provisions routinely are included in contracts. Freedom of information provisions also could be built into arrangements with entities contracting for public services. Contracts, for example, could require that final products and interim documents be accessible to the public. Transparency also could be built into outcome measures in contracts (also see Rosenbloom in this volume).

The final aspect of the authors' framework is the condition of markets with respect to contracting, with the availability of information a key service component of successful markets. Governmental transparency enables the flow of specific kinds of information and not others. For instance, non-bid contracts may serve some purposes, such as expediency, but they do not promote transparency. Consequently, the style, timeliness, and location of proposal requests are important factors for practitioners and scholars to appreciate as they relate to the public's ability to understand the decision to contract out services and the likelihood that a business will see the proposal and submit a bid. In addition, although transparency most clearly fits within the values and institutional portions of the authors' framework, it is relevant to the service market component as well. Businesses have come to rely on FOIA information to assess market competitors. When exceptions exist, market competition—the essence of marketized public administration—may suffer.

Certainly, more study on the intersection of transparency and contracts is needed. One avenue for future research is to identify and analyze transparency programs initiated by local governments. Another is to identify systematically how transparency relates to each of the phases of the contracting cycle. Yet another question is whether organizations contracting with governments should be held to the same standard of openness as the government whose business they are conducting. Freedom of information and open meetings laws generally constrain government managers. With regard to the contracting process, when do these constraints become prohibitive? Work needs to be done to identify what is the appropriate level of openness at all stages in the contracting process.

Commentary

Thomas F. Reilly

Although Brown, Potoski, and Van Slyke do an important service in offering their framework for practitioners to consider as they are involved in contracting, I would add or further elaborate on the following considerations. First, monopolistic companies can manipulate the process to make the contracting entity require more services. Monopolistic companies have no competition. When routine updates, maintenance, or change orders are required, a company can explain that such changes will require a drastic workaround when, in reality, it may be an easy fix. For example, with software companies, often the source code is proprietary and there is no competition to gauge the amount of work actually required. The monopolistic company can also make mistakes, prolong the change, and then charge the entity for those related hours, depending on how the contract is structured. Additionally, some companies may purposely use older technology, which requires a longer time to repair.

Second, the authors posit under contract specification and within the contours of legal requirements that public managers have discretion to specify several features (e.g., vendor tasks, outcome measures, and reporting requirements). I would argue that "legal jurisdiction" also is very important for managers and researchers to consider. *Where* disputes are adjudicated can be critical. Most public entities would want legal terms and disputes defined and settled in their home state, as opposed to states whose laws favor the domiciled company. Third, not only should values, institutions, and markets be aligned but so, too, should service delivery goals; true, realistic, and acceptable costs; and performance measurement. When organizations lack a clear understanding of what the "real" cost is of delivering the service, expectations are not readjusted to either "realistic" or "acceptable" service levels. And without clear key performance indicators, metrics, and costs, comparisons of contracting versus in-house service delivery may do nothing more than compare "apples to oranges."

Fourth, as the authors note, one common aspect of contracting involves the purchase of information technology (IT) software. Governments need to band together to buy widely popular software such as Microsoft. Too often, large IT companies dictate the contract and buying terms. They also dictate the servicing requirements. Banding together affords more purchasing expertise, experience, and leverage to governments than when they act individually. Fifth, although the authors mention that managers may not legally authorize the auditing of vendor records and performance, I would recommend placing audit verbiage in contract clauses. This language is not only possible to incorporate but also essential for accountability. Sixth, I would emphasize, too, that competing workarounds can minimize the efficiency of markets, thus ensuring a cycle of thin markets. Minimizing this problem requires an agreement with elected officials and their appointees that they will be willing to bear the "transaction costs" of an unhappy contractor community.

Seventh, the authors make the important point that principal–agent problems can arise in contract management. I would add, however, that the internal structuring of a department's contract management function can either mitigate or exacerbate these problems. Breaking apart the contracting function by leaving it up to the administrative staff to "manage" a contract runs the risk of losing the program skills needed to provide sufficient arm's-length oversight. This occurs when a contract manager oversees contract processes or performance but without a sense for what constitutes high quality of service provision.

Finally, not only is aligning values, institutions, and markets critical in the contracting process but so, too, is aligning service delivery roles between government organizations and vendors. Done adroitly and within the larger context of the authors' framework, contracting can become a win–win situation for governments, contractors, and the public. Government employees can bring a public interest orientation to the work of vendors, an orientation for which the profit motive is not known. Meanwhile, vendors can fill a need for the public sector by providing highly specialized skills that are needed only intermittently (i.e., staffing for the "valleys" in demand and contracting for the "peaks" in demand). Contractors also can aggregate the demand and costs for these specialized skills among many government customers. In the meantime, vendors can profit by aggregating the fluctuating demand across agencies to stabilize their own workforces.

In sum, the authors demonstrate the importance of contracting out in a way that integrates values, institutions, and service markets. They recognize and seek to conceptualize more broadly what authors such as Goldsmith and Eggers (2004), Newland (2002), and Salamon (2002) contend: that government is finding itself increasingly in the position of managing resources that belong to someone else to address community problems. They also point out that managing this array of service providers is dramatically different from managing internal organizational resources and that most governmental agencies lack the capacity to manage these networks effectively. Relatedly, Ingraham (1995) argues that contracting presents a challenge to "retooling" an existing employee base from specialized "doers" to subject-matter experts with contract management skills. Consider, for example, the government programmer who used to write and support applications but is now responsible for managing new system implementation and its associated contracts and support agreements. Thus, public agencies are in need of an array of employees who not only can perform traditional duties such as planning, budgeting, and deploying staff but also are skilled in facilitation and negotiation, contract negotiations, contract management, risk analysis, and the ability to manage across boundaries (Goldsmith and Eggers 2004; Newland 2002; Salamon 2002). The ability of public agencies, managers, and employees to make these role changes and effectively perform them is in question. But the need to do so is not. Contracting requires public agencies and universities to enhance their traditional training programs to incorporate this new reality. Providing relevant, practical, and value-based guidance such as the framework on contract management advanced by Brown and his colleagues is a step toward such an understanding for practitioners and academics.

Commentary

Andrew B. Whitford

It is hard to offer a small set of contracting prescriptions for managers, even though managers will continue to find contract management difficult in the public sector. Why? First, as Brown, Potoski, and Van Slyke argue, public managers make decisions about contracting while trying to navigate and reconcile political values that are not always in accord with one another. As the authors indicate, these competing values make their way into the rules and regulations—the institutions—that define the public manager's environment. These institutions tell managers how and when to construct governmental markets for service provision—markets consisting of those who depend on the services themselves and the external markets that exist for their provision. Institutions—formal or informal—act as the "rules of the game" (North 1990) for managers making important decisions with significant long-term public consequences.

North's (1990) work on institutions helps one understand how the rules of the game provide a long-term basis for the growth and survival of economies. His position has always been that, over the long-term, the rules of the game help economies become efficient or the rules will not survive; if they do not, the rules are replaced or society does not survive. But I suspect that most public managers can think of many situations where the rules sent to them for guiding their decisions do everything but help them make contracting efficient. Arguing against North, Knight (1992) made this point more generally, claiming that the rules of the game often are meant to reward one at the expense of another or to distribute the benefits of public power disproportionately.

Strategically, one makes different decisions based on assumptions regarding whether the rules of the game are meant to make government and society more efficient or to move resources out of the public sector and to nonprofits and for-profit firms. The authors of this chapter focus on efficiency and argue, "If the goals are innovation and efficiency in service provision, then contracting with a private vendor may be more desirable; private employees typically operate with *higher-powered, compensation-based, and profit-oriented incentives*" (emphasis added). Yet the best evidence from the private sector calls this assumption into question. In fact, private employees are less affected by high-powered incentives than one might suspect (e.g., Tosi et al. 2000), and the incentives in place (e.g., promotion tournaments) often are no different from those in place in many public settings. Moreover, experimental evidence is quite clear that high-powered incentives are neither necessary nor sufficient in many work settings to induce innovation and efficiency (e.g., Bottom et al. 2006).

What these arguments really tell us is that whether you need contracting out or other devices to gain efficiency in government depends on the institutions in place. In some settings, good rules mean governments are probably just as efficient as markets. These arguments also tell us that political rules meant to cause governments to become more efficient will not always achieve this goal—that public managers may have very little latitude to achieve efficiency, especially if the rules of the game are not meant to do so. For evidence of the latter, casual observers need look only to government contracts in the reconstruction of Iraq or to the expanded use of preferred provider organizations in Medicare.

A second reason so few clear prescriptions can be offered for managers is that they often are asked to write contracts and job-out services that should be made in-house, not bought from contractors. Brown and his colleagues also emphasize that managers can try to specify the contract or better manage service delivery under contract. But transaction cost economics (TCE) is fairly clear that there are many situations where contracts are inherently difficult to write. The authors emphasize two dimensions of contract writing: asset specificity and ease of measurement. But TCE also shows that contracting ease expands or contracts based on other dimensions, such as inherent uncertainty or complexity in the contracting environment or the frequency of interaction between contractors and those they serve.

Economists think about contracting in terms of the "necessity of vertical integration" in the firm. They also think of the relationship between a vendor and a contracting government less in principal–agent terms and more in terms of bilateral monopoly (which is more of a bargaining–negotiation problem). The question is whether a government should use a contractor given a combination of asset specificity and uncertainty/complexity. What matters are how the vendor and the contracting government experience asset specificity (together, alone, or not at all) and whether the contracting environment is marked by uncertainty/complexity (low or high). In three of six possible combinations of these factors, vertical integration (no contracting out) is the best governance structure. In one situation, spot contracts are desirable; in another, long-term contracts are preferred. In the last, whether contracts are desired depends on the frequency of the interaction (e.g., Douma and Schreuder 2002; Williamson 1975).

How often can most public managers say that political directives to contract out actually considered these dimensions? Moreover, what is the incidence of those choices with these combinations of the environmental factors of asset specificity, uncertainty/complexity, and frequency? If the incidence is roughly 50 percent, that still leaves 50 percent of the time where vertical integration is probably preferred, where long-term contracts are not preferred, or where spot contracts are unlikely to perform. There are few definitive prescriptions in these cases. A prescription of getting the relational contract right does not necessarily outperform blind management, because relational contracting is only relevant one-sixth of the time—the case where long-term contracts are better than vertical integration or spot contracts, which occurs when both parties face high asset specificity and uncertainty/complexity is low.

In the long run, the added value of this chapter will be to shift our emphasis away from hand-wringing about the benefits of contracts, the costs to public managers of having to write contracts, and the long-term implications of contracts for the public service (although, of course, all are excellent fields of endeavor). Foremost, instead, will be trying to understand how managers should strategically implement political directives to contract out. When the world is complex and the optimal choice is not clear, managers "do the best they can do." That is a strategic problem and well describes where this chapter directs our attention.

Chapter 8

A Return to Spoils? Revisiting Radical Civil Service Reform in the United States[*]

Stephen E. Condrey and R. Paul Battaglio, Jr.

Contents

---

[*] Adapted from Condrey, S. E., and R. P. Battaglio, Jr. 2007. A return to spoils? Revisiting radical civil service reform in the United States. *Public Administration Review* 67(3): 425–436.

Writing over a quarter century ago, Frederick Mosher (1982, 221) observed, "One thing seems clear ... the principles of merit and the practices whereby they were given substance are changing and must change a good deal more to remain viable in our society." He argued in his classic *Democracy and the Public Service* that human resource management (HRM) systems "should be decentralized and delegated to bring them into more immediate relationship with the middle and lower managers they served" (86). More recently, however, administrative reformers have gone significantly further. So-called *radical civil service reform* (RCSR) couched in the neomanagerialist tenets of the new public management (NPM) has grown popular among government reinventors and has resonated as a populist political theme (Barzelay with Armajani 1992; Durant and Legge 2006; Pollitt 1990; Terry 1993). Consonant with NPM advocates who espouse freeing managers from the bonds of bureaucratic constraints to allow them to manage their organizations effectively, proponents of RCSR advocate eliminating job security in favor of at-will employment, eroding merit protections, linking pay to performance, and decentralizing personnel functions to program line managers, largely without checks on managerial excesses.

Not surprisingly under these circumstances, all are not sanguine about the implications of today's NPM-related RCSR agenda (Box et al. 2001; Denhardt and Denhardt 2000; Jos and Tompkins 2004; Kelly 1998; Moe 1994, 2001; Moe and Gilmour 1995; Terry 1993, 1998; Wamsley and Dudley 1998). As Condrey (2002, 123) summarized their critique in assessing the likely prospects of Georgia's first-in-the-nation effort to move toward at-will employment:

> It is too early to see if cronyism, favoritism, and unequal pay for equal work will be the wholesale result of the Georgia reform. However ... the likelihood of these problems occurring has increased due to the diminished role of Georgia's central personnel authority. As other states look at Georgia, it is hoped that they will work to devise strategic partnerships between central and agency personnel authorities, seeking a healthy balance between responsiveness and continuity.

It is still premature to know how accurate the perspectives of proponents or opponents of RCSR have been in Georgia as well as in Florida and Texas, the two other leading states embracing these reforms. Time and prior research have advanced enough at this point, however, to at least begin taking stock of the extent to which the promise and perils of RCSR have occurred. First, we review briefly the logic and history of these initiatives in the United States, examining the substance and pace of adoption across the states. Second, we review prior research conducted in Florida, Georgia, and Texas to see if the worries of opponents of RCSR have materialized. Third, we offer the results of our own survey research in Georgia indicating that, despite dire predictions, there appears to be no wholesale rush to spoils in the state—at least in the eyes of state agency human resource (HR) professionals. Fourth, and derived from this analysis, we offer a set of propositions for practitioners to consider when thinking about adopting RCSR in their states and that researchers might test, elaborate, and extend in their work. We conclude by arguing that a variety of underlying societal, organizational, and political forces suggest that continuing support for RCSR in the U.S. is likely.

Radical Civil Service Reform: Diffusion, Breadth, and Some Early Lessons

RCSR is a direct result of administrative reform prescriptions that frame government as hamstrung by, among other things, overly bureaucratized civil service systems. Instead of modernizing these systems and their myriad policies and procedures, RCSR reformers opt to make organization employees at will—that is, serving without the guarantee of tenure or job security protections. For example, Georgia's former Democratic governor, Zell Miller, blazed the trail for RCSR nationally in 1996 by alleging a recalcitrant and unresponsive state personnel system. His administration abolished civil service protections for newly hired employees as well as for those accepting promotions or transfers to other positions in state government. As of 2006, approximately 76 percent of Georgia's state employees were employed at will (State of Georgia 2006). Following suit, Florida Governor Jeb Bush implemented his Service First and People First programs in 2001, outsourcing key HR functions and placing upper-level managers in at-will status. Texas has long operated under a decentralized, at-will arrangement for delivery of HR services and is the only state that does not have a central personnel agency (Chi 2005). Importantly, although due process protections remain in Georgia and for employees of several Texas agencies, they do not afford protections comparable to traditional civil service systems.

Unsurprisingly, these three state initiatives in RCSR have prompted considerable interest among HRM practitioners and scholars in the United States. Two issues of the *Review of Public Personnel Administration* (Summer 2002 and 2006) were devoted to these types of civil service reform initiatives, with the first focused on Georgia's experience (Condrey 2002; Gossett 2002; Kellough and Nigro 2002; Kuykendall and Facer 2002; Lasseter 2002; West 2002) and the second exploring the impact of RCSR (Battaglio and Condrey 2006; Bowman and West 2006; Coggburn 2006; Hays and Sowa 2006; Wilson 2006). From this and other research, several lessons and testable propositions can be drawn.

Lesson 1: At-will employment practices have diffused quite significantly across states and localities in the United States, with the strength of public employee unions tempering but not precluding its adoption and with the spread of decentralized personnel management coming in its wake.

In 2006, Hays and Sowa surveyed all fifty states to determine whether at-will employment policies were expanding and whether decentralization of the HR function was taking place. The authors found that at-will employment influences have diffused to a majority of state governments. Additionally, of the twenty-eight state governments reporting at-will policy expansion, twenty-five also report some degree of decentralization of their personnel systems.

The result of this decentralized, at-will environment is the substitution of agency-specific, manager-centered HR systems for the conventionally centralized, rule-oriented systems that once characterized these state personnel systems. This result appears to be the case particularly in states with weak employee unions and collective bargaining rights. A case in point is Florida. When Governor Bush implemented his Service First at-will employment scheme, law enforcement and nursing unions were able to exempt themselves from the reform (Bowman and West 2006). As such, practitioners advocating these reforms do well to expect, and researchers might hypothesize, that states with strong and effective employee unions will experience the greatest amount of resistance to RCSR initiatives.

Still, as Bowman and West (2006) chronicle in their research on Florida's experience to date with RCSR, public union opposition may be a limiting, but not precluding, factor in adopting RCSR. Since its inception in 2001, for example, Florida's Service First program has placed approximately 16,000 (out of a total of approximately 124,000 state employees) senior state government managers in at-will status. Additionally, through its People First initiative, Florida has chosen to outsource much of its HR function.

Lesson 2: Claims regarding superior performance have yet to materialize, and views regarding their impacts differ between program and HRM professionals.

As noted, insufficient time, confounding effects, and inadequate databases preclude rigorous empirically grounded answers to the question of whether RCSR has produced improved service delivery. However, it is not too early to assess how deeply and with what obstacles RCSR has sunk into day-to-day personnel management in the states. In Florida, Bowman and West (2006, 139) found that: "The management of human resources is undergoing profound transition in concept and practice. A key component of this transformation is the dissolution of the traditional social contract at work: job security with good pay and benefits in exchange for employee commitment and loyalty." But they also note obstacles to implementing RCSR in Florida. For example, Convergys—the firm to which many routine HR processing functions were outsourced in Florida—experienced delays and "significant problems," including payroll and benefit errors (OPPAGA 2006, 2). Moreover, although proponents claimed the state would save an average of $24.7 million annually, Florida still had not established a "methodology to capture project cost savings" (3). Although state officials in Florida's Selected Exempt Service found the reforms to be "of little consequence at best and harmful at worst," state HR directors were more "sanguine," citing some administrative improvements (155). Meanwhile, in Georgia, Sanders (2004) found RCSR popular among state politicians, but evoking general dissatisfaction among state workers (also see Kellough and Nigro 2002). Sanders's review of recent surveys also found little or no observable improvement in the evaluation and discipline processes among state workers.

Limited evidence also suggests that opponents' fears that RCSR would lead to violations of merit principles can be overstated in states with traditions of decentralized personnel management. Coggburn (2006), for example, reports that because of the maturity of Texas's decentralized management structure, the state's organizational culture has managed to avoid the wholesale cronyism expected to result from reducing employment rights. Fully 97.4 percent of state HR directors surveyed agreed that "even though employment is at-will [sic], most employee terminations in Texas agencies are for good cause" (166).

Lesson 3: RCSR may bring the improvement in processes that proponents claim, but recruitment and retention of employees may suffer if cost savings reduce the attractiveness of employment.

Recent research also suggests, however, that there may be problems with recruitment and retention should a rush to cost savings occur. Although they found that at-will employment contributed to streamlining the dismissal process, Elling and Thompson's (2006) surveys of staff and line managers in ten states in 1982 and 2000 find no significant correlation with the extent of state personnel system deregulation and streamlining of HR processes. Interestingly given its history, the exception was Texas. Texas managers said that they encountered fewer problems in disciplining or dismissing employees. However, these same managers also were more likely to articulate concerns with low pay impeding recruitment and retention. The lesson may be that although deregulation may be a cornerstone to eliminating impediments to effective management, implementation of at-will employment systems must not allow a focus on cost savings to undermine the attractiveness of public employment and retention (e.g., adequate compensation).

Assessing the "Calculus of Dissent" for At-Will Employment in Georgia

In the remainder of this chapter, we offer and test a model for assessing the perceptions of RCSR reforms held by HRM professionals in Georgia state government. We undertook two statewide surveys from January to March 2006. The specifics of our data and methods are discussed in Appendix A. We first asked respondents to indicate their level of agreement with a number of statements evaluating at-will employment. Premised on the findings of prior research, the first eighteen survey items were condensed into three scales that served as our dependent variables (see Appendix A). The first scale tapped into respondents' perceptions of the potential for at-will employment to discourage good government (Battaglio and Condrey 2006; Condrey 2002; Gossett 2002). The second reflected how much respondents saw at-will employment realizing the claims of RCSR proponents regarding enhanced efficiency, accountability, responsiveness, customer satisfaction, motivation, managerial flexibility, performance, streamlining, and modern management techniques (Barzelay with Armajani 1992; Kettl 2000; Light 1997; Osborne and Gaebler 1992; Savas 2000, 2006). The third scale represented respondents' perceptions of how much critics' concerns had materialized regarding at-will employment promoting unfair treatment of employees.

We then identified factors that might explain variations in respondents' perceptions of these three factors. A review of prior research indicated that various demographic and agency-specific characteristics might be at work (see, for example, Brudney, Hebert, and Wright 1999; Brudney and Wright 2002; Kearney, Feldman, and Scavo 2000). We posed twenty-nine questions assessing the age, gender, race/ethnicity, and political views of respondents; their previous HRM private sector experience; their years of service in the public sector; their educational level; and the size of the agency in which they worked (measured as the number of full-time employees). Additionally, we developed three scales measuring the effect of agency-related factors on respondent assessment of at-will employment in Georgia. Specifically, the scales measured perceptions of previous misuses of the HR system, prior "unwarranted reductions in force (RIFs)," and general trust in management (see Appendix A for details of scale construction).

Overall, we found significant splits among HR professionals in their perceptions of how well RCSR led to the performance improvements claimed by proponents. Less than half of the respondents (47 percent) thought that at-will employment had helped "ensure that employees are responsive to the goals and priorities of agency administrators." Only 43 percent found that at-will employment in Georgia state government made the "HR function more efficient," and only 34.9 percent reported that RCSR provided the "needed motivation for employee performance."

We next used multiple regression analysis to test for the independent effects of various demographic and agency-specific characteristics on perceptions about at-will employment in Georgia while simultaneously controlling for (i.e., holding constant) the impact of the other factors. On the basis of the results summarized in Table 8.1, we offer the following propositions for practitioners to consider and researchers to test, elaborate, and refine in future research.

Table 8.1   Impact of Agency-Specific Experiences on General Scales for Attitudes toward At-Will Employment

Explanatory Factors	Discourages Good Government	Supports NPM Claims	Encourages Unfair Employment Practices
Age and Years in Service	.211** (1.99)	–.0545* (–0.55)	.161* (1.91)
Prior Private Sector Experience	.146 (1.23)	.038 (0.34)	.190** (2.01)
Size of Agency	.001 (0.48)	.006** (2.64)	.003 (1.35)
Gender	–.383** (–2.71)	.185 (1.40)	.007 (0.06)
Education	–.091** (–1.97)	.014 (0.32)	–.004 (–0.10)
Political Views—Liberal	–.148 (–1.02)	.020 (0.15)	–.180 (–1.56)
Political Views—Conservative	.036 (0.33)	.045 (0.44)	–.013 (–0.14)
Caucasian	–.180 (–0.66)	–.264 (–1.03)	.069 (0.32)
African American	–.096 (–0.34)	–.435* (–1.63)	.139 (0.61)
Misuse of the HR System	.133* (1.82)	–.002 (–0.04)	.278** (4.79)
Unwarranted RIFs	.062 (1.05)	–.043 (–0.78)	.055 (1.16)
Trust Management	–.444** (–5.31)	.344** (4.41)	–.457** (–6.89)
R-Squared	*.306*	*.184*	*.503*

Note: Column entries include regression coefficients and t-scores in parentheses. $N = 232$ (cases with missing data were dropped from the regression).

* Significant at the .10 level.
** Significant at the .05 level.

Proposition 1: HR professionals with greater tenure in office will be more likely to oppose measures associated with at-will employment in government.

We expected that the more seasoned public sector HRM respondents would be not only more cynical about management fads generally but also more likely to worry that increased managerial discretion would diminish employee protections. As hypothesized, respondents who had a longer tenure in their positions (age and years in service) consistently tended to view at-will employment in Georgia as discouraging good government, not realizing NPM claims, and potentially resulting in unfair employment practices.

Proposition 2: HRM professionals with prior experience in the private sector are no more likely than professionals with only public service experience to support measures associated with at-will employment in government.

We also expected that respondents with prior experience in the private sector would have more favorable views about at-will employment than would respondents who had worked solely in public agencies. The former would be not only less sensitive to the historical import of merit principles but also less invested personally in the merit system and more impressed by private sector models and performance. Statistical significance is achieved for only one of the scales testing this expectation; respondents with only public sector backgrounds were more likely to see at-will employment encouraging unfair employment practices. Respondents with private sector backgrounds were no more or less likely to be wary of an at-will environment.

Proposition 3: Respondents in agencies with greater numbers of full-time employees (FTEs) are more likely to support at-will employment.

Not unlike prior research on NPM reforms more generally (Brudney et al. 1999; Kearney et al. 2000), our analysis indicated that respondents in agencies with greater numbers of FTEs were significantly more likely to find support for

NPM principles than respondents in smaller agencies. Thus, it appears that HRM professionals in large agencies may have bought into the neomanagerialist ideology promulgated by the Georgia reformers, perhaps because at-will employment facilitates the overall management of these agencies or because efficiency is a more overriding principle or concern in such agencies. Moreover, HRM professionals in large agencies may be prone to dedicate professional and technical resources toward experimentation with at-will employment and may be better resourced to do so (Brudney et al. 1999, 25; Kearney et al. 2000, 540).

Proposition 4: Although female and minority HR professionals are likely to be less supportive of at-will employment, those with higher education levels are more likely to support it.

Given historical levels of discrimination against women and minorities in the workplace, we expected female and minority HRM professionals to be less likely to support at-will employment in Georgia. We also expected respondents with higher levels of education to be less skeptical of at-will employment, but we entertained the rival hypothesis that—because of their greater familiarity with the more pro-business and anti-public sector biases of the NPM agenda—the more highly educated would be more wary about loss of public sector jobs and the potential for arbitrariness and abuse of merit principles.

Yet we found that female respondents were significantly *more* likely than male HR respondents to disagree with the notion that at-will employment discourages good government. Perhaps female HR professionals feel their career progression has been slowed by civil service rules that have favored their more-tenured male counterparts. Our initial expectations regarding education, however, were not validated. Respondents with higher levels of education did not agree that at-will employment discourages good government. As such, respondents with higher formal education may have a greater awareness than the less well educated of its potential benefits and less fear of its downsides. They may also be less fearful of being adversely affected by these initiatives because of their higher levels of education.

In contrast, and although the relationship demonstrates only marginal statistical significance, African American respondents were less likely to find support for the neomanagerialist philosophy informing NPM principles. As Wilson (2006, 178) suggests, by giving managers the upper hand in employment relationships, African Americans may view at-will employment as a tool for "discrimination-induced job dismissals." One other possibility is that having a long history with the Democratic Party in Georgia, African Americans either may have felt left out of the reform process as a Republican governor took over the reins of administration for the first time since Reconstruction or simply may have been averse to Republican initiatives generally.

> **Proposition 5:** Overall, political ideology is not a significant predictor of attitudes toward at-will employment initiatives.

Turning to ideology, we also anticipated that HR respondents who saw themselves as politically conservative would be more likely to support at-will employment in Georgia than those viewing themselves as liberals. In contrast to liberals who are less sanguine about the magic of marketized public administration and the application of private sector techniques to government, conservatives are likely to be more supportive of market-based approaches to personnel administration such as at-will employment. However, we found that political ideology was not a statistically significant predictor of support for RCSR in any of our three models. Moreover, statistical significance aside, liberals actually tended to support at-will employment in all three cases, while conservatives viewed it as discouraging good government. It is possible that conservatives are inherently less sympathetic to radical changes of any kind and that might lead to challenges to the status quo in service provision, while liberals are more prone to embracing initiatives that might lead to substantive policy change in state services.

> **Proposition 6:** HR professionals whose experience has involved abuses of employees by managers are less likely to support at-will employment initiatives, making prior and present leadership key factors in employee acceptance.

We expected that HR professionals who anticipated "misuse of the HR system" by managers and "unwarranted RIFs" based on past experiences in the Georgia state system would be less supportive of at-will employment. Equally unlikely to support at-will systems would be respondents who did not trust program managers generally. Our expectations were largely confirmed; respondents who were suspicious about misuse of the HR system were significantly more likely to believe that at-will employment in Georgia discouraged good government and encouraged unfair employment practices. Conversely, respondents who trusted managers to do the right thing in personnel actions were significantly more likely to view at-will employment as an important management tool in government.

Conclusion: An Idea Whose Time Has Come?

The generalizability of our findings aside, we would argue that several large-scale political, social, and organizational forces will continue to make RCSR attractive to elected officials and citizens. These include

- Broad public support for at-will employment and its symbolic appeal to elected officials: At-will employment is a way for elected officials to demonstrate to the public that they are "in charge" and have control over the ship of state. Although there is no evidence to date that at-will employment is improving state operations, it enjoys broad public support. In addition to our findings, a 2006 poll of Georgia citizens indicates that they hold high levels of support for their state's civil service reform initiatives (Peach State Poll 2006).

- Changes in public employment and electoral politics: Interest group politics, lucrative government contracts, and privatization of government functions now are the fuel that power elections and electoral politics. Indeed, the move toward a "hollow state" with extensive privatization and outsourcing of governmental functions has diminished the importance of the individual government employee in electoral coalition building and enhanced the importance of satisfying large private organizational interests. Consequently, jobs are no longer traded for votes on a large-scale basis as they once were. As the preceding review of prior research suggests, critics' fears that at-will employment would bring a return to spoils once employee protections were abolished have not materialized. Although there is anecdotal evidence of this in the state of Florida, little support exists for any widespread return of patronage politics in states adopting at-will employment systems. Our analysis in Georgia indicates that politics did not factor at all into the perceptions of HR professionals about at-will employment. Many HR professionals even expressed their support for at-will employment in their written survey responses. As one respondent stated, "I believe that at-will employment has significantly improved the efficiency and effectiveness of our agency's HR processes. I do not believe the abuses (cronyism, firing competent employees, etc.) are any more common than they were previously."

- The ascendancy of complex bureaucracies and a developed economy: Most state bureaucracies employ tens of thousands of employees, the sheer complexity of which negates coordinated efforts to politicize entire bureaucracies. And our analysis of survey data in Georgia confirms this. It substantiates earlier research (Brudney et al. 1999, 25; Kearney et al. 2000, 540) demonstrating that agency size may indicate a willingness to experiment with reforms to achieve efficiency.

- The changing nature of the workforce and the notion of psychological work contracts: Employment relationships continue to evolve in the U.S.

workforce. Thompson and Mastracci (2005) note the increasing use of contingent or "nonstandard work arrangements" whereby part-time, temporary, and contract workers are used in the public sector workforce. This phenomenon increases the importance of flexible work arrangements and diminishes the notion of full-time, career-based employment upon which traditional civil service systems were based. Prior research also indicates that younger workers no longer expect to form long-term psychological contracts with their employers (Riccucci 2006; Tulgan 1997; West 2005). Likewise, our analysis in Georgia suggests that generational trends may be at play in support for at-will employment, with older respondents less supportive of this initiative. As such, at-will employment may suit the next generation of workers who enter the workforce anticipating that their career path will involve a number of different jobs with different organizations. As one respondent stated, "I think that at-will employment is a nonissue for new and younger employees but a concern for long-term employees." Another respondent observed, "Only classified employees express concern regarding at-will employment."

■ The blurring of public and private sector employment: Arguments for special protections for public employees will hold less weight as the distinctions erode between public and private employment. Even before these initiatives began, scholars pointed to the decline in public–private distinctions (Bozeman 1987). Public sector jobs continue to be attractive because they offer both career employment and civil service protections. As these protections erode and as the generational shift in attitudes mitigates against career employment in a single organization, public and private employment differences are likely to blur even further. At best, this phenomenon will lead to more competitive wages for public sector employment. At worst, and more likely, public agencies without civil service protections and competitive wages could become employers of last resort.

Appendix A

Data and Methods

Our sampling universe consisted of individuals identified by the Georgia State Merit System as having a significant HRM function in their respective agency. Thus, the survey was not limited to director-level positions, making for a more balanced and representative view of the reforms. The surveys were mailed to 534 Georgia HR professionals. A follow-up mailing resulted in a total survey return rate of approximately 51.3 percent, or 274 completed surveys. Because of the exploratory nature of our study, we used both the conventional .05 and the more relaxed .10 levels of statistical significance in our discussion of the findings.

Scale Development and the Dependent Variables

Using a theoretical construct, scales were developed with survey items from the respondents' views regarding at-will employment in general. These views were assessed by the following set of Likert Scale-rated questions:

Part I: At-Will Employment In General

Respondents were asked to circle the number (Coded 1 = Strongly Disagree and 5 = Strongly Agree) corresponding to their level of agreement or disagreement with statements related to the claims of proponents and opponents of at-will employment.

1. Leads to greater customer satisfaction for citizens.
2. Leads to greater government accountability and responsiveness to the public.
3. Has streamlined the hiring/firing process.
4. Helps ensure employees are responsive to the goals and priorities of agency administrators.
5. Provides needed motivation for employee performance.
6. Makes the HR function more efficient.
7. Provides essential managerial flexibility over the HR function.
8. Represents an essential piece of modern government management.
9. Makes employees feel more secure about their jobs.
10. Discourages employees from taking risks that could lead to program or policy innovation.
11. Discourages employees from reporting agency wrongdoing (or "blowing the whistle").
12. Discourages employees from freely voicing objections to management directives.
13. Could—by not requiring a rationale or justification for terminating employees—negatively affect managers' decision-making in other non-HR decisions.
14. Could—by not requiring a rationale or justification for terminating employees—make public employees less sensitive to issues of procedural fairness.
15. Is at odds with the public sector's traditional emphasis on merit in human resources decisions.

16. Makes state government jobs less attractive to current and future employees than would be the case if there was more job security.
17. Gives an upper-hand to employers relative to employees in the employment relationship.
18. Is sometimes used to fire competent employees so other people with friends or connections to government can be hired.

Utilizing principal components analysis and ensuring internal reliability, we developed as dependent variables three scales associated with the notion of radical reform. The scales are composed of the combined mean responses to scale items by respondent. Thus, let's assume that a respondent's answers to the four statements comprising the "Discourages Good Government" scale were 3, 4, 5, and 3, respectively (where 1 = Strongly Disagree and 5 = Strongly Agree). Instead of adding the items in the scale (in this example, 15) and using the totals in the analyses, the means of respondents' scores on the scale (in this example, 3.75) were used in the regression analyses.

The first scale was developed from perceptions that an at-will employment scheme would discourage responsible or "good" government. A "Discourages Good Government" scale was calculated by summing responses for four statements (statements 10–12 and 16) from the survey (see Part I above); higher values are associated with stronger levels of agreement. A higher value on the scale corresponds to a more negative sentiment toward at-will employment and an increased belief that at-will employment discourages good government. The scale has a respectable degree of internal reliability indicated by a Cronbach's alpha of .784, with a mean of 3.05 and a standard deviation of .854.

The second dependent variable is a scale indicating that at-will employment upholds certain tenets of NPM. These "managerialist" beliefs include greater efficiency, accountability, responsiveness, customer satisfaction, motivation, managerial flexibility, performance, streamlining, and modern management (Barzelay with Armajani 1992; Kettl 2000; Light 1997; Osborne and Gaebler 1992; Savas 2000, 2006). This "Supports NPM Principles" scale was developed by summing responses to survey statements 1-8, with a higher value on the scale corresponding to a more positive view of at-will employment. A Cronbach's alpha of .893 indicates a high degree of internal reliability for this scale, with a mean of 3.23 and standard deviation of .766.

A final dependent variable assessed respondents' perceptions that at-will employment resulted in unfair employment practices. This "Encourages Unfair Employment Practices" scale sums responses to five survey questions (13–15, 17, and 18), with a higher value on the scale indicating a more negative sentiment about at-will employment. Thus, a high scale value indicates a belief that at-will employment increases the likelihood of unfair treatment of employees. This scale also has a respectable degree of internal reliability indicated by a Cronbach's alpha of .801, with a mean of 3.06 and a standard deviation of .807.

Scale Development and the Explanatory Variables

In order to gauge the impact of agency-specific effects, an additional three scales were developed from the survey. These scales were derived from the next twenty-six statements on the survey (Part II) and were framed as, "In my agency…," thus capturing agency-specific experiences of the respondents with at-will employment. This "Misuse" scale is comprised of statements 9, 10, 12, and 16. Statements 13–15 make up the "Unwarranted RIFs" scale, and the "Trust" scale includes statements 7, 8, 18, 24, and 25. For all three scales, higher values indicate stronger levels of agreement. While the possibility of interactive effects is possible, further research is necessary to validate that relationship.

Part II: At-Will Employment in Your Agency

Respondents were asked to circle the number (Coded 1 = Strongly Disagree and 5 = Strongly Agree) corresponding to their level of agreement or disagreement with the following statements related to their experiences with at-will employment in their respective agency.

1. Employees are more productive because they are employed at-will.
2. The lack of job security is made up for with competitive compensation (salary and benefits).
3. The lack of job security makes recruiting and retaining employees difficult.
4. Even though employment is at-will, most employee terminations are for good cause.
5. Even if an employee is terminated at-will, we maintain documentation to justify the termination should a lawsuit arise.
6. Concern about wrongful termination and discrimination lawsuits limit our use of at-will termination.
7. Managers treat employees fairly and consistently when it comes to HR decisions.
8. Employees trust management when it comes to HR decisions.
9. I know of a case where a competent employee was fired at-will so that another person with friends or connections to government could be hired.
10. Employees have been terminated at-will because of personality conflicts with management.

11. Employees have been terminated at-will because of poor performance.
12. Employees have been terminated at-will because of changing managerial priorities/objectives.
13. Employees have been terminated at-will in order to meet agency budget shortfalls.
14. Employees have been terminated at-will in order to meet agency downsizing goals.
15. Employees have been terminated at-will in order to meet mandated management-to-staff ratios.
16. Employees have been terminated at-will for politically motivated reasons.
17. At-will employment has led to pay discrepancies among employees with similar duties.
18. Employees feel that they can trust the organization to treat them fairly.
19. We include disclaimers in our policies and procedures manuals and employee handbooks stating that they do not alter the at-will employment relationship.
20. We clearly state in our job announcements and applications that employment with the agency is at-will.
21. We require employees to sign a form acknowledging that they are employed at-will by the agency.
22. We provide training to managers who make HR decisions on the legal exceptions to at-will employment and on how to preserve the at-will employment status.
23. We have improved our employee selection processes to better ensure employees hired fit the job and agency culture.
24. We give employees clear expectations about what is desirable and undesirable performance (e.g., through orientation and annual performance reviews).
25. We provide training to supervisors on how to effectively identify and handle problem employees (to reduce at-will terminations).
26. We have adopted or considered adopting a termination for good cause policy in order to reduce our total litigation risks (e.g., for wrongful termination, discrimination, etc.).

The scales for "Misuse of the HR System" and "Unwarranted Reductions of Force (RIFs)" presume that at-will employment may lead to misuses in the personnel process and unwarranted RIFs. The scales have a high degree of internal reliability indicated by their respective Cronbach's alphas of .823 (with a mean of 2.64 and a standard deviation of .823) and .864 (with a mean of 2.94 and a standard deviation of .864). The "Trust in Management" statements were associated with whether or not HR professionals trust their supervisors to do the right thing in personnel matters. The scale has a respectable degree of internal reliability indicated by a Cronbach's alpha of .777 (with a mean of 3.28 and a standard deviation of .729).

To these explanatory variables were added additional agency-specific and demographic variables culled from the following set of Likert Scale-type questions:

- Age Years in Service: To measure tenure in office, the variables for age and years of service in the public sector were combined and computed as a new variable. This variable was coded 1 = 16 or more years in service and 45 and older; 0 = 15 or less years in service and 44 and younger.
- Prior Private Sector Experience coded as 1 = Yes, 2 = No.
- Size of Agency coded as the number of FTEs authorized for the agency.
- Gender coded as 0 = Male, 1 = Female.
- Education coded as highest level of academic achievement where 1 = high school diploma, 2 = 2-year college degree, 3 = 4-year college degree, 4 = Master's degree, 5 = Law degree, 6 = PhD or equivalent.
- Political Views coded as 1 = Very Conservative, 2 = Conservative, 3 = Moderate, 4 = Liberal, 5 = Very Liberal.
- Respondent Race/Ethnicity coded as 1 = American Indian or Alaska Native, 2 = Asian, 3 = Black or African American, 4 = Hispanic or Latino, 5 = Native Hawaiian or other Pacific Islander, 6 = White, 7 = Some other race.

Commentary

Frank D. Ferris

Condrey and Battaglio have given us very useful measures to assess the technical aspects of the at-will picture in the states. As they suggest, an "at-will employment" campaign platform plank has undeniable voting-booth appeal. It can be explained in the average six-second media sound bite; it suggests a certain frontier toughness by the candidate; it taps into the stereotypical image of civil service employees who have been regularly trashed in presidential campaigns since Jimmy Carter; it enables one to demagogue about the "out-of-touch, pointy-headed, elite, liberal, activist judges" who reinstate employees; and it permits the candidate to say he or she is just doing what good business leaders would do. Of course, little thought is given in the heat of campaigns to the immortal words of H. L. Mencken: "There is always an easy solution to every human problem—neat, plausible, and wrong."

Time for a reality check. Although the popular understanding of at-will employment by citizens is that an employee can be fired for any reason at all, that is not what the law provides. Courts have recognized numerous exceptions to an executive's right to fire at will. They have reversed termination decisions when they find any of the following: (1) a written, oral, or otherwise implied contract of something other than an "at-will" relationship; (2) an implied promise of good faith and fair dealing in the employment relationship; (3) a termination that violates public policy; (4) a fraudulent representation in hiring the employee; (5) an intentional failure to disclose a material fact about the job that harms the employee; (6) an infliction of emotional distress on the employee; (7) the tortuous interference with the employee–employer relationship by a third party; or (8) defamation of the employee (White 1998, 13–26).

An employee also can charge that the termination violates any of more than a dozen statutes that prohibit discrimination based on race, color, gender, age, religion, national origin, disability, pregnancy, sexual orientation, sexual harassment, union activity, whistle-blowing activity, political affiliation, veterans' status, and several other grounds written into state and local jurisdiction codes. In other words, modern at-will employment rights are those that are left over after cutting through the many legal exceptions that, it could be argued, have overtaken the rule. Even Justice John Roberts's Supreme Court has added to the at-will employer's uncertainty. It has endorsed an employee's right to sue an employer for a termination based solely on retaliation for some protected conduct engaged in by the employee (see *Burlington Northern & Santa Fe Railroad v. White*, Supreme Court, No. 05-259 [2006]). Indeed, one need only enter into google.com the search terms "lawsuit" and "discrimination" to see over 1.2 million stories on litigation employment decisions.

Perhaps the most intriguing observation that Condrey and Battaglio provide us is their finding of substantial opposition to the at-will concept among the more experienced human resource managers, suggesting that resistance to at-will reforms will "retire" with this senior generation. However, there likely is even better data to be found on this issue among the first- and second-line managers in public agencies, regardless of age. Federal sector researchers, for example, have found that managers shy away from terminations for many reasons other than the lack of an at-will option: (1) they rarely get to replace the terminated employee in a timely fashion due to budget constraints, which means the employee's workload must now be shared among the good performers who remain; (2) even when replacements are brought in, they are often inexperienced, which requires a great deal of the manager's time in training the substitute; (3) terminations often upset those employees in the workgroup who remain because they are perceived as unfair, a threatening action, or the removal of a long-time friend; and (4) managers get little support or training to help them through a termination (MSPB 1999; OPM 1999). Thus, at-will options are unlikely to have their assumed effect. After all, if the manager gets promoted, the employee is someone else's problem.

As noted, many voters will be attracted to the at-will platform. Yet ask those same voters how happy they would be with giving government managers the unchecked right to throw away a functioning computer solely because the manager no longer liked it. Is there any doubt about the level of public outrage that would occur over the disposal of property? When the public views the employee as its employee (or, crassly, its property) in whom much has been invested, it is easy to anticipate their interest in ensuring that public resources are used wisely, not just at the whim of some other public employee.

Speaking as a labor negotiator with thirty years' experience, radical civil service change is always available to one party at a bargaining table if it is willing to offer other involved parties similar radical *improvements*. It need not even be a one-for-one exchange. But if civil service change advocates continue to design these radical changes in their faculty offices, on their consultant's conference table, at campaign headquarters, or even in the halls of the National Academy of Public Administration and similar organizations of no-longer-active-in-government stakeholders, they will accomplish little.

Commentary

Norma M. Riccucci

Condrey and Battaglio accurately observe at the state level that rather than civil service protections being the solution for improving government performance, they are routinely portrayed as problems diminishing government performance. Efforts to chip away at civil service protections at the federal level date back several decades and are, in fact, promulgated by the demonstration project provisions of the Civil Service Reform Act of 1978. Demonstration projects permit federal agencies to suspend Title V of the U.S. Code—which governs the federal civilian civil service—to explore new and improved approaches to federal personnel management. Likewise, the National Performance Review (NPR 1993, para. 3–4) explicitly attacked civil service protections, stating: "The Federal government's current personnel management 'system'… [is] process-driven; results are a by-product, not a measure of accountability."

More recently, the George W. Bush administration launched MaxHR (later called "Human Capital Operational Plan") and the National Security Personnel System (NSPS) as reform packages to overhaul the personnel systems in the Department of Homeland Security (DHS) and the Department of Defense (DOD), respectively. Under each, civil service rules and provisions that traditionally embraced employee protections would give way to ones that support performance and managerial flexibility and discretion. As Kearney and Hays (1998, 39) put it, "Although wrapped in a blanket of reform and bolstered by a plethora of positive motives, reinventing government's progress may bring with it a weakening of neutral competence, merit professionalism, and related values…."

Can these trends toward eroding public employee protections be halted or even reversed? Is there some tool or mechanism that could counteract the effects of radical civil service reform with respect to employee rights? One only need look at the experience of the Bush administration's efforts to overhaul the personnel systems in DHS and DOD to answer these questions. Both initiatives sought to provide agency leaders and managers with a great deal of discretion over human resources. The two most contentious reforms would have greatly altered collective bargaining rules and compensation. Public employee unions immediately raised objections and sought through court action to block implementation first of the DHS's proposed labor reforms. The regulations would have provided the DHS unilateral authority to negate otherwise lawful collective bargaining contracts.

The first lawsuit was filed in January 2005 by four major public employee unions—the National Treasury Employees Union, the American Federation of Government Employees, the National Association of Agriculture Employees, and the National Federation of Federal Employees. In August 2005, a federal district court judge for the District of Columbia ruled in *NTEU et al. v. Chertoff* (385 F. Supp. 2d 1) that the proposed labor relations rules of the DHS did not guarantee public employees their lawful bargaining rights and therefore rendered the rules invalid. The court stated that the unions' "collective bargaining would be on quicksand, as the Department would retain the right to change the underlying bases for the bargaining relationship and absolve itself of contract obligations while the Unions would be bound" (38). The court went on to say that "while DHS may be required to bargain in good faith, there is no effective way to hold it to that bargain. Under such circumstances, a deal is not a deal, a contract is not a contract, and the process of collective bargaining is a nullity" (41–42).

The court also struck down proposed DHS rules that would have interfered with the Merit System Protection Board's (MSPB) role of protecting public employees from merit abuses. The rules would have prevented the MSPB from altering or vacating DHS penalties imposed on employees for actions or behaviors that the DHS deemed improper or undesirable. The court also struck down DHS's proposed rules to weaken the responsibilities of the Federal Labor Relations Authority (FLRA), which serves as fact-finder and adjudicator in labor disputes in the federal government. The rules would have subsumed the FLRA's responsibilities under a newly appointed Homeland Security Labor Relations Board.

The DHS appealed, and in June 2006, the U.S. Court of Appeals for the District of Columbia unanimously upheld the district court ruling (*NTEU et al. v. Chertoff*, 452 F.3d 839 [D.C. Cir. 2006]). The three-judge panel, which included two Republican-appointed judges, went even further than the district court decision by ruling that DHS unlawfully limited the scope of employee bargaining. It ruled that "in no sense can such a limited scope of bargaining be viewed as consistent with the [Homeland Security] Act's mandate that DHS ensure collective bargaining rights for its employees" (844). Then, in a decisive victory for the unions, the administration indicated that it would not appeal the decision to the U.S. Supreme Court (Rutzick 2006b).

Despite the rulings in *Chertoff*, Pentagon officials attempted to push through proposed labor reforms at the DOD. Thirteen unions, including those previously mentioned and representing DOD civilian employees, prevailed at the district court level (see *AFGE v. Rumsfeld*, 422 F. Supp. 2d 16 [2006]). The DOD appealed, but in the interim, Congress blocked funding of the labor relations' aspects of NSPS for 2007 (Rutzick 2006a). The Pentagon, however, moved a number of nonbargaining personnel into a new pay-for-performance system.

As such, the clear lesson of these efforts is that any significant reform effort at the federal level must take into account such internal stakeholders as public employee unions. Reinvention efforts must also recognize the role of the courts, which are the ultimate enforcers of civil service rules and regulations. At the state level, no clear trends are discernible on the impact of unions and the courts on radical civil service reforms, so a robust research agenda exists for scholars.

Commentary

Frank J. Thompson

Condrey and Battaglio recount how Florida, Texas, and, above all, Georgia have adopted radical at-will employment systems. Insightful as their work is, two caveats deserve note. First, the Texas case is not about reform. In essence, the state fell so far behind in responding to one management reform cycle (the creation of a centralized merit system) that it wound up at the head of the pack in the next (reinvention and deregulation). Second, a fully developed concept of letting managers manage in the human resource arena would include not only at-will employment but other dimensions as well. Additional pertinent aspects of deregulation include the degree to which managers can (1) determine the pay of individual employees based on market and performance considerations, (2) freely reassign employees from one set of duties to another, and (3) modify working conditions without consulting union representatives. Ideally, we should measure each dimension and develop a summative deregulation score. This would facilitate the systematic comparison of states and expedite efforts to explain variations among them.

Condrey and Battaglio also uncover some tendency for older, more experienced workers to view radical deregulation less positively. But does this finding reflect a generational or maturational effect? If the former, it would mean that younger professionals bring a different mindset to employment that will essentially remain with them throughout their careers. It may be, however, that maturational processes are at play. Older, higher-salaried employees may feel that they have fewer career options if they suffer adverse outcomes under at-will systems.

The authors also offer support for the proposition that at-will employment systems buttress hierarchical accountability. They report that 47 percent of respondents feel the reform in Georgia heightened responsiveness "to the goals and priorities of agency administrators." Although the authors portray this as a limited effect, I find the result quite striking. Most administrative reforms would have a difficult time rallying close to a 50 percent endorsement for an impact of this kind. Condrey and Battaglio do not report how many human resource professionals believe that the reform weakened responsiveness (as distinct from having made no difference). But unless this number is much greater than I suspect, the data suggest that at-will systems heighten employee deference to agency executives.

This finding raises the issue of whether at-will systems open the door to enhanced gubernatorial control of personnel processes. The authors report that chief executives in Georgia and Texas do not appear to have used radical deregulation as a vehicle for partisan patronage. Although the authors are probably right to downplay concerns about patronage, two considerations deserve mention. First, one should be careful not to make too much of the Texas experience. Governors in that state are institutionally weak compared with their counterparts elsewhere. This elevates transaction costs for a governor who wants to reward the party faithful with state jobs. Second, even in the absence of well-organized patronage operations, radical deregulation will increase the vulnerability of agencies to interventions from governors and other political principals on matters of hiring and firing. Nearly all gubernatorial administrations face pressures to find jobs for campaign supporters who have marginal credentials for public employment. Governors may well resist these pressures most of the time. Merit systems can help them deflect these pressures; that is, "I'd like to help but my hands are tied."

Of course, governors vary in the attention they pay to public administration in general and human resource management in particular. Hays and Sowa (2006) conclude that Georgia has not had an activist governor who places a priority on using administrative agencies to achieve policy or partisan purposes. Florida's Jeb Bush presents a sharp contrast (Greenblatt 2006). Governor Bush's management agenda suggests the importance of viewing radical deregulation less as a platform for patronage and more as an avenue for governors to shape the outputs and outcomes of programs via the administrative process. Bush's success in subjecting the management echelons in Florida to at-will conditions will make it easier for his successors to pursue an "administrative governorship" where chief executives orchestrate substantial policy shifts without going through the legislative process.

Although radical human resource deregulation opens the door to greater administrative responsiveness to governors and their agency heads, it can erode accountability rooted in a respect for law. At-will employees will be in a weaker position to resist importuning by their superiors to stretch statutory and constitutional interpretations to the limits. Even more important, radical deregulation may impair the efficiency and effectiveness of state agencies. To the degree that at-will systems foster a sense of job insecurity among seasoned civil servants, they may become more reluctant to share their candid assessments with their superiors.

Other threats to performance revolve around the implications of radical deregulation for attracting and sustaining a high-quality workforce. Condrey and Battaglio report no cause for immediate alarm. But surveys should not only continue to target employees but also probe the image of the state government as an employer among the general public. Other research should focus on the quality of human capital (e.g., education and experience), turnover, vacancy rates, and the like. To the extent that state officials fail to compensate for less job security with other incentives that make government work attractive (e.g., pay, benefits, and mission), radical deregulation may well fuel a deterioration in workforce quality.

One of the major risks of radical civil service deregulation is its propensity to crowd out thinking about the substantial gap between policy promises and the resources provided to administrative agents to deliver on these promises. The exhortation to let managers manage via radical deregulation rarely addresses the importance of enabling managers to manage through adequate investments in managerial training and education. Some twenty years ago, the Winter Commission recommended that state and local governments set aside 3 percent of personnel costs for training. This remains a useful benchmark, one especially pertinent in states that have radically deregulated their personnel systems.

It will also be unfortunate if radical civil service reform and the excessive rhetoric that often accompanies it distract us from more promising reforms in the human resource arena. Many merit systems continue to place too many constraints on managers. Targeted incremental deregulation with respect to hiring, removal, and other personnel processes makes considerable sense in many contexts. Reforming personnel systems on the margins is a lot less exciting than throwing out current systems and fashioning new ones. It can be quotidian and even tedious. But incremental change of this kind will ultimately serve government better than the radical reforms described by Condrey and Battaglio.

Chapter 9

A Solution in Search of a Problem? Discrimination, Affirmative Action, and the New Governance[*]

Sally Coleman Selden

Contents

---

[*] Adapted from Selden, S. C. 2006. A solution in search of a problem? Discrimination, affirmative action, and the new public service. *Public Administration Review* 66(6): 911–923.

For over half a century, the United States has pursued a more diverse workforce—first, through an emphasis on equal opportunity and, later, through affirmative action (AA) policies. As Table 9.1 illustrates, these efforts have come through an amalgam of federal and state legislation, executive orders, administrative rules, and judicial decisions. However, this morphing from equal employment opportunity (EEO) to representation ignited one of the most heated and divisive controversies over social policy facing this nation today.

The battle has been led by passionate advocates and opponents (Holzer and Neumark 2000a; Jones 2005; Sabbagh 2003). Proponents of AA argue that remnants of race, ethnicity, and gender discrimination remain in hiring, promotion, and retention decisions in the public, private, and nonprofit sectors of this nation. Relaxing AA pressures would prevent future progress and undermine progress made in these areas over the past four decades. To opponents, however, AA can constitute reverse discrimination that is not needed, precisely because of the progress made to date in the antidiscrimination area. Others argue that premising AA on race and ethnicity makes little sense given the changing mixed-race and ethnicity composition of today's (and likely tomorrow's) citizenry in the United States. Relatedly, others in this "beyond-AA" camp argue that recruitment is not the problem; rather, the problem is retention of diverse workers. Diversity management is thus the key to growing, nurturing, and empowering a heterogeneous workforce.

Has AA's time passed—politically, substantively, in impact? This article focuses on what prior research tells us about three important dimensions of this question that beg understanding before an informed answer can be given. First, what does prior research tell us about where the public stands on AA? Second, what does it tell us about where AA presently stands in terms of state legislatures, the courts, and civil society? Third, as a guide to arguing the merits and demerits of AA in the future, what does prior research tell us about what AA has accomplished in light of its passive and active representation goals?

Divided It Falls?

What does prior research suggest about where Americans stand politically on the issue of AA?

Lesson 1: Citizens remain conflicted about AA, support for AA varies slightly across time and polls, and the results vary across time and by race.

Table 9.1 **Influential Equal Employment Opportunity and Affirmative Action Executive Orders, Statutes, and Referenda in the United States**

Expanding Equal Employment Opportunity and Affirmative Action	Year	Limiting Affirmative Action
Brown v. Board of Education	1954	
Executive Order 10925	1961	
Title VII of the Civil Rights Act	1964	
Executive Order 11246	1965	
Executive Order 11478	1969	
Department of Labor, Order Number 4	1970	
Griggs v. Duke Power Company	1971	
Equal Employment Opportunity Act Executive Order 11625	1972	
Regents of University of California v. Bakke	1977	*Regents of University of California v. Bakke*
Civil Service Reform Act	1978	
United Steelworkers of America, AFL-CIO-CLC v. Weber	1979	
Fullilove v. Klutznick	1980	Ronald Reagan elected president
	1984	*Firefighters Local Union Number 1784 v. Stotts*
	1986	*Wygant v. Jackson Board of Education*
Johnson v. Transportation Agency, Santa Clara County *United States v. Paradise*	1987	
	1989	*Richmond v. J.A. Croson Company*
Metro Broadcasting, Inc. v. FCC	1990	

Continued

Table 9.1 (*Continued*)   Influential Equal Employment Opportunity and Affirmative Action Executive Orders, Statutes, and Referenda in the United States

Expanding Equal Employment Opportunity and Affirmative Action	Year	Limiting Affirmative Action
United States v. Fordice	1992	
	1994	*Adarand Constructors, Inc. v. Peña*
		Podberesky v. Kirwan
	1996	*Hopwood v. University of Texas*
		California Proposition 209
	1998	Washington Initiative 200
	1999	"One Florida" (EO 99-201)
Grutter v. Bollinger	2003	*Gratz v. Bollinger*
	2006	Michigan Civil Rights Initiative

Survey results indicate that support for AA varies slightly across time and opinion polls (Jones 2005). A comparison of public opinion polls administered by CBS News and the Gallup Organization are illustrative. In 2003, CBS News found that 53 percent of respondents believed AA programs should be continued (CBS News Poll 2003). By 2006, 36 percent of persons surveyed believed that it should be continued, a decrease of 17 percent from 2003. In contrast, respondents to a 2005 annual Gallup survey of minority rights and relations were slightly more supportive of AA programs for racial minorities (50 percent) than opposed to such programs (42 percent). Moreover, between 2001 and 2005, the percentage of persons opposed to AA programs actually decreased, albeit marginally, from 44 percent to 42 percent (Jones 2005). And because the percentage of persons who wanted to see a decrease in AA programs fell from 37 percent in 1995 to 26 percent in 2003, Jack Ludwig (2003), director of research for Gallup Poll Social Audits, argued that the public was warming toward AA.

What has been consistent over the years, however, is an enduring racial gap in perceptions of AA, with minorities supporting AA by a margin of at least 20 percentage points in five annual CBS and Gallup surveys (CBS News Poll 2006; Jones 2005; Ludwig 2003). For example, a 2003 Gallup Poll revealed that African Americans and Hispanics were significantly more supportive of AA programs than non-Hispanic whites. In that survey, 70 percent of African American respondents and 63 percent of Hispanic respondents favored AA, whereas 44 percent of white respondents favored AA.

More in-depth exploration of this perceptual gap has led some to conclude that the differences in perspectives between African Americans and whites toward AA programs "likely stem from the belief among a majority of whites (59 percent) that blacks in this country have equal job opportunities with whites, while only 23 percent of blacks agree. Roughly three in four blacks believe that they do not have equal job opportunities in this country" (Jones 2005, 2). Moreover, the percentage of African Americans who believed that the government should make every effort to help blacks and other minorities increased from 59 percent to 67 percent between 1997 and 2003. The trend for white respondents in the CBS and Gallup surveys differed slightly in each, however, with the percentage supporting federal government efforts increasing from 34 percent in 1997 to 41 percent in 2001 but decreasing to 36 percent in 2003.

Affirmative Action on the Defensive: The View from the Courts, Legislatures, and Governors' Offices

Against this leitmotif of eroding public opinion support among large segments of the American public, and perhaps helping to coalesce it, recent years have seen a sustained attack on AA in Washington, DC, in the states, and in the courts.

Lesson 2: A narrowing of AA by the courts has been underway since the late 1980s but with some protections added in the higher education area.

At the federal level, the seeds of President Ronald Reagan's efforts to appoint federal judges "opposed to regulation in general and AA in particular" (Kelly and Dobbin 2001, 95) blossomed after Reagan left office (Kellough 1989; Naff 2004). Before then, and although many of the decisions were split, AA typically received (with few exceptions) the support of the Supreme Court (ibid.). For instance, the court ruled that colleges and universities were permitted to use race or ethnicity as a flexible factor in their admissions decisions. Likewise, public and private employers could voluntarily employ AA programs to address racial, ethnic, or gender imbalances in their workforces, while the federal government could require AA programs from employers receiving federal funding.

Since then, however, AA has been on the defensive in the federal courts. The Supreme Court's first major decision in this regard challenged the legal standing of AA programs at the state and local levels by requiring them to pass a more stringent level of scrutiny by the courts. In *Richmond v. J.A. Croson Co.* (488 U.S. 469

[1989]), the court ruled that the City of Richmond's 30 percent set-aside program for black-owned construction firms was an "unyielding racial quota." The court established that AA programs at the state and local levels could exist but had to show first that racial discrimination was pervasive throughout the industry.

In *Metro Broadcasting, Inc. v. FSS* (497 US 547 [1990]), the Supreme Court held that the minority preference policies of the Federal Communications Commission did not violate the equal protection clause of the Fifth Amendment. But in *Adarand Constructors, Inc. v. Pena* (513 U.S. 1012 [1994]), the court actually struck down its *Metro Broadcasting* decision and ruled that the strict standards established in *Croson* were the proper standards for examining federal set-aside programs. Although the court found that federal AA programs need to serve a "compelling governmental interest," the majority decision affirmed that AA may be justified in particular instances, such as when systematic discrimination exists. Importantly, the aforementioned rulings do not preclude local, state, and federal governments from using AA programs, but they do "raise the standards for their legal justification" (Holzer and Neumark 2000a, 491). In the wake of these decisions, the Clinton administration responded quickly, recognizing that "federal HRM affirmative action for minorities had become constitutionally questionable" (Naylor and Rosenbloom 2004, 151). Thus, although the *Adarand* decision pertained only to government contracting, the administration instructed all federal agencies and departments to apply the decision both to contracting and to employment (Naff 2004; Naylor and Rosenbloom 2004).

Moreover, two other important circuit court decisions called AA into question. In *Podberesky v. Kirwan* (38 F.3d 147 [1994]), the Fourth U.S. Circuit Court of Appeals ruled that the University of Maryland's Banneker scholarship program, which was limited to African Americans, was unconstitutional. The next year, the Fifth Circuit Court of Appeals' *Hopwood v. University of Texas* (518 U.S. 1033 [1996]) decision prohibited consideration of race or ethnicity in admissions decisions, even for the express purpose of creating a diverse student body. According to the court, diversity in higher education did not represent a compelling state interest (Springer 2006). The Fifth Circuit Court held that although addressing past discrimination was a compelling state interest, diversity in the system in general was not. The Supreme Court let the *Hopwood* decision stand without review. Granted, the Supreme Court has more recently ruled more positively on AA in higher education in *Gratz v. Regents of the University of Michigan* (539 U.S. 244 [2003]) and *Grutter v. Regents of the University of Michigan* (539 U.S. 306 [2003]). It did so, however, in ways decidedly more constraining than in the pre-Reagan era.

Lesson 3: Grassroots legislative actions, ballot initiatives, and executive orders threaten AA, but state legislators and governors are not without the tools to hold its demise at bay.

Prompted especially by the Fifth Circuit decision, grassroots anti-AA movements began growing in various states and produced legislative and gubernatorial initiatives. Some have prompted state-level efforts to curb AA through legislation, ballot initiatives, and executive orders (Americans for a Fair Chance 2005). Two states, California (Proposition 209) and Washington (I-200), passed citizen initiatives in 1996 and 1998, respectively, prohibiting state and local governments from discriminating against or granting preferential treatment to any individual or group based on race, sex, color, ethnicity, or national origin. Again, however, racial and ethnic disparities in the voting arose. Polling results suggested that 61 percent of white voters supported Proposition 209 compared with only 25 percent of African American voters and 28 percent of Hispanic voters (Hardy-Fanta 2000). Moreover, even when citizen initiatives have failed or not even reached the ballot, some governors have taken unilateral action to end, limit, or redefine AA. In Florida, for example, Governor Jeb Bush ended AA in the state's employment, contracting, and education systems by issuing Executive Order 99-201, titled the "One Florida Initiative" (U.S. Commission on Civil Rights 2000).

By the same token, however, supporters of AA have worked legislatively with sympathetic governors to limit the impact of anti-AA campaigns and court decisions. In response to the dismantling of AA in higher education admissions by the courts, for instance, legislatures in California, Florida, and Texas adopted "percentage plans" to address the issue of equal educational opportunity. Although these plans differ somewhat from each other, they each grant top high school graduating students admission to the state's university system. Adopted in response to the *Hopwood* decision, for example, the "Texas Ten Percent Plan" allows students in the top 10 percent of their graduating class admission into the University of Texas system. More narrowly, California adopted a plan to guarantee the top 4 percent of its public school graduating students admission to the University of California system (Springer 2006). Meanwhile, Florida's "Talented 20% Plan" allows the top 20 percent of its graduating high school seniors admission into one of the University of Florida's public institutions (Springer 2006).

Has Affirmative Action Attained Its Goals?

Although the majority of empirical research demonstrates the positive impact of AA policies on educational and employment opportunities for minorities and women (Chay 1998; GAO 1991; Goldstein and Smith 1976; Holzer and Neumark 2000a, 2000b; Kellough 1990a, 1990b; Leonard 1990; Naff 2001; Naylor and Rosenbloom 2004; Rodgers and Spriggs 1996), other studies raise questions about its true benefits (Bowen and Bok 1998; Datcher, Garman, and Garman 1993, 1995; Davidson and Lewis 1997; Kane 1998; Sander 2004; Vars and Bowen 1998). Some research shows progress on the critical pipeline dimension of educational opportunity. However, significantly less progress exists when it comes to other major goals such as hiring, equal pay, and the elimination of discrimination once minorities and women are hired. Consequently, future progress likely requires the kinds of "pressure of court decisions, legislation, executive action, and the power of examples in the public and private sector" that were so essential to the progress made since the 1960s (Clinton 1995).

Lesson 4: Substantial and important progress are being made when it comes to the critical area of educational opportunities, but the retention and academic performance measures of some minority students are disappointing, suggesting that different types of efforts are needed.

The impact of AA on educational opportunity has been extensively researched and is clear: more women and minorities are represented on college campuses and in professional programs today than prior to the use of AA (Stephanopoulos and Edley 1995). Studies examining the linkage between AA and student performance, however, are less compelling for minorities; on average, minority students do not perform as well as white students. On the other hand, women perform better academically than men (Berkner, Cuccaro-Alamin, and McCormick 1996; Bierman 2006; Clune, Nuñez, and Choy 2001).

In 1969, about 38 percent of women graduating from high school went to college, compared with 66.5 percent of women in 2003 (NCES 2004b). Between 1974 and 2003, U.S. Department of Education (2004a) data indicate that a larger percentage of graduating high school students across racial and ethnic groups went to college. Specifically, white enrollment rose from 47.8 to 66.2 percent of the available pool during that period, and African American enrollments rose from 32.6 to 57.5 percent. Hispanic enrollment improved only marginally, from 54.1 to 58.6 percent. Thus, the news—although positive—in terms of AA goals on this dimension is not all good. For example, over a thirty-year period, there was a slightly higher rate of growth of African Americans going to college (24.9 percent) than of white students (18.4 percent). But the rate of growth of Hispanics going to college during this same period was significantly lower (4.5 percent) than the growth rate of whites and African Americans. Still, minority students compose a much higher percentage of college and university students today. In 2002, 29.4 percent of undergraduate students were minorities, compared with 15.4 percent in 1976 (NCES 2004d).

Prior research also finds that women and minorities have increased their representation in graduate and professional schools in the last twenty-five years (NCES 2004d, 2004e). In 1969, women represented 38 percent of graduate school enrollments, compared with 58 percent of graduate students in 2003 (NCES 2004c). Between 1976 and 1977, whites received 91.7 percent of first-professional degrees awarded, African Americans 4 percent, Hispanics 1.7 percent, Asians 1.6 percent, and Native Americans 0.3 percent. By 2002–03, however, minorities were receiving a larger percentage of first-professional degrees conferred: African Americans received 7.1 percent, Hispanics 5.1 percent, Asians 12.1 percent, and Native Americans 0.7 percent (NCES 2004e). The progress of women in professional programs is even more impressive. Whereas women received 19 percent of first-professional degrees issued in 1976–77, they received 48 percent of first-professional degrees awarded in 2002–03 (NCES 2004e). Likewise, in 1955–56, women received only 1.1 percent, 5.1 percent, and 3.9 percent of dental, medical, and law degrees conferred, respectively. By 2002–03, however, women received 38.9 percent, 45.3 percent, and 49 percent of dental, medical, and law degrees awarded, respectively, in these fields.

Controversy nonetheless exists over what these gains mean in terms of academic performance (e.g., Bowen and Bok 1998; Datcher et al. 1993, 1995; Davidson and Lewis 1997; Kane 1998; Sander 2004; Vars and Bowen 1998). For example, a recent article by Sander raises and validates the concerns of many AA critics: AA results in minority applicants who are less qualified being accepted to more elite universities. Assessing grade point averages (GPAs) and graduation rates, Sander argues that many African American students struggle in law school academically and fail at higher rates than their white counterparts. Without AA, Sander contends that African American law students would likely perform better, because they would be admitted to less selective programs that better fit their entry credentials (e.g., GPAs and LSAT scores). In turn, better academic performance would lead to better job placement, because many law firms weigh heavily a law student's class ranking in their interview process (Sander 2004). Similarly, in a study of undergraduate performance and earnings, Datcher, Garman, and Garman (1995) find that, at the undergraduate level, African Americans had lower GPAs and graduation rates. However, they find that African Americans were not necessarily worse off because they attended a more selective institution. Still, the authors argue that the gains African Americans receive from attending the more selective colleges are not as significant as those observed for white students.

Lesson 5: The pipeline arguments of AA opponents are not as compelling as they suggest and may not survive a relaxation of pressure on employers to hire a diverse workforce.

A number of studies have examined the effects of AA on the employment of minorities and women across different sectors (Ashenfelter and Heckman 1976; Chay 1998; GAO 1991; Goldstein and Smith 1976; Holzer and Neumark 2000a, 2000b; Kellough 1990a, 1990b; Leonard 1984, 1990; Naff 2001; Naylor and Rosenbloom 2004; Rodgers and Spriggs 1996; Stephanopoulos and Edley 1995).

Many studies used the Employer Information EEO-1 survey data collected by the Equal Employment Opportunity Commission (EEOC) to examine the impact of AA as established by Executive Order 11246 on minority and female employment shares for federal contractors and noncontractors in the private sector. Leonard (1990), for instance, finds that AA is effective because employment gains by women and minorities for the period from 1974 to 1980 rose more significantly for federal contractors than for noncontractors. He also found that the most important predictor of employment gains for minorities and women is enforcement or compliance reviews. Overall, studies using EEO-1 data have shown that AA has significantly and positively impacted the minority employment share in the private sector, particularly in unskilled positions.

Minorities and women, however, are still substantially underrepresented in chief executive officer (CEO) posts compared with their participation in the civilian labor force, with the gap highest for women, African Americans, and Hispanics. According to *Fortune* magazine, in 1992, only three of the Fortune 500 companies were led by African American CEOs (Daniels 2002; editors' note: In 2012, the number rose to twelve). What might help account for this? Some prior research suggests that a lack of representation of minorities and women on boards of directors does not help this situation. In a study of Fortune 100 companies, researchers found that women held 16.9 percent of board seats and minorities held 14.9 percent (Alliance for Board Diversity 2005). Hispanics held only 3.9 percent of board seats. Thus, one approach for remedying the situation is to move aggressively to diversify corporate boards so that they might engage in the active representation needed to foster diversity at all levels of these organizations.

A number of studies also have examined the demographic composition of local, state, and federal workforces (e.g., Cayer and Sigelman 1980; Dometrius 1984; GAO 1991; Gibson and Yeager 1975; Grabosky and Rosenbloom 1975; Hellriegel and Short 1972; Kellough 1990a; Kim 1993; Lewis 1988; McCabe and Stream 2000; Nachmias and Rosenbloom 1973; OPM 2006; Page 1994; Rose and Chia 1978). Unlike studies of federal contractors and noncontractors, however, studies of public organizations cannot isolate the effects of AA from broader civil rights enforcement on the representation of minorities and women. Still, one can discern important trends that are not as persistently promising in showing the kinds of impacts that proponents of AA would hope. They indicate that strong political pressures from Washington may be necessary but hardly sufficient for sustained progress on diversity.

Although earlier studies suggest that African American representation improved significantly into the 1960s and 1970s (Grabosky and Rosenbloom 1975; Hellriegel and Short 1972), other studies indicate that progress slowed at all governmental levels in the 1980s during the Reagan administration (Page 1994). Women and some minorities are today better represented in terms of overall presence in public organizations, but many studies find that they are overrepresented in the lower echelons of bureaucracies and underrepresented in the managerial and executive ranks (Baldwin 1996; Dometrius 1984; GAO 1991; Greene, Selden, and Brewer 2001; Kim 1993;

OPM 2006). In 2006, however, the U.S. Office of Personnel Management reported that minorities were better represented in the federal than in the civilian labor force. The only exception to this was the representation of Hispanics. This finding is similar to research on state governments, where studies have found that Hispanics are grossly underrepresented in state bureaucracies (Greene et al. 2001). Moreover, the disparity between the presence of minorities and women in management and non-management positions in the federal government still remains.

Holzer and Neumark (2000b) employ a different methodology to examine the impact of AA in the private sector. Instead of relying on EEO-1 data or public sector workforce statistics, they survey an array of firms regarding their use of different AA practices and focus on the pipeline activities of recruiting and hiring. Their study of 3,200 employers in four metropolitan areas find that 56 percent of employers used AA in recruiting, compared with 42 percent in hiring. What is more, they find that employers using AA "recruit[ed] applicants much more extensively and screen[ed] them more intensively; rel[ied] more heavily on formal rather than informal means of evaluation (both before and after a worker is hired) and [were] more likely to provide training to candidates they do hire." Firms using AA as part of their recruitment process also received more applications from and hired more women and minorities than firms not doing so.

There is some additional and promising news for AA proponents emanating from the private sector, especially when it comes to the largest corporations in America. Despite ongoing debates about the fairness, impact, and legalities of AA, many employers are shifting their focus to workforce diversity. Some organizations, such as Genworth Financial and IBM (plus the state of New Jersey in the public sector), have committed extensive resources to creating cultures that value and encourage diversity. Using diversity management, these companies have introduced some new practices, including cultural audits that identify internal barriers inhibiting diversity.

Lesson 6: The durability of intentional or unintentional pay discrimination remains high, despite progress in this area.

A number of studies have examined the wages, earnings, and salaries of women and minorities (e.g., Aher and Popkin 1984; Barbezat 1989; Blau 1998; Blau and Kahn 1997; GAO 2003b; Holzer and Neumark 2000a; Katz, Stern, and Fader 2005; Lewis 1998; Stanley and Jarrell 1998; Stephanopoulos and Edley 1995; Willoughby 1991). The consensus across these studies is that although wages have improved, the wage gap between white males and both minorities and women persists, though it is lower in the public sector than in the private sector (Blau 1998; Blau and Kahn 1997; Holzer and Neumark 2000b; Lewis 1996; Smith 1976; Sorensen 1989; Stanley and Jarrell 1998; Stephanopoulos and Edley 1995). For example, in 2004, women working full-time earned 76.5 percent (median salary $31,223) of the annual wages earned by white men (median salary $40,798) at the same education level (Institute for Women's Policy Research 2006).

Moreover, Waldfogel (1998) find that the most significant wage gap exists between men and women with children. It must also be said that although wage gaps often are interpreted as discrimination, some labor economists feel that the omission of factors such as unobserved skills may account for a number of the disparities (e.g., Becker 1985; GAO 2003b). And although Lewis (1985) find that a significant portion of the wage gap between women and men in federal service could be explained by occupational segregation, the U.S. General Accounting Office (GAO 2003b) find that it was unable to explain all of the earnings differences between men and women, even when controlling for work patterns. Might performance explain these differentials? Not if a wage study of manufacturing employees by Hellerstein, Neumark, and Troske (1999) is considered. They find that female employees earned lower wages compared with their male counterparts but exhibited comparable levels of productivity. Indeed, other research concludes that "employer discrimination continues to play a role in generating different labor market outcomes by race and sex" (Holzer and Neumark 2000a, 499).

Lesson 7: The idea that public or business organizations will be more aggressive in pursuing diversity because of profits in global markets or for foreign policy reasons alone is belied by the extent to which employment discrimination still persists.

Although some encouraging news about public and private sector efforts has been reported above, so have other disturbing trends. Consequently, no one should be sanguine about the prospects for continued progress in either the private or public sector absent continued external pressures. In addition to the research already mentioned, for example, a variety of other studies have documented evidence suggesting that women and minorities are subject to labor market discrimination (for examples, see Darity and Mason 1998; Heckman 1998; Kolpin and Singell 1996; Naff 2001; Stephanopoulos and Edley 1995). Moreover, although the EEOC investigates charges of employment discrimination in public and private organizations and litigates cases that are not resolved or deferred to states according to state statutes, their reports and the research informed by them may be only the tip of the iceberg.

The EEOC, after all, is often and rightly criticized as being slow in its processing of EEO complaints (Dodge 1997; GAO 2005), mostly because its enforcement tasks have expanded without anywhere near a commensurate increase in investigative staff (Dodge 1997). Granted, between fiscal years 2001 and 2005, the total number of discrimination charges filed with the EEOC decreased from 80,840 to 75,428, or by 6.7

percent (EEOC 2006). However, although the reported incidence of discrimination may have slowed in the last three years, staffing levels at the EEOC during this four-year period have fallen by 19 percent, almost triple the reduction observed in complaints filed with the EEOC. Moreover, even if the number of complaints is declining, the EEOC received 19,024 complaints against the federal government itself alleging employment discrimination (EEOC 2004). In the process, the number of national origin–based and gender-based discrimination charges increased between fiscal years 1992 and 2005, while the number of race-based discrimination charges dropped.

A recent Gallup Poll also suggests that actual EEOC discrimination filings may underestimate the magnitude of the problem (EEOC 2005). In 2005, nearly 15 percent of U.S. workers surveyed perceived that they had faced some type of employment discrimination or had been treated unfairly. Interestingly, the perceptions of discriminatory treatment at work varied by group, but this time with Asian and African American workers reporting higher levels of perceived discrimination. A full 31 percent of Asians surveyed reported incidents of discrimination, compared with 26 percent of African Americans, 18 percent of Hispanics, 22 percent of white women, and 3 percent of white men (EEOC 2005).

Lesson 8: Mixed evidence, especially regarding women, suggests that active representation is overall a byproduct of diversity in public agencies.

Why does all this matter? Passive representation in public, private, and non-profit organizations is important as a ladder of opportunity and symbol of career mobility. Moreover, although the evidence is a little mixed, particularly for women, on the whole, studies show that passive representation in public organizations—such as the EEOC, the Farmers Home Administration, and schools—leads to policy outcomes that benefit represented groups (e.g., Hindera 1993a, 1993b; Meier 1993; Meier and Stewart 1992; Selden 1997).

Some studies have shown that this type of active representation is more likely to occur in the lower echelons of organizations, where representation of those groups is higher (Meier 1993; Selden 1997). Research also has shown that representation of minorities makes a real difference in how services are delivered and how program resources are allocated, but its ultimate impact on organizational performance is not as well documented (e.g., Andrews et al. 2005; Coleman 1999; Hindera 1993a, 1993b; Hindera and Young 1998; Meier 1993; Meier and Nicholson-Crotty 2006; Meier and Stewart 1992; Selden 1997). For example, Meier and Stewart (1992) find that schools with more African American teachers disciplined African Americans less often, placed fewer African American students in educable mentally retarded classes, and identified more African American students as gifted.

Though several studies have not found a linkage between active and passive representation for women (Meier, Pennington, and Eller 2005; Selden 1997), Meier and Nicholson-Crotty (2006) find evidence that police departments with more women police officers were more effective at getting women to report sexual assaults and at gaining convictions for those crimes. Prior research also suggests that an effective means of ensuring that minority and female interests are represented in administrative decision-making processes is to employ minorities and women. Still, a recent study by Meier, Pennington, and Eller (2005) is less positive; active representation of African Americans in the EEOC itself is declining, with no evidence of a linkage between passive and active representation for women in the EEOC.

Why the variation in linkages? Prior research suggests that the representation linkage is more likely under certain conditions and is enabled by particular factors, including institutional constraints, organizational socialization, perceived administrative roles, policy context, and strategy (Andrews et al. 2005; Brudney, Hebert, and Wright 2000; Dolan 2002; Keiser et al. 2002; Kelly and Newman 2001; Saidel and Loscocco 2005; Selden 1997; Sowa and Selden 2003; Wilkins and Keiser 2006). Much remains to be done, however, before a clear understanding is available of the link between passive and active representation in all types of organizations across sectors in the new governance era.

Conclusion

The preceding review of prior public opinion, educational, employment, and discrimination research suggests that despite the gains achieved by women and minorities since the early 1960s, the challenges of eradicating discrimination in the workplace remain. The educational pipeline for increasing diversity in the workforce is more robust than in the past, but performance and graduation rates of minority students are disappointing. Likewise, although significant progress has been made in employment opportunities, women, Hispanics, and African Americans lag behind white men in their ability to reach the highest ranks of public and private organizations, in their capacity to receive comparable wages, and in their ability to work in a discrimination-free workplace. Thus, affirmative action's time—albeit perhaps in modified form—has not passed.

Commentary

Domonic A. Bearfield

Selden describes affirmative action quite accurately as being on the defense today in the United States. In addition, however, I would argue that changes in the way we understand the challenges facing the policy's traditional target groups also call its future into question—particularly as a recruiting tool used to increase representation in the new public service of networked governance (Light 1999a). In the past, terms used to describe one's gender (male/female), ethnicity (e.g., Irish/Hispanic), or race (e.g., black/white) designated what previously were assumed to be distinct, homogeneous populations. However, research confirms that problems previously believed to impact all people within a given group (e.g., barriers to college admission, employment, or home ownership) often are either limited to certain subgroups within the population or felt differentially by various subgroups (Wilson 1987, 1996). For example, the W. E. B. DuBois classic, *The Philadelphia Negro* (1899), first illuminated the class and cultural differences within this community. As McDaniel (1998, 175) notes, "Although African Americans share a common history and the burden of racism, they differ greatly in their wealth, income, and family structure. In DuBois's analysis, one could understand the African population only by recognizing its diversity." Moreover, as we learn more about how we see ourselves and how we are seen by others (Yanow 2003), the more apparent it becomes that the one-size-fits-all approach to affirmative action is inadequate.

To move beyond the one-size-fits-all approach, we must explore additional characteristics—such as class, ethnicity, culture, and gender—that exist within larger groups. When combined with one another, these characteristics reveal distinct subgroups with their own unique assets and challenges. Certainly, critics of affirmative action who either pose alternatives to it or mount uncompromising counteroffensives against it have seized upon these differences in target groups. They routinely charge that affirmative action policy ignores class differences that exist within historically disadvantaged groups (e.g., Wilson 1987). In response, Wilson calls for a race-neutral or class-based affirmative action approach that can be paired with traditional affirmative action initiatives. He contends that a class-based or race-neutral approach also would acknowledge that additional barriers posed by class deserve our attention during the hiring and promotion processes.

Affirmative action predicated solely on race also ignores a looming "supply-side" problem. During the 1990s, America experienced both an economic boom and a prison boom. Despite the economic boom, labor force participation rates for young black men, particularly those with low education, "continued their long secular decline" (Holzer, Offner, and Sorensen 2005, 329). And during this same period of employment decline for black males, the labor force participation rates for young black women with low education increased considerably, revealing something more than racial discrimination as the reason for the decline. More precisely, America sent a record number of people to prison during this era, including a disproportionate number of young black men (Holzer et al. 2005).

Western (2006, 16) notes that by "2000 ... almost 8 percent of African American men of working age were in prison or jail." He also estimates that black men were nearly twice as likely to go to prison (22.4 percent) than to receive a bachelor's degree (12.5 percent) between 1965 and 1969 (28–29). Although these estimates are more positive than the figures provided by Gates (1997) a few years previously, they still are quite chilling—especially when compared with the estimates of life chances for white men born between 1965 and 1969. Data projections indicate that only 3.2 percent of white men will have their lives interrupted by incarceration and that 31.6 percent of white men born during this period can expect to receive a bachelor's degree. In a different study, Bonczar and Beck (1997) estimate that 28.5 percent of black men can expect to go to either a state or federal prison during their lifetimes, compared with 3.6 percent of black women, 4 percent of white men, and 16 percent of Hispanic men. Unless these trends are ameliorated, young black men will continue to be absent from the pool of available workers. Consequently, it is unlikely that affirmative action alone will be enough to draw a significant subgroup of African American men into the workforce.

Several other developments suggest that all is not entirely lost. But they also suggest that traditional affirmative action initiatives must and can be combined with other policies to improve significantly the levels of representation of African American males in the public sector. Master's degrees in public administration and in the social services, for example, are rising in importance among African Americans. Of the master's degrees awarded in the 2003–04 academic year, public administration trailed only business and education as fields of study for this group. Also, of the degrees in public administration and social services awarded to African Americans during that academic year, 21 percent were awarded to African American men (Snyder, Tan, and Hoffman 2006). At the same time, African American men received 7 percent of all the bachelor's degrees awarded to men during the 1999–2000 academic year (ibid.). Although this figure is well below the percentage of African American men in the population, it marks a dramatic increase over the 1990–91 academic year, when black men accounted for only 4.9 percent of degrees awarded to men (ibid.).

Recognition of the class-based dimensions of the problem is also occurring. Naff (2001) notes that although federal agencies have mostly been focused on creating activities to foster diversity based on the traditional categories of race, gender, and age, several agencies also have started to address additional dimensions such as education and class. Similar recognition of the need for enhancing skill sets also is emerging. Holzer and Offner (2004), for example, argue that public policy, specifically welfare reform, helped to ease the transition of low-income, low-skilled black women into the workforce. Still, many of the policies affecting low-skilled black men in welfare reform and other areas were punitive. The creation of skill acquisition programs in high school to help young black men transition from school to full-time employment thus seems imperative.

Commentary

Lael R. Keiser

I do not necessarily disagree with Selden's lesson that "mixed evidence, especially regarding women, suggests that active representation is overall a byproduct of diversity in public agencies." However, I think the literature allows us to be much more specific and more consistent in its findings than she allows. Scholars consistently have found links between passive and active representation in a variety of policy areas.

In the field of education, for example, several studies have found that increasing passive representation of minorities or female teachers in unrepresented areas leads to educational improvement for minority and female students (Meier 1993; Meier and O'Toole 2006; Meier, Stewart, and England 1989; Pitts 2005). Researchers also have found that increasing African American representation in the Department of Agriculture's Farmers Home Administration and in the Equal Employment Opportunity Commission (EEOC) leads to better outcomes for African Americans (Selden, Brudney, and Kellough 1998). Furthermore, Wilkins and Keiser (2006) find that increasing female representation in child support offices leads to greater enforcement of cases where women, rather than the state, gain financially. Others have found that increasing the number of women in law enforcement agencies increases the reporting and conviction of sexual assault cases (Meier and Nicholson-Crotty 2006).

Selden also argues that a link between passive and active representation is more likely to occur in the lower echelons of organizations, where representation of those groups is higher. A closer reading of the literature shows, however, that both levels are important. For example, several studies find a link between passive and active representation at the upper levels of the bureaucracy (see Brudney, Hebert, and Wright 2000; Dolan 2000; Selden et al. 1998; Wilkins and Keiser 2006). Others find effects at both the upper and lower levels of the bureaucracy (Meier 1993; Meier and Stewart 1992; Pitts 2005), while still others find effects only at the lower levels (Keiser et al. 2002; Meier and O'Toole 2006). For those studies that test for effects at both levels, Pitts (2005) find more effects at the upper levels, Meier (1993) and Meier and Stewart (1992) find more effects at the lower level, and Wilkins and Keiser (2006) find effects only at the upper level. And regardless of organizational level, prior research has demonstrated that the link between passive and active representation is stronger when minorities or women have reached a critical mass (Kanter 1977; Meier 1993).

In terms of claims of reverse discrimination, a few studies suggest that increasing passive representation does not have negative consequences for nonminority groups. My colleagues and I (Keiser et al. 2002) find, for example, that both boys and girls perform better in math when school districts have more female math teachers, although girls benefit more. Similarly, Meier, Wrinkle, and Polinard (1999) find that both minority and nonminority students gain academically in the presence of a representative bureaucracy. In another study, my colleagues and I (Keiser et al. 2005) find that, with an increase in the passive representation of women, girls do not benefit relative to boys in school discipline.

In terms of the effects of affirmative action policy on agency performance, the evidence is more mixed. Diversity may have positive effects by enhancing creativity through the combination of a diverse set of opinions (Pitts 2005). Some research also finds positive effects on organizational performance in workgroups with diversity, although decision making may take longer (Bantel and Jackson 1989; Watson, Kumar, and Michaelson 1993). Still other research finds no effects (Kilduff, Angelmar, and Mehra 2000); others find that diversity increases emotional conflict (Pelled, Eisenhart, and Xin 1999), while still others find it decreases performance on cognitive tasks (Murnighan and Conlon 1991).

Practitioners also should be sensitive to an important distinction that Pitts (2005) makes between representation and diversity. Representation reflects how similar the demographic characteristics of bureaucrats are to the client population, whereas diversity reflects the heterogeneity of the bureaucracy regardless of the characteristics of the clientele. He finds that diversity among managers has no effect on performance, whereas representation among managers enhances performance. At the same time, others find no impact from diversity, but they do find a negative impact from representation when performance is measured by client satisfaction (Murnighan and Conlon 1991). Interestingly, however, when administrative organizational performance data are used as opposed to client surveys, representation has no effect. This suggests the possibility that clients may have negative feelings about making the bureaucracy more representative, even if it does not harm actual organizational effectiveness. Other studies show, however, that when measuring organizational performance by the satisfaction of minority groups rather than all clients, representation increases client satisfaction (Thielemann and Stewart 1996).

Commentary

Sharon H. Mastracci

I would argue that it is important to add the dimension of socioeconomic status—or class—more explicitly to Selden's examination of affirmative action policy. Given the trends that she identifies, beleaguered proponents of affirmative action would do well to reconceptualize the problem and reframe the promotion of their cause as one of class-based discrimination. This is true for several reasons. First, beginning with *Croson*, the Supreme Court has indicated that presuming that race is a proxy for class is not as accepted as it has been previously. Thus, no longer do proactive steps to improve the economic status of blacks and women in general necessarily serve a compelling societal interest.

Second, class is also an important focus when one sees social networks as key to job opportunities. For example, Arrow (1998) argues for a network approach to explaining workplace discrimination. Economic sociologists also use job search models that emphasize the importance of acquaintances, as opposed to close friends and family members, in providing information about a wider variety of job opportunities (Granovetter 1983; Lin 2001; Montgomery 1991, 1994; Rankin 2003).

Rankin, for example, examines the job search strategies of low-income women and finds that "women tend to end up in lower-wage, female-dominated occupations partly because their social networks are composed of greater numbers of women, family and kin, neighbors, and fewer employed members" (286). Drentea (1998) arrives at similar conclusions about women's job search patterns, and others find that blacks and Latinos follow these strategies as well (Elliott 1999; Holzer 1987; McGuire 2000). Moreover, even when gender and race intersect in the workplace, valuable information on how to perform well, who to know, and how to get ahead is found to be withheld from dissimilar coworkers to undermine efforts to diversify the workplace (Reskin and Bielby 2005).

Recognizing these realities would not diminish the importance of race, gender, and ethnicity, and it would keep the focus of policy discussions on economic mobility. What is more, a debate about economic mobility, rather than race, ethnicity, and gender per se, seems a more politically—and now judicially—advantageous agenda to pursue and defend. Emphasizing class status would put affirmative action opponents in the position of having to take a stand against upward economic mobility for all.

RECONCEPTUALIZ-ING INSTITUTIONS FOR NEW POLICY CHALLENGES

As noted in Section I, one of the major challenges facing societies today is discerning how best to deal administratively with wicked policy problems in an increasingly globalized, interconnected, economically competitive, and militarily dangerous world. These challenges, in turn, have led practitioners and researchers to think more closely about "institutions" rather than continue to embrace what Hjern and Porter (1981) famously labeled the "lonely organization" syndrome. Institutions are defined as comprising the rules, norms, values, cultures, and taken-for-granted behaviors of actors operating among fields of organizational actors dealing with specific policy problems. Perhaps nowhere do institutions, their cultures, and their inertia matter more than in three wicked problem areas: advancing economic development in a globalized economy, promoting humanitarian efforts and nation-building by the U.S. military and nongovernmental agencies (NGOs) in conflict-riven developing nations around the world, and adapting existing regulatory structures to deal with global climate change.

In terms of economic development, discerning what globalization means for state and local economic development strategies, structures, and policies remains a formidable governance challenge today. Two very different diagnoses and sets of recommendations for coping with globalization have attracted considerable attention in the popular media: one offered by journalist Thomas Friedman in his book,

The World Is Flat (2005), and the other offered by economic development specialist Richard Florida, author of *The Rise of the Creative Class* (2002). In light of economic development theories, Richard Feiock of Florida State University, Jae Moon of Yonsei University, and Hyung Jun Park of Sungkyunkwan University take stock of and ponder the implications of the Friedman–Florida debate for state and local administrators, elected officials, and stakeholders. Comparing, contrasting, and critiquing the theoretical roots and practical implications of the debate, the authors contend that a regional governance focus is best suited for coping with globalization, a focus that helps bridge the Friedman–Florida divide.

Responding to their arguments, William Lyons, chief policy officer and deputy to the mayor for the City of Knoxville, Tennessee, contests many of the points made by Florida and Friedman and offers examples of regional coordination efforts in eastern Tennessee. Proffering his experience as typical, he contests the conceptualization of the Friedman–Florida debate as two opposite poles on a continuum. Attracting the creative class is most likely a response to the community's citizenry for its own lifestyle purposes rather than an explicit economic development strategy. For Laura Reese, director of the Global Urban Studies Program at Michigan State University, prior research and experience illustrate the flaws in Florida's and Friedman's arguments, call into question the practicality of regional strategies such as Feiock and his colleagues offer, and emphasize what she calls "place luck" rather than strategy in attracting business. In particular, she points to a failure of researchers to link economic development empirically to the presence of a creative class and questions the feasibility of regional cooperation strategies that fail to account for race and the barriers it poses to coordination. John Morris of Old Dominion University and former city manager Douglas Watson of the University of Texas–Dallas also question on political grounds the practicality of regional efforts. Arguing that "coopertition" among cities is the rule rather than the exception, they argue that regional governance approaches fail to account for the very real incentives in place to promote a go-it-alone mentality by individual units of government.

Going-it-alone strategies also offer challenges, choices, and opportunities in conflict-prone areas for the U.S. military and NGOs pursuing peacekeeping and humanitarian missions. Over the past two decades, public administration and public management scholars have significantly increased their research focus on nonprofits and NGOs, cross-sectoral partnering, and (much less often) the U.S. military, but they have largely ignored the military–humanitarian nexus around the world. Nancy Roberts, professor of defense analysis at the Naval Postgraduate School, weighs in on this neglected issue. Integrating personal insight, on-the-ground perspectives, and theoretical acumen, Roberts offers a typology of the military–humanitarian nexus as a framework for thinking about these issues and for building collaboration across the sometimes bloody boundaries separating these institutions.

Reacting to her arguments, Robert "Robin" Dorff, research professor of national security affairs at the Strategic Studies Institute, finds great value in Roberts's work but offers important refinements to it. Finding value in her typology, he hastens to note that no clear dividing lines exist between the "battle space" and the "humanitarian space." At the same time, he argues that the perceptions that matter most are not those of the military or civilians toward each other but rather those of the combatants. He also contends that a structural solution to the problem may be necessary, but integrating multiple organizations in a strategically coherent manner is inherently constrained by the National Security Act of 1947. More positively, however, structural reform may not be necessary if the promise of communities of practice can be realized. He remains, nonetheless, pessimistic about resolving these issues soon.

Finally, efforts to reduce greenhouse gas emissions are falling far short of what a consensus of scientists argues is necessary to avoid potentially catastrophic increases in the mean global temperature. Consequently, attention has shifted toward understanding the vulnerability and adaptability of social and ecological systems to climate change in particular areas of the world. In the western United States and other semi-arid regions of the world, possibly the most immediate, direct impacts of climate change involve the availability of water resources. Scientific evidence suggests that the West is likely to become hotter and drier and will experience greater variability in precipitation. These changes will affect tens of millions of residents in western states and nearly every sector of the economy, especially agriculture, and will threaten their food, economic, and health security.

In their chapter, Edella Schlager of the University of Arizona and Tanya Heikkila of the University of Colorado–Denver cull lessons from the logic of common-pool resource (CPR) theory to assess the institutional barriers to adapting to climate change in the regions covered by interstate water compacts. They conclude that vulnerability and adaptive capacity are problematic but vary across compacts. Premised on these same principles, and incorporating case evidence from a prior fourteen-compact study funded by the National Science Foundation, Heikkila and Schlager recommend immediate attention to the problem by state legislatures, investments in transparent monitoring and conflict resolution processes, and coordination of water demand and supply-side strategies.

Elisabeth Graffy, a professor of practice at Arizona State University and a senior sustainability scientist in the Global Institute of Sustainability, reacts quite positively to Heikkila's and Schlager's analysis and arguments. Where she parts company, however, is over the framing of the issue, critiquing the authors for paying insufficient attention to the social construction of problems and the policy implications those "frames" will have on future vulnerability and adaptability of water policy in the West. The "high and dry" telling of the water scarcity story used by Schlager and Heikkila reveals strong managerial and scientific narratives and an absence of what she calls an "ecological" narrative. Doing so, she argues, creates a dysfunctional impression of insulation from ecological factors, which may be caused or at least compounded by an institutional design that appears to limit the scope of participation in collective choice (Heikkila, Schlager, and Davis 2011).

Promoting a "socioecological" management paradigm for addressing water issues, Graffy argues that "if recommendations to reopen and renegotiate allocation rules proactively do not fully account for the social risks of a lack of institutional change, they are unlikely to be adopted no matter how much biophysical risk they identify."

Chapter 10

Is the World "Flat" or "Spiky"? Rethinking the Governance Implications of Globalization for Economic Development*†

Richard C. Feiock, M. Jae Moon, and Hyung Jun Park

Contents

* Adapted from Feiock, R. C., M. J. Moon, and H. J. Park. 2008. Is the world "flat" or "spiky"? Rethinking the governance implications of globalization for economic development. *Public Administration Review* 68(1): 24–35.
† Recipient of the 2009 William and Frederick Mosher Award for Best Article by an Academician in *Public Administration Review*.

In his best-selling book, *The World Is Flat*, Thomas Friedman (2005) argues that the information age accompanying globalization has diminished the importance of location as a competitive edge in fostering economic growth. If Friedman is correct that the world is flat, American communities no longer have a great advantage in innovation. Technologies such as the Internet and wireless communication increasingly allow anyone, anywhere in the world, to be players in the global economy, particularly in places where wages for highly educated and skilled persons are lower. In these locales, a business-centered strategy for economic development makes sense—one wherein localities reduce the costs of doing business through subsidies and incentives for regulatory relief.

In contrast, Richard Florida, author of *The Rise of the Creative Class* (2002) and *The Flight of the Creative Class* (2005a, 2005b), argues that although globalization has exposed many regions to heightened competition, the world is far from flat. It is still quite mountainous, or "spiky," because it is full of clusters where location matters, most notably in cities. His data suggest that those cities doing better in a global economy are luring creative people to their environs by offering amenities (e.g., the arts) and cultural climates (e.g., a tolerance of diversity) that appeal to a creative class of young, upwardly and geographically mobile professionals who tend to stay single longer and look instead to the community. These localities have combinations of infrastructure, technology, specialty activities, entrepreneurial culture, human capital, and a quality of life that offer them competitive economic advantages over others. Cities thus "need a [friendly] 'people climate' even more than they need a [friendly] business climate" (2002, 283).

This chapter critically examines the Friedman–Florida debate and offers a quite different perspective and strategy for economic development in a global economy. After presenting their arguments in greater depth, we explore their continuities and discontinuities through four major pillars of economic development strategy in the

United States. We then argue that the true governance implications of Friedman's and Florida's work—a focus on regions—have gone unrecognized. The world is neither flat nor spiky. Instead, it is rough and uneven, marked by regional clusters that require intergovernmental coordination and regional governance strategies for successful economic development. We next illustrate how a regional governance perspective can become a bridge spanning Friedman's and Florida's perspectives. Finally, we review various strategies for overcoming the collective action problems inherent in building regional governance institutions. We do this by reviewing several lessons that policy makers should *not* draw from the perspectives covered in our article.

The Friedman–Florida Debate: Competing Visions of the Global Economic Development Landscape

The World Is Flat!

In *The World Is Flat*, Friedman argues that technology has made the world smaller and flatter by breaking down geographic, political, and other boundaries to information flow, international trade, and collaboration. Throughout the twentieth century, natural and political geography and the high costs of communication created "mountains and oceans" of worldwide barriers, making it difficult for people to work together. These provided a strategic advantage to nations, regions, and cities that could capitalize on transportation, communication, and political cost advantages. Thus, economic development strategies focused on such investments made sense for attracting businesses to their jurisdictions.

Friedman argues, however, that a series of events has converged that no longer makes geography a barrier to global commerce. The widespread availability of inexpensive computers, standardized file formats and transfer protocols, excess international fiber-optic cable capacity, outsourcing, and a handful of other trends have greatly leveled the international playing field. The dominant forces in this new flat world are not governments or corporations but individuals with good ideas, high skill levels, and access to capital, regardless of location, especially when the products of intellectual capital can move instantaneously around the globe. Concomitantly, repetitive tasks can now be done wherever costs are low and there are enough moderately skilled workers available. Moreover, in a flat world, locating a business depends far less than it used to on proximity to raw materials and physical access to consumer markets.

Friedman is certainly not alone in noting trends such as these. Like Friedman, others note that the economic vitality of U.S. cities and towns is challenged by rapid growth in global trade as well as the mobility of labor and capital across borders. This is especially true in manufacturing. American firms in labor-intensive, lower-productivity manufacturing—for example, textiles or auto parts—face stiff competition from foreign firms that use the same technology but have much lower labor costs. Similar effects occur in services such as data entry, software, and call centers, but impacts on manufacturing have garnered the most public attention. In response, many cities and towns have tried to overcome these globalization effects by offering a variety of tax incentives, deregulatory measures, subsidies, and infrastructure commitments to businesses they hope to retain or attract to their jurisdictions.

No, the World Is Spiky!

In contrast to the challenges that Friedman sees globalization posing for U.S. cities and localities, Florida sees no leveling of communities competing to retain and attract businesses for economic development. In his "spiky" world, globalization creates and sustains inequalities among communities. Although global competition is worldwide, only some places experience economic prosperity; others fall into economic valleys. Florida argues that traditional infrastructure tools—such as subsidies and regulatory relief for the wrong kinds of industries—may actually decrease the competitive power of cities and localities. More important, he contends, are what he calls the "people climate" rather than the more venerable "business climate" historically targeted by cities.

Enhancing the people climate means actively nurturing a community that embraces diversity (racial, gender, ethnic, and sexual preference) and that invests in sports and retail shopping complexes, the arts, urban parks, school systems, public safety, and bike trails. Why? These are desirable to young and mobile professionals who stay single longer and make up a significant proportion of the creative class needed in a postindustrial era. Florida questions why people who can work anywhere would move to, or stay in, a community with high taxes and poor-quality services and amenities.

Not unlike Friedman's arguments, Florida's also are not without precedent. For example, Florida's arguments share much in common with Tiebout's (1956) thesis that people vote with their feet on the cost and quality of public goods by moving to whatever community provides the bundle of services they prefer. Florida's quality-of-life factors certainly are at least partially determined by public service provision in areas such as transportation, health care, parks, recreational opportunities, public safety, and taxes. Likewise, although his claim is not novel that returns to human capital and entrepreneurial activity have become more important than physical capital in production, this insight is still important. Teske and his colleagues (1993) found, for example, that the market for local public goods is driven by a small set of affluent informed citizens. By analogy, if innovative and entrepreneurial people are mobile, what matters for economic development strategies is where higher proportions of talented people choose to locate.

To support his argument, Florida shows that many regions tend to attract highly educated workers and occupations and that wage premiums for highly educated workers have been surging in recent decades. Some cities attract this critical workforce through actively encouraging in-migration of creative types—including artists, gays, and techies—by removing discriminatory barriers and proactively promoting diversity and inclusiveness. The policy goal is to create safe, high-density, central-city neighborhoods characterized by a vibrant day- and nightlife. Moreover, the quantity and quality of education, public services, and constructed amenities are directly shaped by state and local governments.

Is There Anything New under the Sun?

Despite the seeming breadth of their analyses and the hype given to them in popular media outlets, both Friedman and Florida paint only a part of the economic development picture and provide a limited treatment of a complex phenomenon. To better understand this complexity, as well as the real contributions and implications of their ideas for economic development strategies in the United States, a review of four leading economic development and growth theories related to their work is useful. These are the comparative production factor advantage theory, institutional theory, human capital theory, and social capital theory. Table 10.1 summarizes how Friedman's and Florida's arguments build from and add to these theories.

Table 10.1   Four Theories of Economic Growth

Theories	Focus	Friedman	Florida
Comparative Advantage Theory	Resources	Low wages	Cultural wealth
Institutional Theory	Institutional transaction costs	Decreasing transaction costs from information and communications technologies International regimes	Reducing barriers to entry for creative-class workers
Human Capital Theory	Education and skills	Developing human capital through education	Attracting human capital through amenities and culture
Social Capital Theory	Trust, community, relationships	Technology-driven collaboration Personalization of distance relationships	Social capital, cultural capital, economic capital Weak-tie relationships

Comparative Production Factor Advantage

For most of the last century, economic growth theory emphasized relative production factor costs and comparative advantage created by differences in production and transaction costs. Geography, of course, creates natural advantages in production costs. Proximity to land, labor, raw materials, transportation lines, and markets for finished goods endows some places with a strategic advantage. Yet this advantage has become a less compelling factor today due to the development of transportation and communication technologies. Thus, even were the world not flat, some types of goods and services can be produced anywhere in the world, and proximity to factors of production is no longer strongly correlated with production quality or cost.

Florida builds on the comparative advantage approach in a more nuanced way. Some place-based factors no longer matter, he argues, but others matter more than ever. If production can be carried out anywhere as Friedman contends, then desirable place-based characteristics of communities and regions increase rather than decrease in importance. This, again, is not an entirely new insight; research on chief executive officers' considerations in business relocation decisions indicates the importance of cultural amenities and the quality of life that a community offers. What is different, however, is the centrality, sequence, and priority that Florida assigns to people-friendly climates. Business activity does not automatically attract workers to cities and localities. According to the sequence described by Florida, local governments must first take action to create livable urban environments valued by talented and creative people. These policies then induce creative-class workers to remain in or move to their cities, which then attract business and capital and produce economic growth.

Institutional Theory

Aspects and embellishments of institutional theory can also be found in both Friedman's and Florida's arguments. Nobel Prize-winning economist Douglass North (1990) describes institutions as the humanly devised constraints that structure human interaction. They consist of formal constraints (rules, laws, and constitutions), informal constraints (norms of behavior, conventions, and self-imposed codes of conduct), and their enforcement characteristics. Together, the institutions and technologies employed determine the transaction and transformation costs that add up to the costs of production.

Obviously, subnational governments play an important role in defining the rights, rules, organizations, and institutions that structure local economies, including property rights, governance mechanisms, financial resources, operational rules, and regulations. Among these, however, regulatory tools are unique in that they influence more than just the costs of production. In this vein, Denver Mayor John Hickenlooper (2005) warned that "local government cannot be an impediment to economic vitality," and he advocated cutting red tape in areas such as development permitting and building inspection. Relatedly, if future rights and regulations cannot be anticipated, local governments create perceptions of risky investment environments and increased capital costs (Clingermayer 1989). For example, recent research demonstrates that economic growth is enhanced when transaction costs are lessened by administrative arrangements that reduce uncertainty over property rights (Feiock and Stream 2001). Nor is the stringency of regulations affecting land-use decisions alone a burden; so, too, are long development reviews and uncertainty of approval (Jeong 2006).

Thus, reforms in regulatory processes that make property rights more secure and the future more predictable can provide a strategic advantage in development competition. Extending this logic to the international realm, Friedman describes China's decision to participate in the World Trade Organization as facilitating offshoring, outsourcing, and the flattening of the global economy. Both state and international initiatives such as these, in turn, have ripple effects on local economic development because of the mobility of labor and capital.

Institutions, of course, can be private as well as public. As an example, Friedman describes agreement on Internet protocols as one of the forces that flatten the world. Florida, however, elaborates and extends conventional applications of this concept to economic development by arguing that diversity is a key factor in enabling places to mobilize technology and talent. This can be seen as an institutional argument, because informal institutional arrangements that discriminate are believed to disadvantage a community systematically in the competition for talented creative people.

Human Capital Theory

Theories of endogenous economic growth also are notable in Florida's and Friedman's work, with Florida extending the insights of human capital theory beyond what is typically offered. As posited by human capital theory, long-term growth is a function of both technological and human capital development (Romer 1990). Enhancing a nation's knowledge and skill base leads to economic growth through development of new forms of technology and efficient and effective means of production. Moreover, although physical capital is subject to diminishing returns, the accumulation of human capital leads to increasing returns. Knowledge increases not only individuals' productivity but also the skill level and productivity of the whole work group (see Lucas 1988; Romer 1990).

It is also important to note that in endogenous growth models, an educated workforce plays a special role in determining the long-term rate of technological innovation and long-run growth. The greater the accumulation of human knowledge, the greater the long-range technological progress and productivity gain (Gould and Ruffin 1993). Consequently, government provision of education, training, research, and development influences returns on the factors of production. Public education reduces firm-level production costs and increases the net return to these same productive factors (Storm and Feiock 1999). Nor does the power of educational investment rest exclusively in expenditures for primary and secondary education. Recent marketplace shifts make it necessary for higher education institutions to play a more prominent role in the development and commercialization of new technologies.

Florida and Friedman also both recognize that technology has enabled more people to participate in the global economy. Friedman asserts a need to provide better education in science, technology, engineering, and math to ensure Americans are competent in advanced technologies, whether they are product- or service-oriented. Florida, however, concentrates on the environments that encourage this new class of creative and highly educated people to choose one location over another. His focus on talent is thus an extension of human capital theories of growth.

Although human capital is typically measured by education, Florida substitutes a measure of creative occupations as a measure of human capital, thus emphasizing current work over past educational achievements. Places are endowed with certain stocks of technology or talent, and these stocks account for different rates of innovation and growth. But human capital is different from more traditional factors of production, such as land or raw materials, because it is a flow, not a fixed, stock. Creative people are a highly mobile element of production that flows into and out of places. Thus, cities and localities that ignore or cannot meet the quality-of-life concerns of geographically mobile artists, gays, and techies in the creative class risk forfeiting the economic development game to their rivals.

Social Capital Theory

Finally, Florida's (more than Friedman's) analysis draws upon and extends contemporary theories of social capital as they relate to economic development. Opportunities for affiliation with like-minded and diverse others matter for economic development. Research by Coleman (1990) and Putnam (1993) previously linked the effective performance of economies and democratic governance to strong norms of interpersonal trust and civic community. In their view, building trust and consensual allocations of rights establishes norms valued by individuals (Coleman 1990, 300), norms that are key elements of commercial and employment transactions (Miller 1992). Moreover, activities and exchange that require agents to rely on the future performance of others can be accomplished with lower transaction costs in an environment of mutual trust where each actor's commitments are taken as credible and enduring. Conversely, a lack of norms of trust and voluntary cooperation drives up transaction costs and makes exchange more costly (North 1990). Cooperative norms also act as constraints on opportunism, leading individuals to contribute to the provision of public goods.

Several mechanisms link social capital and economic development. Institutional (Miller 1992; North 1990) and common-pool resource (Ostrom 1990) economics point, for example, to the critical role of trust, cooperation, and credible commitment for effective markets. Social capital may also effect economic development indirectly through its influences on government performance (Knack and Keefer 1997). Civic involvement also might provide a check on rent seeking (i.e., corruption) and the proliferation of socially inefficient public programs by helping citizens overcome collective action problems.

The question of how communities can enhance their stock of social capital to gain competitive advantage has attracted much attention from practitioners and researchers. Some scholars link human capital and social capital by arguing that civic education is critical to the development of norms of trust and cooperation (McGinn 1996). Putnam (1993) links social capital to participation in social organizations. By joining and participating in voluntary associations, citizens build norms and habits of behavior that foster effective collective action as they acquire knowledge, skills, attitudes, and behaviors that enhance self-governance. Putnam also posits that civic community determines both civic involvement and economic development.

Little effort has been made, however, to test theories about the relationship between social capital and economic development. In an analysis of Italian regions using data from the early 1900s to the 1980s, Putnam (1993) finds that civic involvement was strongly correlated with economic development. Conversely, a comparative study of civic community and economic development in the United States by Jennings and Haist (1998) finds little support for a positive relationship between organizational activity and development. Yet more support for this thesis comes from a cross-country study of social capital and economic development by Knack and Keefer (1997). Like Jennings and Haist, they find no positive relationship between organizational activity and economic performance. However, when they directly measure trust, civic cooperation, and confidence in government with survey data, they find a strong positive relationship between norms of trust and cooperation and economic growth.

Recent work at the local level also finds that development programs seeking to reduce inequality are effective in improving community-wide economic development (Tao and Feiock 1999). One explanation for this relationship is that reducing income inequality has resulted in social capital gains that translate into enhanced growth. A growing literature also points to the importance of face-to-face interactions and interpersonal networks for both the development of social capital (Ostrom 2005) and the formation of economic alliances that create strategic advantage (Gulati and Gargiulo 1999).

In these regards, Florida focuses on the broad relationship between culture and economic growth; this is a significant elaboration on social capital theory. He argues that culture operates by enabling and mobilizing, rather than constraining, the range of human creative possibilities. An expansive, open culture that does not discriminate on the basis of race, gender, ethnicity, or sexual preference allows people to validate their varied identities. It also unleashes human creative potential, thus spurring innovation, entrepreneurship, and economic development.

Missing Links: Thinking Regionally, Governing Proactively, Working Cooperatively

Although both Friedman and Florida attempt to explain great economic and social trends that shape current societies and their economic development prospects and strategies, they differ markedly in many respects. Summarized in Table 10.2, these differences include focus, major actors, movement/orientation, primary driving forces, linkages among different capitals (e.g., human and social), importance of place (geographic boundary), and the role of government and economic development professionals.

Friedman's focus is on globalization processes propelled by transnational corporations, while Florida pays most attention to the rising creative class in American communities and regions. This leads to different views on the direction and nature of society's trajectory, creating a kind of chicken-and-egg dilemma. The basis of Friedman's framework for understanding globalization is that connectedness, outsourcing, and borderless movements of human and economic "capitals" propel the process of international division of labor. In contrast, Florida argues that the concentrating or clustering of the creative class within a particular geographical boundary is an essential phenomenon for economic development. Friedman seems to view the supremacy of human capital in terms of skills and wages as primary assets that engage a society with the global economy and then produce economic capital and possibly cultural enrichment. However, Florida suggests that cultural wealth needs to come first to draw creative-class members, who later become the engine of economic growth.

The authors also differ over the importance of "place" (or location) and the role of government. Due to the emphasis on globalization and borderless outsourcing by multinational corporations, Friedman suggests that place becomes a less important factor for productivity and economic growth. But Florida views place as central for understanding the role of the creative class. What both do share, however, is a constrained view of the role of governance in economic development. Friedman gives a limited role to government in the area of education, primarily from a national level. Florida offers more roles for government (e.g., in culture-based urban revitalization, economic growth, and education), primarily at the local level. He describes the rise of the creative class in terms of regional forces, patterns, and trends. The unit of analysis then shifts from regions to cities in discussing policy prescriptions to develop a friendly "people climate" for attracting and retaining the creative class. This reflects the reality of fragmented local political authority in the United States.

Consequently, both authors pay insufficient attention to the role of *regions* and *regional governance* in promoting economic development. Metropolitan regions now are central to economic development in a globalized world. This is the case as regions become "clusters" of agglomerated industries. In the process, however, collective action problems arise among decentralized governmental authorities still seeking to create competitive economic advantage over each other. Thus, the world is metaphorically rough and uneven ("clustered") rather than flat or spiky.

As typically conceived, regionalism as a development approach is distinctive. It encompasses the role of industry-specific regional clusters and the provision of regional public goods and infrastructure as necessary for development (Feiock 2004). But although regionalism is a distinct approach to economic development, we argue that it can also be a *bridge* or *link* between the global perspective of Friedman and the local perspective of Florida on globalization and what implications globalization holds for economic growth strategies in the United States. Returning to Table 10.2, readers can appreciate this point by comparing a regional governance approach, introduced elsewhere by Feiock (2007), with Friedman's and Florida's approaches.

Toward a Regional Governance Perspective

Turning to the specifics of this comparison, Friedman focuses on global competition where the important actors are entrepreneurial individuals, firms, and nation states. Florida acknowledges the importance of regions and international competition, but his policy focus is on competition among American cities to keep and attract creative-class workers. Instead, a regional governance approach seeks to align political and economic boundaries. Metropolitan regions are the building blocks of local, national, and global economies. Economists believe that metropolitan areas constitute coherent and at least partially integrated areas large enough to achieve economies of scale (Faruqee et al. 2006; Porter 2000). Yet metropolitan regions are also small enough to allow businesses to create working relationships and develop trust among partners that are difficult to achieve on a global, national, or state level.

Friedman also sees economic activity as shaped and driven by network connections to entities (firms, governments, systems of regulation, and populations) that do not co-locate and that may locate outside any one metropolitan area. Cities and regions are merely local nodes within global webs. Agglomerative forces are not irrelevant. However, they coexist in dynamic tension with technological and organizational innovations that facilitate relationships at a distance. In contrast, a regional perspective views trust as built through proximity and repeated interaction, which then stimulates collaboration, new technologies, and innovation.

It is also well established that firms and workers often find one another through the intersection of their regional social networks (Granovetter 1985). North Carolina's Research Triangle and California's Silicon Valley are prominent examples of face-to-face interactions where network-based trust stimulated growth and innovations (Dreier, Mollenkopf, and Swanstrom 2001; Orfield 1997; Pastor et al. 2000; Pierce 1993; Porter 2000). Moreover, the tendency of firms to locate near one another produces regional specialization that fosters efficiency and innovation through the mix of competitive and cooperative relationships among firms, local institutions, and local governments.

Table 10.2 Comparison of Friedman's, Florida's, and Feiock's Frames

Dimension	Friedman	Florida	Feiock
Focus	Globalization	Localization	Regional governance
Imperative	Economic imperative	Sociocultural imperative	Administrative imperative
Main Actor	Multinational corporations (e.g., IBM, Microsoft)	Creative class (creative core and creative professionals)	Local governments
Movement/Orientation	Connecting Borderless outsourcing Convergence (flattening)	Concentrating and bounded clustering Divergence (spikiness)	Coordination and collaboration Agglomeration Regional governance
Driving Forces	Development of information and communication technologies Human capital with comparative advantage of wage and skill International division of labor	Emergence of creative class Human capital with comparative advantage of creativity	Economy of scale for public services Interjurisdictional collaboration Industry clusters

	Human capital (comparative advantage in skills and wage) • Economic capital • Cultural capital	Cultural capital • Human capital (comparative advantage in creativity) • Economic capital	Administrative capital • Economic capital
Capital Linkages			
Importance of Place	Low	High	Medium/High (distance among local government matters)
Role of Government	Limited (to education)	Medium/High	High
Context	Competition among nations	Competition among regions and cities	Competition among regions and collaboration within regions
Policy Implication	Education-focused economic development	Culture-based economic revitalization	Regional governance and development partnerships

Toward Regional Governance Tools?

As noted, conventional economic development strategies have focused on building better business climates. In the process of offering various business incentives, competition among state and local governments operates like an economic market. Rather than functioning in a perfectly operating global market for jobs and new development, however, local governments operate in a quasi-market that is subject to market failures and driven by political, not just economic, considerations (Feiock 2002). As such, we agree with Friedman and Florida that the flattening of the world and the rise of the creative class have important implications for economic development strategies. But in contrast to them, we believe that local officials need to develop the regional institutions to mobilize physical, human, and social capital to enhance their economic position. They must then direct local government programs and fiscal policies to attract or produce that environment.

In *City Limits*, Peterson (1981) contends that the critical pool of labor for cities to capture is affluent taxpayers who will directly enhance the revenue-acquiring capacity of city governments. Reflective of Tiebout's (1956) hypothesis, Peterson also argues that local governments seek to improve their market position and attractiveness as a locale for economic activity through policies that maximize the economic capacity of land, labor, and capital. Because land is fixed at the local level, local government strategies are confined to creating an institutional environment that promotes growth through land-use regulation and other institutions. Because labor and capital are not fixed at the local level, local governments seek to develop them internally or compete in a political market with each other to acquire desirable labor and capital through services, incentives, and inducements.

Florida builds on this work but narrows its target labor pool and reverses the causal mechanism between labor and capital. To him, the critical pool of labor is highly educated, young, and innovative people who indirectly enhance the economic position of a city by attracting technology and innovation-focused businesses, rather than vice versa. Moreover, although Peterson (1981) also argues that progressive or redistributive policies have pushed out affluent taxpayers, Florida claims that this critical labor force of educated, young, technologically savvy, and innovative persons is attracted to cities that offer a mix of arts and cultural amenities. All this, however, may mean higher rather than lower taxes.

We argue that a regional governance perspective bridges these approaches. Human capital is particularly productive when deployed in dense urban environments where the interaction of knowledge workers generates spillovers. Consequently, firms are more dependent on regional labor pools, whereas workers are attracted by networks of jobs and occupations rather than by specific firms. Prior research also suggests that investments in the physical infrastructure and human capital of regions significantly affect economic development and agglomeration economies, especially in information and innovation-based industries (Dahlenberg, Partridge, and Rickman 1998).

Economic development organizations, administrators, and institutions also need to move beyond "city limits" and coordinate regional networks of local governments and other actors. The difficulty is that in providing infrastructure and public goods at a regional level, network collaboration among local governments and private actors is critical. Coordination among local governments is inherently challenging, however, because information, agency cost, and division-of-gains problems typically pose barriers to joint action. Incomplete information and differences in information levels frequently prevent governments from recognizing the potential gains from partnering. They also increase concerns about the motivations or trustworthiness of potential partners, because actors suspect each other of seeking to gain a strategic advantage. Agency costs arise if the preferences of public officials negotiating development agreements depart from the preferences of the citizens they represent, and bargaining and division problems frequently impede regional strategies. Even if everyone in the region gains, agreement may not be reached if the parties cannot settle on how to divide the economic gains (Carr and LeRoux 2005).

Nevertheless, theoretical and empirical work demonstrates that local governments can overcome transaction cost barriers to promote cooperation (Feiock 2004, 2007; Feiock, Park, and Steinacker 2007; Park and Feiock 2006; Parks and Oakerson 1993). Standard solutions focus on establishing positive reputations, repeating interactions among participants, making credible commitments, creating compatible incentive structures, and linking issues (Dixit 1996; Heckathorn and Maser 1987). And when it comes to regional economic development, the conditions for these collective action problem solutions can be found in various formal and informal networks that link communities in a region (Feiock 2007). Existing agreements among the parties increase the likelihood of future cooperative action by reducing information and enforcement-related transaction costs. Moreover, existing networks add information beyond that found in the simple dyadic (one-to-one) relationship between contracting local government units. If each organization also participates in related agreements with other local governments, the ensuing series of dyadic relationships evolves into a regional network.

Over time, these embedded relationships capture each participant's reputation for reliability and competency (Gulati and Gargiulo 1999). Cities choose partners for new collaborative ventures on the basis of their direct prior experience with other governments as well as their indirect knowledge of other units through common third parties in the network (Granovetter 1985). The common party in effect vouches for the government units that have not had direct experience with each other. As the network grows more extensive, information about all participants increases, because members will have at least indirect information about competency and past performances of other government units.

Regional intergovernmental networks also increase the credibility of any commitments made by transforming short-term relationships into repeated ones and linking participants across policy domains. Increased in the process are opportunities for punishment if a city engages in opportunistic behavior in any of the regional interactions. A highly clustered, dense network structure also contributes to building social capital within regions by providing extensive monitoring mechanisms and by facilitating development of mutual reciprocity, trust, and conformance to the rules of the game (Coleman 1990). Regional strategies can also streamline the regulatory and development approval process, thus reducing transaction costs for firms needing development approvals from multiple agencies (Feiock and Jeong 2002).

When they occur, regional economic development partnerships become "alliance[s] formed by local governments, often with the help of private sector firms and nonprofit organizations, which ha[ve] a mission of enhancing the economy of a multi-jurisdictional area" (Olberding 2002, 253). As Putnam (1995) argues, participation by community leaders in business and civic networks increases collaboration and reduces mistrust among those leaders when they interact in the public policy arena. Moreover, regional reform has evolved in places into partnerships that both coordinate and support marketing and recruitment efforts as well as impose constraints on member governments (Feiock, Tao, and Johnson 2004; Olberding 2002; Park and Feiock 2006). For example, thirty-two mayors in the Denver area recently collaborated on what the city's mayor termed the "most ambitious transit initiative in the country" (Hickenlooper 2005). Prior research also suggests that innovation, research and technology transfers, and job searches are more efficient when embedded in social networks (Weissbourd and Berry 2004).

Learning the Right Lessons

Understanding the mechanisms by which growth occurs is fundamental to promoting and researching economic development. Yet economic growth is a complex phenomenon, and Friedman's, Florida's, or our own integrative prescriptions should not be interpreted as the basis for simplistic or misguided policy prescriptions. Culture-based urban regeneration projects aimed at rediscovering heritage, promoting environmental sustainability, attracting cultural workers and artists, and creating cultural infrastructure are sometimes good examples of what not to do, as are the efforts of some cities to build collaborative institutional arrangements among different sectors (e.g., governments, cultural organizations, and businesses) for cultural enrichment.

Trumpeted internationally as a successful culture-based urban regeneration project, for example, the Newcastle/Gateshead case in the United Kingdom did not focus on luring the creative class into its environs (Bailey, Miles, and Stark 2004). Rather, designers focused on tourism. Another simplistic application of Florida's ideas was an effort to create "cool cities" led by mayors and policy gurus from Berlin and London to Sydney and San Francisco. Florida argues that governmental efforts should emphasize uniqueness and authenticity, but many readers have not heard that message. The most cited example is Michigan Governor Jennifer Granholm's call to create "cool cities" in her 2004 State of the State address: "Over the last year, we've begun an important dialogue about how we can stimulate the rise of such cool cities in Michigan—cities that attract these young workers and the businesses that rely on their talents" (5). But Michigan had no unique advantage in this regard, a strategy that frequently fails. Critics also claim that focusing on lifestyle issues diverts attention from underlying social and economic problems that are the real barriers to economic development (Kotkin 2005).

Conclusion

We have argued that globalization has produced a world that is neither flat nor spiky. More apt is a metaphor portraying the economic world as more "clustered" and rough (regionally focused) than flat (globally focused) or spiky (locally focused). Put simply, economic development success gravitates toward interconnected regional entities whose competitive advantage lies in collaboration. Thus, regional strategies matter most, can serve as bridges linking flat and spiky world diagnoses and prescriptions, and require proactive and effective governance to overcome collective action disincentives to cooperate. Whether focused on cities, regions, or both, however, building business- or people-friendly environments requires public investment in the infrastructure needed to create future growth.

At the same time, regional approaches are risky strategies for economic development officials; they typically operate in political environments with short-term rather than long-term time horizons. In fact, the wrong lessons and misapplications of Friedman's and Florida's ideas described here probably reflect the desire for either short-term solutions or quick fixes for declining economies. Recent studies of the policy instruments used in pursuit of economic development also reveal that these kinds of perverse political incentives lead local governments to employ zero-sum targeted incentives that produce no net gains for a region (Feiock, Jeong, and Kim 2003). As we have suggested, many institutional and organizational vehicles are available for advancing regional governance. They range from voluntary networks of bilateral and multilateral contracting among jurisdictions and other actors to regional partnership organizations in which either public or private organizations can take a leading role (Feiock 2007). But in each case, local actors must overcome collective action difficulties as they try to initiate, nurture, and sustain such partnerships.

Commentary

William Lyons

The authors' premise is that economic development professionals have two significant models of choice to guide their work, and they then offer a third model (regional cooperation) as a melding of the two. Conceptualizing Florida's and Friedman's arguments as a continuum, they argue that, at one end, those following Friedman's logic are to concentrate on creating direct incentives and an educated workforce; at the other end, those following Florida's logic must concentrate their resources on providing amenities that would draw creative people to the community. The authors argue, however, that these models miss the point: economic development follows regional rather that "flat" patterns (Friedman) or "spiky" patterns (Florida).

To some degree, this is a straw-person argument. The polls of their continuum are not really in as much opposition as they posit. When Friedman writes of a "flat" world, he is talking about an international-level playing field supported by an advanced telecommunications infrastructure, one that allows individuals and companies all over the world to compete. In this sense, geography does not matter, or at least it does not matter as much as it did. At the same time, Friedman is not writing about those who create the knowledge or technological advances that are so critical to economic development. Rather, he is focused on those who perform support services for those creating the knowledge. This occurs through the analysis or entry of data, the provision of customer support, or the delivery of like services.

My experience is that recruiting businesses in a flat world is a matter of a relatively short-term strategy, while drawing the creative class is a long-term strategy. Thus, any strategy that supports the creative class is most likely a response to the existing community's own lifestyle purposes rather than an explicit economic development calculus. Indeed, our experience in Knox County, Tennessee, is that the creative-class argument addresses a relevant but decidedly indirect weight in the equation in economic recruitment. The City of Knoxville explicitly participates in a regional strategy to recruit industry. The selling points revolve around the advantages of doing business in the area. These include the costs of doing business, distribution advantages, low cost of living for employees, natural beauty of the area, and other livability factors. Certainly, these livability factors include many elements that are logical extensions of the creative-class argument. However, it would be a stretch to say that they represent an explicit use of a general strategy based on a creative-class approach to economic development.

On balance, I would emphasize that a missing component of all three models offered is the type of industry involved. The world may be flat and, to some degree, so is the nation when it comes to the location of service centers. The nation is less flat when it comes to distribution and manufacturing. Most communities, thinking regionally, deal with the immediacy of meeting the needs of companies looking to relocate or expand by stressing the advantages they have over other cities in their region and by offering incentives. To be sure, Florida's model certainly has utility for these strategies, at the very least in the margins relative to the amenities that managers might prefer. But its application is much more long-term and diffuse.

One other challenge correctly posed by the authors is both the necessity and difficulties involved in creating regional cooperative strategies. Knoxville's regional cooperative strategy is multifaceted and built largely around a multicounty regional approach known as "Jobs Now." This program is funded by local governments and local businesses. Its leaders help recruit businesses to the region by facilitating necessary discussions with local leaders when needed, while avoiding competition among jurisdictions. Local governments extend this cooperation by agreeing not to offer incentives for the relocation of existing businesses within the region. This approach replaces a haphazard system often characterized by a lack of cooperation that had become painfully inadequate and counterproductive for both the city and the region.

Of course, locating a company within the corporate limits of Knoxville provides the greatest benefit to city residents. However, locating a company in the region is clearly a win as well. Thus, the city's strategy has been regional in scope, with an explicit aim of pooling resources and using a third party to recruit and locate businesses in the most suitable location within the region. Thus, I agree with the authors of this article that collective action problems can arise in the system, but their point is also valid that they can be overcome by "establishing positive reputations, repeating interactions among participants, making credible commitments, creating compatible incentive structures, and linking issues."

Commentary

Laura A. Reese

I have concerns with all three development strategies presented in this chapter: Friedman's flat world, Florida's spiky world, and the authors' uneven one. One of the most often criticized aspects of the creative-class approach is the amorphous nature of the concept itself. The connections and processes required for the growth chain to operate have not been sufficiently tested empirically, and the assumptions embedded within creative-class arguments have raised many questions among academics and other policy evaluators (see, e.g., Ley 2003; Peck 2005; Scott 2006; Thomas and Darnton 2005). Findings, particularly those related to measures of high technology and creativity, are sensitive to how variables are operationalized, what time periods are used, and which particular set of cities or regions are examined (Chapple et al. 2004).

The internal components of the diversity or melting-pot concepts are also problematic. For example, relationships between the presence of African Americans and economic growth or decline have not been fully explored (Madden 2001; Thomas and Darnton 2005), but we know that race serves as an intractable barrier to regional cooperation and has been one of the more problematic elements of Florida's creative-class argument (Thomas and Darnton). Neither has the impact of immigrants by skill level been examined (Borjas 1995), nor has an assessment been made of the extent to which ethnic and racial enclaves are voluntary (Qadeer 2005). In turn, measures of "gays" are highly problematic as well due to the reliance on census data that may well underrepresent single gays and fail to differentiate among different types of gay households (Thomas and Darnton). Likewise, the tolerance concept has been measured almost exclusively by proxies that assume the mere presence of diversity implies tolerant individuals.

It seems unlikely that measuring the extent of regional cooperation will be much easier. Although there have been studies counting the number of regional or cooperative agreements (LeRoux and Carr 2007) and some promising early work on networks of regional actors (Ansell and Reckhow 2007), assessing the quality of regional cooperation may be as slippery as that of measuring the creative class. Further, much research on city–county or multicity consolidations shows little positive impact on economic growth, reductions in intraregional competition, and prolonged cost savings (among many others, Carr and Feiock 1999; Reese 2006).

There is also a growing body of research exploring whether the creative class actually leads to, or is even correlated with, economic growth. As yet, no discernible relationship exists between improved economic health (economic growth) and any of the commonly used creative-class indicators. Although higher numbers of same-sex households and creative, racially, and ethnically diverse residents are correlated with economic health at static points in time, none of the creative-class attributes is related to actual economic improvement (Sands and Reese 2008). Other research indicates that education and skill development appear more important than culture or amenities in economic growth (Glaeser, Kolko, and Saiz 2001).

A number of scholars also suggest that policies commonly derived from creative-class theories, in particular, are misguided at best. Creativity is not something that can be simply imported into the city on the backs of peripatetic computer hackers, skateboarders, gays, and assorted bohemians (Scott 2006, 15). Local creative scenes must develop generatively; growth is the result of a complex of factors, including economic, social, political, and even historical forces. Cities high on the creative-class index also have gotten there because of a variety of forces having nothing to do with local public policy. "Place luck" allows cities with natural or climatic features—such as Denver, Portland, San Diego, and San Francisco—to prosper. Historical market forces have allowed New York to maintain its position as a cultural and economic mecca and Washington, DC, as a political node. Local generative cultural and musical movements have lent a unique flavor to cities such as Kansas City, Nashville, and New Orleans.

Commentary

John C. Morris and Douglas J. Watson

We agree that cooperation and collaboration are important weapons in the economic development "arsenal." However, we believe the authors' conclusions fail to account for the realities of economic development in American states and communities. In short, the problem of a regional governance approach is that it fails to account for the very real incentives in place to promote a go-it-alone approach by individual units of government.

Over the past twenty-five years, all fifty states and almost all of America's local governments over a population of 10,000 have committed resources to economic development. Some have established departments within their own governments, others have created city–county agencies, and others have partnered with the private sector. This, however, has led to a highly competitive situation among state and local governments, with a dizzying escalation in the types and magnitude of incentives offered by these governments. Many cities fund and operate business incubators for start-up companies, often as partnerships of state and local governments and research universities; others offer grants or loans, allow free utility connections, build infrastructure, construct speculative buildings, and provide free land for larger projects. These programs are in addition to tax abatements that are offered by most state and local governments.

Unlike the way they are evaluated on other expenditures for local services, economic development professionals are judged by the number and size of projects that they bring to the jurisdiction. This has led to a situation that Rubin (1988) describes as, "Shoot anything that flies; claim anything that falls." And success breeds imitation. For example, when Alabama provided approximately $350 million in incentives to Mercedes-Benz to locate near Tuscaloosa in 1993, officials from Georgia and other competing states were shocked by the size of Alabama's incentive package (Watson 1995, 69–70). But in the years since the location of Mercedes-Benz, Honda, Hyundai, and dozens of suppliers have moved to the state, creating thousands of good-paying jobs for Alabama residents. Thus, the political pressure to attract large employers has led to increasingly larger incentive packages. At the same time, economic development can also be inherently local and, as a result, produce winners and losers.

Thus, to achieve the vision suggested by Feiock and his colleagues would require a significant revision to substate governmental structure—not an insignificant exercise. Moreover, it would require the creation of overlapping regional structures, as the relative benefits of some economic development projects will be more or less than those of other projects. The outcome might well be new levels of complex and overlapping jurisdictions placed over existing jurisdictions.

In spite of the concerns, we do agree that there is an important and appropriate role for regional action in economic development. Indeed, such activity is already in place. For instance, the "Team New England" project conceived and facilitated by Northeast Utilities Services has as its goal the continued economic development of the northeast region (Lombard 2008). The fundamental presumption is that these states, and individual cities within these states, can cooperate with one another to attract new economic development to the region. By pooling their resources, they can be more competitive collectively than they can individually. Conversely, the outcomes are unevenly distributed—a project that locates in Hartford, Connecticut, for example, concentrates the benefits in Hartford to the exclusion of Springfield, Massachusetts. Thus, although they work together to attract new development to the region, they compete to be the specific location of the development because there are clear benefits that flow to the winner. We have termed this process *coopertition* (see Watson and Morris 2008), a process that produces "spiky" results.

Chapter 11

Spanning "Bleeding" Boundaries: Humanitarianism, NGOs, and the Civilian–Military Nexus in the Post–Cold War Era[*]

Nancy C. Roberts

Contents

[*] Adapted from Roberts, N. C. 2010. Spanning "bleeding" boundaries: Humanitarianism, NGOs, and the civilian-military nexus in the post-Cold War era. *Public Administration Review* 70(2): 212–222.

Over the past two decades, one of the most challenging developments for civilian–military (civ–mil) relations around the world has been finding ways to work together. The transformation of warfare in the post–Cold War era fuels conflicts between civ–mil organizations. Diminished in the process has been the effectiveness of the co-located and interdependent operations of both communities.

How do civ–mil organizations cope with their interdependencies in the human security domain as the boundaries between them blur? What mechanisms exist to coordinate field activities and overcome the perceptual and real differences between the two communities? Public administration researchers have been largely silent on these questions, despite their import and relevance. This chapter first identifies the sources of tensions that have arisen between civ–mil organizations in the post–Cold War era. It then offers a typology of civ–mil operations based on the level of threat (Crocker, Hampson, and Aall 2001) and the level of domain consensus. The chapter concludes by identifying a range of formal and informal interorganizational cooperation (IOC) mechanisms used in civ–mil operations, each with its own constraints and limitations.

The Civilian–Military Conundrum in the Post–Cold War Era

One of the most striking developments in contemporary warfare is the blurring of the dividing line between soldiers and civilians. Taliban spokesman Zabiullah Mujahid, for example, speaks for many in claiming there is no distinction between civilian and military personnel when justifying the Taliban's attacking and killing of International Rescue Committee workers in Logar, Afghanistan. They were the "foreign invader forces." They were "not working for the interests of Afghanistan and they belonged to those countries whose forces … took Afghanistan's freedom" (BBC News 2008).

Insisting on guidelines to separate civilians and combatants when the nature of combat and adversaries makes those boundaries obsolete is unlikely to produce successful outcomes for either civilians or the military. Civ–mil organizations both operate in the domain of human security, framed from a military perspective as freedom from personal attacks and violence and from a civilian perspective as providing both emergency relief and the long-term basic needs of life such as food, clothing, shelter, medical care, and employment. Both are interdependent, are co-located in threatening environments, and confront very challenging problems—peacekeeping, disaster relief, postconflict reconstruction, and warfare. Civilians need the military to provide information about the terrain, operations, and affected populations, and in high-threat conditions, they often rely on military transportation and logistics. The military needs civilians for humanitarian assistance and for their knowledge and expertise in the reconstruction and development of devastated areas.

Lesson 1: Although civ–mil organizations increasingly are co-located and need each other to deal effectively with theater challenges, differences in cultures, organizational structures, beliefs, and priorities have made effective coordination challenging.

Better coordination between civ–mil organizations is needed to protect human life; however, differences in philosophies and operating procedures have made civ–mil relations difficult during field-based operations (Sommers 2000; Whelan and Harmer 2006). Although all members share a "commitment to service, a willingness to work among the dead and dying, and also an acceptance of significant risk in their daily lives," their organizational characteristics are "profoundly different" (Seiple 1996, v) in terms of cultures, structural features, and behavior (Aall, Miltenberger, and Weiss 2000; Frandsen 2002; James 2003; Seiple 1996). Civilian organizations, especially nongovernmental organizations (NGOs), believe that human suffering should be relieved without regard for nationality, political or ideological beliefs, race, religion, sex, or ethnicity. They fulfill their mandates by being autonomous, neutral, and impartial; resist instructions from those outside their organizations; and eye with suspicion any attempts to organize or integrate with others lest they compromise their freedom of operation. Their organizational designs are typically decentralized to adapt field operations quickly to austere conditions. They assemble on an as-needed basis and execute on the fly while striving toward transparency, accountability, and consensus-based decision making.

In contrast, military organizations epitomize hierarchical authority, clear lines of command and control, and explicit rules of engagement. Their mandate is to establish and maintain public order and ensure operational security and force protection, making them less inclined to share information. They pride themselves on advanced planning and systematic execution of operational orders and seek a positive public image.

In general, civilians believe that close alignment with the military in political disputes or political positions compromises their principles of humanity, impartiality, and neutrality (IASC 2004; Phelan and Wood 2005). Their fear is that, if viewed as partial, their members will not be able to gain access to vulnerable populations, will be exposed to greater risks in the field, and will even be targeted by combatants (Dziedzic and Seidl 2005; IASC 2004). This perception has been reinforced by recent attacks against the United Nations (UN) in Afghanistan and Iraq and by the assassination of Margaret Hassan, director of Care International's operations in Iraq. Interaction potential between the military and civilians also is limited because of their mutual suspicions. These derive from a host of factors, such as a perceived lack of common goals and values and the absence of a common task-related language for discourse. Frandsen (2002, 140) writes of military–NGO relations: "NGO personnel have many feelings about the military: general disdain, nervousness (around weapons, camouflage, saluting, the "hoo-ah" attitudes), ignorance (which often leads to nervousness or disdain), previous bad experience (Kent State University, Somalia, etc.), or philosophical opposition." Moreover, NGOs sometimes "perceive the military as responsible for the destruction of homes, crops and livestock and guilty of serious offenses such as rape, torture, genocide and violations of human rights. And when the conflict does end, they see the military leaving behind unexploded ordnance and landmines that cause long-term human damage" (Ford, Hogan, and Perry 2002, 12).

The military also directs a "slew of … verbiage aimed at NGO inefficiencies, whimsical patterns, media hunger and lack of absolute independent logical capabilities" (Frandsen 2002, 140). Likewise, Ford, Hogan, and Perry (2002, 12) note that "from the military side, NGOs are often viewed as difficult to work with…. They want support yet they demand autonomy. NGOs will not respond to orders given by the military even if their personal safety is at stake." They "will openly criticize the military, while at the same time request logistics, communications and transportation support from" them (ibid., 13).

Civilian–Military Operations: An Analytical Perspective

Although the organizational theory literature confirms that not all civ–mil interaction needs to be addressed in the same way, it also overlooks the level of threat facing potential partners—a critical component of this relationship.

> **Lesson 2:** In the civ–mil nexus, environmental threat interacts with domain consensus to create four analytically distinct categories of civ–mil operations that should be considered when crafting coordination mechanisms.

Various dimensions have been used by organizational theorists to characterize environments in terms of their technological, legal, political, economic, demographic, ecological, and cultural elements (Aldrich 1979; Hall 1999). To conduct their studies, theorists have reduced and simplified these content areas into analytical dimensions, such as the level of munificence, complexity, and dynamism in a particular environment (Dess and Beard 1984; Van de Ven and Ferry 1980). However, one dimension that is critical to the security domain is not addressed by organizational theorists: the level of threat to human life. Most researchers assume the existence of competitive forces but not of life-ending ones. Yet threat level is a central dimension in understanding the human security domain and the range of tasks and operations that are conducted within it. These include intelligence, policing, justice and legal administration, emergency management, and national security.

Within the national security domain, civilians tend to focus on affected populations, while the military tends to focus on combatants. But, as noted, separating combatants from civilians is difficult. When this blurring occurs, not only are security risks heightened for all, including the populations that both are trying to protect, but blurred boundaries between civ–mil organizations prompt conflicts over which organizations have the "right" to be where, at what time, and for what purpose. Yet domain consensus, a critical dimension in IOC research (Aldrich 1979; Aldrich and Marsden 1988), has been found to be a "necessary precondition" for organizations to coordinate (Alexander 1995).

Combining threat level and domain consensus into a two-by-two matrix makes it possible to map civ–mil operations (Figure 11.1): peacekeeping (quadrant I); disaster relief (quadrant II); development and reconstruction, stabilization/security/transition/reconstruction, peace-building, and nation-building operations (quadrant

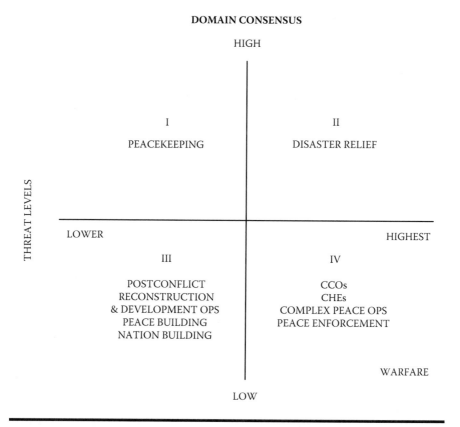

Figure 11.1 Civilian and military operations under varying conditions of threat and domain consensus.

III); and complete humanitarian emergencies (CHEs), complex contingency operations, peace enforcement, and warfare (quadrant IV). Each presents different civ–mil coordination challenges.

Peacekeeping involves the use of civ–mil personnel to separate combatants, police demilitarized zones, and monitor cease-fires after they have been negotiated and accepted by all belligerents (Jett 2000). The general threat level is reduced because a cease-fire has been accepted by all parties, although a potential threat remains if the combatants do not maintain their agreements. Domain consensus, however, remains high for both the military and civilians who monitor agreements. Both operate under restricted "rules of engagement": civilians monitor the cease-fires and elections, and the military keeps former combatants separated and polices the demilitarized zones. The challenges for IOCs in these cases result from "mission creep," where the goals of operations are redefined and expanded, thus requiring renegotiation of the rules of engagement for both civilians and the military. Examples of peacekeeping operations include UN interventions into Cyprus and the Golan Heights (ibid.).

Disaster relief refers to any response to natural disasters and environmental emergencies that pose a threat to human life (Auf der Heide 1989). Threats range from low to high levels, depending on their scale. However, military involvement in disaster relief tends to occur when the threat levels are high and calamities overwhelm the ability of civilian responders to provide immediate care. In terms of domain consensus, civ–mil organizations generally agree that their missions are similar: to provide emergency food, water, shelter, and medical care to those in need. Although both the military and civilians end up working in the same humanitarian space, friction points tend to be fewer because both acknowledge their mutual dependencies and the complementarity of their efforts. The military contributes transportation, "lift," and advanced communication and information technology; civilians provide in-depth cultural and historical knowledge and functional expertise in disaster relief.

The third type of civ–mil operations—*postconflict reconstruction and development operations*—is defined by the UN as *peace-building* operations; by the U.S. military as *stabilization, security, transition*, and *reconstruction operations* (DOD 2005); and by others as *nation building* (Dobbins et al. 2003, 2007). Still others have referred to these activities as "fourth-generation peacekeeping" or "complex peacekeeping" (Rittberger 2007). Activities include the following (Dobbins et al. 2007, xxiii):

- *Security:* Peacekeeping, rule of law, law enforcement, and security sector reform
- *Humanitarian relief:* Return of refugees and provision of medical care, food, and shelter
- *Governance:* Resumption of public services and restoration of public administration

- *Economic stabilization:* Establishment of a stable currency and a legal and regulatory framework for the resumption of local and international commerce
- *Democratization:* Creation of political parties, free press, civil society, and a legal and constitutional framework for elections
- *Development:* Economic growth, poverty reduction, and infrastructure improvements

As major combat subsides, one expects the domain conflicts between civ–mil organizations to lessen. This can be the outcome, as nation-building exercises in Bosnia and Kosovo have demonstrated (Dobbins et al. 2003). However, despite the official endings of war, U.S. operations in Afghanistan and Iraq still activate domain conflicts between civ–mil organizations. Several factors contribute to the ongoing tensions. First, Afghanistan and Iraq are considered nonpermissive environments where military forces are still engaged as combatants. Even though operations transitioned from major combat to stabilization, friction between civ–mil organizations exists around information sharing and securing a humanitarian space. Development space is also contested when the military engages in civic action projects such as building schools and medical clinics, although those involved in reconstruction and development appear to be "less wedded to the concepts of independence and impartiality" (Dziedzic and Seidl 2005, 6). Even coordination mechanisms to assist in stabilization and reconstruction, such as the Provincial Reconstruction Teams (PRTs) in Afghanistan and Iraq, are contentious.

The PRTs combine civ–mil personnel from various government agencies, as well as diplomats and specialists, in economic development, stabilization, and reconstruction activities (Dziedzic and Seidl 2005; Perito 2007). To accomplish their mission, they interact with regional political, military, and community leaders and sponsor various civic engagement and reconstruction projects (Dobbins et al. 2003). Despite their many contributions, however, tensions have arisen (Dziedzic and Seidl 2005, 7). Development NGOs and international organizations (IOs) see PRTs expanding the military's role into their development space, thus challenging their areas of comparative advantage. Meanwhile, the military sees the PRTs as born of the unstable situation in Afghanistan and the changing nature of warfare, where insurgents and terrorists view anyone aligned with the Afghan government as the enemy, including humanitarian and development organizations that provide easy, soft targets.

More serious domain conflicts surfaced with the publication of the Department of Defense's Directive 3000.05 (DOD 2005). The U.S. military was given a new mandate—support for stability, security, transition, and reconstruction—atop combat operations. Once stability is restored to an area, or even during large-scale combat operations, the military's short-term goal is to reestablish essential services and meet humanitarian needs. Its long-term goal is to develop indigenous capacity for ensuring essential services, a market economy, the rule of law, democratic institutions, and a robust civil society.

The promulgation of this new directive sent shock waves through the civilian community. Although it states that operational tasks are best performed by indigenous, foreign, or U.S. civilian professions, U.S. military forces are now to perform all tasks when civilians cannot do so. Tasks involve rebuilding indigenous institutions, including security forces, correctional facilities, and judicial systems; reviving or rebuilding the private sector, including encouraging citizen-driven, bottom-up economic activity and constructing the necessary state infrastructure; and developing representative government institutions (Counterinsurgency 2006). From the concerned perspective of civilian organizations, military organizations are now pitted against the civilian reconstruction and development organizations that challenge the military's expanding roles into civil society.

Finally, domain conflicts are high in quadrant IV. As noted, various terms are used to describe these operations: *multidimensional peacekeeping, second-generation peacekeeping, robust peacekeeping, third-generation peacekeeping, complex humanitarian emergencies, complex contingency operations,* or *complex peace operations* that often require peace enforcement (Byman et al. 2000; Pirnie 1998; Rittberger 2007). These operations occur "where there is total or considerable breakdown of authority resulting from internal or external conflict" (IASC 2004, 5). They often result in massive numbers of refugees and internally displaced persons, gross violations of human rights, and large-scale disruption of people's livelihoods. Thus, typical of quadrant IV operations is the forcible restoration of peace without the consent of the parties in the armed conflict (e.g., the no-fly zones in Iraq and Bosnia).

During the early stages of CHEs, emergency relief in the form of food, water, and shelter is a priority, yet its distribution can be hampered by a lack of security, supportive government, or social infrastructure. The civilian component of these interventions has a large contingent of humanitarian relief organizations populated by NGOs and IOs whose purposes are to relieve human suffering and "to protect the human rights of victims of violence, persecution, and other misfortunes" (Sommers 2000, 99). Depending on the intervention, the military component could be composed of UN, regional (e.g., NATO), or national security forces (e.g., U.S. military; Byman et al. 2000; Pirnie and Francisco 1998; USIP 2000; White House 1997). Apart from taking a more coercive role in disarming adversaries, restoring public order, demobilizing and reintegrating former combatants, and enforcing peace agreements, the military also supports and facilitates civilian activities. These include the distribution of assistance; the provision of safety for refugees, displaced persons, and civilian NGOs and IOs; the protection of relief supplies in unstable situations by securing warehouses, convoy routes, and distribution points; and the provision of logistical expertise to civilian organizations. Depending on the mission, the military may also work with civilians in demining, reuniting divided societies, organizing elections, and promoting representative governments and economic growth (Dobbins et al. 2007).

Lesson 3: To understand the challenges and opportunities for civ–mil coordination, pay attention to the temporal coincidence or sequencing of humanitarian and military operations.

The temporal coincidence of security operations and assistance complicates IOC for civ–mil organizations, as occurred in Somalia, the former Republic of Yugoslavia, and Kosovo (Oliker et al. 2004; Studer 2001). At issue is "humanitarian space" (Studer 2001; Whelan and Harmer 2006): civilian organizations must be able to "cross the 'lines' of conflict," which in contemporary warfare are fluid and vary over time (Dziedzic and Seidl 2005, 6). Association with any of the combatant parties puts them and those they are helping at risk. The safest action is to avoid any association with belligerents. Therefore, the goal for civilian organizations is to establish and preserve a neutral, impartial humanitarian space in which to work without undue interference from combatants or governments during peace operations (Dziedzic and Seidl 2005; Whelan and Harmer 2006).

Even civilian humanitarians within the UN system take pains to distance themselves from UN-sanctioned military actions, noting that "whenever we are associated with political strategies, we increase our own vulnerabilities and risk" (Reindorp and Wiles 2001, 44). If the distribution of aid, which humanitarians consider to be a civilian task, is militarized, it "blurs the boundaries" and heightens security risks by turning humanitarian facilities and staff into perceived enemy targets (Bessler and Seki 2006; Whelan and Harmer 2006). For example, the attempt to apprehend the warlord Mohammed Aideed in Somalia was viewed by his supporters as the United States and the UN taking sides in the conflict.

Lesson 4: Although the military sees NGOs and IOs as "force multipliers," NGOs and IOs see the military as trying to "politicize humanitarianism."

Civilians also resist and resent the military's attempts to treat them as "force multipliers" for the purpose of "winning hearts and minds" (Oliker et al. 2004; Tomb 2005). During an insurgency, the military may support displaced civilians and initiate civic action projects in order to cultivate popular support among the locals, increase force protection, and reduce the overall threat level in the area

(Counterinsurgency 2006). NGOs have serious concerns about being co-opted into a military strategy and becoming pawns in a "politicization of humanitarianism" (James 2003; Whelan and Harmer 2006).

For the military, humanitarian aid dispensed during a conflict is not a neutral act (Seiple 1996). It can sustain a conflict because the combatants, as well as their supporters, are reinforced rather than weakened. The military cites civilian difficulties in disentangling assistance from the political objectives of governments and warring factions, which affects their ability to be seen as neutral actors in Afghanistan. The military notes, for example, that "NGOs were perceived by Afghans ... and by the Taliban in particular as partisan" (Oliker et al. 2004, 37).

In addition, given the tensions between civ–mil organizations over what constitutes security, as well as the number and diversity of civilian organizations, security in the humanitarian space is difficult to establish. The UN-affiliated Union of International Associations recognizes more than 14,500 different international NGOs (Jett 2000). Reports indicate that some 1,700 NGOs were active in Bosnia (Pollick 2000, 59) and more than 800 are registered in Afghanistan (Tomb 2005). Nor do these figures include those operating without the consent of the governing authority, all of which makes coordination complex. Civilian organizations also tend to be independent and widely dispersed geographically. Each has its own specific area of expertise and competes with others for funding and media coverage to attract more funds (Abiew 2003; Oliker et al. 2004; Reindorp and Wiles 2001). Thus, it is difficult for civilians to coordinate with one another to establish humanitarian space, let alone coordinate as a whole with military organizations (Donini 2000).

Lesson 5: Civ–mil relations are likely to deteriorate during warfare when the military engages in humanitarian efforts.

Domain conflict reaches a high point when a situation is deemed too dangerous for civilians to continue their work, so the military steps in to dispense humanitarian aid. The military now assumes a dual role—combatant and provider of humanitarian assistance, as it did in the cases of Kosovo, East Timor, and Operation Enduring Freedom in Afghanistan. In this situation, coordination becomes a "complicated and vexing matter in an environment where the UN and NGO community fear that association with one of the combatant forces imperil[s] its perceived neutrality, increase[s] the security threat, and limit[s] its ... ability to accomplish its missions over the longer term" (Oliker et al. 2004, 82). When some civil affairs military units put on civilian clothes to distribute aid, relations reached their low point (InterAction 2002). The blurred lines between civ–mil organizations apparent during CHEs (Whelan and Harmer 2006) become literal "bleeding boundaries" in warfare (Phelan and Wood 2005).

Interorganizational Theory, Administrative Constraints, and the Civilian–Military Nexus

Certainly, increasing linkages between and among organizations have their advantages, as studies in other policy arenas have documented (e.g., Alter and Hage 1993; Huxham and Vongen 2005; Provan and Milward 1995). But tighter connections among organizations also have their challenges. They can increase their interdependencies (Alexander 1995; Gray 1985, 1989; Luke 1991; Pfeffer and Salancik 1978; Scott 2003), which, in turn, have to be managed if interorganizational relationships are to be maintained (Alexander 1995; Hatch 1997).

Given the mix of organizational characteristics, coordinating costs, and interaction potential in IOCs, organizations consider a range of coordination mechanisms and choose those that they perceive fit the situation and its requirements (Alexander 1995). In the case of civ–mil organizations, experimentation has been underway for some time as they try to move beyond the "blight of adhocracy" (Reindorp and Wiles 2001, 50), an unsatisfactory condition in which organizations operate without regard to others in their domain. Finding the right balance between self-interests and domain interests is a delicate maneuver; each organization seeks mechanisms that enable it to coordinate with others and yet not be coordinated by others.

Lesson 6: Mechanisms for coordinating civ–mil relations during theater operations are similar to those identified by Galbraith in his intraorganizational information-processing approach, and each has run into formidable constraints on effectiveness.

Although Galbraith's (1973) information-processing approach to coordination focuses on intraorganizational coordination, it provides a useful framework to examine coordination mechanisms used in civ–mil relations. Galbraith identifies five different coordination strategies: rules and programs, hierarchy, goals and targets, reduction of the need to process information, and increased capacity to process information laterally. Applying Galbraith's model of information processing and coordination to civ–mil relations, we find that all of his strategies have been attempted to date to some extent. Standard operating procedures are evident in attempts to establish *rules* to govern humanitarian space. But with changes in threat levels in the post–Cold War era, the rules of humanitarian space have been challenged, straining civ–mil relations. When efforts to reaffirm rules are inadequate, as Galbraith would predict, the organizations involved then turn to *hierarchy* as a mechanism of coordination. One example is the UN's experiment with the Strategic Framework, an effort to create a top-down mechanism to coordinate all in-country organizations in Afghanistan. Although it did have some limited success (Roberts and Bradley 2005), it was discontinued after its second deployment in Sierra Leone failed to integrate political (which includes military), humanitarian, and development strategies.

Even when there has been a political consensus—for example, when a UN resolution authorizing peace operations is signed by major civ–mil organizations—the weak international authority structure makes it difficult to rely on a single hierarchical chain of command as a mechanism of coordination. No one authority exists that all IOs, governments, and NGOs acknowledge. Even the special representatives of the secretary-general, nominally the head of UN missions in a country, do not exercise control over independent heads of such UN agencies as the resident representative of the UN Office for the Coordination of Humanitarian Affairs, much less over NGOs or military forces.

Without agreement on hierarchical authority, Galbraith's third coordination strategy is also constrained. There is no leadership that is able to establish *goals and targets* to guide all intervention efforts. Vertical information transfers likewise suffer from the same limitations of hierarchy, goal, and target setting. Without agreement on an overarching authority, no one can initiate, develop, and implement a vertical information system for the purpose of integrating all civ–mil organizations in any given theater. Each organization tends to have its own system and limits access to others (Holohan 2005).

Galbraith's fourth strategy—*the reduction of the need to process information*—is used by both military and civilian organizations. It involves two options, and each has its constraints. First, organizations can lower the number of exceptions with which they have to contend by reducing their expected performance levels. For example, they can allow for extra time and resources to work together. They can be more accepting of delays in information processing between and among organizations. They can be willing to tolerate budget overruns as a result of coordination problems. Of course, these examples of slack increase costs and reduce overall system efficiency, potentially eroding effectiveness as benefits to needy people decline. Alternatively, either because of conflicting mandates or because they find the transaction costs too high, they can ignore or refuse to work with other organizations in the human security domain, with human security becoming less than it could be.

The remaining strategy in Galbraith's typology—*the creation of lateral relations*—is the most widely recognized mechanism of information processing and coordination. Direct contacts are prevalent where organizations operate without formal lateral mechanisms to orchestrate concerted action. Coordination ends up reliant on informal, ad hoc, and personal relationships among organizational members who are forced to discover and renegotiate all of their connections afresh at the onset of each international intervention, often with uncertain results (Reindorp and Wiles 2001).

Liaison roles, individual positions created to link specific organizations, are evidenced by the civ–mil liaison officers who are appointed to handle interorganizational contacts and coordination. Task forces and teams also are prevalent, as demonstrated in the Integrated Mission Task Forces, the Civil-Military Operations Task Force, and the Provincial Reconstruction Teams. Examples of new organizational units include the UN On-Site Operations Coordination Center, Civil-Military Operations Centers, and the Afghanistan NGO Security Office. But these, too, are hardly panaceas, as some civilian organizations opt out when military personnel are involved for fear of compromising their neutrality.

Toward Communities of Practice? Preliminary Lessons from the Front Lines

Although the preceding has chronicled a variety of formal coordination mechanisms and their constraints, there are important undercurrents beneath the formal level that also must be acknowledged in civ–mil relations. Surfacing in all four quadrants are communities of practice (COPs)—"groups of people who share a concern, a set of problems, or a passion about a topic, and who deepen their knowledge and expertise ... by interacting on an ongoing basis" (Wenger, McDermott, and Snyder 2002, 4).

Lesson 7: Self-emergent hubs—or (COPs)—are promising ways to avoid coordination constraints.

Examples of COPs can be grouped within the four general types of civ–mil operations outlined in Figure 11.1. Peacekeeping hubs attract those interested in training and preparing for upcoming assignments. These include efforts by the Pearson Peacekeeping Centre, the Hawaii Center for Excellence in Disaster Management and Humanitarian Assistance, and the Asia Pacific Peace Operations Capacity Building Program. They gather civilians from federal governments, UN personnel, civilian police, and international and nongovernmental agencies. Together with military personnel, they practice dealing with the complexities of peace operations. The U.S. Army Peacekeeping and Stability Operations Institute also offers peace operations training and education for mid- to senior-level audiences, including U.S. military services, interagency programs, civilian organizations, foreign militaries, and IOs/NGOs.

Similar hubs exist for disaster relief, including the UN's Office for the Coordination of Humanitarian Affairs and AlertNet, sponsored by the Reuters Foundation. These programs afford access to documents, articles, and links to sites on topics such as satellite images, children and war, working in relief, refugees, and technology. Another good example is the Strong Angel exercises. Originally sponsored by a small group of interested civilian and military personnel, Strong

Angel demonstrations experiment with the use of cutting-edge techniques and technologies to facilitate improved information flow and cooperation in disaster relief situations.

COPs also are emerging around stabilization and reconstruction issues. One example is the Center for Stabilization and Reconstruction Studies, a teaching institute located at the Naval Postgraduate School in Monterey, California. It provides educational opportunities for the full spectrum of actors—U.S. and international armed forces, government civilian agencies, and representatives from NGOs and IOs. Practitioner-oriented programs include games/table-top exercises, short courses, workshops, conferences, and applied research initiatives on topics such as security sector reform, disarmament, demobilization, reintegration, cross-cultural understanding, information sharing, and skill development in collaboration and negotiation.

There also are a growing number of COPs within the development area. The United States Institute of Peace has brought together civ–mil organizations to address IOC challenges concerning complex emergencies. It has launched efforts to improve the designs of new information management and planning capabilities involving humanitarian relief, human rights, and militaries engaged in complex emergencies. It has also developed guidelines to preserve humanitarian space in high-conflict environments in Afghanistan and Iraq (USIP 2007). Examining the impact of these COPS in more systematic ways than we have done historically is an important focus for future research.

Commentary

Robert "Robin" H. Dorff

Roberts has rightfully identified the civilian–military nexus as central to the international strategic environment of the twenty-first century. Several points related to Roberts's lessons are important to bear in mind as we struggle with this dilemma. First, unlike in her typology, there are no clear dividing lines between the battle space and the humanitarian space. For example, it is important to recognize that stabilization is required across the entire range of crises we are discussing. In the aftermath of the Indonesia tsunami, the inability of some local and national governments to govern effectively opened the door not only for increased natural human tragedy but also for exploitation by nefarious actors. In Somalia in the 1990s, humanitarian attempts to provide food led to efforts by those competing for the authority to "govern" to seize the food and control its distribution as another form of "combat."

Second, the kinds of divisions that might exist between the humanitarian and battle spaces shift over time and often remain highly fluid. Consequently, although it is useful to work with the typology of civilian–military operations developed by Roberts, the operational and, hence, strategic dilemma is that the theoretically useful quadrants in such a typology do not remain equally distinct in practice. This suggests that we must have either a single organization with the ability to conduct all the operations in an integrated fashion or find ways to integrate the capabilities of multiple organizations in a strategically coherent manner. However, any changes made would be constrained by the National Security Act of 1947. Thus, policy makers must consider whether that act is still appropriate for designing and implementing the kind of integrated strategy we need in an era of asymmetric warfare.

Roberts also points to operational challenges arising from (1) the temporal coincidence or sequencing of humanitarian and military operations in any given theatre of operation and (2) both the military perception that "humanitarian aid dispensed during a conflict is not a neutral act" and the civilian view that the military wants to "politicize humanitarianism." But the reality is that temporal coincidence is the most frequent reality in many, if not all, theater operations. Moreover, the perception that matters most is not that of the military or even the civilians but that of the combatants. For example, because the provision of humanitarian aid is by definition "political" to many of these actors in fragile or failed states (or, perhaps better, "contested states"), they do not have to be politicized by the military. Politicization is a function of the very nature of the acts of providing aid and comfort to civilians in societies that are contested. Thus, the "indigenous combatants" who frequently cause the need for a foreign military presence (United States, UN, or other) will do whatever they can to blur this distinction. And, clearly, the proliferation of civilian organizations, their wide dispersion, their competition for funding and media coverage, and, at times, their freewheeling independence (the desire to act in a country without consent from any entity because of the overriding importance of human security) virtually guarantee that it will continue to be "difficult for civilians to coordinate with one another to establish humanitarian space, let alone coordinate as a whole with military operations."

Roberts's discussions of coordination strategies and communities of practice are useful in focusing our attention on areas and questions where additional research can help identify courses of action that can be implemented in practice. But multiple organizations can achieve strategic success even in the absence of clear coordinating strategies. The key to this is achieving some kind of overarching acceptance of shared goals and objectives. More structure, whether in the form of organizational hierarchy or rules, does little to address the complex problems and often serves to bog down the operations and to stifle the adaptability, innovation, and flexibility that are needed.

It is also currently in vogue to call for increasing civilian capabilities and capacity. The problem has been that we have seen very little movement in the direction of reorienting government agencies (State Department and USAID, as well as others) to undertake operations in the "stabilization space" and even less interest on the part of the U.S. Congress to resource such a strategic shift. Virtually no movement along any of the major lines of reorganization is as yet visible. It would be nice if even some consolidation and coordination of the "civilian" side of the equation could be accomplished, if for no other reason than to reduce somewhat the numbers of competing civilian actors trying to operate independently in the humanitarian space.

So if organizational reform or reorientation is not going to come to the rescue, a kind of "gap-bridging company" is needed (Dorff 2007). This would most likely be a private sector company—a nongovernmental organization perhaps—that would specialize in working in the identified stabilization space. It would require personnel and policies to accommodate both the civilian and military organizations that are likely to be found in all three spaces. But its specialty would be the ability to operate effectively in the stabilization space—or, in the language of this chapter, to operate across the domains. Although it would not have any command authority over these other organizations, it would have an enhanced ability to help forge shared purpose and shared effort across them.

Chapter 12

Left High and Dry? Climate Change, Common-Pool Resource Theory, and the Adaptability of Western Water Compacts*

Edella Schlager and Tanya Heikkila

Contents

---

* Adapted from Schlager, E., and T. Heikkila. 2011. Left high and dry? Climate change, common-pool resource theory, and the adaptability of western water compacts. *Public Administration Review* 71(3): 461–470.

As efforts to reduce greenhouse gas emissions fall far short of what a consensus of scientists argues is necessary to avoid potentially catastrophic increases in the mean global temperature, mounting efforts and attention are being devoted to understanding both the vulnerability and adaptability of our social and ecological systems to climate change (Adger 2000, 2006; Gallopín et al. 2001; IPCC 2007). Vulnerability is largely a function of the levels of exposure and sensitivity in populations to the different stresses resulting from climate change, such as increasing temperatures, rising sea levels, and more frequent and extreme weather events (Adger 2000, 2006; IPCC 2007). Vulnerability also depends on the adaptability of communities, or the changes undertaken to minimize the effects of climate impacts.

In the western United States, one of the most immediate and direct effects of climate change involves the availability of water resources (IPCC 2007). On average, states west of the 100th meridian receive less than 20 inches of rainfall per year (except for the coastal region of the Pacific Northwest), with areas of the Southwest and Intermountain West receiving less than 10 inches of rainfall per year. Moreover, the hydrologic cycles of the West are changing; not only may the hottest and driest region of the United States become even drier, but the availability of water is likely to be much more variable (Climate Change Science Program 2008; also see Barnett and Pierce 2008, 2009; Barsugli et al. 2009; Brikowski 2008; Wiley and Palmer 2008). For instance, Barnett and Pierce (2009, 7336) estimate that a 10 percent reduction in runoff in the Colorado River Basin will lead to requested water deliveries exceeding sustainable deliveries by 2040. If climate change impacts are greater—say, a 20 percent reduction in runoff—then water delivery shortfalls will occur by 2025.

Historically, interstate river compacts have been the primary means for resolving conflicts over competing water demands in the West by establishing allocation rules for stream flows, thus ensuring downstream users a defined share of water from rivers. When the federal government began pouring billions of dollars into this infrastructure in the early twentieth century, interstate compacts helped states to ensure that water resource development would be orderly, with minimal conflict. A majority of compacts also established rules for how water would be allocated from reservoirs built on interstate rivers. By capturing and storing snowmelt and spring runoff and making it available to water users during the summer months when demand is high, large-scale reservoirs also provide multiyear storage to minimize state vulnerability to droughts in the West lasting up to a decade.

But will the current design of these interstate compacts be well matched to new conditions driven by climate change? How effectively can these institutions induce rule compliance through monitoring and conflict resolution? To what degree are they capable of adapting? To inform the answers to these questions, we turn to scholarship on the management of common-pool resources (CPRs; Ostrom 1990; Ostrom, Gardner, and Walker 1994). After showing how common-pool resource theory (CPRT) applies to interstate compacts, we cull five propositions informed by CPRT and illustrate their validity in this management arena with examples from an earlier comparative study of fourteen western interstate water compacts that focus largely on supply-side efforts (Schlager and Heikkila 2009). We conclude with four recommendations grounded in CPRT for adapting interstate water compacts to climate changes. We argue that state and interstate compact officials need to give greater thought to CPRT principles before designing water supply and demand solutions.

Common-Pool Resource Theory, Natural Resources, and the Importance of Institutional Arrangements

The theory of CPR management has been used to understand the factors that are associated with both the robustness and the fragility of governing arrangements for a range of natural resources such as water, fisheries, and forests (e.g., Ostrom 1990; Ostrom et al. 1994; Schlager 2004). CPRT, which is developed within a broader research framework on institutional analysis (Ostrom 2005), points to critical institutional features that can help one anticipate how interstate river compacts might perform in the face of climate change and what institutional changes might improve interstate water management. Interstate rivers are CPRs. Excluding would-be water users from accessing a river is costly, and water withdrawn and consumed is not available for others to use (Ostrom and Ostrom 1977). These two defining characteristics—costly exclusion and subtractability of resource units—mean that resources can be easily overused and severely degraded unless their many users are coordinated and governed.

Coordination and governance occur through institutional arrangements. Institutional arrangements are rules and property rights systems that guide, direct, and constrain people's actions with respect to CPRs (Ostrom 2005). Rules define what actions must, must not, or may be taken in any given action situation (Crawford and Ostrom 1995). Water allocation rules are the foundation of interstate river compacts and typically specify the actions that an upstream state must or must not take to ensure that a downstream state receives its water allotment.

When assessing how vulnerable or how adaptable compacts are to climate change, we begin with an analysis of these rules. In particular, CPRT posits that the performance of institutions depends on how well the rules are matched to the biophysical and social settings in which they are applied (Ostrom et al. 1994). For instance, a water allocation rule that allocates more water than is available in a river is not well matched to its setting. Equally important is how well rules reflect important social norms and practices, particularly in how they distribute the benefits and burdens of governing a CPR (Ostrom 2005). In general, if benefits and burdens are proportionately distributed, a CPR institution will be viewed as fair and will be supported by resource users. Thus, water allocation rules that focus the risk of water shortages on a single state or type of water user tend to generate conflict, whereas water allocation rules that distribute risk among all water users tend to inspire more cooperative behavior.

Institutional performance also depends on whether people are following the rules. When the majority of resource users participate in devising rules, and when the authority of resource users to make decisions is not likely to be usurped by higher authorities, people are more likely to buy into the rules. Rule-following behavior is also advanced by monitoring rule compliance and by providing users information on how the resource responds to the rules (Ostrom 2005).

The CPR literature recognizes that conflict resolution mechanisms are needed to settle differences over the interpretation of rules and to hold accountable resource users and those administering the rules (Ostrom 1990). Developing and maintaining a common understanding of what rules require, especially in dynamic biophysical settings such as those occasioned by climate change, are essential for effective regimes. In complex CPR settings such as interstate watersheds, the theory emphasizes that CPR institutions—their rules, monitoring, and conflict resolution mechanisms—should be nested and aligned across levels of governance.

The literature on CPR management also recognizes that the institutional arrangements devised to govern highly salient CPRs such as scarce water supplies are not static. As people learn about the CPR, each other's behavior, and how that behavior affects the resource, they revise the arrangements to match the biophysical and social setting better (Ostrom 2005). However, both free-riding and haggling over fair distribution of benefits and costs can be issues.

Assessing Compact Vulnerability and Adaptability to Climate Change

With these CPR expectations in mind, we can now assess the vulnerability and adaptability of existing interstate water compacts in light of climate change predictions. Starting in the 1920s, western states entered into more than twenty compacts to allocate water from interstate rivers, signing the majority of these prior to the 1950s. All remain in force, including the fourteen listed in Table 12.1 from our previous 2009 study. Many of them established active governance commissions composed of state water officials and, often, water users. The commissions administer the water allocation rules, address problems and conflicts, engage in studies, monitor, and report on different water use and supply issues in the compact river basin. Other compacts eschew commissions and are enforced by state water agencies. Over time, as compact commissioners and states have faced disagreements

Table 12.1   Interstate River Compacts

Compacts	Member States	Date Formed	Governing Structure	Jurisdictional Scope
Arkansas	Colorado, Kansas	1942	Commission	Surface water Groundwater
Bear	Idaho, Utah, Wyoming	1958, 80	Commission	Surface water Groundwater Water quality
Belle Fourche	South Dakota, Wyoming	1943	None	Surface water
Big Blue	Kansas, Nebraska	1971	Commission	Surface water Groundwater Water quality
Costilla Creek	Colorado, New Mexico	1944, 63	Commission	Surface water
Klamath	California, Oregon	1956	Commission	Surface water Water quality
La Plata	Colorado, New Mexico	1922	Commission	Surface water
Pecos	New Mexico, Texas	1949	Commission	Surface water Water quality
Republican	Colorado, Kansas, Nebraska	1943	Commission	Surface water Groundwater
Rio Grande	Colorado, New Mexico, Texas	1938	Commission	Surface water Water quality
Snake	Idaho, Wyoming	1949	Commission	Surface water
South Platte	Colorado, Nebraska	1923	None	Surface water
Upper Niobrara	Nebraska, Wyoming	1962	None	Surface water
Yellowstone	Montana, North Dakota, Wyoming	1950	Commission	Surface water

over compliance with or interpretation of the rules under new circumstances, they have adapted in various ways. Two compacts have been modified, a few have been revised due to court cases, and a number have invested in new strategies and capacity building (Heikkila and Schlager 2008).

Effective institutional change is not guaranteed, however. Premised on CPRT principles, four general categories of expectations about the vulnerability and adaptability of existing compacts to climate change are discernible and offer analytical guidance to policy makers: those applicable to the nature of the rules, the scope of the rules, levels of state adaptive capacity, and the potential for interstate water commission adaptation.

Rule Types

Compact water allocation rules consist of different "types" (e.g., fixed or proportionate), which may apply at different times of the year, to different segments of rivers, or to different water users or states (see Table 12.2). Each type of rule, in turn, has subcategories of rules within it. These features determine how well matched the different compacts are to the physical context imposed by climate change. Who is likely to be most vulnerable also depends on how the rules apportion benefits to the users in the CPR setting.

Proposition 1: Fixed allocation rules squarely place the risk of water shortages on specific states, making it likely that they are less adaptive than proportional rules to climate change.

Two kinds of fixed allocation rules differentially affect western states' vulnerabilities and adaptive capacities to projected climate change. One type of fixed rule allocates a specified amount of water to each state. The Republican River Compact originally allowed Colorado and Nebraska, the two upstream states, to take their fixed allocation regardless of whether sufficient water remained in the river to meet the fixed allocation of Kansas. Thus, Kansas was vulnerable to the actions of the upstream states.

A more commonly used fixed allocation rule is the minimum flow rule. Upstream states commit to delivering a specified amount of water to downstream states. Consequently, the upstream states bear the effects of a changing hydrologic regime. In the case of the Big Blue Compact and the South Platte Compact, upstream states commit to providing minimum daily stream flows during the irrigation season. During particularly dry years, even if the upstream state fully complies with all of the administrative requirements of the compact, it still will be out of compliance. This very scenario occurred in the Big Blue River Basin for the first

Table 12.2   Water Allocation Rules of Western Interstate River Compacts

Compact	Rule Type	Seasonality	Users Subject to Compact Regulation
Arkansas	Stream flows fixed; reservoir proportionate	November 1–March 31 winter storage; April 1–October 31 summer storage	Post-1948 Colorado water users
Bear	Stream flows proportionate; reservoir fixed	Low flows trigger regulation	All water users
Belle Fourche	Proportionate	None	Post-1943 water users
Big Blue	Stream flows fixed	May 1–September 30 irrigation season	Post-November 1, 1968 Nebraska water users
Costilla Creek	Proportionate	May 16–September 30 irrigation season; October 1–May 15 storage season	All water users
Klamath	Prior appropriation	None	Post-1957 water users
La Plata	Proportionate	February 15–December 1	Colorado water users
Pecos	Fixed	None	New Mexico water users
Republican	Fixed	None	Post-1948 Nebraska water users
Rio Grande	Proportionate	None	Colorado and New Mexico water users
Snake	Proportionate	None	All water users

Continued

Table 12.2 (*Continued*)   Water Allocation Rules of Western Interstate River Compacts

Compact	Rule Type	Seasonality	Users Subject to Compact Regulation
South Platte	Fixed	April 1–October 15 irrigation season	Post-June 14, 1897 Colorado water users Washington County east to state line
Upper Niobrara	Prior appropriation	None	Post-1957 water users
Yellowstone	Proportionate	None	Post-January 1, 1950 water users

time in 2003 as a severe drought unfolded. Even though Nebraska limited intrastate water use—as required by the compact—for three years, it consistently failed to deliver the required minimum flows to Kansas during the irrigation season (Big Blue River Compact Commission 2004, 2005).

Proposition 2: Proportionate allocation rules can be effective in sharing the risk of water shortages among states and thus are more adaptive to climate change conditions, but upstream users may be vulnerable to greater shortages than they have been historically.

Proportionate allocation rules spread the risk of water shortages among the states rather than concentrating them on an upstream or a downstream state. These rules can provide either a set percentage for each state or the proportion may vary depending on water flows. The Bear River Compact of 1958, for example, allocates supplies as a set percentage for each state, prompted whenever stream flows drop below a specified level (Bear River Compact Commission 1958–70; Jibson 1997).

Under a drier and more variable climate, however, fixed proportionate rules lead to new vulnerabilities, particularly for water users in upstream states who may have to forego historical water usage in deference to downstream users. For instance, the La Plata River Compact requires Colorado, the upstream state, to shepherd 50 percent of the flow of the river to the New Mexico border. Colorado must absorb all water transit losses in getting this flow to the border. During the middle of the summer, transit losses may be quite high. Furthermore, Colorado water users who have very "senior" (or long-standing and historical) rights to water must be prevented from diverting the water before it reaches New Mexico, something that they have resisted (Knox 2001). Although the compact allows some leeway for states to manage extreme water shortages, the number of times that Colorado is unable to deliver water supplies to the border is likely to increase throughout the year under climate change, even if Coloradoans do not divert water.

Some compacts, such as those of the Rio Grande and Costilla Creek, use "variable" proportionate rules that stipulate how the amount of water allocated differs depending on water flows. Although these rules may appear more flexible to changing climate conditions, their percentages are based on hydrologic models that may be ill calibrated to new climate conditions. For instance, under the Rio Grande Compact, Colorado is committed to a schedule of water deliveries to New Mexico, using a model that estimates the relationships between inflows at the head of the river and outflows at the state line with New Mexico. Under climate change, droughts may be more frequent or rainfall and snowmelt patterns may change, meaning that the actual relationships between inflows and outflows are less likely to fit the model. The upstream state will then find it more difficult, if not impossible, to meet its water delivery commitments.

Rule Scope

CPRT also indicates that the scope of water allocation rules must be matched to climate change needs or users will be vulnerable to shortages. Scope specifies when compact rules apply, how much water they apply to, and which water users are affected by them.

Proposition 3: When the scope of compact rules targets particular seasons, encompasses a large portion of river flows, or targets particular users over others, vulnerabilities to climate change are likely to be greater.

As noted, most compact water allocation rules are particularly restrictive during the irrigation season or summer season. Outside of the irrigation season, a number of compacts devote stream flows to filling reservoirs. As climate change unfolds, however, the dates defining seasons may no longer correspond to the actual seasons. With warmer temperatures, farmers may want to irrigate into the fall or may need to start planting and irrigating earlier in the spring. Yet compacts with seasonal rules restrict such options, and those with seasonal fixed allocation rules may be particularly vulnerable. Moreover, with earlier snowmelt and runoff, upstream states may no longer be credited with providing minimum flows guaranteed during a particular season by the upstream state, as peak flows may begin occurring out of season.

How much water a compact rule encompasses may also prove to be as important as the seasonality of the rule. For instance, the Big Blue Compact's minimum flow rules apply only during the irrigation season from May through September. During those months, Nebraska is required to deliver to Kansas between 3 and 17 percent of the mean monthly flow of the Big and Little Blue rivers, providing Nebraska with a larger "water cushion" to meet compact requirements. In contrast, in 1947, the Republican Compact water allocation rule divided about 75 percent of the average annual surface flows among the states, providing much less leeway for states to meet their compact requirements. Thus, Nebraska has had a much easier time complying with the Big Blue River Compact. It has struggled, however, especially during drought seasons, to comply with the Republican River Compact. This also places Kansas in a more vulnerable position with respect to the challenges Nebraska will face in complying with the Republican River Compact's allocation rules as climate change exacerbates drought conditions.

As noted, the targets of compact rules will also affect water vulnerabilities. Many compacts explicitly exclude water users with allocation rights prior to the signing of the agreement from facing use restrictions. The idea was that only new water users would need to be limited in order to ensure future interstate "comity." For instance, the 1947 Arkansas River Compact states that the flows of the river may not be materially depleted. This has been interpreted to mean that after 1947, new water uses that deplete the river, such as groundwater pumping, have to replace the depleted water, thus limiting the compact's scope. But under changing climate conditions, the vulnerabilities of those who are subject to the compact are likely to increase, a condition that CPR theory views as problematic for success, because the pain will not be shared by all users.

A related challenge is that very few compacts originally included both surface water and groundwater users in the allocation rules. As several compact members have already found, the hydrologic connection between groundwater and surface water means that groundwater pumping, which often increases during drought years, can reduce flows downstream. The Republican River, for example, is hydrologically connected to the Ogallala groundwater aquifer; pumping in the Republican River Basin has been slowly reducing surface water flows so that the total amount of water that the allocation rule governs exceeds the average annual discharge of the river (Szilagyi 1999). This led to a lawsuit by Kansas against Nebraska and Colorado, the upstream states, that went all the way to the U.S. Supreme Court.

The lawsuit settlement required the two upstream states to count a portion of their groundwater pumping against their compact water allocations. Counting groundwater placed both states out of compliance with the compact and required them to attempt strict regulation of groundwater wells. Such strategies may enhance adaptability for the states; Nebraska, for instance, invested in integrated ground and surface water modeling expertise to enhance its capacity to administer the compact's water allocation rules. However, placing new regulations on established water users—rather than all users—increases tensions. The Nebraska Department of Natural Resources has had to work for almost a decade with groundwater users to align them better with state compact commitments.

State Capacity

A fundamental take-home message from CPRT, however, is that no single best allocation rule is applicable to all river basins or even the same river basin over time (Ostrom 1990, 2005). Many of the problems identified earlier, such as seasonality mismatches or the nature of the hydrologic connection between rivers and groundwater basins, became apparent only after years of administering the water allocation rules and learning how they work in practice. Consequently, another key issue identified by CPRT is whether learning can inform rule revisions or new strategies to make rules perform better. This is especially true in upstream states, because they are likely to be the first responders to climate impacts, and even more so for states in compacts with allocation rules requiring minimum flows to downstream users.

Proposition 4: Under climate change conditions, states with a history of adaptation to groundwater and surface water allocation shifts informed by established administrative capacities could become models of how best to induce compact compliance and thus mitigate vulnerabilities.

CPR research clearly shows that climate change vulnerability and adaptability are a function of both state physical features (needs) and administrative capacities and that these will vary across states and times. Take Colorado, which is an upstream and "headwater" state in five compacts that we examined (Arkansas, Costilla Creek, Republican, Rio Grande, and South Platte), as a case in point. In each of these five river basins, Colorado's water supplies are either fully allocated or overallocated. Consequently, its water compact administrators have little flexibility to ensure that more water flows downstream to meet interstate compact requirements as they face climate vulnerabilities.

Although Colorado is largely constrained by its commitments to surface water rights, it has demonstrated some degree of adaptive capacity when groundwater is involved. Beginning in the 1960s, conflicts emerged over access to increasingly scarce water supplies, primarily between Colorado's groundwater and surface water users and between Colorado and downstream states. At the heart of the intrastate and interstate conflicts has been the effects of groundwater pumping on surface water flows. Colorado's policy makers, water users, and state engineer's office created restrictions on pumping groundwater that is "tributary" to surface water. Groundwater users also could continue pumping at certain times of the year if they provided "replacement" water for the portion of the surface water that pumping depleted from the stream.

Importantly, the state of Colorado invested tens of millions of dollars in decision support systems that carefully track water rights and water diversions from the major river basins in the state. Basin-centered arrangements have been developed that also foster water governance capacity. Citizens in the Arkansas River Valley created a conservancy district with taxing powers. The revenues are used to purchase or lease Arkansas River water rights that would otherwise be sold to water users in other river basins, thus keeping the water in basin to meet water demands (Lower Arkansas Valley Water Conservancy District 2010).

Most importantly, however, Colorado used and invested in institutional arrangements that align with CPR principles. First, water users have actively participated in designing the rules governing ground and surface water allocation and use. Opportunities to engage in water governance occur through a variety of venues. Those with water rights or those who want water rights have access to water courts to create, revise, enforce, and extinguish existing water rights. The state engineer actively engages water users in devising rules and regulations. Once the state engineer finalizes rules and regulations, a water court is asked to rule on the validity of the rules, providing water users another opportunity to weigh in. Colorado also allows water users to devise their own governing arrangements, as the water users in the Arkansas River Basin did in creating a conservancy district. Second, careful attention is paid to resolving conflicts among competing water users and between water users and state water officials. Water courts are used not only to devise water rights and rules but also to address and resolve conflicts among water users and officials. Third, as CPRT advises, Colorado has invested in extensive water monitoring systems, from local water commissioners who administer water rights on the ground to sophisticated decision support systems that track water rights and their use in real time.

In comparison, Wyoming does not face the same problems that Colorado faces of having overappropriated water rights in its compact basins. In fact, in 2001, Wyoming predicted that it was in a position to develop more storage and new water allocations while remaining in compliance with compact obligations (Wyoming Water Development Commission 2001). As such, pressures to enhance capacity building have not been as strong. Nonetheless, it is not clear how long this will last. Although Wyoming has a small population, its water demands from the energy sector are growing. Additionally, in the Bear and Yellowstone river basins, increasing water scarcity is beginning to place pressure on Wyoming to administer water rights more actively so that downstream states receive compact allocations. Consequently, the state has begun paying closer attention to the potential effects of climate change on its water supplies, especially given reliance on snowpack to feed its rivers (Gray and Andersen 2009).

Interstate Commission Rules

Upstream states, of course, did not enter into compacts alone. Although they may be forced into the position of first responders to the effects of climate change, they also have the opportunity to work together with downstream states via interstate commissions to adapt to the challenges facing compacts. In the process, the importance of nesting cannot be overemphasized.

Proposition 5: How well rules are nested will determine the success of adaptation efforts.

We illustrate this point by again looking at the interstate administrative capacities of the two compacts in which Wyoming, as an upstream state, is likely to have less physical wiggle room to adapt to climate change—the Bear and Yellowstone river compacts. Over time, the Bear River Compact Commission has invested in establishing real-time automated monitoring of stream flows over the length of the river, combined with regular communication between state watermasters, who monitor intrastate water rights diversions, and the compact water administrator (Barnett 2006; Jibson 1997). Based on real-time stream flow information, the compact administrator determines whether flows have dropped below a level that triggers regulation and then communicates to the state watermasters which water users to shut down and when. When flows exceed the "trigger" level or when the end of the growing season is reached, administration of interstate allocation rules ceases. This type of nested, multilevel rule set facilitates transparency, consistent expectations among the states and water users, and quick responses to changes in resource availability, while meeting compact obligations.

In contrast, the Yellowstone River Compact Commission has not invested in nested administrative capacity to account for water use and to monitor water allocations. Supplies have generally been more than sufficient to meet water demands in the basin, so the states historically have not had to administer the compact. However, concern has periodically arisen among the commissioners that supply limitations are on the horizon and that procedures and mechanisms will be needed to administer the compact more actively before these limitations are realized (Yellowstone River Compact Commission 1950–2005).

Starting in 2000, drought in the basin brought these questions to the forefront of discussions at the commission, with Montana raising concerns that Wyoming may not be effectively complying with the compact. Although Wyoming argues it has not violated the compact, the state openly admits that the "official gauging stations established by the Compact to effect a regulation" are inadequate to determine when water supply conditions should trigger water administration (Wyoming Water Development Commission 2002, I-9). Thus, this compact lacks the nested design principles that CPRT says will induce rule compliance or foster adaptation.

Toward CPRT-Informed Institutional Adaptation to Climate Change

Building on the insights of CPRT, we offer and assess the obstacles to realizing four important goals that compact administrators, water managers, and water users should pursue in light of their vulnerabilities, capacities, and fiscal realities.

Recommendation 1: States should not wait to reopen and renegotiate the water allocation rules of compacts.

With climate change underway in the western states, policy makers in most states should begin redesigning water allocation rules immediately. Three obstacles will make these negotiations difficult. First, when compacts were initially signed, all participants anticipated being made better off, or at least not worse off. Most compacts also grandfathered in existing water rights, providing water users with more secure rights in the process. In addition, many compacts resulted in the federal government building large surface water storage projects that provided more water and more reliable sources of water to states and their citizens. Even with all this, however, it often took a decade or more for compact adoption. Moreover, the compact negotiating context is very different today. The federal government is unlikely to entice compact revisions by investing in new surface storage facilities. Also, in attempting to make water allocation rules better match a drier environment, states will be attempting to reallocate less water. It is unclear how states will gain sufficient support to reduce or eliminate water rights.

Second, the different processes for negotiating and renegotiating compacts present states with the worrisome possibility that they could lose control of the process. If initiated by states and commissions, compacts must still be ratified by the states' legislatures and Congress. This opens the compact to the scrutiny of disaffected farmers who feel that their water rights are being taken from them, of municipalities who want more water for their growing populations, and of environmentalists who seek to protect riparian areas and endangered species. Another approach is for Congress to redesign the water allocation rules, but states are even more likely to lose control over this process than the previous one. Both of these processes are also likely to expose compacts to the requirements of federal environmental laws. As noted, most compacts were adopted prior to the enactment of federal environmental laws. As environmental issues have arisen in compact-governed river basins, they have largely been addressed through means separate from compacts. That would almost certainly change if either states or Congress tried to revise compacts.

Third, states could try to alter existing compacts with a U.S. Supreme Court case. But no state has ever attempted explicitly to revise water allocation rules this way, and it is not clear that the Supreme Court would accept this role. In the interstate river compact cases that it has decided thus far, the court has accepted compliance, monitoring, and penalty proposals by states, but it has refused to redesign what it has considered key aspects of compacts, such as the structure and voting rules of commissions.

Recommendation 2: Press for investments in well-developed and transparent monitoring systems, compliance mechanisms, and information-sharing procedures among stakeholders.

States should also invest in adequate monitoring systems to support robust governance—especially when water supplies are scarce. Monitoring lessens the mistrust and tensions between states that are likely to result when they face differing degrees of climate vulnerability. As the hydrologic systems of the western United States change and become drier and more variable, downstream states will find it difficult to determine whether compact violations are attributable (1) to upstream states allowing additional water development, (2) to upstream states failing to limit intrastate water use effectively, (3) to a changing hydrologic regime, or (4) to a combination of all three. Most existing compacts also need to be much clearer about how upstream states are to come into compliance with water allocation rules in a timely fashion, as well as how they are to make up the water that was due the downstream state but not delivered. Both of these issues hinge on more complete and transparent monitoring systems.

Developing additional information and investing in more extensive monitoring networks will, over time, address some of the uncertainty. However, how well they do depends on the design of monitoring networks and the sharing of various types of information. CPRT suggests that any extensive monitoring networks developed need to be transparent across all member states and need to provide assurances that upstream states are acting in good faith when complying with compact allocation rules. Most compact commissions operate an extensive system of gauges that monitor surface water stream flows. However, few compact commissions have access to data on intrastate water diversions or water consumption. Nor do they have detailed information on the operation of reservoirs that they do not directly control, or on groundwater pumping and its effects on surface flows. In addition, most compact commissions have not invested in developing hydrologic models that further understanding of the interaction between surface and groundwater diversions, the operation of reservoirs, and water consumption on the behavior of river systems. But without top-notch hydrologic models, it is difficult for compact commissions to determine the sources of declining flows.

Although well-designed and extensive water monitoring systems and hydrologic models seem reasonable and practical, a number of hurdles must be overcome to put them in place. First, the benefits and costs of such systems are unevenly distributed among the states. The costs of extensive monitoring systems are largely borne by the upstream state, as it and its water users invest in measuring (e.g., metering wells), monitoring (e.g., additional watermasters), and reporting. The benefits of such systems are largely enjoyed by the downstream state, which is provided with better information, allowing it more ably to assess the sources of increasingly variable flows. Second, well-designed and extensive water monitoring systems expose the upstream state to additional water regulation or at least demands for it by downstream states. As downstream states demand more stringent water regulation, upstream states bristle at perceived incursions into their state sovereignty. Third, although allowing greater insight into the interactions of the various parts of the river basin, hydrologic modeling does not remove all uncertainty, thus allowing downstream states to continue making demands for more water from upstream states. Still, the benefits of having these systems in place outweigh the risks, especially if accompanied by conflict resolution approaches to resolving the disagreements that do arise.

Recommendation 3: Press for investments in conflict resolution mechanisms that are relatively low cost and easily accessible, rather than only relying on commissions or the courts.

Investing in monitoring and compliance may help minimize distrust, but it cannot eliminate disagreements over the interpretation of monitoring and compliance activities and requirements. One long-standing CPR principle is the necessity of relatively low-cost conflict resolution mechanisms. Presently, most compacts have two forms of conflict resolution—compact commissions and the Supreme Court. Certainly, both types of mechanisms have strengths, but they also have limitations. Even though they use unanimity rules and address a wide range of conflicts, commissions consistently fail to address claims made by downstream states that upstream states are violating water allocation rules (Schlager and Heikkila 2009). And although states can use the authority of the Supreme Court to bring their very reluctant partner(s) in a dispute before the bench to settle the issue, cases may last a decade or more and cost tens of millions of dollars to develop hydrologic models and round up expert witnesses.

Consequently, we argue that different forms of mediation and arbitration are better alternatives that compact commissions could experiment with to supplement the work of commissions and the Supreme Court. In particular, an independent third-party option may allow states to identify and explore acceptable solutions to the more challenging conflicts with which commissions struggle, in the process avoiding time-consuming delays and exorbitant court costs. Moreover, access to conflict resolution mechanisms should be made relatively simple but not so simple that every conflict leads to alternative dispute resolution. This would undermine the conflict resolution roles of commissions. By the same token, CPRT suggests that the processes should be relatively flexible so as not to recreate the discovery and burden-of-proof requirements of a full-fledged court case.

In the end, however, alternative dispute resolution mechanisms work only as well as wanted by the participants. In the one compact that does allow for binding arbitration (Arkansas River), the states have not agreed on the issues for its use and thus have not used it. In the only compact that allows for nonbinding arbitration (Republican River), the states have used arbitration but have rejected the proposed solutions. Thus, the Supreme Court and commissions are still likely to play an important conflict resolution role as climate changes accelerate.

Recommendation 4: States and commissions must look for opportunities to coordinate actions that limit water demand and increase water supply.

The challenge for compacts facing climate change will be to identify flexible management opportunities that are workable under new supply constraints while still reliably meeting the water demands of member states (e.g., Blomquist 2007; Gleick 2003; Lall et al. 2008). We argue that the key to doing so is integrating supply-and-demand approaches to dealing with the water problems occasioned by climate change. According to CPRT, these opportunities, in turn, require coordination (i.e., nesting) of approaches with state and local water managers who face similar challenges.

One option is to move water toward more "higher-valued" uses to encourage more efficiency in use both within and between states, such as through water leasing. States that have high-value demands, such as municipal use or industrial use, may be able to pay other states to refrain from using their water for lower-valued uses (e.g., certain crops). This allows more water to be available for higher-valued uses in times of shortages. Alternatively, compact commissions might consider interstate water banking, whereby one state that has excess resources in a wet season or year is paid by another state to store that water so that it can be made available in times of shortages. They also could assist states in saving more water by investing in water demand reductions or efficiency improvements in irrigated agriculture, which consumes nearly 80 percent of western water supplies. For instance, compact states could share the costs of lining the canals of irrigation systems and, in turn, share the water that is saved, which could be devoted to compact purposes.

In basins that have not yet faced overappropriation and still have sources of supply to develop, states also may need to invest over the long term in more storage capacity to buffer the increasing variability of stream flows and longer-term droughts. In the Bear River Basin, Wyoming has acknowledged the need for more storage in the coming years to ensure compact compliance during low-flow scenarios (Wyoming Water Development Commission 2001). Utah also has been looking for more upstream storage on the Bear River for years, and recently, it has been feeling increasing pressure from growth in Salt Lake City to capture more of those resources. The rub is that gaining political approval for new dams has proven difficult at best in the West since the 1970s. Storage of surface water in groundwater basins is an additional option for enhancing long-term storage in such settings, depending on local hydrogeology and institutional feasibility (Blomquist, Schlager, and Heikkila 2004).

This seems the most immediately promising of the lessons we have drawn, because leasing water rights, operating water banks, investing in irrigation efficiencies, and developing groundwater recharge projects are all familiar types of projects to western states. Still, success depends on states contributing the necessary resources in time to meet the vulnerabilities they are experiencing with changing climates—hardly a given in today's era of fiscal stress. Regardless, demand-side solutions focused on water conservation must aggressively complement supply-side strategies—whether by individual states or commissions—if institutional adaptation is to have any hope of keeping up with the challenges of climate change in the region.

Conclusion

Little doubt exists among climate scientists, hydrologists, and water managers that the availability of water supplies in the western United States, especially in the Southwest and Intermountain West, is going to be more limited and more variable in the coming decades. The vulnerability of different basins, states, and water users to these changes depends not only on the degree of the physical changes but also on the institutional arrangements that westerners have developed or will create to govern water supplies. We have argued that CPRT, with its emphasis on the design and performance of institutional arrangements, provides a useful starting point for assessing vulnerabilities, adaptation capacities, and institutional responses to climate change.

CPRT alerts policy makers to the importance of having rules align with the physical and social settings in which they are applied. Thus, among other things, compacts with fixed water allocation rules and seasonal rules are more vulnerable to climate change, because they provide little leeway or flexibility in dealing with a changing hydrologic regime. Moreover, CPRT posits that such mismatches are more readily addressed if resource users participate in meaningful ways in revising the rules. States such as Colorado have been able to respond to increasing water scarcity in part because water users have access to different venues that allow them to participate in rule design. CPRT also reminds us that rules are not self-implementing or self-enforcing and should be nested to be effective.

Looking to the future, we expect that institutional investments to enhance monitoring, compliance, and conflict resolution mechanisms in interstate compacts will be essential to their ability to deal with vulnerabilities, as the likelihood of renegotiating existing compacts is low. In light of ongoing changes in western state climates, interstate compact officials are going to have to (1) make such investments; (2) work closely with states and local water users to promote, integrate, and nest more flexible supply- and demand-side water management strategies; and (3) encourage more efficient water use and conservation to ensure that the West's precious water resources will fuel their economies. And in doing so, ignoring CPRT insights is to court disappointment, if not severe social, economic, and lifestyle changes.

Commentary

Elisabeth A. Graffy

Water scarcity is frequently presumed to be a biophysical dilemma, but it is also socially constructed. How the phenomenon is understood can dramatically affect how it is identified as a problem; its scope, urgency, and potential for causing harm; and the options or justifications for a collective response. This key component escapes the scrutiny of Schlager and Heikkila, although their arguments are important for future progress in addressing climate adaptation in the American West.

Presently, five distinct narratives characterize water scarcity discourse—scientific, managerial, governance, ecological, and development—each corresponding to very different social constructions of the problem and applicable solutions (Graffy 2006). Some elements of these narratives contradict each other philosophically and some readily harmonize toward coordination in a variety of policy coalitions over time. Yet, in the water policy domain as a whole, managerial and scientific narratives tend to characterize historical water management regimes, whereas development, governance, and ecological narratives are relative newcomers.

The "high and dry" telling of the water scarcity story in this chapter reveals strong managerial and scientific narratives associated with interstate compacts. By applying common-pool resource theory and making recommendations for enhanced inclusiveness as a principle of good institutional design, the authors introduce elements of the governance narrative. Still, surprisingly little voice is given to the ecological narrative. This creates a dysfunctional impression of insulation, which may be caused or at least compounded by an institutional design that appears to limit the scope of participation in collective choice (Heikkila, Schlager, and Davis 2011). Best practices and theory remain elusive, but it may suffice to describe this distinct and still-emerging management paradigm that I offer as *socioecological governance*.

Socioecological governance reflects the mainstreaming of environmental legislation since the 1970s, as well as assumptions about the importance of public participation and the necessity of a more collaborative rather than hierarchical relationship between science and society. It does not reject economic development as an objective, but as a management paradigm, it rests on different philosophical foundations than the economic development orientation that prevailed in natural resource management in the twentieth century, when most of the compacts now in force were signed. However, concerns about equity and tradeoffs spill out beyond the boundaries of the traditional water management sector. These social and political questions need to be addressed by socioecological governance models—and have issues framed in ways prompting reforms.

As the authors concede, scientific forecasts of water scarcity, no matter how severe, will not automatically translate into a social response; the latter requires a process through which new information is understood, invested with social meaning, and framed in a way that enables goal-setting and implementation through formal and informal institutional channels (Graffy 2006, 2008). In the case of interstate compacts, reluctance to adopt recommendations may reflect the incompleteness of such a process. For instance, if recommendations to reopen and renegotiate allocation rules proactively do not fully account for the social risks of a lack of institutional change, they are unlikely to be adopted no matter how much biophysical risk they identify.

Despite conventional wisdom insisting that only crises can trigger far-reaching reform such as that needed in the West in response to climate change, symbolic events framed in ways stressing ecological and social impacts can afford the impulse for reform among galvanized politicians, lawyers, environmental groups, scientists, agency administrators, and many members of the general public. In addition, greater inclusiveness in the deliberative process in putting solutions together is necessary to achieve institutional legitimacy and a willingness to comply with reforms. Granted, barriers and incentives for interstate water compacts to undertake reforms in anticipation of climate change-induced scarcity can be complex and highly situation-specific. And resolving these issues is only likely to become more vexing. Arguably, progress can be better made by reframing the issue from one of science to one of socioecological impacts, as well as by affording meaningful public engagement for legitimacy and redress.

References

Aall, P., D. Miltenberger, and T. Weiss. 2000. *Guide to IGOs, NGOs, and the military in peace and relief operations.* Washington, DC: United States Institute of Peace.

Abiew, F. 2003. From civil strife to civic society: NGO-military cooperation in peace operations. Occasional Paper no. 39, Centre for Security and Defence Studies, Carleton University. http://www.carleton.ca/csds/docs/occasional_papers/npsia-39.pdf (accessed November 19, 2009).

Abramson, M. A., and P. R. Lawrence. 2001. The challenge of transforming organizations: Lessons learned about revitalizing organizations. In *Transforming organizations*, edited by M. A. Abramson and P. R. Lawrence, 1–10. Lanham, MD: Rowman & Littlefield.

Adger, N. 2000. Social and ecological resilience: Are they related? *Progress in Human Geography* 24(3): 347–364.

Adger, N. 2006. Vulnerability. *Global Environmental Change* 16(3): 268–281.

Agranoff, R. 2005. Managing collaborative performance. *Public Performance & Management Review* 29(1): 18–45.

Agranoff, R. 2008. Enhancing performance through public sector networks: Mobilizing human capital in communities of practice. *Public Performance & Management Review* 31(3): 320–347.

Aher, M., and J. Popkin. 1984. The effect of gender and race differences on public-private wage comparisons: A study of postal workers. *Industrial and Labor Relations Review* 38(1): 16–25.

Aldrich, H. E. 1979. *Organizations and environments.* Englewood Cliffs, NJ: Prentice Hall.

Aldrich, H. E., and P. Marsden. 1988. Environments and organization. In *Handbook of sociology*, edited by N. J. Smelser, 361–392. Newbury Park, CA: Sage Publications.

Alexander, E. R. 1995. *How organizations act together: Interorganizational coordination in theory and practice.* Luxembourg: Gordon and Breach.

Alford, J. 2009. *Engaging public sector clients: From service-delivery to co-production.* London: Palgrave Macmillan.

Allan, P., and S. Rosenberg. 1986. Assessment of merit pay administration under New York City's managerial performance evaluation system: Three years of experience. *Public Personnel Management* 15(3): 297–309.

Alliance for Board Diversity. 2005. New report shows severe under-representation of women and minorities on corporate boards. News release, May 11. www.catalystwomen.org/files/pr/ABD_pr.pdf (accessed August 2, 2006).

Alter, C., and J. Hage. 1993. *Organizations working together.* Newbury Park, CA: Sage Publications.

American Civil Liberties Union of Northern California. 2002. Bush administration vs. the Constitution: A civil liberties scorecard, September 2002. www.aclunc.org/911/scorecard.html (accessed September 27, 2006).

Americans for a Fair Chance. 2005. *Anti-affirmative action threats in the states: 1997-2004.* Leadership Conference on Civil Rights Education Fund. http://fairchance.civilrights.org/the_facts/reports/aa_state_2005.pdf (accessed February 20, 2006).

Amis, J., T. Slack, and C. R. Hinings. 2002. Values and organizational change. *Journal of Applied Behavioral Science* 38(4): 436–466.

Amis, J., T. Slack, and C. R. Hinings. 2004. The pace, sequence, and linearity of radical change. *Academy of Management Journal* 47(1): 15–39.

Andersen, L. B. 2007. Professional norms, public service motivation, or/and economic incentives: What motivates public employees? Presented at the Annual Conference of the European Group of Public Administration, Madrid, Spain, September 19–22.

Andersen, L. B., and T. Pallesen. 2008. "Not just for the money?" How financial incentives affect the number of publications at Danish research institutions. *International Public Management Journal* 11(1): 28–47.

Andrews, R., G. A. Boyne, K. J. Meier, L. J. O'Toole, Jr., and R. M. Walker. 2005. Representative bureaucracy, organizational strategy, and public service performance: An empirical analysis of English local government. *Journal of Public Administration Research and Theory* 15(4): 489–504.

Anklam, P. 2007. *Net work: A practical guide to creating and sustaining networks at work and in the world.* Boston, MA: Elsevier/Butterworth-Heinemann.

Ansell, C. K., and S. E. Reckhow. 2007. Linking networks to interview results: A study of the Oakland school reform network. Presented at the Annual Meeting of the American Political Science Association, Chicago, IL, August 30–September 2.

Appleby, P. H. 1945. *Big democracy.* New York: Alfred A. Knopf.

Armenakis, A. A., and A. G. Bedeian. 1999. Organizational change: A review of theory and research in the 1990s. *Journal of Management* 25(3): 293–315.

Armenakis, A. A., S. G. Harris, and H. S. Feild. 2001. Paradigms in organizational change: Change agent and change target perspectives. In *Handbook of organizational behavior,* edited by R. T. Golembiewski, 631–658. New York: Marcel Dekker.

Arnstein, S. R. 1969. A ladder of citizen participation. *Journal of the American Planning Association* 35(4): 216–224.

Arrow, K. J. 1998. What has economics to say about racial discrimination? *Journal of Economic Perspectives* 12(2): 91–100.

Artz, K. W., and T. H. Brush. 2000. Asset specificity, uncertainty, and relational norms: An examination of coordination costs in collaborative strategic alliances. *Journal of Economic Behavior & Organization* 41: 337–362.

Ashenfelter, O., and J. Heckman. 1976. Measuring the effect of an antidiscrimination program. In *Evaluating the labor market effects of social programs,* edited by O. Ashenfelter and J. Blum, 46–84. Princeton, NJ: Princeton University Press.

Aucoin, P. 1990. *The new public management: Canada in comparative perspective.* Montreal: IRPP.

Auf der Heide, E. 1989. Disaster response: Principles of preparation and coordination. http://orgmai12.coe-dmha.org/dr/index.html (accessed November 19, 2009).

Axelrod, R. H. 2000. *Terms of engagement.* San Francisco, CA: Berrett-Koehler Publishers.

Baar, K. K. 2001. Open competition, transparency, and impartiality in local government contracting out of public services. In *Navigation to the market: Regulation and competition in local utilities in Central and Eastern Europe*, edited by T. M. Horváth and G. Péteri, 99–140. Budapest, Hungary: Local Government and Public Service Reform Initiative, Open Society Institute.

Bailey, C., S. Miles, and P. Stark. 2004. Culture-led regeneration and the revitalisation of identities in Newcastle, Gateshead and the North East of England. *International Journal of Cultural Policy* 10(1): 47–65.

Baiocchi, G. 2001. Participation, activism, and politics: The Porto Alegre experiment and deliberative democratic theory. *Politics and Society* 29(1): 43–72.

Baker, B., D. Besendorfer, and L. J. Kotlikoff. 2002. Intertemporal state budgeting. National Bureau for Economic Research, Working Paper W9067. http://www.nber.org/papers/w9067 (accessed July 16, 2007).

Baker, G., R. Gibbons, and K. J. Murphy. 2002. Relational contracts and the theory of the firm. *Quarterly Journal of Economics* 117(1): 39–84.

Baldassare, M. 1998. *When government fails: The Orange County bankruptcy*. Berkeley: University of California Press.

Baldwin, J. N. 1996. Female promotions in the male-dominant organizations: The case of the United States military. *Journal of Politics* 58(4): 1184–1197.

Balogun, J., P. Gleadle, V. H. Hailey, and H. Willmott. 2005. Managing change across boundaries: Boundary-shaking practices. *British Journal of Management* 16(4): 261–278.

Bantel, K. A., and S. E. Jackson. 1989. Top management and innovations in banking: Does the composition of the top team make a difference? *Strategic Management Journal* 10(S1): 107–124.

Barber, B. R. 1984. *Strong democracy: Participatory politics for a new age*. Berkeley: University of California Press.

Barber, B. R. 2003. *Strong democracy: Participatory politics for a new age*. 20th anniversary ed. Berkeley: University of California Press.

Barbezat, D. 1989. Affirmative action in higher education: Have two decades altered salary differentials by sex and race? *Research Labor Economics* 10: 107–156.

Barnett, J. 2006. Engineer-Manager, Bear River Compact Commission. Personal communication.

Barnett, T. P., and D. W. Pierce. 2008. When will Lake Mead go dry? *Water Resources Research* 44(3).

Barnett, T. P., and D. W. Pierce. 2009. Sustainable water deliveries from the Colorado River in a changing climate. *Proceedings of the National Academy of Sciences* 106(18): 7334–7338.

Barsugli, J. J., K. Nowak, B. Rajagopalan, J. R. Prairie, and B. Harding. 2009. Comment on when will Lake Mead go dry? by T. P. Barnett and D. W. Pierce. *Water Resources Research* 45(9).

Bartol, K. M., and D. C. Martin. 1989. Effects of dependency, dependency threats, and pay secrecy on managerial pay allocations. *Journal of Applied Psychology* 74(1): 105–113.

Barzelay, M. 2001. *The new public management: Improving research and policy dialogue*. Berkeley: University of California Press.

Barzelay, M., with B. J. Armajani. 1992. *Breaking through bureaucracy*. Berkeley: University of California Press.

Battaglio, R. P., Jr., and S. E. Condrey. 2006. Civil service reform: Examining state and local cases. *Review of Public Personnel Administration* 26(2): 118–138.

Battaglio, R. P., Jr., and S. E. Condrey. 2009. Reforming public management: Analyzing the impact of public service reform on organizational and managerial trust. *Journal of Public Administration Research and Theory* 19(4): 689–707.

BBC News. 2008. Aid women killed in Afghanistan. August 13. http://news.bbc.co.uk/2/hi/south_asia/7558076.stm (accessed November 19, 2009).

Bear River Compact Commission. 1958–70. *Annual meeting minutes.* Logan, UT: Bear River Compact Commission.

Bebchuk, L. A., and J. M. Fried. 2004. Executive compensation as an agency problem. Centre for Economic Policy Research Discussion Paper 3961. http://papers.ssrn.com/sol3/papers.cfm?abstract_id=438720 (accessed August 20, 2008).

Becker, G. S. 1985. Human capital, effort, and the sexual division of labor. *Journal of Labor Economics* 3(1): S33–58.

Behn, R. D. 2001. *Rethinking democratic accountability.* Washington, DC: Brookings Institution Press.

Beierle, T. C., and J. Cayford. 2002. *Democracy in practice: Public participation in environmental decisions.* Washington, DC: Resources for the Future.

Berkner, L., S. Cuccaro-Alamin, and A. C. McCormick. 1996. *Descriptive summary of 1989–90 beginning postsecondary students: 5 years later, with an essay on postsecondary persistence and attainment.* U.S. Department of Education, National Center for Education Statistics. Washington DC: U.S. Printing Office, NCES 96–155.

Berman, E., and X. Wang. 2000. Performance measurement in U.S. counties: Capacity for reform. *Public Administration Review* 60(5): 409–420.

Bernheim, D. B., and M. D. Whinston. 1998. Incomplete contracts and strategic ambiguity. *American Economic Review* 88(4): 902–932.

Berry, F. S., R. Chackerian, and B. Wechsler. 1999. Reinventing government: Lessons from a state capital. In *Public management reform and innovation: Research, theory, and application*, edited by H. G. Frederickson and J. M. Johnston, 329–355. Tuscaloosa: University of Alabama Press.

Berry, J. M., K. E. Portney, and K. Thomson. 1993. *The rebirth of urban democracy.* Washington, DC: Brookings Institution Press.

Bertelli, A. 2006. Motivation crowding and the federal civil servant: Evidence from the U.S. Internal Revenue Service. *International Public Management Journal* 9(1): 3–23.

Bessler, M., and K. Seki. 2006. Civil-military relations in armed conflicts: A humanitarian perspective. *Liaison: A Journal of Civil-Military Humanitarian Relief Collaborations* 3(3): 4–10. http://coe-dmha.org/Liaison/Vol_3No_3/Dept01.htm (accessed November 19, 2009).

Bierman, N. 2006. Women are besting men in college, but not salary. *Miami Herald*, April 28. http://www.miami.com/mld/miamiherald/news/local/14448191.htm (accessed May 28, 2006).

Big Blue River Compact Commission. 2004. *Thirtieth annual report.* Beatrice, NE: Big Blue River Compact Commission.

Big Blue River Compact Commission. 2005. *Thirty-first annual report.* Beatrice, NE: Big Blue River Compact Commission.

Bingham, L. B. 2008. Legal frameworks for collaboration in governance and public management. In *Big ideas in collaborative public management*, edited by L. B. Bingham and R. O'Leary, 247–269. Armonk, NY: M.E. Sharpe.

Bingham, L. B., C. J. Hallberlin, D. A. Walker, and W. T. Chung. 2009. Dispute system design and justice in employment dispute resolution: Mediation at the workplace. *Harvard Negotiation Law Review* 14: 1–50.

Bingham, L. B., and C. R. Wise. 1996. The Administrative Dispute Resolution Act of 1990: How do we evaluate its success? *Journal of Public Administration Research and Theory* 6(3): 383–414.

Bishop, P. C., and A. J. Jones, Jr. 1993. Implementing the Americans with Disabilities Act of 1990: Assessing the variables of success. *Public Administration Review* 53(2): 121–128.

Blau, F. 1998. Trends in the well-being of American women, 1970–1995. *Journal of Economic Literature* 36(1): 112–165.

Blau, F., and L. M. Kahn. 1997. Swimming upstream: Trends in the gender wage differential in the 1980s. *Journal of Labor Economics* 15(1): 1–42.

Blomquist, W. 2007. Water 2010: A "near-sighted" program of water resource management improvements for the western United States. National Water Research Institute, White Paper. http://www.nwri-usa.org/pdfs/2007%20Water%202010%20Report.pdf (accessed February 15, 2011).

Blomquist, W., E. Schlager, and T. Heikkila. 2004. *Common waters, diverging streams: Linking institutions and water management in Arizona, California, and Colorado.* Washington, DC: Resources for the Future Press.

Bonczar, T. P., and A. J. Beck. 1997. Lifetime likelihood of going to state or federal prison. In *Bureau of Justice Statistics Bulletin, NCJ 160092.* Washington, DC: U.S. Department of Justice.

Bonné, J. 2003. Ambition and frustration at NASA. http://msnbc.msn.com/id/3077640 (accessed September 27, 2006).

Bonosaro, C. 2008. Senior Executives Association. *Pay for Performance Systems: Hearings before the Subcommittee on Federal Workforce, Postal Service, and the District of Columbia of the House Committee on Small Business.* 110th Cong., 2nd sess., February 12.

Bordia, P., E. Hunt, N. Paulsen, D. Tourish, and N. DiFonzo. 2004. Uncertainty during organizational change: Is it all about control? *European Journal of Work and Organizational Psychology* 13(3): 345–365.

Borins, S. 2000. Loose cannons and rule breakers, or enterprising leaders? Some evidence about innovative public managers. *Public Administration Review* 60(6): 498–507.

Borjas, G. J. 1995. The economic benefits from immigration. *Journal of Economic Perspectives* 9(2): 3–22.

Boskin, M. J. 2000. Economic measurement: Progress and challenges. *American Economic Review* 90(2): 247–252.

Bottom, W. P., J. Holloway, G. J. Miller, A. Mislin, and A. B. Whitford. 2006. Building a pathway to cooperation: Negotiation and social exchange between principal and agent. *Administrative Science Quarterly* 51(1): 29–58.

Bowen, C. D. 1966. *Miracle at Philadelphia: The story of the Constitutional Convention, May to September 1787.* Boston, MA: Little, Brown.

Bowen, W. G., and D. Bok. 1998. *The shape of the river: Long-term consequences of considering race in college and university admissions.* Princeton, NJ: Princeton University Press.

Bowerman, B. L., R. T. O'Connell, and A. B. Koehler. 2005. *Forecasting, time series, and regression: An applied approach.* 4th ed. Belmont, CA: Thomas Brooks/Cole.

Bowman, J. S., and J. P. West. 2006. Ending civil service protections in Florida government: Experiences in state agencies. *Review of Public Personnel Administration* 26(2): 139–157.

Box, R. C., G. S. Marshall, B. J. Reed, and C. M. Reed. 2001. New public management and substantive democracy. *Public Administration Review* 61(5): 608–619.

Boyne, G. A. 1998. Bureaucratic theory meets reality: Public choice and service contracting in U.S. local government. *Public Administration Review* 58(6): 474–484.

Boyne, G. A. 2003. Sources of public service improvement: A critical review and research agenda. *Journal of Public Administration Research and Theory* 13(3): 367–394.

Bozeman, B. 1987. *All organizations are public: Bridging public and private organizational theories.* San Francisco, CA: Jossey-Bass.

Bradbury, M. D., R. P. Battaglio, Jr., and J. Crum. 2010. Continuity amid discontinuity? George W. Bush, federal employment discrimination, and "big government conservatism." *Review of Public Personnel Administration* 30(4): 445–466.

Bramson, R. A., and T. Buss. 2002. Methods for whole system change in public organizations and communities: An overview of the issues. *Public Organization Review* 2(3): 211–221.

Brehm, J., and S. Gates. 1997. *Working, shirking, and sabotage: Bureaucratic response to a democratic public.* Ann Arbor: University of Michigan Press.

Brewer, G. A. 2003. Building social capital: Civic attitudes and behavior of public servants. *Journal of Public Administration Research and Theory* 13(1): 5–26.

Brewer, G. A., and S. C. Selden. 1998. Whistle blowers in the federal civil service: New evidence of the public service ethic. *Journal of Public Administration Research and Theory* 8(3): 413–439.

Bridges, W. 2003. *Managing transitions.* 2nd ed. Cambridge, MA: Perseus Books Group.

Brikowski, T. H. 2008. Doomed reservoirs in Kansas, USA? Climate change and groundwater mining on the Great Plains lead to unsustainable surface water storage. *Journal of Hydrology* 354(1–4): 90–101.

Brodkin, E. Z. 1990. Implementation as policy politics. In *Implementation and the policy process: Opening the black box*, edited by D. J. Palumbo and D. J. Calista, 107–118. Santa Barbara, CA: Greenwood Press.

Brown, J., and P. Duguid. 2001. Knowledge and organization: A social-practice perspective. *Organization Science* 12(2): 198–213.

Brown, M. 2001. Merit pay preferences among public sector employees. *Human Resource Management Journal* 11(4): 38–54.

Brown, M. M., and J. L. Brudney. 1998. A "smarter, better, faster, and cheaper" government: Contracting and geographic information systems. *Public Administration Review* 58(4): 335–345.

Brown, T. L., and M. Potoski. 2003a. Managing contract performance: A transaction cost approach. *Journal of Policy Analysis and Management* 22(2): 275–297.

Brown, T. L., and M. Potoski. 2003b. Transaction costs and institutional explanations for government service production decisions. *Journal of Public Administration Research and Theory* 13(4): 441–468.

Brown, T. L., and M. Potoski. 2004. Managing the public service market. *Public Administration Review* 64(6): 656–668.

Brown, T. L., and M. Potoski. 2005. Transaction costs and contracting: The practitioner perspective. *Public Performance & Management Review* 28(3): 326–351.

Brown, T. L., and M. Potoski. 2006. Contracting for management: Assessing management capacity under alternative service delivery arrangements. *Journal of Policy Analysis and Management* 25(2): 323–346.

Bruce, D., W. F. Fox, and M. H. Tuttle. 2006. Tax base elasticities: A multi-state analysis of long run and short run dynamics. *Southern Economic Journal* 73(2): 315–341.

Brudney, J. L., and S. E. Condrey. 1993. Pay for performance: Explaining the differences in managerial motivation. *Public Productivity & Management Review* 17(2): 129–144.

Brudney, J. L., F. T. Hebert, and D. S. Wright. 1999. Reinventing government in the American states: Measuring and explaining administrative reform. *Public Administration Review* 59(1): 19–30.

Brudney, J. L., F. T. Hebert, and D. S. Wright. 2000. From organizational values to organizational roles: Examining representative bureaucracy in state administration. *Journal of Public Administration Research and Theory* 10(3): 491–512.

Brudney, J. L., and D. S. Wright. 2002. Revisiting administrative reform in the American states: The status of reinventing government during the 1990s. *Public Administration Review* 62(3): 353–361.

Bruhn, J. G., G. Zajac, and A. A. Al-Kazemi. 2001. Ethical perspectives on employee participation in planned organizational change: A survey of two state public welfare agencies. *Public Performance & Management Review* 25(2): 208–228.

Bryer, T. A. 2009. Explaining responsiveness in collaboration: Administrator and citizen role perceptions. *Public Administration Review* 69(2): 271–283.

Bryson, J. M. 2004a. *Strategic planning for public and nonprofit organizations.* 3rd ed. San Francisco, CA: Jossey-Bass.

Bryson, J. M. 2004b. What to do when stakeholders matter. *Public Management Review* 6(1): 21–53.

Bryson, J. M., and S. R. Anderson. 2000. Applying large-group interaction methods in the planning and implementation of major change efforts. *Public Administration Review* 60(2): 143–162.

Bullock, R. J. 1983. Participation and pay. *Group and Organization Studies* 8(1): 127–136.

Bunker, B. B., and B. T. Alban. 1997. *Large group interventions: Engaging the whole system for rapid change.* San Francisco, CA: Jossey-Bass.

Burke, W. W. 2002. *Organization change: Theory and practice.* Thousand Oaks, CA: Sage Publications.

Burnside, C. 2004. Assessing new approaches to fiscal sustainability analysis. Prepared for the World Bank, Latin America and Caribbean Department. http://www.duke.edu/~acb8/res/fs_assmnt2.pdf (accessed July 16, 2007).

Burroughs, J. D. 1982. Pay secrecy and performance: The psychological research. *Compensation Benefits Review* 14(3): 44–54.

Burt, R. T. 1976. Positions in networks. *Social Forces* 55(1): 93–122.

Burt, R. T. 1980. Models of network structure. *Annual Review of Sociology* 6(1): 79–141.

Byman, D., I. Lesser, B. Pirnie, C. Benard, and M. Waxman. 2000. *Strengthening the partnership: Improving military coordination with relief agencies and allies in humanitarian operations.* Santa Monica, CA: RAND.

Camilleri, E. 2007. Antecedents affecting public service motivation. *Personnel Review* 36(3): 356–377.

Campbell, J. 2005. Lawmakers should let sun shine on quasi-public groups. *Quill Magazine* (Society of Professional Journalists), March 22–23.

Carnall, C. 1995. *Managing change in organizations.* New York: Prentice Hall.

Carpenter, S. L., and W. J. D. Kennedy. 2001. *Managing public disputes: A practical guide for government, business, and citizens' groups.* San Francisco: Jossey-Bass.

Carpini, M. X. D., F. L. Cook, and L. R. Jacobs. 2004. Public deliberations, discursive participation, and citizen engagement: A review of the empirical literature. *Annual Review of Political Science* 7: 315–344.

Carr, J. B., and R. C. Feiock. 1999. Metropolitan government and economic development. *Urban Affairs Review* 34(3): 476–488.

Carr, J. B., and K. LeRoux. 2005. Which local governments cooperate on public safety? Lessons from Michigan. Working Group on Interlocal Services Cooperation, Wayne State University Digital Commons. http://digitalcommons.wayne.edu/interlocal_coop/4/(accessed October 24, 2007).

Caudle, S. 2006. Basic practices aiding high-performance Homeland Security regional partnerships. *Homeland Security Affairs* II(3). http://www.hsaj.org (accessed December 12, 2008).

Cayer, N. J., and L. Sigelman. 1980. Minorities and women in state and local government: 1973–1975. *Public Administration Review* 40(5): 443–450.

CBS News Poll. 2003. U.S. favors affirmative action. January 23. http://www.cbsnews.com/stories/2003/04/01/opinion/polls/main547089.shtml (accessed February 20, 2006).

CBS News Poll. 2006. *Pollingreport.com*, January 5–8. www.pollingreport.com/race.htm (accessed February 24, 2006).

Chackerian, R., and P. Mavima. 2000. Comprehensive administrative reform implementation: Moving beyond single issue implementation research. *Journal of Public Administration Research and Theory* 11(3): 353–378.

Chapple, K., A. Markusen, D. Yamamoto, G. Schrock, and P. Yu. 2004. Gauging metropolitan "high tech" and "I-tech" activity. *Economic Development Quarterly* 18(1): 10–29.

Chaskin, R. J. 2003. Fostering neighborhood democracy: Legitimacy and accountability within loosely coupled systems. *Nonprofit and Volunteer Sector Quarterly* 32(2): 161–189.

Chaskin, R. J., P. Brown, S. Venkatesh, and A. Vidal. 2001. *Building community capacity*. Piscataway, NJ: Aldine Transaction.

Chay, K. 1998. The impact of federal civil rights policy on black economic progress: Evidence from the Equal Opportunity Act of 1972. *Industrial Labor Relations Review* 51(4): 608–632.

Chen, B. 2008. Assessing interorganizational networks for public service delivery. *Public Performance & Management Review* 31(3): 348–363.

Chi, K. S. 2005. State civil service systems. In *Handbook of human resource management in government*, 2nd ed., edited by S. E. Condrey, 76–94. San Francisco, CA: Jossey-Bass.

Chisholm, D. 1989. *Coordination without hierarchy: Informal structures in multiorganizational systems*. Berkeley: University of California Press.

Cho, Y. H., and B. Choi. 2004. E-government to combat corruption: The case of Seoul metropolitan government. *International Journal of Public Administration* 27(10): 719–735.

Cleveland, H. 1986. Government is information (but not vice versa). *Public Administration Review* 46(6): 605–607.

Climate Change Science Program and Subcommittee on Global Change Research. 2008. *The effects of climate change on agriculture, land resources, water resources, and biodiversity*. Washington, DC: U.S. Environmental Protection Agency.

Clingermayer, J. 1989. Regulatory uncertainty, investment climates, and state economic growth. Presented at the Annual Meeting of the Southeastern Conference on Public Administration, Jackson, MO, October 3–5.

Clinton, W. J. 1995. Remarks by William Jefferson Clinton on affirmative action. *National Archives*, July 19. http://clinton4.nara.gov/Initiatives/OneAmerica/19970610-1444.vcs (accessed February 24, 2006).

Clune, M. S., A. Nuñez, and S. P. Choy. 2001. Competing choices: Men's and women's paths after earning a bachelor's degree. *National Center for Education Statistics*. http://nces.ed.gov/programs/quarterly/vol_3/3_3/q4-5.asp (accessed February 24, 2006).

CNN. 2006. ABA: Bush violating Constitution. July 24.

Coase, R. 1937. The nature of the firm. *Economica* 4: 386–405.

Coch, L., and J. R. P. French, Jr. 1948. Overcoming resistance to change. *Human Relations* 1: 512–532.

Coggburn, J. D. 2006. At-will employment in government: Insights from the state of Texas. *Review of Public Personnel Administration* 26(2): 158–177.

Coggburn, J. D., R. P. Battaglio, Jr., J. S. Bowman, S. E. Condrey, D. Goodman, and J. P. West. 2010. State government human resource professionals' commitment to employment at will. *American Review of Public Administration* 40(2): 189–208.

Cohen, M. D., and P. Bacdayan. 1994. Organizational routines are stored as procedural memory: Evidence from a laboratory study. *Organization Science* 5(4): 554–568.

Cohen, S., and W. Eimicke. 1994. Project-focused total quality management in the New York City Department of Parks and Recreation. *Public Administration Review* 54(5): 450–456.

Colella, A., R. L. Paetzold, A. Zardkoohi, and M. J. Wesson. 2007. Exposing pay secrecy. *Academy of Management Review* 32(1): 55–71.

Coleman, J. S. 1990. *Foundations of social theory.* Cambridge, MA: Harvard University Press.

Coleman, M. G. 1999. Merit, cost, and the affirmative action policy debate. *Review of Black Political Economy* 27(1): 99–127.

Conant, J. K. 2006. Wisconsin: Institutions, processes, and policies. In *Budgeting in the states: Institutions, processes, and politics,* edited by E. J. Clynch and T. P. Lauth, 235–256. Westport, CT: Praeger Publishers.

Condrey, S. E. 2002. Reinventing state civil service systems. *Review of Public Personnel Administration* 22(2): 114–124.

Condrey, S. E., and J. L. Brudney. 1992. Performance-based managerial pay in the federal government: Does agency matter? *Journal of Public Administration Research and Theory* 2(2): 157–174.

Connor, P. E., L. K. Lake, and R. W. Stackman. 2003. *Managing organizational change.* 3rd ed. Westport, CT: Praeger Publishers.

Cook, B. J. 2007. Woodrow Wilson's ideas about local government reform: A regime perspective on the new push for citizen engagement in public administration. *Administration & Society* 39(2): 294–314.

Cooper, H., and L. V. Hedges. 1994. Research synthesis as a scientific enterprise. In *Handbook of research synthesis,* edited by H. Cooper and L. V. Hedges, 3–14. New York: Russell Sage Foundation.

Cooper, P. J. 1986. The Supreme Court, the First Amendment, and freedom of information. *Public Administration Review* 46(6): 622–628.

Cooper, P. J. 1996. Understanding what the law says about public responsibility. In *Handbook of public administration,* edited by J. L. Perry, 115–135. San Francisco, CA: Jossey-Bass.

Cooper, T. L., and T. A. Bryer. 2007. William Robertson: Exemplar of politics and public management rightly understood. *Public Administration Review* 67(5): 816–824.

Cooper, T. L., T. A. Bryer, and J. W. Meek. 2008. Outcomes achieved through citizen-centered collaborative public management. In *Big ideas in collaborative public management,* edited by R. O'Leary and L. Bingham, 211–229. Armonk, NY: M.E. Sharpe.

Cornia, G. C., R. D. Nelson, and A. Wilko. 2004. Fiscal planning, budgeting, and rebudgeting using revenue semaphores. *Public Administration Review* 64(2): 164–179.

Counterinsurgency. 2006. Army Field Manual No. 3-24. Marine Warfighting Publication 3-33.5. Washington, DC: U.S. Department of the Army, Department of the Navy.

Crawford, S., and E. Ostrom. 1995. A grammar of institutions. *American Political Science Review* 89(3): 582–600.

Crawley, V., and B. Adelsberger. 2004. Abu Ghraib reports fault contracting, leadership. *Federal Times*, August 30, 12.

Cresswell, A. M., T. A. Pardo, F. Thompson, and J. Zhang. 2006. Trust and collaboration: Knowledge sharing in public sector IT innovations. In *Knowledge transfer for eGovernment*, edited by R. Traumuller, 92–103. Linz, Austria: Trauner Verlag.

Crewson, P. E. 1997. Public-service motivation: Building empirical evidence of incidence and effect. *Journal of Public Administration Research and Theory* 7(4): 499–518.

Crocker, C., F. Hampson, and P. Aall, eds. 2001. *Turbulent peace: The challenges of managing international conflict*. Washington, DC: United States Institute of Peace.

Cronon, W. 2011. Wisconsin's radical break. *New York Times*, March 21. http://teamsters952. org/wisconsin's_radical_break_-_nytimes-com.pdf (accessed December 5, 2011).

Dahl, R. A. 2001. *How democratic is the American Constitution?* New Haven, CT: Yale University Press.

Dahlenberg, D. R., M. D. Partridge, and D. S. Rickman. 1998. Public infrastructure: Pork or job creator? *Public Finance Review* 26(1): 24–52.

Daley, D. 1987. Merit pay enters with a whimper: The initial federal civil service reform experience. *Review of Public Personnel Administration* 7(2): 72–79.

Daniels, C. 2002. The most powerful black executives in America meet 50 black business men and women who wield unprecedented clout. *Fortune*, July 22. http://money.cnn.com/ magazines/fortune/fortune_archive/2002/07/22/326294/index.htm (accessed August 2, 2006).

Darity, W. A., and P. L. Mason. 1998. Evidence on discrimination in employment: Codes of color, codes of gender. *Journal of Economic Perspective* 12(2): 63–90.

Datcher, L., L. Garman, and D. Garman. 1993. Affirmative action in higher education. *American Economic Review* 83(2): 99–103.

Datcher, L., L. Garman, and D. Garman. 1995. College selectivity and earnings. *Journal of Labor Economics* 13(2): 289–308.

Davenport, T. H., D. W. DeLong, and M. C. Beers. 1998. Successful knowledge management projects. *Sloan Management Review*, Winter: 43–57.

Davidson, J. 2011. Unions blast GOP plan to extend federal pay freeze. *Washington Post*, December 1. http://www.washingtonpost.com/blogs/federal (accessed December 6, 2011).

Davidson, R., and E. Lewis. 1997. Affirmative action and other special consideration admissions at the University of California, Davis School of Medicine. *Journal of American Medical Association* 278(14): 1153–1158.

Davidson, S. M., L. M. Manheim, M. M. Hohlen, S. M. Werner, B. K. Yudkowsky, and G. V. Fleming. 1992. Prepayment with office-based physicians in publicly funded programs: Results from the Children's Medicaid Program. *Pediatrics* 89(4): 761–767.

Dawes, S. S. 1995. Interagency information sharing: Expected benefits, manageable risks. *Journal of Policy Analysis and Management* 15(3): 377–394.

Dawes, S. S., M. Gharawi, and G. B. Burke. 2012. Transnational public sector knowledge networks: Knowledge and information sharing in a multi-dimensional context. *Government Information Quarterly* 29(1): S112–S120.

Deadrick, D. L., and K. D. Scott. 1987. Employee incentives in the public sector: A national survey of urban mass transit authorities. *Public Personnel Management* 16(2): 135–143.

Deci, E. L., R. Koestner, and R. M. Ryan. 1999. A meta-analytic review of experiments examining the effects of extrinsic rewards and intrinsic motivation. *Psychological Bulletin* 125(6): 627–668.

Deci, E. L., and R. M. Ryan, eds. 2004. *Handbook of self-determination research*. Rochester, NY: University of Rochester Press.

Deckop, J. R., R. Mangel, and C. C. Cirka. 1999. Getting more than you pay for: Organizational citizenship behavior and pay-for-performance plans. *Academy of Management Journal* 42(4): 420–428.

DeHoog, R. H. 1984. *Contracting out for human services: Economic, political, and organizational perspectives*. Albany: State University of New York Press.

DeHoog, R. H. 1990. Competition, negotiation, or cooperation: Three models for service contracting. *Administration & Society* 22(3): 317–340.

DeHoog, R. H. 1997. Legal issues in contracting for public service: When business does government. In *The handbook of public law and public administration*, edited by P. Cooper and C. Newland, 528–545. San Francisco, CA: Jossey-Bass.

de Lancer Julnes, P., and M. Holzer. 2001. Promoting the utilization of performance measures in public organizations: An empirical study of factors affecting adoption and implementation. *Public Administration Review* 61(6): 693–708.

deLeon, P. 1995. Democratic values and the policy sciences. *American Journal of Political Science* 39(4): 886–905.

Delli Carpini, M. X., F. L. Cook, and L. R. Jacobs. 2004. Public deliberation, discursive participation, and citizen engagement: A review of the empirical literature. *Annual Review of Political Science* 7(1): 315–344.

DeLong, D. W., and L. Fahey. 2000. Diagnosing cultural barriers to knowledge management. *Academy of Management Executive* 14(4): 113–127.

Deng, X., Q. Tian, S. Ding, and B. Boase. 2003. Transparency in the procurement of public works. *Public Money & Management* 23(3): 155–162.

Denhardt, J. V., and R. B. Denhardt. 2007. *The new public service: Serving, not steering*. Armonk, NY: M.E. Sharpe.

Denhardt, R. B., and J. V. Denhardt. 1999. *Leadership for change: Case studies in American local government*. Washington, DC: IBM Center for the Business of Government.

Denhardt, R. B., and J. V. Denhardt. 2000. The new public service: Serving rather than steering. *Public Administration Review* 60(6): 549–558.

Denhardt, R. B., and J. V. Denhardt. 2008. The new public service: Serving rather than steering. In *The age of direct citizen participation*, edited by N. C. Roberts, 63–77. Armonk, NY: M.E. Sharpe.

Department of Homeland Security (DHS). 2005. Office of Management and Budget, The Executive Office of the President. http://www.whitehouse.gov/omb/budget/fy2005/homeland.html.

Dess, G., and D. Beard. 1984. Dimensions of organizational task environments. *Administrative Science Quarterly* 29(1): 52–73.

Dewey, J. 1988. The public and its problems. In *The later works of John Dewey, 1925–1952*, edited by J. A. Boydston, vol. 2, 238–372. Carbondale: Southern Illinois University Press.

DiIulio, J. D., Jr. 1994. Principled agents: The cultural bases of behavior in a federal government bureaucracy. *Journal of Public Administration Research and Theory* 4(3): 277–318.

DiMaggio, P. J., and W. W. Powell. 1983. The iron cage revisited: Institutional isomorphism and collective rationality in organizational fields. *American Sociological Review* 48(2): 147–160.

DiNome, J., S. Yaklin, and D. H. Rosenbloom. 1999. Employee rights: Avoiding legal liability. In *Human resource management in local government: An essential guide*, edited by S. F. Freyss, 93–131. Washington, DC: International City/County Management Association.

Dixit, A. K. 1996. *The making of economic policy: A transaction-cost politics perspective*. Boston, MA: MIT Press.

Dobbins, J., S. Jones, K. Crane, and B. DeGrasse. 2007. *The beginner's guide to nation-building*. Santa Monica, CA: RAND.

Dobbins, J., J. McGinn, K. Crane, S. Jones, R. Lal, A. Rathmell, R. Swanger, and A. Timilsina. 2003. *America's role in nation-building*. Santa Monica, CA: RAND.

Dodge, L. R. 1997. Intergovernmental relations and the administrative enforcement of equal employment opportunity laws. *Public Administration Review* 57(5): 431–440.

Doig, J. W., and E. C. Hargrove, eds. 1990. *Leadership and innovation: Entrepreneurs in government*. Abridged ed. Baltimore: The Johns Hopkins University Press.

Dolan, J. 2000. The Senior Executive Service: Gender, attitudes, and representative bureaucracy. *Journal of Public Administration Research and Theory* 10(3): 513–530.

Dolan, J. 2002. Representative bureaucracy in the federal executive: Gender and spending priorities. *Journal of Public Administration Research and Theory* 12(3): 353–375.

Dometrius, N. C. 1984. Minorities and women among state agency leaders. *Social Science Quarterly* 65(3): 127–137.

Donahue, J. D. 1989. *The privatization decision: Public ends, private means*. New York: Basic Books.

Donini, A. 2000. The strategic framework for Afghanistan: A preliminary assessment. Prepared for the World Bank/ADB Asia Regional Consultation on Social Cohesion and Conflict Management, Manila, March 16–17.

Dorff, R. H. 2007. Bridging the gap: Integrating civilian-military capabilities in security and reconstruction operations. In *The interagency and counterinsurgency warfare: Stability, security, transition, and reconstruction roles*, edited by J. R. Cerami and J. W. Boggs, 389–406. Carlisle Barracks, PA: U.S. Army War College, Strategic Studies Institute.

Dothan, M. U., and F. Thompson. 2006. Optimal budget rules: Making government spending sustainable through present-value balance. Presented at the Annual Conference of the Association for Budgeting and Financial Management, Atlanta, GA, October 20. http://ssrn.com/abstract=939815 (accessed August 4, 2007).

Douma, S., and H. Schreuder. 2002. *Economic approaches to organizations*. 3rd ed. Upper Saddle River, NJ: Financial Times/Prentice Hall.

Dowling, B., and R. Richardson. 1997. Evaluating performance-related pay for managers in the National Health Service. *The International Journal of Human Resource Management* 8(3): 348–366.

Dreier, P., J. Mollenkopf, and T. Swanstrom. 2001. *Place matters: Metropolitics for the 21st century*. Lawrence: University Press of Kansas.

Drentea, P. 1998. Consequences of women's formal and informal job search methods of employment in female-dominated jobs. *Gender & Society* 12(3): 321–338.

DuBois, W. E. B. 1899/1996. *The Philadelphia Negro: A social study*. Philadelphia: University of Pennsylvania Press.

Dunleavy, P., and C. Hood. 1994. From old public administration to new public management. *Public Management and Money* 14(3): 9–16.

Durand, R., and R. Colari. 2006. Sameness, otherness? Enriching organizational change theories with philosophical considerations on the same and the other. *Academy of Management Review* 31(1): 93–113.

Durant, R. F., and J. S. Legge, Jr. 2006. "Wicked problems," public policy, and administrative theory: Lessons from the GM food regulatory arena. *Administration & Society* 38(3): 309–334.

Durant, R. F., J. S. Legge, Jr., and A. Moussios. 1998. People, profits, and service delivery: Lessons from the privatization of British Telecom. *American Journal of Political Science* 42(1): 117–140.

Dye, R. F., and D. F. Merriman. 2004. State revenue stability: Alternative conceptualizations. Presented at the 97th Annual Conference on Taxation, National Tax Association, Minneapolis, MN, November 11–13.

Dziedzic, M., and M. Seidl. 2005. *Provincial reconstruction teams and military relations with international and nongovernmental organizations in Afghanistan.* Washington, DC: United States Institute of Peace.

Earley, P.C. 1993. East meets West meets Mideast: Further exploring collectivistic and individualistic work groups. *Academy of Management Journal* 36(3): 319–348.

Edmondson, A. C., R. M. J. Bohmer, and G. P. Pisano. 2001. Disrupted routines: Team learning and new technology implementation in hospitals. *Administrative Science Quarterly* 46(4): 685–716.

Egger-Peitler, I., G. Hammerschmid, and R. Meyer. 2007. Motivation, identification, and incentive preferences as issues for modernization and HR strategies in local government—First evidence from Austria. Presented at the European Group of Public Administration Annual Conference, Madrid, Spain, September 19–22.

Eglene, O., S. S. Dawes, and C. A. Schneider. 2007. Authority and leadership patterns in public sector knowledge networks. *American Review of Public Administration* 37(1): 91–113.

Eisner, R. 1986. *How real is the federal deficit?* New York: Free Press.

Elangovan, A. R. 1995. Managerial third-party dispute intervention: A prescriptive model of strategy selection. *Academy of Management Review* 20(4): 800–830.

Elangovan, A. R. 1998. Managerial intervention in organizational disputes: Testing a prescriptive model of strategy selection. *International Journal of Conflict Management* 9(4): 301–335.

Elkin, S. L. 2006. *Reconstructing the commercial republic: Constitutional design after Madison.* Chicago, IL: University of Chicago Press.

Elling, R. C., and T. L. Thompson. 2006. Human resource problems and state management performance across two decades: The implications for civil service reform. *Review of Public Personnel Administration* 26(4): 302–334.

Elliott, G. 2006. Bush and Blair reflect on failures. *The Australian,* May 26.

Elliott, J. R. 1999. Social isolation and labor market insulation: Network and neighborhood effects on less-educated urban workers. *Sociological Quarterly* 40(2): 199–216.

Elmore, R. F. 1979–80. Backward mapping: Implementation research and policy decisions. *Political Science Quarterly* 94(4): 601–616.

Fagotto, E., and A. Fung. 1995. Revitalizing Minneapolis. http://www.archonfung.net/docs/cases/NRPcaseOct05.pdf (accessed September 30, 2010).

Faruqee, H., D. Laxton, D. Muir, and P. A. Pesenti. 2006. Would protectionism defuse global imbalances and spur economic activity? A scenario analysis. Federal Reserve Bank of New York, Staff Report No. 268. http://www.newyorkfed.org/research/staff_reports/sr268.pdf (accessed October 24, 2007).

Feeley, M., and R. Hanson. 1990. The impact of judicial intervention on prisons and jails. In *Courts, corrections, and the Constitution: The impact of judicial intervention on prisons and jails*, edited by J. J. DiIulio, Jr., 12–46. New York: Oxford University Press.

Feinberg, L. E. 1986. Managing the Freedom of Information Act and federal information policy. *Public Administration Review* 46(6): 615–621.

Feinberg, L. E. 1997. Open government and freedom of information: Fishbowl accountability. In *Handbook of public law and administration*, edited by P. J. Cooper and C. A. Newland, 376–399. San Francisco, CA: Jossey-Bass.

Feinberg, L. E. 2004. FOIA, federal information policy, and information availability in a post-9/11 world. *Government Information Quarterly* 21(4): 439–460.

Feiock, R. C. 2002. A quasi-market framework for development competition. *Journal of Urban Affairs* 24(2): 123–142.

Feiock, R. C. 2004. *Metropolitan governance: Conflict, competition and cooperation*. Washington, DC: Georgetown University Press.

Feiock, R. C. 2007. Rational choice and regional governance. *Journal of Urban Affairs* 29(1): 49–65.

Feiock, R. C., and M. Jeong. 2002. Regulatory reform and urban economic development. *State and Local Government Review* 34(3): 153–160.

Feiock, R. C., M. Jeong, and J. Kim. 2003. Credible commitment and council manager government: Implications for policy instrument choice. *Public Administration Review* 63(5): 568–577.

Feiock, R. C., H. J. Park, and A. Steinacker. 2007. Institutional collective action and economic development joint ventures. Working paper, Devoe Moore Center, Program in Local Governance. http://www.fsu.edu/~localgov/publication_files/joint%20ventures.pdf (accessed October 24, 2007).

Feiock, R. C., and J. Scholz, eds. 2007. *Self-organizing governance: Providing public goods and managing resources in federalist systems*. Manuscript.

Feiock R. C., A. Steinacker, and H. J. Park. 2009. Institutional collective action and economic development joint ventures. *Public Administration Review* 69(2): 256–270.

Feiock, R. C., and C. Stream. 2001. Environmental protection and economic development: A false tradeoff? *Public Administration Review* 61(3): 313–321.

Feiock, R. C., J. Tao, and L. Johnson. 2004. Institutional collective action: Social capital and the formation of regional partnerships. In *Metropolitan governance: Conflict, competition, and cooperation*, edited by R. Feiock, 147–159. Washington, DC: Georgetown University Press.

Feiser, C. D. 2000. Protecting the public's right to know: The debate over privatizing and access to government information under state law. *Florida State University Law Review* 27: 825–864.

Fernandez, S., and H. G. Rainey. 2006. Managing successful organizational change in the public sector. *Public Administration Review* 66(2): 168–176.

Fischer, F. 2006. Participatory governance as deliberative empowerment: The cultural politics of discursive space. *American Review of Public Administration* 36(1): 19–40.

Fisher, R., W. Ury, and B. Patton. 1991. *Getting to yes: Negotiating agreement without giving in*. 2nd ed. New York: Houghton Mifflin.

Fishkin, J. S. 2009. *When the people speak: Deliberative democracy and public consultation*. Oxford: Oxford University Press.

Fix, M., and R. J. Struyk. 1992. An overview of auditing for discrimination. In *Clear and convincing evidence: Measurement of discrimination in America*, edited by M. Fix and R. J. Struyk. Washington, DC: Urban Institute Press.

Fletcher, C., and R. Williams. 1996. Performance management, job satisfaction, and organizational commitment. *British Academy of Management* 7(2): 169–179.

Florida, R. 2002. *The rise of the creative class: And how it's transforming work, leisure, community, and everyday life*. New York: Basic Books.

Florida, R. 2005a. *The flight of the creative class: The new global competition for talent*. New York: Harper Business.

Florida, R. 2005b. The world is spiky. *The Atlantic* 296(3): 48–51.

Fluke, C., and L. Kump. 2004. Beyond the balance sheet: Social scorecard. *Forbes*, December 14. www.forbes.com/free_forbes/2004/1213/171tab.html (accessed September 27, 2006).

Foerstel, H. N. 1999. *Freedom of information and the right to know: The origins and applications of the Freedom of Information Act*. Westport, CT: Greenwood Press.

Follett, M. P. 2003. *Dynamic administration: The collected papers of Mary Parker Follett*, edited by H. C. Metcalf and L. Urwick. New York: Routledge.

Food Research and Action Center. 2005. School breakfast scorecard: 2005. www.frac.org/pdf/2005_SBP.pdf (accessed September 27, 2006).

Ford, T., J. Hogan, and M. Perry. 2002. *Communication during complex humanitarian emergencies: Using technology to bridge the gap*. Monterey, CA: Naval Postgraduate School.

Forester, J. 1999. *The deliberative practitioner: Encouraging participatory planning processes*. Cambridge, MA: MIT Press.

Fox, W. F. 2003. Three characteristics of tax structures have contributed to the current state fiscal crises. *State Tax Notes* 29: 375–383.

Frandsen, G. 2002. *A guide to NGOs: A primer about private, voluntary, non-governmental organizations that operate in humanitarian emergencies globally*. Bethesda, MD: Center for Disaster and Humanitarian Assistance Medicine.

Frederickson, H. G. 1997. *The spirit of public administration*. San Francisco, CA: Jossey-Bass.

Freeman, R. E. 2005. The development of stakeholder theory: An idiosyncratic approach. In *Great minds in management: The process of theory development*, edited by K. G. Smith and M. A. Hitt, 417–435. Oxford: Oxford University Press.

Freudenberg, W. R. 2004. Can we learn from failure? Examining US experiences with nuclear repository siting. *Journal of Risk Research* 7(2): 153–169.

Frey, B. S. 1997a. A constitution for knaves crowds out civic virtues. *Economic Journal* 107(July): 1043–1053.

Frey, B. S. 1997b. *Not just for the money: An economic theory of personal motivation*. Cheltenham, UK: Edward Elgar.

Frey, B. S., and R. Jegen. 2001. Motivation crowding theory. *Journal of Economic Surveys* 15(5): 589–611.

Frey, B. S., and M. Osterloh. 2005. Yes, managers should be paid like bureaucrats. *Journal of Management Inquiry* 14(1): 96–111.

Friedman, T. L. 2005. *The world is flat: A brief history of the twenty-first century*. New York: Farrar, Straus & Giroux.

Fung, A. 2003. Recipes for public spheres: Eight institutional design choices and their consequences. *Journal of Political Philosophy* 11(3): 338–367.

Fung, A. 2004. *Empowered participation: Reinventing urban democracy*. Princeton, NJ: Princeton University Press.

Fung, A. 2006. Varieties of participation in democratic governance. *Public Administration Review* 66(S1): 66–75.

Fung, A., M. Graham, and D. Weil. 2007. *Full disclosure: The perils and promise of transparency.* Cambridge, UK: Cambridge University Press.

Fung, A., and E. O. Wright. 2001. Deepening democracy: Innovations in empowered participatory governance. *Politics and Society* 29(1): 5–41.

Gabris, G. T. 1986. Can merit pay systems avoid creating discord between supervisors and subordinates? Another uneasy look at performance appraisal. *Review of Public Personnel Administration* 7(1): 70–89.

Gabris, G. T., and D. M. Ihrke. 2000. Improving employee acceptance toward performance appraisal and merit pay systems: The role of leadership credibility. *Review of Public Personnel Administration* 20(1): 41–53.

Gabris, G. T., and K. Mitchell. 1986. Personnel reforms and formal participation structures: The case of the Biloxi merit councils. *Review of Public Personnel Administration* 6(3): 94–144.

Gabris, G. T., and K. Mitchell. 1988. The impact of merit raise scores on employee attitudes: The Matthew effect of performance appraisal. *Public Personnel Management* 17(4): 369–386.

Gaertner, G. H., K. N. Gaertner, and D. M. Akinnusi. 1984. Environment, strategy, and the implementation of administrative change: The case of civil service reform. *Academy of Management Journal* 27(3): 525–543.

Gaertner, K. N., and G. H. Gaertner. 1985. Performance-contingent pay for federal managers. *Administration & Society* 17(1): 7–20.

Galaskiewicz, J. 1985. Interorganizational relations. *Annual Review of Sociology* 11: 281–304.

Galbraith, J. R. 1973. *Designing complex organizations.* Reading, MA: Addison-Wesley.

Gallopín, G. C., S. Funtowicz, M. O'Connor, and J. Ravetz. 2001. Science for the twenty-first century: From social contract to the scientific core. *International Social Science Journal* 53(168): 219–229.

Gallup Poll. 2003. Race and ethnicity (polling data). Pollingreport.com, June 12–18. www.pollingreport.com/race.htm (accessed August 2, 2006).

Gates, H. L., Jr. 1997. *Thirteen ways of looking at a black man.* New York: Random House.

Gaus, J. M. 1923–1924. The new problem of administration. *Minnesota Law Review* 8: 217–231.

Gentry, W. F., and H. F. Ladd. 1994. State tax structure and multiple policy objectives. *National Tax Journal* 47(4): 747–772.

Gherardi, S., and D. Nicolini. 2000. To transfer is to transform: The circulation of safety knowledge. *Organization* 7(2): 320–348.

Gibson, F. K., and S. Yeager. 1975. Trends in the federal employment of blacks. *Public Personnel Management* 4(3): 189–195.

Glaeser, E. L., J. Kolko, and A. Saiz 2001. Consumer city. *Journal of Economic Geography* 1(1): 27–50.

Gleick, P. 2003. Global freshwater resources: Soft path solutions to 21st-century water needs. *Science* 320: 1524–1528.

Goldsmith, S. 1999. *The twenty-first century city: Resurrecting urban America.* Lanham, MD: Rowman & Littlefield.

Goldsmith, S., and W. D. Eggers. 2004. *Governing by network: The new shape of the public sector.* Washington DC: Brookings Institution Press.

Goldstein, M., and R. Smith. 1976. The estimated impact of the antidiscrimination program aimed at federal contractors. *Industrial Labor Relations Review* 29(3): 524–543.

Golembiewski, R. T. 1985. *Humanizing public organizations*. New York: Lomond.

Goodnow, F. J. 1900. *Politics and administration: A study in government*. New York: Macmillan.

Gore, A. 1993. *Creating a government that works better and costs less: The report of the National Performance Review*. Washington, DC: Government Printing Office.

Gore, A. 1995. *Common sense government: Works better and costs less*. Washington, DC: Government Printing Office.

Gossett, C. W. 2002. Civil service reform: The case of Georgia. *Review of Public Personnel Administration* 22(2): 94–113.

Gould, D. M., and R. J. Ruffin. 1993. What determines economic growth? *Economic and Financial Policy Review: Federal Reserve Bank of Dallas*, April, 25–40.

Grabosky, P. N., and D. H. Rosenbloom. 1975. Racial and ethnic integration in federal service. *Social Science Quarterly* 56(2): 71–84.

Graffy, E. A. 2006. Expert forecasts and the emergence of water scarcity on public agendas. *Society and Natural Resources* 19(5): 465–472.

Graffy, E. A. 2008. Meeting the challenges of policy-relevant science: Bridging theory and practice. *Public Administration Review* 68(6): 1087–1100.

Granholm, J. 2004. Our determination, our destination: A 21st century economy. State of the State Address, Lansing, MI, January 27. http://www.michigan.gov (accessed October 24, 2007).

Granovetter, M. S. 1973. The strength of weak ties. *American Journal of Sociology* 78(6): 1360–1380.

Granovetter, M. S. 1983. The strength of weak ties: A network theory revisited. *Sociological Theory* 1(2): 201–233.

Granovetter, M. S. 1985. Economic action and social structure: The problem of embeddedness. *American Journal of Sociology* 91(3): 481–510.

Grant, A. M. 2008. Employees without a cause: The motivational effects of prosocial impact in public service. *International Public Management Journal* 11(1): 48–66.

Graves, B. n.d. OSHA's "cooperative" compliance program. PF Online. www.pfonline.com/columns/0798edit.html (accessed September 27, 2006).

Gray, B. 1985. Conditions facilitating interorganizational collaboration. *Human Relations* 38(10): 911–936.

Gray, B. 1989. *Collaborating: Finding common ground for multiparty problems*. San Francisco, CA: Jossey-Bass.

Gray, S. T., and C. Andersen. 2009. Assessing the future of Wyoming's water resources: Adding climate change to the equation. William D. Ruckelshaus Institute of Environment and Natural Resources, University of Wyoming–Laramie. http://www.uwyo.edu/enr/_files/docs/UofW-Water_Climate_final_comp.pdf (accessed February 15, 2011).

Greenblatt, A. 2006. Jebocracy. *Governing* 20(3): 32–38.

Greene, V., S. Selden, and G. Brewer. 2001. Measuring power and presence: Bureaucratic representation in the American states. *Journal of Public Administration Research and Theory* 11(3): 379–402.

Greiner, J. M., R. E. Dahl, H. P. Hatry, and A. P. Millar. 1977. *Monetary incentives and work standards in five cities: Impacts and implications for management and labor*. Washington, DC: Urban Institute Press.

Greiner, L. E. 1967. Patterns of organizational change. *Harvard Business Review* 45(3): 119–128.

Grizzle, G. A., and C. D. Pettijohn. 2002. Implementing performance-based program budgeting: A system-dynamics perspective. *Public Administration Review* 62(1): 51–62.

Groves, H. M., and C. H. Kahn. 1952. The stability of state and local tax yields. *American Economic Review* 42(1): 87–102.

Guerra, F. J., M. Marks, M. Barreto, S. Nuno, J. Magnabosco, and N. Woods. 2007. Los Angeles riots 15th anniversary resident follow-up survey report: April 23, 2007, final topline results. Los Angeles: Leavey Center for the Study of Los Angeles, Loyola Marymount University.

Gulati, R. 1995. Does familiarity breed trust? The implications of repeated ties for contractual choice in alliances. *Academy of Management Journal* 38(1): 85–112.

Gulati, R., and M. Gargiulo. 1999. Where do interorganizational networks come from? *American Journal of Sociology* 104(5): 1439–1493.

Guo, C., and J. A. Musso. 2007. Representation in nonprofit and voluntary organizations: A conceptual framework. *Nonprofit and Voluntary Sector Quarterly* 36(2): 308–326.

Guttman, D. 2000. Public purpose and private service. *Administrative Law Review* 52(3): 859–926.

Hall, R. H. 1999. *Organizations: Structures, processes, and outcomes.* 7th ed. Upper Saddle River, NJ: Prentice Hall.

Hannan, M. T., and J. Freeman. 1984. Structural inertia and organizational change. *American Sociological Review* 49(2): 149–164.

Hannan, M. T., L. Polos, and G. R. Carroll. 2003. The fog of change: Opacity and asperity in organizations. *Administrative Science Quarterly* 48(3): 399–432.

Hansman, H. 1987. The role of nonprofit enterprise. *Yale Law Journal* 89(5): 835–901.

Hardy-Fanta, C. 2000. A Latino gender gap? Evidence from the 1996 election. *Milenio Series*, no. 2 (February). Austin, TX: Inter-University Program for Latino Research.

Harokopus, K. A. 2001. Transforming the Department of Defense: Creating the new Defense procurement system. In *Transforming organizations*, edited by M. A. Abramson and P. R. Lawrence, 11–55. Lanham, MD: Rowman & Littlefield.

Harris, C. 1999. Lack of procedure kills OSHA reinvention program. *Federal Times*, April 26, 3.

Harris, S. 2004a. Bad to worse. *Government Executive*, September 15. www.govexec.com/features/0904-15/0904-15newsanalysis2.htm (accessed September 27, 2006).

Harris, S. 2004b. GSA canceled Guantánamo interrogator contract. *Government Executive*, July 16. www.govexec.com/dailyfed/0704/071604h1.htm (accessed September 27, 2006).

Hart, O. 2003. Incomplete contracts and public ownership: Remarks, and an application to public-private partnerships. *The Economic Journal* 113(March): C69–C76.

Hart, O., and J. Moore. 1999. Foundations of incomplete contracts. *Review of Economic Studies* 66: 115–138.

Hart, O., A. Shleifer, and R. W. Vishny. 1997. The proper scope of government: Theory and an application to prisons. *Quarterly Journal of Economics* 112(4): 1126–1161.

Hatch, M. J. 1997. *Organization theory: Modern, symbolic, and postmodern perspectives.* New York: Oxford University Press.

Hatry, H. P., J. M. Greiner, and R. J. Gollub. 1981. *An assessment of local government management motivational programs: Performance targeting with and without monetary incentives.* Washington, DC: Urban Institute Press.

Hays, S. W., and J. E. Sowa. 2006. A broader look at the "accountability" movement: Some grim realities in state civil service systems. *Review of Public Personnel Administration* 26(2): 102–117.

Heckathorn, D., and S. Maser. 1987. Bargaining and the sources of transaction costs: The case of government regulation. *Journal of Law, Economics, and Organization* 3(1): 69–98.

Heckman, J., C. Heinrich, and J. Smith. 1997. Assessing the performance of performance standards in public bureaucracies. *American Economic Review* 87(2): 389–395.

Heckman, J. J. 1998. Detecting discrimination. *Journal of Economic Perspectives* 12(2): 101–116.

Heery, E. 1998. A return to contract? Performance related pay in a public service. *Work, Employment & Society* 12(1): 73–95.

Heikkila, T., and E. Schlager. 2008. The role of information infrastructure needs in improving the organizational capacity for interstate water management and conflict resolution. Presented at the Annual Meeting of the Association for Public Policy Analysis and Management, Los Angeles, CA, November 6–8.

Heikkila, T., E. Schlager, and M. W. Davis. 2011. The role of cross-scale institutional linkages in common pool resource management: Assessing interstate river compacts. *Policy Studies Journal* 39(1): 121–145.

Heinrich, C. J. 2007. False or fitting recognition? The use of high performance bonuses in motivating organizational achievements. *Journal of Policy Analysis and Management* 26(2): 281–304.

Hellerstein, J., D. Neumark, and K. R. Troske. 1999. Wages, productivity, and worker characteristics: Evidence from plan-level production functions and wage equations. *Journal of Labor Economics* 17(3): 409–446.

Hellriegel, D., and L. Short. 1972. Equal employment opportunity in the federal government: A comparative analysis. *Public Administrative Review* 32(6): 851–867.

Heneman, H. G., and I. P. Young. 1991. Assessment of a merit pay program for school district administrators. *Public Personnel Management* 20(1): 35–47.

Heneman, R. L., D. B. Greenberger, and S. Strasser. 1988. The relationship between pay-for-performance perceptions and pay satisfaction. *Personnel Psychology* 41(4): 745–759.

Hennessey, J. T. 1998. "Reinventing" government: Does leadership make the difference? *Public Administration Review* 58(6): 322–332.

Hibbing, J. R., and E. Theiss-Morse. 2002. *Stealth democracy: Americans' beliefs about how government should work*. Cambridge, MA: Cambridge University Press.

Hickenlooper, J. 2005. Speech delivered at the National League of Cities Forum on Local Economic Vitality, Denver, CO, June 16–17. http://www.nlc.org (accessed September 4, 2007).

Hickson, G. B., W. A. Altemeier, and J. M. Perrin. 1987. Physician reimbursement by salary or fee-for-service: Effects on physician practice behavior in a randomized perspective trial. *Pediatrics* 80(3): 344–350.

Hill, K. Q., and T. Matsubayashi. 2005. Civic engagement and mass-elite policy agenda agreement in American communities. *American Political Science Review* 99(2): 215–224.

Hill, M., and P. Hupe. 2009. *Implementing public policy: An introduction to the study of operational governance*. 2nd ed. Los Angeles, CA: Sage Publications.

Hindera, J. J. 1993a. Representative bureaucracy: Further evidence of active representation in the EEOC district offices. *Journal of Public Administration Research and Theory* 3(4): 415–429.

Hindera, J. J. 1993b. Representative bureaucracy: Imprimis evidence of active representation in the EEOC district offices. *Social Science Quarterly* 74(1): 95–108.

Hindera, J. J., and C. D. Young. 1998. Representative bureaucracy: The theoretical implications of statistical interaction. *Political Research Quarterly* 51(3): 655–671.

Hinkelmann, C., and S. Swidler. 2004. Using futures contracts to hedge macroeconomic risks in the public sector. *Derivatives Use, Trading, and Regulation* 10(1): 54–69.

Hinkelmann, C., and S. Swidler. 2005. State government hedging with financial derivatives. *State and Local Government Review* 37(2): 127–141.

Hjern, B., and D. O. Porter. 1981. Implementation structures: A new unit of administrative analysis. *Organization Studies* 2(3): 211–227.

Hogan-Esche, T. 2002. Recapturing suburbia: Urban secession and the politics of growth in Los Angeles, Boston, and Seattle. PhD dissertation, University of Southern California.

Holcombe, R. G., and R. S. Sobel. 1997. *Growth and variability in state tax revenue: An anatomy of state fiscal crises.* Westport, CT: Greenwood Press.

Holohan, A. 2005. *Networks of democracy: Lessons from Kosovo for Afghanistan, Iraq, and beyond.* Stanford, CA: Stanford University Press.

Holzer, H. J. 1987. Informal job search and black youth unemployment. *American Economic Review* 77(3): 446–452.

Holzer, H. J., and D. Neumark. 2000a. Assessing affirmative action? *Journal of Economic Literature* 38(3): 483–568.

Holzer, H. J., and D. Neumark. 2000b. What does affirmative action do? *Industrial and Labor Relations Review* 53(2): 240–272.

Holzer, H. J., and P. Offner. 2004. The puzzle of black male unemployment. *Public Interest* 154(Winter): 74–84.

Holzer, H. J., P. Offner, and E. Sorensen. 2005. Declining employment among young black less-educated men: The role of incarceration and child support. *Journal of Policy Analysis and Management* 24(4): 329–350.

Holzer, M., and K. Callahan. 1998. *Government at work: Best practices and model programs.* Thousand Oaks, CA: Sage Publications.

Hood, C., and G. Peters. 2004. The middle aging of new public management: Into the age of paradox? *Journal of Public Administration Research and Theory* 14(3): 267–282.

Hosmer, L. T., and C. Kiewitz. 2005. Organizational justice: A behavioral science concept with critical implications for business ethics and stakeholder theory. *Business Ethics Quarterly* 15(1): 67–91.

Hou, Y. 2006. Budgeting for fiscal stability over the business cycle: A countercyclical fiscal policy and the multiyear perspective on budgeting. *Public Administration Review* 66(5): 730–741.

Houston, D. J. 2000. Public-service motivation: A multivariate test. *Journal of Public Administration Research and Theory* 10(4): 713–727.

Houston, D. J. 2006. "Walking the walk" of public service motivation: Public employees and charitable gifts of time, blood, and money. *Journal of Public Administration Research and Theory* 16(1): 67–86.

Houston, D. J. 2008. Behavior in the public square. In *Motivation in public management: The call of public service*, edited by J. L. Perry and A. Hondeghem, 177–199. Oxford: Oxford University Press.

Human Rights Campaign. n.d. U.S. Congress and scorecards. www.hrc.org/content/navigationmenu/hrc/get_informed/congress_and_scorecard/index.htm (accessed September 27, 2006).

Hutchison, B., S. Birch, J. Hurley, J. Lomas, and F. Stratford-Devai. 1996. Do physician-payment mechanisms affect hospital utilization? A study of health service organizations in Ontario. *Canadian Medical Association Journal* 154(5): 653–661.

Huxham, C. 2003. Theorizing collaboration practice. *Public Management Review* 5(3): 401–423.

Huxham, C., and S. Vongen. 2005. *Managing to collaborate: The theory and practice of collaborative advantage*. London: Routledge.

Ingraham, P. W. 1993a. Of pigs in pokes and policy diffusion: Another look at pay-for-performance. *Public Administration Review* 53(4): 348–356.

Ingraham, P. W. 1993b. Pay for performance in the states. *American Review of Public Administration* 23(3): 189–200.

Ingraham, P. W. 1995. *The foundation of merit: Public service in American democracy*. Baltimore, MD: The Johns Hopkins University Press.

Ingram, H., and A. Schneider. 1990. Improving implementation through framing smarter statutes. *Journal of Public Policy* 10(1): 67–88.

Inman, R. P. 2003. Transfers and bailouts: Enforcing local fiscal discipline with lessons from U.S. federalism. In *Fiscal decentralization and the challenge of hard budget constraints*, edited by J. Rodden, G. S. Eskeland, and J. Litvack, 35–83. Cambridge, MA: MIT Press.

Institute for Women's Policy Research. 2006. *The gender wage ratio: Women's and men's earnings*. Washington, DC: Institute for Women's Policy Research.

InterAction. 2002. Humanitarian leaders ask White House to review policy allowing American soldiers to conduct humanitarian relief programs in civilian clothes. News release, April 2.

Inter-Agency Standing Committee (IASC). 2004. Civil-military relationships in complex emergencies. Reference paper, United Nations Office for the Coordination of Humanitarian Affairs.

Intergovernmental Panel on Climate Change (IPCC). 2007. Climate change 2007—Impacts, adaptation, and vulnerability. Contribution of Working Group II to the Fourth Assessment Report of the IPCC. http://www.ipcc.ch/-ipccreports/ar4-wg2.htm (accessed February 15, 2011).

Irvin, R. A., and J. Stansbury. 2004. Citizen participation in decision making: Is it worth the effort? *Public Administration Review* 64(1): 55–65.

James, E. 2003. Two steps back: Relearning the humanitarian-military lessons learned in Afghanistan and Iraq. *Journal of Humanitarian Assistance*, October. http://www.jha.ac/articles/a125.htm (accessed November 19, 2009).

Jennings, E. T., and M. P. Haist. 1998. Civic community, interest groups, and economic development in the states. Presented at the Annual Meeting of the American Political Science Association, Boston, MA, September 3–6.

Jeong, M. 2006. Local choices for development impact fees. *Urban Affairs Review* 41(3): 338–357.

Jett, D. C. 2000. *Why peacekeeping fails*. New York: Palgrave Macmillan.

Jibson, W. N. 1997. History of the Bear River Compact. http://waterrights.utah.gov/techinfo/bearrivc/history.html (accessed February 15, 2011).

Johnson, G., and W. Leavitt. 2001. Building on success: Transforming organizations through an appreciative inquiry. *Public Personnel Management* 30(1): 129–136.

Jones, C., W. S. Hesterly, and S. P. Borgatti. 1997. A general theory of network governance: Exchange conditions and social mechanisms. *Academy of Management Review* 22(4): 911–945.

Jones, J. 2005. Race, ideology, and support for affirmative action. *The Gallup Poll*, August 23. http://poll.gallup.com/content/default.aspx?ci=18091 (accessed March 20, 2006).

Jos, P. H., and M. E. Tompkins. 2004. The accountability paradox in an age of reinvention: The perennial problem of preserving character and judgment. *Administration & Society* 36(3): 255–281.

Judson, A. S. 1991. *Changing behavior in organizations: Minimizing resistance to change.* Cambridge, MA: Basil Blackwell.

Jun, K. 2007. Event history analysis of the formation of Los Angeles neighborhood councils. *Urban Affairs Review* 43(1): 107–122.

Jurkiewicz, C. J., T. K. Massey, Jr., and R. G. Brown. 1998. Motivation in public and private organizations. *Public Productivity & Management Review* 21(3): 230–250.

Kammen, M. G. 1986. *A machine that would go of itself: The Constitution in American culture.* New York: Alfred A. Knopf.

Kane, T. 1998. Racial preferences and higher education. In *The black-white test score gap*, edited by C. Jencks and M. Phillips, 431–456. Washington, DC: Brookings Institution Press.

Kanter, R. M. 1977. *Men and women of the corporation.* New York: Basic Books.

Kanter, R. M. 1983. *The change masters.* New York: Simon and Schuster.

Kaplan, R. S., and D. P. Norton. 1992. The balanced scorecard: Measures that drive performance. *Harvard Business Review* 70(1): 71–79.

Kaplan, R. S., and D. P. Norton. 1996. Using the balanced scorecard as a strategic management system. *Harvard Business Review* (January–February): 75–85.

Karl, B. 1963. *Executive reorganization and reform in the New Deal: The genesis of administrative management, 1900–1939.* Cambridge, MA: Harvard University Press.

Kathi, P. C., and T. L. Cooper. 2005. Democratizing the administrative state—Connecting neighborhood councils and city agencies. *Public Administration Review* 65(5): 559–567.

Katz, M. B., M. J. Stern, and J. J. Fader. 2005. Women and the paradox of economic inequality in the twentieth-century. *Journal of Social History* 39(1): 65–88.

Kearney, R. C., B. M. Feldman, and C. P. F. Scavo. 2000. Reinventing government: City manager attitudes and actions. *Public Administration Review* 60(6): 535–548.

Kearney, R. C., and S. W. Hays. 1998. Reinventing government, the new public management and civil service systems in international perspective: The danger of throwing the baby out with the bathwater. *Review of Public Personnel Administration* 18(4): 38–54.

Keiser, L. R., M. L. Overby, K. J. Meier, and D. Hawes. 2005. Does passive representation lead to active representation in organizations lacking historical bias? Why public schools are biased against boys in punishment. Presented at the Annual Meeting of the Midwest Political Science Association, Chicago, IL, April 7–10.

Keiser, L. R., V. M. Wilkins, K. J. Meier, and C. A. Holland. 2002. Lipstick and logarithms: Gender, institutional context, and representative bureaucracy. *American Political Science Review* 96(3): 553–564.

Kellough, J. E. 1989. *Federal equal employment opportunity policy and numerical goals and timetables: An impact assessment.* Westport, CT: Greenwood Press.

Kellough, J. E. 1990a. Federal agencies and affirmative action for blacks and women. *Social Science Quarterly* 71(1): 83–92.

Kellough, J. E. 1990b. Integration in the public workplace: Determinants of minority and female employment in federal agencies. *Public Administration Review* 50(5): 557–566.

Kellough, J. E. 2006. *Understanding affirmative action: Politics, discrimination, and the search for justice.* Washington, DC: Georgetown University Press.

Kellough, J. E., and H. Lu. 1993. The paradox of merit pay in the public sector: Persistence of a problematic procedure. *Review of Public Personnel Administration* 13(2): 45–64.

Kellough, J. E., and L. G. Nigro. 2002. Pay for performance in Georgia state government: Employee perspectives on GeorgiaGain after 5 years. *Review of Public Personnel Administration* 22(2): 146–166.

Kellough, J. E., and S. C. Selden. 1997. Pay-for-performance systems in state government: Perceptions of state agency personnel managers. *Review of Public Personnel Administration* 17(1): 5–21.

Kelly, E., and F. Dobbin. 2001. How affirmative action became diversity management. In *Color lines: Affirmative action, immigration, and civil rights options for America*, edited by J. D. Skrentny, 87–117. Chicago, IL: University of Chicago Press.

Kelly, R. M. 1998. An inclusive democratic polity, representative bureaucracies, and the new public management. *Public Administration Review* 58(8): 201–208.

Kelly, R. M., and M. Newman. 2001. The gendered bureaucracy: Agency mission, equality of opportunity, and representative bureaucracies. *Women & Politics* 22(3): 1–33.

Kelman, S. J. 2002a. Contracting. In *The tools of government: A guide to the new governance*, edited by L. M. Salamon, 282–318. New York: Oxford University Press.

Kelman, S. J. 2002b. Strategic contracting management. In *Market-based governance: Supply side, demand side, upside, and downside*, edited by J. D. Donahue and J. S. Nye, Jr., 88–102. Washington, DC: Brookings Institution Press.

Kelman, S. J. 2005. *Unleashing change: A study of organizational renewal in government*. Washington, DC: Brookings Institution Press.

Kelman, S. J. 2007. Trends in the next decade: Interorganizational collaboration. In *The Business of Government Forum: Collaborative Governance*, edited by A. Morales, 53–56. Washington, DC: IBM Center for the Business of Government.

Kemp, E. J., Jr., R. J. Funk, and D. C. Eadie. 1993. Change in chewable bites: Applying strategic management at EEOC. *Public Administration Review* 53(2): 129–134.

Kerno, S. J. 2008. Limitations of communities of practice: A consideration of unresolved issues and difficulties in the approach. *Journal of Leadership & Organizational Studies* 15(1): 69–78.

Kerr, D. 2002. The balanced scorecard in the public sector. *Performance Magazine* 1(8): 4–9.

Kessler, I., and J. Purcell. 1992. Performance related pay: Objectives and application. *Human Resource Management Journal* 2(3): 16–33.

Kets de Vries, M. F. R., and K. Balazs. 1999. Transforming the mind-set of the organization. *Administration & Society* 30(6): 640–675.

Kettl, D. F. 1993. *Sharing power: Public governance and private markets*. Washington, DC: Brookings Institution Press.

Kettl, D. F. 2000. *The global public management revolution: A report on the transformation of governance*. Washington, DC: Brookings Institution Press.

Kilduff, M., R. Angelmar, and A. Mehra. 2000. Top management team diversity and firm performance. *Organization Science* 11(1): 21–34.

Kim, P. S. 1993. Racial integration in the American federal government: With special reference to Asian-Americans. *Review of Public Personnel Administration* 13(1): 52–66.

Kim, S. 2006. Public service motivation and organizational citizenship behavior in Korea. *International Journal of Manpower* 27(8): 722–740.

King, C. S., K. M. Feltey, and B. O. Susel. 2008. The question of participation: Toward authentic public participation in public administration. In *The age of direct citizen participation*, edited by N. C. Roberts, 383–400. Armonk, NY: M.E. Sharpe.

Klitgaard, R., and G. F. Treverton. 2003. *Assessing partnerships: New forms of collaboration.* Washington, DC: IBM Center for the Business of Government.

Knack, S., and P. Keefer. 1997. Does social capital have an economic payoff? A cross-country investigation. *Quarterly Journal of Economics* 112(4): 1251–1288.

Knight, J. 1992. *Institutions and social conflict.* Cambridge, UK: Cambridge University Press.

Knox, K. 2001. The La Plata River Compact: Administration of an ephemeral river in the arid Southwest. *University of Denver Water Law Review* 5: 104–120.

Kolpin, V., and L. Singell. 1996. The gender composition and scholarly performance of economics departments: A test for employment discrimination. *Industrial Labor Relations Review* 49(3): 408–423.

Kotkin, J. 2005. Uncool cities. *Prospect Magazine*, October. http://www.prospect-magazine. co.uk/article_details.php?id=7072 (accessed October 24, 2007).

Kotlikoff, L. J. 1986. Deficit delusion. *Public Interest* 84(Summer): 53–65.

Kotlikoff, L. J., and S. Burns. 2004. *The coming generational storm: What you need to know about America's economic future.* Cambridge, MA: MIT Press.

Kotter, J. P. 1995. Leading change: Why transformation efforts fail. *Harvard Business Review* (March–April): 59–67.

Kotter, J. P. 1996. *Leading change.* Watertown, MA: Harvard Business School Press.

Kouides, R. W., N. M. Bennett, B. Lewis, J. D. Coppuccio, W. H. Barker, and F. M. LaForce. 1998. Performance-based physician reimbursement and influenza immunization rates in the elderly. *American Journal of Preventive Medicine* 14(2): 89–95.

Kraatz, M. S. 1998. Learning by association? Interorganizational networks and adaptation to environmental changes. *Academy of Management Journal* 41(6): 621–643.

Kraft, M. E., and B. B. Clary. 1991. Citizen participation and the NIMBY syndrome: Public response to radioactive waste disposal. *Western Political Quarterly* 44(2): 299–328.

Krasnik, A., P. P. Groenewegen, P. A. Pedersen, P. von Scholten, G. Mooney, A. Gottschau, H. A. Flierman, and M. T. Damsgaard. 1990. Changing remuneration systems: Effects on activity in general practice. *British Medical Journal* 300(6741): 1698–1701.

Kriz, K. A. 2003. The optimal level of local government fund balances: A simulation approach. *State Tax Notes* 27(10): 887–892.

Kuykendall, C. L., and R. L. Facer, II. 2002. Public employment in Georgia state agencies: The elimination of the merit system. *Review of Public Personnel Administration* 22(2): 133–145.

Kweit, R. W., and M. G. Kweit. 1980. Bureaucratic decision-making: Impediments to citizen participation. *Polity* 12(4): 647–666.

LaBombard, R. 1998. OSHA's "cooperative" compliance program faces uncertain future. www.bcnys.org/capital/osha0319.htm (accessed September 27, 2006).

Lagemann, E. C., ed. 1999. *Philanthropic foundations: New scholarship, new possibilities.* Bloomington: Indiana University Press.

Lall, U., T. Heikkila, C. Brown, and T. Siegfried. 2008. Water in the 21st century: Defining the elements of global crises and potential solutions. *Journal of International Affairs* 61(2): 1–17.

Lambright, W. H. 2001. Transforming the National Aeronautics and Space Administration: Dan Goldin and the remaking of NASA. In *Transforming organizations*, edited by M. A. Abramson and P. R. Lawrence, 91–137. Lanham, MD: Rowman & Littlefield.

Landsbergen, D., and G. Wolken. 2001. Realizing the promise: Government information systems and the fourth generation of information technology. *Public Administration Review* 61(2): 206–220.

Langbein, L. 2006. Measurement by results: Student evaluation of faculty teaching and the mis-measurement of performance. *Economics of Education Review* 27(4): 417–428.

LaPorte, T. R., and D. S. Metlay. 1996. Hazards and institutional trustworthiness: Facing a deficit of trust. *Public Administration Review* 56(4): 341–347.

Lasseter, R. W. 2002. Georgia's merit system reform, 1996–2001: An operating agency's perspective. *Review of Public Personnel Administration* 22(2): 125–132.

Laurent, A. 2003. Entrepreneurial government: Bureaucrats as business people. In *New ways of doing business*, edited by M. A. Abramson and A. M. Kieffaber, 13–47. Lanham, MD: Rowman & Littlefield.

Laurian, L. 2004. Public participation in environmental decision making: Findings from communities facing toxic waste cleanup. *Journal of the American Planning Association* 70(1): 53–65.

Lavery, K. 1999. *Smart contracting for local government services: Processes and experience.* Westport, CT: Praeger.

Lawler, E. E., III. 1990. *Strategic pay.* San Francisco, CA: Jossey-Bass.

Lawrence, P. R., and J. W. Lorsch. 1967. *Organization and environment: Managing differentiation and integration.* Boston, MA: Graduate School of Business Administration, Harvard University.

Lee, J. 2011. Pay freeze through 2015 part of ISSA's supercommittee recs. *Federal News Radio*, October 15. http://www.federalnewsradio.com/?nid=146&si (accessed December 6, 2011).

Lee, S., and A. B. Whitford. 2008. Exit, voice, loyalty, and pay: Evidence from the public workforce. *Journal of Public Administration Research and Theory* 18(4): 647–671.

Leisink, P., and B. Steijn. 2008. Recruitment, attraction, and selection. In *Motivation in public management: The call of public service*, edited by J. L. Perry and A. Hondeghem, 118–135. Oxford: Oxford University Press.

Leonard, J. S. 1984. Employment and occupational advance under affirmative action. *Review of Economics and Statistics* 66(3): 377–385.

Leonard, J. S. 1990. The impact of affirmative action regulation and equal employment opportunity law on black employment. *Journal of Economic Perspectives* 4(4): 47–63.

LeRoux, K., and J. B. Carr. 2007. Explaining local government cooperation on public works: Evidence from Michigan. *Public Work Management & Policy* 12(1): 344–358.

Levin, J. 2003. Relational incentive contracts. *American Economic Review* 93(3): 835–857.

Levine, C. H. 2008. Citizenship and service delivery: The promise of coproduction. In *The age of direct citizen participation*, edited by N. C. Roberts, 78–92. Armonk, NY: M.E. Sharpe.

Levinson, A. 1998. Balanced budgets and business cycles: Evidence from the states. *National Tax Journal* 51(4): 715–732.

Levitt, M. A. 2002. War on terrorism scorecard. *Middle East Quarterly*, Summer: 39–52. http://www.meforum.org/article/494 (accessed September 27, 2006).

Lewicki, R. J., D. J. McAllister, and R. J. Bies. 1998. Trust and distrust: New relationships and realities. *Academy of Management Review* 23(3): 438–458.

Lewin, K. 1947. Group decision and social change. In *Readings in social psychology*, edited by T. M. Newcomb, E. L. Hartley, and others. New York: Holt, Rinehart, and Winston.

Lewin, K. 1951. *Field theory in social science.* New York: Harper & Row.

Lewis, G. P. 1985. Sexual segregation of occupations and earnings differentials in federal employment. *Public Administration Quarterly* 9(3): 274–290.

Lewis, G. P. 1988. Progress toward racial and sexual equality in the federal civil service? *Public Administration Review* 50(3): 700–706.

Lewis, G. P. 1996. Gender integration of occupations in the federal civil service: Extent and effects on male-female earnings. *Industrial and Labor Relations Review* 49(3): 472–483.

Lewis, G. P. 1998. Continuing progress toward racial and gender pay equality in the federal service: An update. *Review of Public Personnel Administration* 18(2): 23–40.

Lewis, G. B., and S. A. Frank. 2002. Who wants to work for the government? *Public Administration Review* 62(4): 395–404.

Ley, D. 2003. Artists, aestheticisation, and the field of gentrification. *Urban Studies* 40(12): 426–441.

Light, P. C. 1997. *The tides of reform.* New Haven, CT: Yale University Press.

Light, P. C. 1999a. *The new public service.* Washington, DC: Brookings Institution Press.

Light, P. C. 1999b. *The true size of government.* Washington, DC: Brookings Institution Press.

Lin, N. 2001. *Social capital: A theory of social structure and action.* New York: Cambridge University Press.

Lindblom, C. E. 1990. *Inquiry and change: The troubled attempt to understand and shape society.* New Haven, CT: Yale University Press.

Link, A. S., ed. 1966–1994. *The papers of Woodrow Wilson* (69 vols.). Princeton, NJ: Princeton University Press.

Lintner, J. 1965. The valuation of risk assets and the selection of risky investments in stock portfolios and capital budgets. *Review of Economics and Statistics* 47(1): 13–39.

Lippmann, W. 1957. *A preface to morals.* New York: Time-Life Books.

Lippmann, W. 1961. *Drift and mastery: An attempt to diagnose the current unrest.* Englewood Cliffs, NJ: Prentice-Hall, Inc.

Lombard, J. R. 2008. Crossing state borders: Utility-led interstate economic development cooperation in New England. In *Building the local economy: Cases in economic development,* edited by D. J. Watson and J. C. Morris, 79–94. Athens: Carl Vinson Institute of Government, University of Georgia.

Long, N. E. 1962. *The Polity.* Chicago: Rand McNally.

Lovrich, N. P., Jr. 1987. Merit pay and motivation in the public workforce: Beyond technical concerns to more basic considerations. *Review of Public Personnel Administration* 7(2): 54–71.

Lower Arkansas Valley Water Conservancy District. 2010. History. http://www.lavwcd.org/history.html (accessed February 15, 2011).

Lucas, R. E. 1988. On the mechanics of economic development. *Journal of Monetary Economics* 22(1): 3–42.

Ludwig, J. 2003. Public warming to affirmative action as Supreme Court hears Michigan case. *Gallup Poll,* April 1. http://poll.gallup.com/content/default.aspx?ci=8092 (accessed April 20, 2006).

Luke, J. 1991. Managing interconnectedness. In *Shared power: What is it? How does it work? How can we make it work better?* edited by J. M. Bryson and R. C. Einsweiler, 25–50. Lanham, MD: University Press of America.

Lynn, L. E., Jr. 2001. The myth of the bureaucratic paradigm: What traditional public administration really stood for. *Public Administration Review* 61(2): 144–160.

Mabin, V. J., S. Forgeson, and L. Green. 2001. Harnessing resistance: Using the theory of constraints to assist change management. *Journal of European Industrial Training* 25(2): 168–191.

MacManus, S. 1991. Why businesses are reluctant to sell to governments. *Public Administration Review* 51(4): 328–343.

Macy, B. A., and H. Izumi. 1993. Organizational change, design, and work innovation: A meta-analysis of 131 North American field studies, 1961–1991. In *Research in organizational change and development*, edited by R. W. Woodman and W. A. Pasmore, 235–313. Greenwich, CT: JAI Press.

Madison, J. 1788/2001. Federalist No. 51. In *The Federalist*, edited by G. W. Carey and J. McClellan. Indianapolis, IN: Liberty Fund.

Madison, J. 1999. To William T. Barry, August 4, 1822. In *James Madison: Writings*, edited by J. Rakove, 790–794. New York: Library of America.

Magrini, P. 2005. *The transparency in public e-procurement: The Italian perspective.* Naples, Italy: Organisation of Economic Co-operation and Development, GOV/PGG/ETH(2005)3.

Makridakis, S., S. C. Wheelwright, and R. J. Hyndman. 1998. *Forecasting: Methods and applications.* 3rd ed. New York: Wiley & Sons.

Mani, B. G. 1995. Old wine in new bottles tastes better: A case of TQM implementation in the IRS. *Public Administration Review* 55(2): 147–158.

Mansbridge, J. J. 1980. *Beyond adversary democracy.* New York: Basic Books.

March, J. G., and J. P. Olsen. 1983. Organizing political life: What administrative reorganization tells us about government. *American Political Science Review* 77(2): 281–296.

Markowitz, H. M. 1952. Portfolio selection. *Journal of Finance* 7(1): 77–91.

Marsden, D. 2004. The role of performance-related pay in renegotiating the "effort bargain": The case of the British public service. *Industrial and Labor Relations Review* 57(3): 350–370.

Marsden, D., and R. Richardson. 1994. Performing for pay? The effects of "merit pay" on motivation in a public service. *British Journal of Industrial Relations* 32(2): 243–261.

Marus, R. 2006. U.S. allies among worst on freedom scorecard. *Christian Century* 123(11): 19–20.

Matland, R. E. 1995. Synthesizing the implementation literature: The ambiguity-conflict model of policy implementation. *Journal of Public Administration Research and Theory* 5(2): 145–174.

Mattoon, R. 2004. Creating a national state rainy day fund: A modest proposal to improve future state fiscal performance. *State Tax Notes* 31(4): 271–289.

Mazmanian, D. A., and P. A. Sabatier. 1989. *Implementation and public policy: With a new postscript.* Latham, MD: University Press of America.

McCabe, B. C., and C. Stream. 2000. Diversity by the numbers: Changes in state and local government workforces 1980–1995. *Public Personnel Management* 29(1): 93–106.

McCubbins, M. D., and T. Schwartz. 1984. Congressional oversight overlooked: Police patrols versus fire alarms. *American Journal of Political Science* 28(1): 165–179.

McDaniel, A. 1998. The "Philadelphia Negro" then and now: Implications for empirical research. In *W. E. B. Dubois, race, and the city: The Philadelphia Negro and its legacy*, edited by M. B. Katz and T. J. Sugrue, 155–193. Philadelphia: University of Pennsylvania Press.

McGinn, N. F. 1996. Education, democratization, and globalization: A challenge for comparative education. *Comparative Education Review* 40(4): 341–357.

McGlinchey, D. 2005. DHS management directives spark union outrage. *Government Executive*, June 23. www.govexec.com/dailyfed/0605/062305d1.htm (accessed September 28, 2006).

McGuire, G. 2000. Gender, race, ethnicity, and networks: The factors affecting the status of employees' network members. *Work and Occupations* 27(2): 501–523.

McLeod, P. L., S. A. Lobel, and T. H. Cox, Jr. 1996. Ethnic diversity and creativity in small groups. *Small Group Research* 27(2): 248–264.

Meier, K. J. 1993. Latinos and representative bureaucracy testing the Thompson and Henderson hypotheses. *Journal of Public Administration Research and Theory* 3(4): 393–414.

Meier, K. J., and D. R. McFarlane. 1995. Statutory coherence and policy implementation: The case of family planning. *Journal of Public Policy* 15(3): 281–298.

Meier, K. J., and J. Nicholson-Crotty. 2006. Gender, representative bureaucracy, and law enforcement: The case of sexual assault. *Public Administration Review* 66(6): 850–860.

Meier, K. J., and L. Nigro. 1976. Representative bureaucracy and policy preferences: A study in the attitudes of federal executives. *Public Administration Review* 36(4): 458–469.

Meier, K. J., and L. J. O'Toole, Jr. 2006. *Bureaucracy in a democratic state: A governance perspective*. Baltimore, MD: John Hopkins University Press.

Meier, K. J., M. S. Pennington, and W. S. Eller. 2005. Race, sex, and Clarence Thomas: Representation change in the EEOC. *Public Administration Review* 65(2): 171–179.

Meier, K. J., and J. Stewart, Jr. 1992. The impact of representative bureaucracies: Educational systems and public policies. *American Review of Public Administration* 22(3): 157–171.

Meier, K. J., J. Stewart, Jr., and R. E. England. 1989. *Race, class and education: The politics of second-generation discrimination*. Madison: University of Wisconsin Press.

Meier, K. J., R. D. Wrinkle, and J. L. Polinard. 1999. Representative bureaucracy and distributional equity: Addressing the hard question. *Journal of Politics* 61(4): 1025–1039.

Mesch, D. J., and P. M. Rooney. In press. Executive compensation and organizational performance: A longitudinal study of nonprofit organizations. *Nonprofit Management & Leadership*.

Mettler, S. 1998. *Dividing citizens: Gender and federalism in New Deal public policy*. Ithaca, NY: Cornell University Press.

Meyer, J. W., and B. Rowan. 1977. Institutionalized organizations: Formal structure as myth and ceremony. *American Journal of Sociology* 83(2): 340–363.

Meyers, M. K., and N. Dillon. 1999. Institutional paradoxes: Why welfare workers cannot reform welfare. In *Public management reform and innovation: Research, theory, and application*, edited by H. G. Frederickson and J. M. Johnston, 230–258. Tuscaloosa: University of Alabama Press.

Milkovich, G. T., and A. K. Wigdor. 1991. *Pay for performance: Evaluating performance appraisal and merit pay*. Washington, DC: National Academy Press.

Miller, G. J. 1992. *Managerial dilemmas: The political economy of hierarchy*. New York: Cambridge University Press.

Miller, G. J., and A. B. Whitford. 2007. The principal's moral hazard: Constraints on the use of incentives in hierarchy. *Journal of Public Administration Research and Theory* 17(2): 213–233.

Miller, T. I., and M. A. Miller. 1991. Standards of excellence: U.S. residents' evaluations of local government services. *Public Administration Review* 51(6): 503–514.

Milward, H. B., and K. G. Provan 2000. Governing the hollow state. *Journal of Public Administration Research and Theory* 10(2): 359–380.

Milward, H. B., and H. G. Rainey. 1983. Don't blame the bureaucracy. *Journal of Public Policy* 3(2): 149–168.

Mink, O. G., P. W. Esterhuysen, B. P. Mink, and K. Q. Owen. 1993. *Change at work: A comprehensive management process for transforming organizations.* San Francisco, CA: Jossey-Bass.

Moe, R. C. 1994. The "reinventing government" exercise: Misinterpreting the problem, misjudging the consequences. *Public Administration Review* 54(2): 111–122.

Moe, R. C. 1996. Managing privatization: A new challenge to public administration. In *Agenda for excellence 2: Administering the state,* edited by B. G. Peters and B. A. Rockman, 135–148. Chatham, NJ: Chatham House.

Moe, R. C. 2001. The emerging federal quasi government: Issues of management and accountability. *Public Administration Review* 61(3): 290–312.

Moe, R. C. 2004. Governance principles: The neglected basis of federal management. In *Making government manageable: Executive organization and management in the twenty-first century,* edited by T. H. Stanton and B. Ginsberg, Chapter 2. Baltimore, MD: The Johns Hopkins University Press.

Moe, R. C., and R. S. Gilmour. 1995. Rediscovering principles of public administration: The neglected foundation of public law. *Public Administration Review* 55(2): 135–146.

Mohrman, S., and E. Lawler. 1983. *Quality of work life.* Los Angeles: University of Southern California Graduate School of Business, Center for Effective Organizations.

Montgomery, J. D. 1991. Social networks and labor market outcomes: Toward an economic analysis. *American Economic Review* 81(6): 1408–1418.

Montgomery, J. D. 1994. Weak ties, employment, and inequality: An equilibrium analysis. *American Journal of Sociology* 99(5): 1212–1236.

Montjoy, R. S., and L. J. O'Toole, Jr. 1979. Toward a theory of policy implementation: An organizational perspective. *Public Administration Review* 39(5): 465–476.

Morgan, D. R., and R. E. England. 1988. The two faces of privatization. *Public Administration Review* 48(4): 979–986.

Mosher, F. C. 1982. *Democracy and the public service.* 2nd ed. New York: Oxford University Press.

Moynihan, D. P., and S. K. Pandey. 2007. The role of organizations in fostering public service motivation. *Public Administration Review* 67(1): 40–53.

Murnane, R. J., and D. K. Cohen. 1986. Merit pay and the evaluation problem: Why most merit pay plans fail and a few survive. *Harvard Educational Review* 56(1): 1–17.

Murnighan, J. K., and D. E. Conlon. 1991. The dynamics of intense work groups: A study of British string quartets. *Administrative Science Quarterly* 36(2): 165–186.

Musso, J. A., M. Sithole, C. Weare, and M. Elliot. 2007. Implementing participatory budgeting: The case of neighborhood councils in Los Angeles. Presented at the Annual Meeting of the Midwest Political Science Association Conference, Chicago, IL, April 12–15.

Musso, J. A., C. Weare, M. Elliot, A. Kitsuse, and E. Shiau. 2007. *Toward community engagement in city governance: Evaluating neighborhood council reform in Los Angeles.* Los Angeles: Neighborhood Participation Project, School of Policy, Planning, and Development, University of Southern California.

Nabatchi, T. 2010. Addressing the citizenship and democratic deficits: The potential of deliberative democracy for public administration. *American Review of Public Administration* 40(4): 376–399.

Nachmias, D., and P. J. Moderacki. 1982. Patterns of support for merit pay and EEO performance: The inherent difficulties of implementing innovation. *Policy Studies Journal* 11(2): 318–327.

Nachmias, D., and D. H. Rosenbloom. 1973. Measuring bureaucratic representation and integration. *Public Administration Review* 33(6): 590–597.

Nadler, D. A., and M. B. Nadler. 1998. *Champions of change: How CEOs and their companies are mastering the skills of radical change.* San Francisco, CA: Jossey-Bass.

Naff, K. C. 2001. *To look like America: Dismantling barriers for women and minorities in government.* Boulder, CO: Westview Press.

Naff, K. C. 2004. From *Bakke* to *Grutter* and *Gratz*: The Supreme Court as a policymaking institution. *Review of Policy Research* 21(3): 405–426.

Nalbandian, J. 2008. Facilitating community, enabling democracy: New roles for local government managers. In *The age of direct citizen participation*, edited by N. C. Roberts, 49–62. Armonk, NY: M.E. Sharpe.

Naylor, L. A., and D. H. Rosenbloom. 2004. *Adarand, Grutter*, and *Gratz*: Does affirmative action in federal employment matter? *Review of Public Personnel Administration* 24(2): 150–174.

Neal, D., and W. Johnson. 1998. The role of premarket factors in black-white wage differences. *Journal of Political Economy* 104(5): 869–895.

Neumark, D. 1996. Sex discrimination in the restaurant industry: An audit study. *Quarterly Journal of Economics* 3(3): 915–941.

Newland, C. A. 2002. Building the futures of local government politics and administration. In *The future of local government administration*, edited by H. G. Frederickson and J. Nalbandian, 231–263. Washington, DC: International City/County Management Association.

Nigro, L. G. 1981. Attitudes of federal employees toward performance appraisal and merit pay: Implications for CSRA implementation. *Public Administration Review* 41(1): 84–86.

Niskanen, W. A. 1971. *Bureaucracy and representative government.* Chicago, IL: Aldine Atherton.

Niven, P. 2003. *Balanced scorecard step-by-step for government and nonprofit agencies.* Hoboken, NJ: Wiley & Sons.

North, D. C. 1990. *Institutions, institutional change and economic performance.* New York: Cambridge University Press.

North, D. C. 1991. Institutions. *Journal of Economic Perspectives* 5(1): 97–112.

Office of the Pardon Attorney. 1996. *Civil disabilities of convicted felons: A state-by-state survey.* Washington, DC: U.S. Department of Justice.

Office of Program Policy Analysis and Government Accountability (OPPAGA), Florida Legislature. 2006. While improving, People First still lacks intended functionality, limitations increase state agency workload and costs. Report 06-39, April.

Office of the Secretary of Defense. 2007. *National Security Personnel System documents.* Washington, DC: Office of the Secretary of Defense. http://www.cpms.osd.mil/nsps/documents.html (accessed December 18, 2007).

Olberding, J. C. 2002. Does regionalism beget regionalism? The relationship between norms and regional partnerships for economic development. *Public Administration Review* 62(4): 480–491.

O'Leary, R., and L. B. Bingham. 2007. *A manager's guide to resolving conflicts in collaborative networks.* Washington, DC: IBM Center for the Business of Government.

Oliker, O., R. Kauzlarich, J. Dobbins, K. Basseuner, D. Sampler, J. McGinn, M. Dziedzic, A. Grissom, B. Pirnie, N. Bensahel, and A. I. Guven. 2004. *Aid during conflict interaction between military and civilian assistance providers in Afghanistan, September 2001–June 2002.* Santa Monica, CA: RAND.

Orfield, M. 1997. *Metropolitics: A regional agenda for community stability.* Washington, DC: Brookings Institution Press.

Orvis, B. R., J. R. Hosek, and M. G. Mattock. 1993. *Pacer Share productivity and personnel management demonstration: Third-year evaluation.* Santa Monica, CA: National Defense Research Institute.

Osborne, D., and T. Gaebler. 1992. *Reinventing government: How the entrepreneurial spirit is transforming the public sector.* Reading, MA: Addison-Wesley.

Osborne, D., and P. Hutchinson. 2004. *The price of government: Getting the results we need in an age of permanent fiscal crisis.* New York: Basic Books.

Osborne, D., and P. Plastrik. 2000. *The reinventor's fieldbook: Tools for transforming your government.* San Francisco, CA: Jossey-Bass.

Osterloh, M., B. S. Frey, and J. Frost. 2001. Managing motivation, organization, and governance. *Journal of Management and Governance* 5(3–4): 231–239.

Ostrom, E. 1990. *Governing the commons: The evolution of institutions for collective action.* New York: Cambridge University Press.

Ostrom, E. 2005. *Understanding institutional diversity.* Princeton, NJ: Princeton University Press.

Ostrom, E., R. Gardner, and J. Walker. 1994. *Rules, games, and common-pool resources.* Ann Arbor: University of Michigan Press.

Ostrom, V., and E. Ostrom. 1977. Public goods and public choices. In *Alternatives for delivering public services: Toward improved performance*, edited by E. S. Savas, 7–49. Boulder, CO: Westview Press.

O'Toole, D. E., and J. R. Churchill. 1982. Implementing pay-for-performance: Initial experiences. *Review of Public Personnel Administration* 2(3): 13–28.

Otsuka, Y. P., and B. M. Braun. 1999. The random coefficient approach for estimating tax revenue stability and growth. *Public Finance Review* 27(6): 665–676.

Oztas, N. 2004. Neighborhood network structure of social capital: A multilevel analysis of the Los Angeles experiment. PhD dissertation, University of Southern California.

Page, P. 1994. African-Americans in Executive Branch agencies. *Review of Public Personnel Administration* 14(1): 25–50.

Pandey, S. K., and H. G. Rainey. 2006. Public managers' perceptions of organizational goal ambiguity: Analyzing alternative models. *International Public Management Journal* 9(2): 85–112.

Pandey, S. K., and E. C. Stazyk. 2008. Antecedents and correlates of public service motivation. In *Motivation in public management: The call of public service*, edited by J. L. Perry and A. Hondeghem, 101–117. Oxford: Oxford University Press.

Pandey, S. K., and B. E. Wright. 2006. Connecting the dots in public management: Political environment, organizational goal ambiguity, and the public manager's role ambiguity. *Journal of Public Administration Research and Theory* 16(4): 511–532.

Pandey, S. K., B. E. Wright, and D. P. Moynihan. 2008. Public service motivation and interpersonal citizenship behavior in public organizations: Testing a preliminary model. *International Public Management Journal* 11(1): 89–108.

Pardo, T. A., A. M. Cresswell, F. Thompson, and J. Zhang. 2006. Knowledge sharing in cross-boundary information system development in the public sector. *Information Technology and Management* 7(4): 293–313.

Park, H. J., and R. C. Feiock. 2006. Social capital and regional partnerships: Overcoming the transaction costs of institutional collective action. Working paper, Devoe Moore Center, Program in Local Governance. http://www.fsu.edu/~spap/feiock/papers/ICA_&_local_governance.pdf (accessed October 24, 2007).

Park, S. M., and H. G. Rainey. 2008. Leadership and public service motivation in U.S. federal agencies. *International Public Management Journal* 11(1): 109–142.

Parks, R., and R. Oakerson. 1993. Comparative metropolitan organization: Service production and governance structure in St. Louis, MO, and Allegheny County, PA. *Publius* 23(1): 19–39.

Pascale, R. T., and J. Sternin. 2005. Your company's secret change agents. *Harvard Business Review* 83(5): 72–81.

Pasmore, W. A. 1994. *Creating strategic change: Designing the flexible, high-performing organization*. New York: Wiley & Sons.

Pastor, M., Jr., P. Dreier, J. E. Grigsby, III, and M. López-Garza. 2000. *Regions that work: How cities and suburbs can grow together*. Minneapolis: University of Minnesota Press.

Pate, S., W. E. Watson, and L. Johnson. 1998. The effects of competition on the decision quality of diverse and nondiverse groups. *Journal of Applied Social Psychology* 28(10): 912–923.

Peach State Poll. 2006. Survey conducted by the Carl Vinson Institute of Government, University of Georgia, Athens, January 27–February 5.

Pearce, J. L., and J. L. Perry. 1983. Federal merit pay: A longitudinal analysis. *Public Administration Review* 43(4): 315–325.

Pearce, J. L., W. B. Stevenson, and J. L. Perry. 1985. Managerial compensation based on organizational performance: A time series analysis of the effects of merit pay. *Academy of Management Journal* 28(2): 261–278.

Peck, J. 2005. Struggling with the creative class. *International Journal of Urban and Regional Research* 29(4): 740–770.

Pelled, L., K. Eisenhart, and K. Xin. 1999. Exploring the black box: An analysis of work group diversity, conflict, and performance. *Administrative Science Quarterly* 44(1): 1–27.

Perito, R. 2007. Provincial reconstruction teams in Iraq. Special Report 185. Washington, DC: Institute of Peace.

Perry, J. L. 1986. Merit pay in the public sector: The case for a failure of theory. *Review of Public Personnel Administration* 7(1): 57–69.

Perry, J. L. 1988. Making policy by trial and error: Merit pay in the federal service. *Policy Studies Journal* 17(2): 389–405.

Perry, J. L. 1992. The merit pay reforms. In *The promise and paradox of civil service reform*, edited by P. W. Ingraham and D. H. Rosenbloom, 199–215. Pittsburgh, PA: University of Pittsburgh Press.

Perry, J. L. 2000. Bringing society in: Toward a theory of public-service motivation. *Journal of Public Administration Research and Theory* 10(2): 471–488.

Perry, J. L., and A. Hondeghem, eds. 2008a. *Motivation in public management: The call of public service*. Oxford: Oxford University Press.

Perry, J. L., and A. Hondeghem. 2008b. Preface. In *Motivation in public management: The call of public service*, edited by J. L. Perry and A. Hondeghem, vii–x. Oxford: Oxford University Press.

Perry, J. L., D. Mesch, and L. Paarlberg. 2006. Motivating employees in a new governance era: The performance paradigm revisited. *Public Administration Review* 66(4): 505–514.

Perry, J. L., B. A. Petrakis, and T. K. Miller. 1989. Federal merit pay, round II: An analysis of the Performance Management and Recognition System. *Public Administration Review* 49(1): 29–37.

Perry, J. L., and L. R. Wise. 1990. The motivational bases of public service. *Public Administration Review* 50(3): 367–373.

Peterson, P. 1981. *City limits*. Chicago, IL: University of Chicago Press.

Pfeffer, J., and N. Langton. 1993. The effect of wage dispersion on satisfaction, productivity, and working collaboratively: Evidence from college and university faculty. *Administrative Science Quarterly* 38(3): 382–407.

Pfeffer, J., and G. R. Salancik. 1978. *The external control of organizations: A resource dependence perspective*. New York: Harper & Row.

Phelan, J., and G. Wood. 2005. *Bleeding boundaries: Civil-military relations and the cartography of neutrality*. Woking, Surrey, UK: Ockenden International.

Piderit, S. K. 2000. Rethinking resistance and recognizing ambivalence: A multidimensional view of attitudes toward an organizational change. *Academy of Management Review* 25(4): 783–794.

Pierce, N. 1993. *City states*. Washington, DC: Seven Locks Press.

Piotrowski, S. J., and D. H. Rosenbloom. 2002. Non-mission-based values in results-oriented public management: The case of freedom of information. *Public Administration Review* 62(6): 643–657.

Pirnie, B. 1998. *Civilians and soldiers: Achieving better coordination*. Santa Monica, CA: RAND.

Pirnie, B., and C. Francisco. 1998. *Assessing requirements for peacekeeping, humanitarian assistance, and disaster relief*. Santa Monica, CA: RAND.

Pitts, D. W. 2005. Diversity, representation, and performance: Evidence about ethnicity in public organizations. *Journal of Public Administration Research and Theory* 15(4): 323–339.

Platt, S. 1989. Respectfully quoted: A dictionary of quotations. http://209.10.134.179/73/1593.html (accessed September 29, 2006).

Poister, T. H., and G. Streib. 1999. Performance measurement in municipal government: Assessing the state of the practice. *Public Administration Review* 59(4): 325–335.

Pollick, S. 2000. Civil-military cooperation: A tool for peacekeepers. *Canadian Military Journal* 1(3): 57–63.

Pollitt, C. 1990. *Managerialism and the public services*. Oxford: Blackwell Publishers.

Pollitt, C., and G. Bouckaert. 2000. *Public management reform*. Oxford: Oxford University Press.

Porter, M. E. 2000. Location, competition, and economic development: Local clusters in a global economy. *Economic Development Quarterly* 14(1): 15–34.

Poston, B., and P. Marley. 2008. Dozens of state workers have bigger paychecks than the governor. *Milwaukee Journal Sentinel*, April 20. ABI/INFORM Dateline database, document ID 1465310921 (accessed May 19, 2008).

Poterba, J. M. 1995. Balanced budget rules and fiscal policy: Evidence from the states. *National Tax Journal* 48(3): 329–336.

Powell, W. 1990. Neither market nor hierarchy: Network forms of organization. In *Research in organization behavior*, vol. 12, edited by B. Staw and L. L. Cummings, 295–336. Greenwich, CT: JAI Press.

Powell, W. W. 1998. Learning from collaboration: Knowledge and networks in the biotechnology and pharmaceutical industries. *California Management Review* 40(3): 228–240.

Powell, W. W., K. W. Koput, and L. Smith-Doerr. 1996. Interorganizational collaboration and the locus of innovation: Networks of learning in biotechnology. *Administrative Science Quarterly* 41(1): 116–145.

Praeger, J. 1994. Contracting out government services: Lessons from the private sector. *Public Administration Review* 54(2): 176–184.

President's Committee on Administrative Management (PCAM). 1937. *Report of the committee*. Washington, DC: Government Printing Office.

Press, E. 2003. Faith based furor. In *Representative bureaucracy*, edited by J. Dolan and D. H. Rosenbloom, 185–188. Armonk, NY: M.E. Sharpe.

Probst, G., and S. Borzillo. 2008. Why communities of practice succeed and why they fail. *European Management Journal* 26(5): 335–347.

Provan, K. G., and H. B. Milward. 1995. A preliminary theory of network effectiveness: A comparative study of four community mental health systems. *Administrative Science Quarterly* 30(1): 1–33.

Provan, K. G., and H. B. Milward. 2001. Do networks really work? A framework for evaluating public-sector organizational networks. *Public Administration Review* 61(4): 414–423.

Provan, K. G., and J. G. Sebastian. 1996. Interorganizational cooperation in community mental health: A resource-based explanation of referrals and case coordination. *Medical Care Research and Review* 53(1): 94–119.

Putnam, R. 1993. *Making democracy work*. Princeton, NJ: Princeton University Press.

Putnam, R. 1995. Bowling alone: America's declining social capital. *Journal of Democracy* 6(1): 65–78.

Qadeer, M. A. 2005. Ethnic segregation in a multicultural city. In *Desegregating the city: Ghettos, enclaves, and inequality*, edited by D. P. Varady, 49–61. Albany: State University of New York Press.

Radin, B. 2006. *Challenging the performance movement: Accountability, complexity, and democratic values*. Washington, DC: Georgetown University Press.

Rainey, G. W., and H. G. Rainey. 1986. Breaching the hierarchical imperative: The modularization of the social security claims process. In *Bureaucratic and governmental reform*, edited by D. J. Calista, 171–195. Greenwich, CT: JAI Press.

Rainey, H. G. 1982. Reward preferences among public and private managers: In search of the service ethic. *American Review of Public Administration* 16(4): 288–302.

Rainey, H. G. 2003. *Understanding and managing public organizations*. 3rd ed. San Francisco, CA: Jossey-Bass.

Rainey, H. G., R. W. Backoff, and C. L. Levine. 1976. Comparing public and private organizations. *Public Administration Review* 36(2): 233–246.

Rainey, H. G., and B. Bozeman. 2000. Comparing public and private organizations: Empirical research and the power of the a priori. *Journal of Public Administration Research and Theory* 10(2): 447–470.

Rankin, B. 2003. How low-income women find jobs and its effects on earnings. *Work and Occupations* 30(3): 281–301.

Reese, L. A. 2006. Metropolitan reorganization: Same governance, different day? *Review of Policy Research* 21(4): 595–611.

Reindorp, N., and P. Wiles. 2001. *Humanitarian coordination: Lessons from recent field experience*. London: Overseas Development Institute.

Relyea, H. C. 1986. Access to government information in the information age. *Public Administration Review* 46(6): 635–639.

Relyea, H. C. 2003. Government secrecy: Policy depths and dimensions. *Government Information Quarterly* 20(4): 395–418.

Renn, O., T. Webler, H. Rakel, P. Dienel, and B. Johnson. 1993. Public participation in decision making: A three-step procedure. *Policy Sciences* 26(3): 189–214.

Reskin, B. F., and D. D. Bielby. 2005. A sociological perspective on gender and career outcomes. *Journal of Economic Perspectives* 19(1): 71–86.

Riccucci, N. M. 2006. Managing diversity: Redux. In *Public personnel management: Current concerns, future challenges,* 4th ed., edited by N. M Riccucci, 58–69. New York: Longman Publishers.

Ring, P. S., and A. H. Van de Ven. 1992. Structuring cooperative relationships between organizations. *Strategic Management Journal* 13(7): 483–498.

Risher, H., and C. H. Fay. 2007. *Managing for better performance: Enhancing federal performance management practices.* Washington, DC: IBM Center for the Business of Government.

Rittberger, V. 2007. UN peacekeeping and peace-building: Taking stock. Presented at the Conference on Public Administration Meets Peace-Building—Peace Operations as Political and Managerial Challenges, Konstanz, Germany, June 15–16.

Rittel, H. J. W., and M. Webber. 1973. Dilemmas in a general theory of planning. *Policy Sciences* 4(2): 155–169.

Roberts, A. S. 2000. Less government, more secrecy: Reinvention and the weakening of freedom of information law. *Public Administration Review* 60(4): 308–320.

Roberts, A. S., and H. Darbishire, eds. 2003. *National security and open government: Striking the right balance.* Syracuse, NY: Campbell Public Affairs Institute.

Roberts, N. C., ed. 2008a. *The age of direct citizen participation.* Armonk, NY: M.E. Sharpe.

Roberts, N. C.. 2008b. Direct citizen participation: Coming of age. In *The age of direct citizen participation,* edited by N. C. Roberts, 491–500. Armonk, NY: M.E. Sharpe.

Roberts, N. C., and R. Bradley. 2005. Organizing for peace operations. *Public Management Review* 7(1): 111–133.

Robertson, P. J., D. R. Roberts, and J. I. Porras. 1993. Dynamics of planned organizational change: Assessing empirical support for a theoretical model. *Academy of Management Journal* 36(3): 619–634.

Robertson, P. J., and S. J. Seneviratne. 1995. Outcomes of planned organizational change in the public sector: A meta-analytic comparison to the private sector. *Public Administration Review* 55(6): 547–558.

Rodgers, W., and W. Spriggs. 1996. The effect of federal contractor status on racial differences in establishment-level employment shares, 1979–1992. *American Economic Review* 86(2): 290–293.

Rohr, J. A. 1986. *To run a constitution: The legitimacy of the administrative state.* Lawrence: University Press of Kansas.

Romer, P. M. 1990. Endogenous technological change. *Journal of Political Economy* 98(5): S71–S02.

Rose, W. H., and T. P. Chia. 1978. The impact of the Equal Employment Opportunity Act of 1972 on black employment in the federal service: A preliminary analysis. *Public Administration Review* 38(3): 245–251.

Rosenbloom, D. H. 1971. *Federal service and the Constitution: The development of the public employment relationship.* Ithaca, NY: Cornell University Press.

Rosenbloom, D. H. 1983. Public administrative theory and the separation of powers. *Public Administration Review* 43(3): 219–227.

Rosenbloom, D. H. 2005. Taking social equity seriously in MPA education. *Journal of Public Affairs Education* 11(3): 247–252.

Rosenbloom, D. H., and S. J. Piotrowski. 2005. Outsourcing the Constitution and administrative law norms. *American Review of Public Administration* 35(2): 103–121.

Rosener, J. B. 2008. Making bureaucrats responsive: A study of the impact of citizen participation and staff recommendations on regulatory decision making. In *The age of direct
citizen participation*, edited by N. C. Roberts, 374–382. Armonk, NY: M.E. Sharpe.

Rossotti, C. O. 2005. *Many unhappy returns*. Boston, MA: Harvard Business School Press.

Rotolo, T., and J. Wilson. 2006. Employment sector and volunteering: The contribution of
nonprofit and public sector workers to the volunteer labor force. *Sociological Quarterly*
47(1): 21–40.

Rourke, F. E. 1978. *Bureaucracy, politics, and public policy*. 2nd ed. Boston, MA: Little Brown.

Rourke, F. E. 1993. Whose bureaucracy is this anyway? *PS: Political Science and Politics*
26(4): 687–692.

Rousseau, D. M. 1995. *Psychological contracts in organizations*. London: Sage Publications.

Rubin, H. J. 1988. Shoot anything that flies, claim anything that falls: Conversations with
economic development practitioners. *Economic Development Quarterly* 2(3): 236–251.

Rubin, I. S. 2005. The state of state budget research. *Public Budgeting and Finance* 25(4S):
46–67.

Rutzick, K. 2005a. Homeland Security appeals decision blocking personnel reforms.
Government Executive, November 14. www.govexec.com/dailyfed/1105/111405r1.
htm (accessed September 28, 2006).

Rutzick, K. 2005b. Pentagon fine-tunes personnel reforms. *Government Executive*, October
26. www.govexec.com/dailyfed/1005/102605r1.htm (accessed September 28, 2006).

Rutzick, K. 2005c. Pentagon releases long-awaited details on personnel reforms. *Government
Executive*, November 29. www.govexec.com/dailyfed/1105/112905r1.htm (accessed
September 28, 2006).

Rutzick, K. 2006a. Congress blocks funding for the Pentagon labor system.
Government Executive, September 27. http://www.govexec.com/story_page.
cfm?articleid=35132&ref=rellink (accessed March 7, 2007).

Rutzick, K. 2006b. Officials forgo Supreme Court appeal in DHS labor case. *Government
Executive*, September 26. http://www.govexec.com/dailyfed/0906/092606r1.htm
(accessed March 7, 2007).

Rydin, Y., and M. Pennington. 2000. Public participation and local environmental planning:
The collective action problem and the potential of social capital. *Local Environment*
5(2): 153–169.

Sabbagh, D. 2003. Judicial uses of subterfuge: Affirmative action reconsidered. *Political
Science Quarterly* 118(3): 411–438.

Saidel, J. R., and K. Loscocco. 2005. Agency leaders, gendered institutions, and representative bureaucracy. *Public Administration Review* 65(2): 158–170.

Salamon, L. M. 1995. *Partners in public service: Government-nonprofit relations in the modern
welfare state*. Baltimore, MD: The Johns Hopkins University Press.

Salamon, L. M., ed. 2002. *The tools of government: A guide to the new governance*. New York:
Oxford University Press.

Sander, R. S. 2004. A systematic analysis of affirmative action in American law schools.
Stanford Law Review 57(2): 367–483.

Sanders, R. M. 2004. GeorgiaGain or GeorgiaLoss? The great experiment in state civil service
reform. *Public Personnel Management* 33(2): 151–164.

Sanderson, T., D. Gordon, and G. Ben-Ari. 2008. *International collaborative online networks*.
Washington, DC: Center for Strategic & International Studies.

Sands, G., and L. A. Reese. 2008. Cultivating the creative class: And what about Nanaimo?
Economic Development Quarterly 22(1): 8–23.

Sassen, S. 1991. *The global city: New York, London, Tokyo*. Princeton, NJ: Princeton University Press.

Savas, E. S. 1987. *Privatization: The key to better government*. Chatham, NJ: Chatham House.

Savas, E. S. 2000. *Privatization and public–private partnerships*. New York: Chatham House.

Savas, E. S. 2006. *Privatization in the city: Successes, failures, lessons*. Washington, DC: CQ Press.

Sayre, W. S. 1951. Trends of a decade in administrative values. *Public Administration Review* 11(1): 1–9.

Schay, B. W. 1988. Effects of performance-contingent pay on employee attitudes. *Public Personnel Management* 17(2): 237–250.

Schlager, E. 2004. Common-pool resource theory. In *Environmental governance reconsidered: Challenges, choices, and opportunities*, edited by R. F. Durant, D. J. Fiorino, and R. O'Leary, 145–175. Cambridge, MA: MIT Press.

Schlager, E., and T. Heikkila. 2009. Resolving water conflicts: A comparative analysis of interstate river compacts. *Policy Studies Journal* 37(3): 367–392.

Schunk, D., and D. P. Woodward. 2005. Spending stabilization rules: A solution to recurring state budget crises? *Public Budgeting and Finance* 25(4): 105–124.

Schuster, J. R., and J. A. Colletti. 1973. Pay secrecy: Who is for and against it? *Academy of Management Journal* 16(1): 35–40.

Sclar, E. D. 2000. *You don't always get what you pay for: The economics of privatization*. Ithaca, NY: Cornell University Press.

Scott, A. J. 2006. Creative cities: Conceptual issues and policy questions. *Journal of Urban Affairs* 28(1): 1–17.

Scott, W. R. 2003. *Organizations: Rational, natural, and open systems*. 5th ed. Upper Saddle River, NJ: Prentice Hall.

Seidman, H. 1998. *Politics, position, and power: The dynamics of federal organizations*. 5th ed. New York: Oxford University Press.

Seiple, C. 1996. *The U.S. military/NGO relationship in humanitarian interventions*. Carlisle, PA: Peacekeeping Institute, Center for Strategic Leadership, U.S. Army War College.

Selden, S. C. 1997. *The promise of representative bureaucracy: Diversity and responsiveness in a government agency*. Armonk, NY: M.E. Sharpe.

Selden, S. C., J. L. Brudney, and E. J. Kellough. 1998. Bureaucracy as a representative institution: Toward a reconciliation of bureaucratic government and democratic theory. *American Journal of Political Science* 42(3): 719–744.

Serra, G. 1995. Citizen-initiated contact and satisfaction with bureaucracy: A multivariate analysis. *Journal of Public Administration Research and Theory* 5(2): 175–188.

Shareef, R. 1994. Subsystem congruence: A strategic change model for public organizations. *Administration & Society* 25(4): 489–517.

Sharpe, W. F. 1964. Capital asset prices: A theory of market equilibrium under conditions of risk. *Journal of Finance* 19(3): 425–442.

Shaw, J. D., M. K. Duffy, A. Mitra, D. E. Lockhart, and M. Bowler. 2003. Reactions to merit pay increases: A longitudinal test of a signal sensitivity perspective. *Journal of Applied Psychology* 88(3): 538–544.

Shetterly, D. R. 2000. The influence of contract design on contractor performance: The case of residential refuse collection. *Public Performance & Management Review* 24(1): 53–68.

Shiller, R. J. 2003. *The new financial order: Risk in the 21st century*. Princeton, NJ: Princeton University Press.

Shleifer, A., and R. W. Vishny. 1998. *The grabbing hand: Government pathologies and their cures.* Cambridge, MA: Harvard University Press.

Shoop, T. 2005. Unions file suit challenging Defense personnel system. *Government Executive,* November 7. www.govexec.com/dailyfed/1105/110705ts1.htm (accessed September 28, 2006).

Siegel, G. B. 1987. The jury is still out on merit pay in government. *Review of Public Personnel Administration* 7(3): 3–15.

Singer, P. 2006. Humanitarian principles, private military agents: Some implications of the privitised military industry for the humanitarian community. In *Resetting the rules of engagement: Trends and issues in military-humanitarian relations,* edited by V. Wheeler and A. Harmer, 67–79. London: Overseas Development Institute.

Sirianni, C., and L. Friedland. 2001. *Civic innovation in America: Community empowerment, public policy, and the movement for civic renewal.* Berkeley: University of California Press.

Skowronek, S. 1982. *Building a new American state: The expansion of national administrative capacities, 1877–1920.* New York: Cambridge University Press.

Slaughter, A. 2004. *A new world order.* Princeton, NJ: Princeton University Press.

Smith, B. W. 2003. The impact of police officer diversity on police-caused homicides. *Policy Studies Journal* 31(2): 147–162.

Smith, S. P. 1976. Government wage differentials by sex. *Journal of Human Resources* 11(2): 185–199.

Snyder, T. D., A. G. Tan, and C. M. Hoffman. 2006. *Digest of education statistics, 2005 (NCES 2006030).* U.S. Department of Education, National Center for Educational Statistics. Washington, DC: Government Printing Office.

Snyder, W. M., and X. de Souza Briggs. 2003. *Communities of practice: A new tool for government managers.* Washington, DC: IBM Center for the Business of Government.

Sobel, R. S., and R. G. Holcombe. 1996. Measuring the growth and variability of tax bases over the business cycle. *National Tax Journal* 49(4): 535–552.

Sommers, M. 2000. The dynamics of coordination. Occasional Paper 40, Thomas J. Watson Institute for International Studies, Brown University.

Sonenshein, R. J. 2004. *The city at stake: Secession, reform, and the battle for Los Angeles.* Princeton, NJ: Princeton University Press.

Sorensen, E. 1989. Measuring the effect of occupational sex and race composition on earnings. In *Pay equity: Empirical inquiries,* edited by R. T. Michaels, H. I. Hartmann, and B. O'Farrell, 49–69. Washington, DC: National Academy Press.

Sowa, J. E., and S. C. Selden. 2003. Administrative discretion and active representation: An expansion of the theory of representative bureaucracy. *Public Administration Review* 63(6): 700–710.

Sparrow, M. K. 1994. *Imposing duties: Government's changing approach to compliance.* Westport, CT: Praeger.

Springer, A. 2006. Update on affirmative action in higher education: A current legal overview, updated January 2006. *American Association of University Professors.* www.aaup.org/issues/affirmativeaction/aalegal.htm (accessed April 5, 2006).

Stanley, T. D., and S. B. Jarrell. 1998. Gender wage discrimination bias? A meta-regression analysis. *Journal of Human Resources* 33(4): 947–973.

State of Georgia, Georgia Merit System. 2006. Personal correspondence, March 30.

Steijn, B. 2008. Person-environment fit and public service motivation. *International Public Management Journal* 11(1): 13–27.

Stephanopoulos, G., and C. Edley, Jr. 1995. Review of federal affirmative action programs. Unpublished White House document.

Stillman, R. J. 1999. *Preface to public administration: A search for themes and direction.* 2nd ed. Burke, VA: Chatelaine Press.

Stock, W. A. 1994. Systematic coding for research synthesis. In *The handbook of research synthesis,* edited by H. Cooper and L. V. Hedges, 125–138. New York: Russell Sage Foundation.

Stoker, R. 1989. A regime framework for implementation analysis: Cooperation and reconciliation of federalist imperatives. *Policy Studies Review* 9(1): 29–49.

Storm, R., and R. C. Feiock. 1999. State support for higher education and economic development. *State and Local Government Review* 31(2): 97–105.

Studer, M. 2001. The ICRC and civil-military relations in armed conflict. *International Review of the Red Cross* 83(842): 367–391.

Sunstein, C. R. 2003. The law of group polarization. In *Debating deliberative democracy,* edited by J. S. Fishkin and P. Laslett, 80–101. Malden, MA: Blackwell Publishing.

Swidler, S. M., R. J. Buttimer, and R. Shaw. 1999. Government hedging: Motivation, implementation, and evaluation. *Public Budgeting and Finance* 19(4): 75–90.

Swindell, D., and J. M. Kelly. 2000. Linking citizen satisfaction data to performance measures: A preliminary examination. *Public Performance & Management Review* 24(1): 30–52.

Szilagyi, J. 1999. Streamflow depletion investigations in the Republican River Basin: Colorado, Nebraska, and Kansas. *Journal of Environmental Systems* 27(3): 251–263.

Tadelis, S. 2002. Complexity, flexibility, and the make-or-buy decision. *American Economic Review Papers and Proceedings* 92(2): 433–437.

Tao, J., and R. C. Feiock. 1999. Directing benefits of need: Evaluating the distributive consequences of urban economic development. *Economic Development Quarterly* 13(1): 55–66.

Terry, L. D. 1993. Why we should abandon the misconceived quest to reconcile public entrepreneurship with democracy. *Public Administration Review* 53(4): 393–395.

Terry, L. D. 1998. Administrative leadership, neomanagerialism, and the public management movement. *Public Administration Review* 58(3): 194–200.

Teske, P., M. Schneider, M. Mintrom, and S. Best. 1993. Establishing the micro foundations of a macro theory: Information, movers, and the competitive local market for public goods. *American Political Science Review* 87(3): 702–713.

Thielemann, G. S., and J. J. Stewart, Jr. 1996. A demand-side perspective on the importance of representative bureaucracy: AIDS, ethnicity, gender, and sexual orientation. *Public Administration Review* 56(2): 168–173.

Thomas, H. 2006. Bush admits mistakes, but not the big ones. http://thebostonchannel.com/print/9336547/detail.html (accessed September 28, 2006).

Thomas, J. C. 1986. *Between citizen and city: Neighborhood organizations and urban politics in Cincinnati.* Lawrence: University Press of Kansas.

Thomas, J. C. 1995. *Public participation in public decisions: New skills and strategies for public managers.* San Francisco, CA: Jossey-Bass.

Thomas, J. C. 2010. When should the public be involved in public management? Design principles with case applications. In *The future of public administration, public management, and public service around the world: The Minnowbrook perspective,* edited by R. O'Leary, D. M. Van Slyke, and S. Kim, 167–176. Washington, DC: Georgetown University Press.

Thomas, J. M., and J. Darnton. 2005. Social diversity and economic development in the metropolis. Presented at the Annual Meeting of the Association of Collegiate Schools of Planning, Kansas City, MO, October 27–30.

Thompson, F. 1994. Mission-driven, results-oriented budgeting: Financial administration and the new public management. *Public Budgeting and Finance* 14(3): 90–105.

Thompson, F. J. 2002. Reinvention in the states: Ripple or tide? *Public Administration Review* 62(3): 362–367.

Thompson, J. R., and S. L. Fulla. 2001. Effecting change in a reform context: The National Performance Review and the contingencies of "microlevel" reform implementation. *Public Performance & Management Review* 25(2): 155–175.

Thompson, J. R., and S. H. Mastracci. 2005. Toward a more flexible public workforce: Issues and implications. In *Handbook of human resources management in government*, 2nd ed., edited by S. E. Condrey, 125–142. San Francisco, CA: Jossey-Bass.

Thompson, J. R., and R. P. Sanders. 1997. Strategies for reinventing federal agencies. *Public Productivity & Management Review* 21(2): 137–155.

Thurmaier, K. M., and K. G. Willoughby. 2001. *Policy and politics in state budgeting*. Armonk, NY: M.E. Sharpe.

Tichy, N. M. 1983. *Managing strategic change: Technical, political, and cultural dynamics*. New York: Wiley & Sons.

Tiebout, C. M. 1956. A pure theory of local public expenditures. *Journal of Political Economy* 64(5): 416–424.

Tomb, N. 2005. *Humanitarian roles in insecure environments*. Monterey, CA: Center for Stabilization and Reconstruction Studies, Naval Postgraduate School.

Tosi, H. L., S. Werner, J. P. Katz, and L. R. Gomez-Mejia. 2000. How much does performance matter? A meta-analysis of CEO pay studies. *Journal of Management* 26(2): 301–339.

Tulgan, B. 1997. *The manager's pocket guide to Generation X*. Amherst, MA: HRD Press.

Tushman, M. L., and E. Romanelli. 1985. Organizational evolution: A metamorphosis model of convergence and reorientation. In *Research in organizational behavior*, edited by L. L. Cummings and B. M. Staw, vol. 7. Greenwich, CT: JAI Press.

U.S. Bureau of Labor Statistics. 2006. *Current population survey*. www.bls.census.gov/cps/cpsmain.htm (accessed October 1, 2006).

U.S. Commission on Civil Rights. 2000. *Toward an understanding of percentage plans in higher education: Are they effective substitutes for affirmative action?* Washington, DC. http://www.usccr.gov/pubs/percent/stmnt.htm (accessed March 20, 2006).

U.S. Congress. 1940. Congressional Record 86, 76th Cong., 3rd sess. Washington, DC: Government Printing Office.

U.S. Congress. 1989. *Examination of the use of consultants and contractors by the Environmental Protection Agency and the Department of Energy*. Hearings before the Senate Committee on Governmental Affairs, Subcommittee on Federal Services, Post Office, and Civil Service. 101st Cong., 1st sess., February 3.

U.S. Department of Defense (DOD). 2005. Directive 3000.05: Military support for stability, security, transition, and reconstruction (SSTR). November 28.

U.S. Department of Education, National Center for Education Statistics (NCES). 2004a. Higher education general information survey, table 182: College enrollment and enrollment rates of recent high school completers, by race/ethnicity: 1960 to 2003. http://nces.ed.gov/programs/digest/d04/tables/dt04_182.asp (accessed April 1, 2006).

U.S. Department of Education, National Center for Education Statistics (NCES). 2004b. Higher education general information survey, table 183: College enrollment and enrollment rates of recent high school completers, by sex: 1960 to 2003. http://nces.ed.gov/programs/digest/d04/tables/dt04_183.asp (accessed April 1, 2006).

U.S. Department of Education, National Center for Education Statistics (NCES). 2004c. Higher education general information survey, table 187: Total graduate fall enrollment in degree-granting institutions, by attendance status, sex of student, and control of institution: 1969 to 2002. http://nces.ed.gov/programs/digest/d04/tables/dt04_187.asp (accessed April 1, 2006).

U.S. Department of Education, National Center for Education Statistics (NCES). 2004d. Higher education general information survey, table 206: Total fall enrollment in degree-granting institutions, by race/ethnicity, sex, attendance status, and level of student: Selected years, 1976 to 2002. http://nces.ed.gov/programs/digest/d04/tables/dt04_206.asp (accessed April 1, 2006).

U.S. Department of Education, National Center for Education Statistics (NCES). 2004e. Higher education general information survey, table 271: First-professional degrees conferred by degree-granting institutions, by racial/ethnic group and sex of student. http://nces.ed.gov/programs/digest/d04/tables/dt04_271.asp (accessed April 1, 2006).

U.S. Equal Employment Opportunity Commission (EEOC). 2004. Annual report on the federal work force: Fiscal year 2004. http://www.eeoc.gov/federal/fsp2004/index.html (accessed February 20, 2006).

U.S. Equal Employment Opportunity Commission (EEOC). 2005. New Gallup Poll on employment discrimination shows progress, problems 40 years after founding of EEOC. News release, December 8. www.eeoc.gov/press/12-8-05.html (accessed August 2, 2006).

U.S. Equal Employment Opportunity Commission (EEOC). 2006. Charge statistics: FY 1992 through FY 2005. http://www.eeoc.gov/stats/charges.html (accessed February 20, 2006).

U.S. General Accounting Office (GAO). 1984. *A 2-year appraisal of merit pay in three agencies.* Washington, DC: GAO.

U.S. General Accounting Office (GAO). 1991. *Federal workforce: Continuing need for federal affirmative employment.* Washington, DC: GAO/GGD-92-27BR.

U.S. General Accounting Office (GAO). 1997. *Privatization: Lessons learned by state and local governments.* Washington, DC: GAO/GGD-97-48.

U.S. General Accounting Office (GAO). 2001. *Information sharing: Practices that can benefit critical infrastructure protection.* Washington, DC: GAO-02-24.

U.S. General Accounting Office (GAO). 2003a. *Homeland Security: Information sharing responsibilities, challenges, and key management issues.* Washington, DC: GAO-03-1165T.

U.S. General Accounting Office (GAO). 2003b. *Women's earnings: Work patterns partially explain differences between men's and women's earnings.* Washington, DC: GAO-04-35.

U.S. Government Accountability Office (GAO). 2005. *Equal employment opportunity: DOD's EEO pilot program under way.* Washington, DC: GAO-06-538.

U.S. Institute of Peace (USIP). 2000. Taking it to the next level: Civilian-military cooperation in complex emergencies. http://www.usip.org/virtualdiplomacy/publications/reports/nextlevel.html.

U.S. Institute of Peace (USIP). 2007. Guidelines for relations between U.S. armed forces and non-governmental humanitarian organizations in hostile or potentially hostile environments. http://www.usip.org/resources/guidelines-relations-between-us-armed-forces-and-nghos-hostile-or-potentially-hostile-envi (accessed November 19, 2009).

U.S. Merit Systems Protection Board (MSPB). 1999. *Federal supervisors and poor performers.* Washington, DC: Merit Systems Protection Board, July.

U.S. National Performance Review (NPR). 1993. *Reinventing human resource management.* Washington, DC, September. http://govinfo.library.unt.edu/npr/library/reports/hrmexe.html (accessed March 7, 2007).

U.S. Office of Management and Budget (OMB). 2001. President's Management Agenda. Washington, DC: Government Printing Office. www.whitehouse.gov/omb/budget/fy2002/mgmt.pdf (accessed September 28, 2006).

U.S. Office of Management and Budget (OMB). 2003. Circular no. A-76 (revised), Performance of commercial activities. www.whitehouse.gov/omb/circulars/(accessed September 28, 2006).

U.S. Office of Management and Budget (OMB). 2006a. Agency scorecards. www.whitehouse.gov/omb/budintegration/scorecards/agency_scorecards.html (accessed September 28, 2006).

U.S. Office of Management and Budget (OMB). 2006b. President's Management Agenda. http://www.whitehouse.gov/omb/budintegration/pma_index.html (accessed September 29, 2006).

U.S. Office of Personnel Management (OPM). 1999. *Poor performers in government: A quest for the true story.* Washington, DC: Office of Merit Systems Oversight and Effectiveness, Report of a Special Study, January.

U.S. Office of Personnel Management (OPM). 2006. *Federal Equal Opportunity Recruitment Program: FY 2005.* http://www.opm.gov/feorpreports/2005/feorp2005.pdf (accessed May 15, 2006).

U.S. Senate. 1974. Committee on the Judiciary, Subcommittee on Administrative Practice and Procedure. *Freedom of Information Act source book: Legislative materials, cases, articles.* 93rd Cong., 2nd sess., S. Doc. 93-82.

Vandenabeele, W., A. Hondeghem, and T. Steen. 2004. The civil service as an employer of choice in Belgium: How work orientations influence the attractiveness of public employment. *Review of Public Personnel Administration* 24(4): 319–333.

Van de Ven, A. H. 1993. Managing the process of organizational innovation. In *Organizational change and redesign: Ideas and insights for improving performance*, edited by G. P. Huber and W. H. Glick, 269–294. New York: Oxford University Press.

Van de Ven, A. H., and D. Ferry. 1980. *Measuring and assessing organizations.* New York: Wiley & Sons.

Van de Ven, A. H., and M. S. Poole. 1995. Explaining development and change in organizations. *Academy of Management Review* 20(3): 510–540.

Van Eerde, W., and H. Thierry. 1996. Vroom's expectancy models and work-related criteria: A meta-analysis. *Journal of Applied Psychology* 81(5): 575–589.

Van Slyke, D. M. 2003. The mythology of privatization in contracting for social services. *Public Administration Review* 63(3): 296–315.

Van Slyke, D. M. 2007. Agents or stewards: Using theory to understand the government-nonprofit social service contracting relationship. *Journal of Public Administration Research and Theory* 17(2): 157–187.

Van Slyke, D. M., and C. A. Hammonds. 2003. The privatization decision: Do public managers make a difference? *American Review of Public Administration* 33(2): 146–163.

Van Slyke, D. M., C. S. Horne, and J. C. Thomas. 2005. The implications of public opinion for public managers: Charitable choice and faith-based organizations. *Administration & Society* 37(3): 321–344.

Vars, F. E., and W. G. Bowen. 1998. Scholastic aptitude, test scores, race, and academic performance in selective colleges and universities. In *The black-white test score gap*, edited by C. Jencks and M. Phillips, 457–479. Washington, DC: Brookings Institution Press.

Ventriss, C. 2008. Toward a public philosophy of public administration: A civic perspective of the public. In *The age of direct citizen participation*, edited by N. C. Roberts, 38–48. Armonk, NY: M.E. Sharpe.

Verba, S., K. L. Schlozman, and H. Brady. 1995. *Voice and equality: Civic voluntarism in American politics*. Cambridge, MA: Harvard University Press.

Vogel, B. 2005. Linking for change: Network action as collective, focused and energetic behavior. *Long Range Planning* 38(6): 531–553.

Von Zielbauer, P. 2005. As health care in jails goes private, 10 days can be a death sentence. *New York Times*, February 27.

Wagner, G. A., and E. M. Elder. 2004. Recessions and rainy day funds in U.S. states: What are the odds your state is saving enough? Working paper, Duquesne University.

Waldfogel, J. 1998. Understanding the "family gap" in pay for women with children. *Journal of Economic Perspective* 12(1): 137–156.

Waldo, D. 1948. *The administrative state: A study of the political theory of American public administration*. New York: Ronald Press.

Waldo, D. 1980. *The enterprise of public administration*. Novato, CA: Chandler & Sharp Publishers.

Waldo, D. 1984. *The administrative state: A study of the political theory of American public administration*. 2nd ed. New York: Holmes & Meier.

Wallin, B. A. 1997. The need for a privatization process: Lessons from development and implementation. *Public Administration Review* 57(1): 11–20.

Wamsley, G. L., and L. S. Dudley. 1998. From reorganization to reinventing: Sixty years and we still don't get it. *International Journal of Public Administration* 21(2–4): 323–374.

Wamsley, G. L., and J. F. Wolf, eds. 1996. *Refounding democratic public administration: Modern paradoxes, postmodern challenges*. Thousand Oaks, CA: Sage Publications.

Wang, R. Y., and D. M. Strong. 1996. Beyond accuracy: What data quality means to data consumers. *Journal of Management Information Systems* 12(4): 5–33.

Warren, K. 2004. *Administrative law in the American political system*. 4th ed. Boulder, CO: Westview.

Warshaw, S. A. 2006. The administrative strategies of President George W. Bush. *Extensions*, Spring, 19–23.

Warwick, D. P. 1975. *A theory of public bureaucracy*. Cambridge, MA: Harvard University Press.

Watson, D. J. 1995. *The new civil war: Government competition for economic development*. Westport, CT: Praeger Publishers.

Watson, D. J., and J. C. Morris, eds. 2008. *Building the local economy: Cases in economic development*. Athens: Carl Vinson Institute of Government, University of Georgia.

Watson, W., L. Johnson, and D. Merritt. 1998. Team orientation, self orientation, and diversity in task groups: Their connection to team performance over time. *Group and Organization Management* 23(2): 161–188.

Watson, W., K. Kumar, and L. Michaelson. 1993. Cultural diversity's impact on interaction processes and performance: Comparing homogeneous and diverse task groups. *Academy of Management Journal* 36(4): 590–602.

Weare, C., J. A. Musso, and K. Jun. 2008. Democracy by design: The institutionalization of community participation networks in Los Angeles. Presented at the Annual Meeting of the Midwest Political Science Association, Chicago, IL, April 12–15.

Weber, E. P., and A. M. Khademian. 2008. Wicked problems, knowledge challenges, and collaborative capacity builders in network settings. *Public Administration Review* 68(2): 334–349.

Weissbourd, R., and C. Berry. 2004. The changing dynamics of urban America. CEOs for Cities, March 30. http://artsmarketing.org/marketingresources/files/changing_dynamics-full_report.pdf (accessed October 24, 2007).

Weissert, C. S., and M. L. Goggin. 2002. Nonincremental policy change: Lessons from Michigan's Medicaid managed care initiative. *Public Administration Review* 62(6): 206–216.

Welsh, M. 2004. Fast-forward to a participatory norm: Agency response to public mobilization over oil and gas leasing in Pennsylvania. *State and Local Government Review* 36(2): 186–197.

Wenger, E. 1998. *Communities of practice: Learning, meaning, and identity.* New York: Cambridge University Press.

Wenger, E., R. McDermott, and W. Snyder. 2002. *Cultivating communities of practice.* Boston, MA: Harvard Business School Press.

West, J. P. 2002. Georgia on the mind of radical civil service reformers. *Review of Public Personnel Administration* 22(2): 79–93.

West, J. P. 2005. Managing an aging workforce: Trends, issues, and strategies. In *Handbook of human resources management in government*, 2nd ed., edited by S. E. Condrey, 164–188. San Francisco, CA: Jossey-Bass.

Western, B. 2002. The impact of incarceration on wage mobility and inequality. *American Sociological Review* 67(4): 526–546.

Western, B. 2006. *Punishment and inequality in America.* New York: Russell Sage Foundation.

Western, B., and B. Pettit. 2000. Incarceration and racial inequality in men's employment. *Industrial and Labor Relations Review* 54(1): 3–16.

Wettenhall, W. 2003. The rhetoric and reality of public-private partnerships. *Public Organization Review* 3(1): 77–107.

Whelan, V., and A. Harmer, eds. 2006. *Resetting the rules of engagement: Trends and issues in military-humanitarian relations.* London: Overseas Development Institute.

White House. 1997. The Clinton administration's policy on managing complex contingency operations: Presidential decision directive 56 white paper. Washington, DC, May.

White, H. D. 1994. Scientific communication and literature retrieval. In *The handbook of research synthesis*, edited by H. Cooper and L. V. Hedges, 41–56. New York: Russell Sage Foundation.

White, R. H. 1998. *Employment law and employment discrimination: Essential terms and concepts.* New York: Aspen Law and Business.

Wildavsky, A. 1979. *Speaking truth to power: The art and craft of policy analysis.* New Brunswick, NJ: Transaction Publishers.

Wiley, M. W., and R. N. Palmer. 2008. Estimating the impacts and uncertainty of climate change on a municipal water supply system. *Journal of Water Resources Planning and Management* 134(3): 239–246.

Wilkins, V. M., and L. R. Keiser. 2006. Linking passive and active representation by gender: The case of child support agencies. *Journal of Public Administration Research and Theory* 16(1): 87–102.

Williamson, A., and A. Fung. 2005. *Mapping public deliberation: A report to the William and Flora Hewlett Foundation.* Cambridge, MA: Taubman Center for State and Local Government, Harvard University.

Williamson, O. E. 1975. *Markets and hierarchies: Analysis and antitrust implications.* New York: Free Press.

Williamson, O. E. 1981. The economics of organization: The transaction cost approach. *American Journal of Sociology* 87(3): 548–577.

Williamson, O. E. 1991. Comparative economic organization: The analysis of discrete structural alternatives. *Administration Science Quarterly* 36(2): 269–296.

Williamson, O. E. 1993. Calculativeness, trust, and economic organization. *Journal of Law and Economics* 36(1): 453–486.

Williamson, O. E. 1995. Transaction cost economics and organization theory. In *Organization theory: From Chester Barnard to the present and beyond,* edited by O. E. Williamson, 207–256. New York: Oxford University Press.

Williamson, O. E. 1996. *The mechanisms of governance.* New York: Oxford University Press.

Willoughby, K. 1991. Gender-based wage gap: The case of the state budget analyst. *Review of Public Personnel Administration* 12(1): 33–46.

Wilson, G. 2006. The rise of at-will employment and racial inequality in the public sector. *Review of Public Personnel Administration* 26(2): 178–187.

Wilson, J., and M. A. Musick. 1997. Work and volunteering: The long arm of the job. *Social Forces* 76(1): 251–272.

Wilson, W. 1997. The study of administration. In *Classics of public administration,* 4th ed., edited by J. Shafritz and A. Hyde, 14–26. Fort Worth, TX: Harcourt Brace.

Wilson, W. J. 1987. *The truly disadvantaged: The inner city, the underclass, and public policy.* Chicago, IL: University of Chicago Press.

Wilson, W. J. 1996. *When work disappears: The world of the new urban poor.* New York: Knopf, distributed by Random House, Inc.

Wisdom, B., and D. Patzig. 1987. Does your organization have the right climate for merit? *Public Personnel Management* 16(2): 127–133.

Wise, L. R. 2002. Public management reform: Competing drivers of change. *Public Administration Review* 62(5): 555–567.

Wittmer, D. 1991. Serving the people or serving for pay: Reward preferences among government, hybrid sector, and business managers. *Public Productivity & Management Review* 14(4): 369–383.

Wooten, K. C., and L. P. White. 1999. Linking OD's philosophy with justice theory: Postmodern implications. *Journal of Organizational Change Management* 12(1): 7–21.

Wyoming Water Development Commission. 2001. Bear River Basin water plan. http://waterplan.state.wy.us/plan/bear/bear-plan.html (accessed February 15, 2011).

Wyoming Water Development Commission. 2002. Powder/Tongue River Basin plan final report. http://waterplan.state.wy.us/plan/powder/finalrept/finalrept.html (accessed February 15, 2011).

Yanow, D. 2003. *Constructing "race" and "ethnicity" in America: Category-making in public policy and administration.* Armonk, NY: M.E. Sharpe.

Yellowstone River Compact Commission. 1950–2005. *Annual reports.* Lakewood, CO: U.S. Geological Survey.

Young, G. J. 2001. Transforming the Veterans Health Administration: The revitalization of VHA. In *Transforming organizations,* edited by M. A. Abramson and P. R. Lawrence, 139–172. Lanham, MD: Rowman & Littlefield.

Young, I. M. 2003. Activist challenges to deliberative democracy. In *Debating deliberative democracy,* edited by J. S. Fishkin and P. Laslett, 102–120. Malden, MA: Blackwell Publishing.

Yukl, G. A. 2002. *Leadership in organizations*. 5th ed. Upper Saddle River, NJ: Prentice Hall.

Zhang, J., and S. S. Dawes. 2006. Expectations and perceptions of benefits, barriers, and success in public sector knowledge networks. *Public Performance & Management Review* 29(4): 433–466.

Zucker, L. G., M. R. Darby, M. B. Brewer, and Y. Peng. 1996. Collaboration structure and information dilemmas in biotechnology: Organizational boundaries as trust production. In *Trust in organizations: Frontiers of theory and research*, edited by R. M. Kramer and T. R. Tyler, 90–113. Thousand Oaks, CA: Sage Publications.

Index